Aging:
An Encyclopedia for Adding Years to Your Life and Life to Your Years

Aging:
An Encyclopedia for Adding Years to Your Life and Life to Your Years

ﻌﻌ

ARTHUR F. BERINGAUSE, PhD

Library of Congress Number: 00-191404

ISBN #:   Hardcover   0-7388-2723-1

                  Softcover   0-7388-2724-X

This book was printed in the United States of America.

To order additional copies of this book, contact:
Xlibris Corporation
1-888-7-XLIBRIS
www.Xlibris.com
Orders@Xlibris.com

For Barbara

We lived through the Great Depression and fought and won WWII. We are survivors.

We were before television, before penicillin, before polio shots, frozen foods, Xerox, contact lenses, Frisbees and the Pill. We were before radar, credit cards, split atoms, laser beams, and ball-point pens. We were before pantyhose, dishwashers, clothes dryers, electric blankets and automatic shift. We got married first and then lived together. How quaint can you be!

In our time closets were for clothes, not for "coming out of." Bunnies were small rabbits, and rabbits were not Volkswagens. We thought a deep cleavage was something a butcher did. Designer jeans were scheming girls named Jean or Jeanne, and having a meaningful relationship meant getting along well with your cousin. We thought fast food was what you ate during Lent, and Outer space was the balcony of the local theater. We were before house-husbands, gay rights, computer dating, dual careers and commuter marriages. We were before day-care centers, group therapy and nursing homes. We never heard of FM radio, computer chips, tape decks, electric typewriters, artificial hearts, word processors, yogurt and guys wearing earrings. We'd have thought ERA and JFK, DOT and LUD were lovers' initials lettered on a school jacket or in a slam book.

We hit the scene when there were 5-and-10 cent stores where you bought things for five and ten cents. The ice cream store sold ice-cream cones for a nickel or a dime. For one nickel you could make a phone call, buy a Coke or enough stamps to mail one letter and two postcards, and mail was delivered twice a day. You could buy a new Chevy coupe for $590, but who could afford one? And a pity, too, because gas was only 12 cents a gallon!

In our day cigarette smoking was fashionable, Grass was mowed, Coke was a cool drink at the corner drug store, and Pot was something you cooked in. Break dancing was something Charlie Henderson played for in the gym at the lunch period. Rock music was grandmother's lullaby, and Aids were helpers in the cafeteria.

We were certainly not before the differences between the sexes was discovered, but we were surely before the sex change. We made do with what we had. And we were the last generation that was so dumb as to think you needed a husband to have a baby.

But . . . we survived!

Anonymous

Also by Arthur F. Beringause:

Brooks Adams: A Biography
Classics of Jewish Literature, co-editor
English Literature from 1940, editor
The Range of College Reading, co-editor
The Spoken Word: A Record Library, editor

Parts of *Aging* have appeared in abbreviated form in *Renaissance*

PLEASE NOTE

This volume cannot replace the services of a physician and other trained and licensed health care professionals. *AGING: AN ENCYCLOPEDIA* is intended solely to impart accurate and balanced information. What readers do with the information is at their own discretion and risk.

Painstaking effort has been made to obtain permission for use of copyrighted material. Inadvertent errors of omission or commission will be corrected in future editions.

PANEL OF CONSULTANTS

Now when a doctor's patients are perplexed,
A consultation comes in order next.

Oliver Wendell Holmes, MD

Aging: An Encyclopedia has benefited substantially from the keen-eyed scrutiny and wise counsel of experts in many varied fields. The names of those who agreed to public mention of my gratitude are:

Richard J. Allen, Sgt., Long Hill Township Police Dept., NJ
Barnet Berin, Actuary
Irving Begelman, Hospital Administrator
Albert Begleiter, Manager, Supermarket
Matthew Drake, CEO, Drake Construction, Inc.
Francois Farron-Furstenthal, Realtor
Susan Forsberg, RD
Menek Goldstein, MD, PhD, Biochemist-Pharmacologist
Lillian Gutner, Travel Agent
Walter Heitzman, DJ, Lawyer and Insurance Counsellor
Ira Kepes, MD, Anesthetist
Mark Marotta, Financial Adviser, Merrill Lynch
Bette Messing, MS, Social Worker
Paul Messing, DJ, Public Defender
Arlene Most, Head, Stirling Library, and Her Staff
Alice Ozaroff, Advertising Executive
Barbara Petrack, PhD, Biochemist, Senior Researcher, RISE Institute
Vincent Pistone, MD, Internist
Deborah A. Price, Librarian, Mt. Sinai Medical Library
Harriet Ribot, RN
Seymour Ribot, MD, Nephrologist
Ronald Robson, PhD, Pharmacologist
Jeffrey Spielberger, Prof., CUNY
Melvin Stern, Retirement and Tax Consultant

John Tamerin, MD, Psychiatrist
Naomi Tamerin, MD, Pathologist
Eric Wahl, MD, Gynecologist
Robert Wolff, MD, Oncologist
Greg Wong, Computers

Every man desires to live long, but no man would be old.

Jonathan Swift

To know how to grow old is the master work of wisdom, and one of the most difficult chapters in the great art of living.

Henri Frederic Amiel

In the middle of the journey of life
I found myself in a dark wood,
For I had lost the right path.

Dante Alighieri

They who would be young when they are old,
must be old when they are young.

John Ray

"You are old, Father William," the young man cried.
"The few locks which are left you are gray;

You are hale, Father William, a hearty old man,—
Now tell me the reason I pray."
"In the days of my youth," Father William replied,
"I remembered that youth could not last,
I thought of the future, whatever I did,
That I never might grieve for the past.

Robert Southey

If I had known that I was going to live this long,
I would have taken better care of myself.

Eubie Blake

The rapid progress "true" science now makes, occasions my
regretting sometimes that I was born so soon. . . . all disease
may by sure means be prevented or cured, not excepting
even that of old age, and our lives lengthened at pleasure
even beyond the antediluvian standard.

Benjamin Franklin

The first thing that must be asked about future man is whether he will be alive, and will know how to keep alive, and not whether it is a good thing that he should be alive.

Charles Darwin

It is our duty ... to resist old age; to compensate for its defects by watchful care; to fight against it as we would fight against disease; to practice moderate exercise; and to take just enough of food and drink to restore our strength and not to overburden it. Nor, indeed, are we to give our attention solely to the body; much greater care is due to the mind and soul. . . .

Cicero

Do not go gentle into that good night,
Old age should burn and rave at close of day,
Rage, rage against the dying of the light.

Dylan Thomas

Die, my dear doctor, that's the last thing I shall do!

Lord Palmerston

Contents

PART TWO: DISEASES AND DISORDERS

THE AGE OF LONGEVITY: AN OVERVIEW

There is nothing more difficult to take in hand . . . than to take the lead in the introduction of a new order of things.

Nicolo Machiavelli

Most of the fundamental ideas of science are essentially simple, and may, as a rule, be expressed in a language comprehensible to everyone.

Albert Einstein

What is needed today more than ever before, and not just by the elderly, is information–up-to-date and accurate–about aging and the aged. Demographic and economic assumptions of earlier and simpler eras are no longer valid. Not only was life expectancy markedly shorter in previous eras, the idea that the natural limit of human life span had been reached was commonly accepted. No longer. Unparalleled in the history of evolution, the rate and degree of extension of human life expectancy are still increasing today.

Americans lack preparation for growing old although the United States is now an aging society. For the first time in history, a large percentage of the population is surviving to old age. More than 2/3 of all persons who ever lived beyond the age of 65 are alive today. At the turn of the twentieth century, 4% of the population was over age 65. At the end of the century, the percentage had risen to 13% and is still climbing: 1 American turns 50 every 7.6 seconds. There are more individuals 65 and older in this country than the combined total population of New England (Connecticut, Maine, Massachusetts, New Hampshire, Rhode Island and Vermont) and the Mountain States (Arizona, Colorado, Idaho, Montana, Nevada, New Mexico, Utah and Wyoming). Already, infants and children are in the minority. By 2050 there will be as many 65-year-olds as 21-year-olds.

People are living longer than was anticipated a decade or two ago. On average, and barring accidents, anyone now 65 will live beyond 85. If medicine continues to conquer disease, size of the older population in the twenty-first century will exceed even current high estimates. Chance of living into the 90s increases with each passing year. By 2050, the number of those aged 65-74 may increase by more than 90%, of those 75-84 by 350%, of those 85+ by 600%. There will probably be 25,000+ centenarians. Optimistic demographers project that life expectancy at birth for 2080 may reach 100 years, making Homo sapiens the longest-lived mammalian species on earth.

As the number of old persons increases dramatically, information is the one thing both the young who are trying to take care of the old and the elderly who are trying to take care of themselves need to assuage concerns and solve problems that advancing years bring. Like their young counterparts, the old know shockingly little about care and upkeep, not only of the automobile, but—more important—of the human body.

Aging: An Encyclopedia concretely and accurately summarizes the latest research in geriatrics and gerontology while presenting strategies for adding years to your life and life to your years. Not just basic questions are answered, such as those involving the onset of cancer, but also seemingly peripheral ones, such as descriptions of government and non-profit agencies that can be reached for information and help. Included are practical aids, such as checklists for choosing a nursing home, a doctor, a financial planner. Theory and application are kept separate. Avoided are the false hopes and sensationalism too often found in news coverage of aging. Only solutions to problems of aging which are medically sound and applicable to everyday life are dealt with.

This volume does not pretend to state or to answer every question that at present can be raised concerning aging. There is no attempt at simple solutions to complex problems. The intention is that enough information be included to support and exemplify statements made. Although I am immensely indebted to the many researchers upon whose work I have leaned so heavily, there are few footnotes, acknowledgments and attributions in the text, for the attempt here is to bring out essentials clearly without scholarly encumbrances, such as raised numbers trailed by sets of dots.

A guidebook, this volume is easy to use and small enough to be carried everywhere. The format is designed as a reference to be consulted for particular concerns. Essays are organized in more than 80 topics arranged alphabetically. Entries are self-contained, so that a reader can start anywhere.

Where it is possible to retain accuracy, language familiar to lay people has been substituted for scientific jargon. Technical terms are explained in the glossary at the end of the volume. For more in-depth information, titles of articles and books are cited in the bibliography and in particular areas although it is wise to remember that publishers and organizations are continually revising or bringing out new writings to reflect research with the most recent data and discoveries.

Whereas scientific investigation of aging is new, the search for eternal youth and immortality has always been a target of pseudoscience, an uneasy amalgam of myth and magic. Completed about 2,000 B.C.E., the first recorded epic, the legend of Gilgamesh, has as its major theme a quest for immortality. Babylonian physicians claimed to have created death-prevention elixirs, and the Hebrews described the Garden of Eden, where seemingly death did not occur. In China, the foremost original goal of Taoism was for unending life. The ancient Greeks with tales of the Hyperboreans introduced myths of long-lived youth to literature, as in modern times James Hilton did with Shangri-La. As late as the Renaissance, alchemy was used in an effort to counter old age. Even in the eighteenth century, at the beginning of the modern era, Benjamin Franklin is said to have sought rejuvenation through chemical nostrums. Where Ponce de Leon tried to find the fountain of youth, youth-seekers today go in quest of hot tubs—not to mention ingesting hormones and other products, both internal and cosmetic, despite government warnings.

Theories of aging are often translated by the mass media into cures and over-the-counter remedies, especially by increasing intake of vitamins and wonder chemicals, for so-called ravages of old age. Beta carotene and lecithin are but two examples of many highly touted *elixirs* in popular use, even though scientists have found no conclusive evidence of their efficacy. Special diets with food supplements, such as wheat germ, have replaced snake oil although high doses of some of these materials may be toxic. There is much to be studied, even more to be learned.

Like other age groups, the elderly are diverse and their behavior adaptive. Often discussed but not defined, human aging is a concept, relative and multifaceted. Aging, never static, never immutable, is a slow process of ongoing time-related change in many directions. So many factors influence its manifestations that science as yet has no unifying theory; gerontology, no definition. Which combinations cause the changes people undergo as they age? Precisely how biological, cultural, environmental, historical and psychological variables interact is not known.

Frequently referred to in general terms as a progressive impairment of function, structure and adaptive response as time passes after sexual maturation until the limit of longevity is reached for all members of the species, aging can easily be mistaken for the taking on of disease. There is a wide range of heterogeneity in manifestations of human aging. Gerontologists characterize aging as *primary* (changes in a living organism that over time occur in the absence of disease) or as *secondary* (changes that over time occur in the presence of disease, environmental damage, stress and toxins). The dividing line is rarely sharp, and much is unknown about cause and effect.

The idea is commonly accepted that the more people age the more disease they suffer. With the passage of time, profound changes in appearance and function ensue in all living organisms. But scientists do not *know* to what extent declines in chronologically older individuals are age-related or the result of disease. Many characteristics of illness change from youth to age. Manifestations of aging vary over time from individual to individual and from culture to culture. Processes involved in aging occur in numerous intertwined contexts: cultural, demographic, economic, environmental, ethnic, historical, personal, physiological, psychosocial, societal, temporal.

Is a person sick because of age or aged because of sickness? There are various ways of defining disease, none fully satisfactory. There is no accepted definition of aging. Indeed, science knows of no valid reason for aging to occur. As Stephen Vincent Benet laments:

> A stone's a stone
> And a tree's a tree,
> But what was the sense
> of Aging me?

How then to distinguish between aging and disease, between the undefined as yet and the indefinable as of now? Aging is a normal process; disease, abnormal. Aging is universal; disease, not. Aging affects all bodily operations; disease acts upon specific tissues. The impact of aging may not be noticeable; the occurrence of disease is usually obvious. Aging is slow and progressive; disease proceeds at different rates and may even be regressive. Disease may strike at almost any time. Aging begins only after development of the individual is complete.

Human development can be defined as the course of biological change during which a fertilized egg becomes an adult. Among immediately apparent signs of aging are crow's feet, graying of hair, skin spots. Predominant but not so obvious characteristics of aging, due in part perhaps to disease, are decreasing speed of performance and diminishing capacity to adapt—all until the end of life. Aging kills; disease varies in harmful effect.

But the cause of death in old people is frequently unknown, if not unknowable. Geriatricians who perform autopsy studies have found no acceptable cause of death in more than 25% of cases. Not Alzheimer's disease but increased vulnerability to onset and development of Alzheimer's is the true cause of death in many elderly. Is that susceptibility an inevitable product of the aging process or is it the chance result of disease? One way of answering that question is to remember that change and/or loss characteristic of aging occurs in cells, tissues and organs of all old human beings, but age-related changes owing to disease occur in only some of the elderly.

What is aging, and of what does the aging process consist? Each species can be characterized by maximum life span and pattern of aging. Longevity among mammals ranges from that of small rodents, about 3 years, to that of human beings, about 120 years–close to twice that of the next most longevous mammal. Potentially, some plants and animals are immortal. Certain plants and animals can propagate asexually. Examples include the forsythia, which roots branches in the soil, and the hydra, which buds offspring. Some animals–lobsters, sea anemones, sharks and turtles among them–seem neither to decay with age nor to have a fixed limit to life span. Certain cells, such as germ cells and some cancer cells (HeLa and other strains), apparently neither age nor die.

Although all living things are composed of similar elements–differences between mouse and human DNA are not so much in kind as in arrangement of chemicals, and even roundworms age in some ways that correspond to those of human aging–common causes of human death differ from those of other animals. While annual rings in tree trunks specifically indicate age, evidently there is no similar measurement for *Homo sapiens* although the rate of accumulation of age pigments (viewed at microscopic levels in tissues such as nerve and muscle) may be a good indication of chronological age. An intricate biochemical puzzle, human aging is difficult to describe, define or explain–as the following attempt in the *Oxford Textbook of Geriatric Medicine* (1992), p. 119, makes clear: "A complex interaction between an individual and his or her environment over time is an appropriate definition of human ageing."

Although a slow process, human aging advances in bodily systems of an individual at varying rates. Some parts can continue to function for a longer time than others. Focal areas for anatomical changes accompanying aging are principally tissues that have limited doubling capacity, such as bone, myocardial, neuronal and reproductive cells. These so-called *hot-spots* of aging appear to be evolution's strategy for limiting human life span approximately to the years of reproductive capability plus the years of parenting requisite to viability of the species. When life of the elderly is no longer essential to survival of the species, the last phase of aging, death, occurs unless occasioned earlier by illness or accident.

What might be markers of human aging? Speculation and theories abound. Hundreds and hundreds of seemingly age-related changes have been observed in the human body, but none has been absolutely validated as a primary biomarker of aging. Some scientists think that programmed development of the human embryo and the later synchronous aging of many cells, tissues and organs indicate existence of master regulatory genes.

Other researchers think of human physiology as an information processing system, with DNA storing programs much like a camcorder on a one-dimensional tape. Cells using the information to instruct assembly and operation of molecules in tissues and organs, are subject to many potential sources of error that may lead to mistakes or hindrances in the flow of information, such that aging eventually results in death. But it is exceedingly difficult to separate changes ascribed to internal aging from those occurring in all directions due to climate, diet, toxins and other extrinsic influences. Chance may not be all, but it is always inevitable as genetic, environmental and lifestyle factors interact.

A person casts off millions of cells every day. Most of the cells present in an adult body now were not there ten years ago. The rate of cell change varies among tissues and organs and from person to person. Although cells of the heart, arteries, veins and capillaries do not divide and replicate, their molecules are replenished as a result of metabolic processes. Even so, the cardiovascular system eventually wears out. To what extent is the death of such non-dividing cells responsible for aging of the entire organism?

Literally, a human being is different from day to day. If a person were cut and a small section of skin and a bit of flesh removed, the body would regenerate what was lost. Obviously, some parts of the body are older than others. Because the body is composed of atoms, which have been the same since creation of the planet, a person can be said to be billions of years old–but only temporarily. Physicists suspect that most subatomic particles decay. Paradoxically, the same person is also immortal, for as a carrier of germ plasm the individual is perpetuating the continuity of life of the species.

Study of aging and the aged is called gerontology (from the Greek, *geron*, an old man). It seeks to find out how and why people age and in what ways the aging process can be brought under control. Its companion, geriatrics (from the Greek, *geras*, old age), deals with health care of the elderly. Despite speedy advances in technology making possible new methods of research, progress in gerontology has been relatively slow. Geriatrics and gerontology are almost new disciplines. Examination for a certificate of special competency in geriatrics was first administered by United States medical boards in 1988. Gerontology, somewhat older than geriatrics, is considered a relatively new science because of the preponderance of recent effort and interest. The Gerontological Society of America was founded in 1945. The International Association of Gerontology has a broad mandate, encompassing such disciplines as the behavioral and social sciences, biology, medicine and social planning.

Because the human body is an almost incredibly complicated and dynamic biological system in which many ongoing activities occur simultaneously, the relationship between senescence and growth rate is not simple, and root causes of aging remain unknown. Still, scientists have achieved a measure of control over the rate and degree of aging, and researchers expect far-reaching development in the future, possibly within the lifetime of many of us. At the present time, the aging process can be modified somewhat by ability to adapt to role changes like retirement and widowhood, diet, exercise, healthful lifestyle, social involvement.

Humankind is in a biochemical race with destiny. If major advances in genetic engineering and medical technology are forthcoming, a vast array of social as well as biological interventions will be possible, including a significant extension of longevity. Already specialists in geriatrics have managed to delay the onset, reduce the severity and eliminate some of the diseases previously thought to be inevitable accompaniments of old age. Analyses and cures which once took months can now be achieved in days. Further knowledge will yield huge financial savings to the nation and enhance the well-being of young and old.

Without doubt, the successful animal cloning experiments announced in 1997 will spur research into many aspects of aging. Cloning may even help answer a key question currently vexing biogerontologists. If cloned sheep develop and age the way other sheep do, is the implication that aging is programmed, perhaps primarily through the activity of telomeres (strings of special purpose DNA in cell nuclei)? Should researchers discover how to mimic in somatic (body) cells the conditions in germ (reproductive) cells, scientists will have realized one of humankind's most pervasive desires for longevity since the time of Methuselah. Even more: cells of young people could be harvested and reprogrammed in old people into whatever cell types are required. Still more: xenotransplantation, the employment of human organs grown in animals, may make possible replacement of body parts. Already, transgenic animals whose genetic structure has been altered to produce human proteins in their milk are appearing on experimental dairy farms. Goats, for example, are used in production of pharmaceuticals. Thus far, medicines from transgenic animals have not appeared on the market, but several are undergoing testing for the US Food and Drug Administration. Success begets success. As more efficient techniques are developed, dairy farms may produce, in addition to cheese and milk, medicines to fight cancer and other diseases.

Some day researchers may prevent aging. Many scientists think such a goal undesirable, if not unattainable, asking how will it be possible to evade or overcome the inevitable breakdown of chemical bonds and deterioration of bodies according to the Second Law of Thermodynamics. In their opinion, emphasis should be placed not on a quest for immortality but on a higher quality of life for the aged, not on extending life span indefinitely but on increasing the health span by maintaining the strength and vigor to enjoy life now. They point out that a longer life is not necessarily a better life. They caution that considerable thought and research should be devoted to consequences, not only to society but also to the individual, of getting control over the life span.

Classicists among scientists issue an indirect warning by referring to the Greek myth in which Zeus granted immortality but not eternal youth to Tithonus, who as he aged shriveled and shriveled until he turned into a grasshopper. They talk in modern terms of a demographic catastrophe, a pandemic afflicting everyone–young, middle-aged and old. Others warn: the increase in life expectancy has occurred so suddenly that society's leaders when shaping future policies have not taken into full account the many transformations it is wreaking economically, politically, socially.

Within three short decades, many of the estimated 76,000,000 baby boomers will be 85 years old. At present, more and more elderly are moving into the oldest-old category, where chronic diseases are prevalent and need for supportive services is formidable. Those elderly have children 65+ who themselves will experience similar problems. If current trends continue, America will be characterized as a society of older women: among persons now 75+, more than half are women living alone and fewer than 1/5 are men.

Economists divide the number of persons 18-64 by the number of those 65+ to get a ratio indicating the percentage of workers whose earnings will be available to pay retirement and old-age benefits. In 1935, when Social Security began, the ratio was about 10:1; in 2035, the ratio will be about 3:1. Can service and benefit levels necessary to maintain current standards of living be sustained for a population in which the proportion and care declines?

Americans are living longer and working shorter. Would life extension, coupled with early retirement that high technology brings, rupture the economic and social fabric of society? How will the young fare in a society where the elderly live on and on? Immense human and financial outlays will be necessary. Many a married couple may face responsibility for taking care of four aged parents and eight grandparents even older, in addition to their own children. Anticipating such a situation, Heartland Business Park, NY, established in 1998 a day-care center for children *and* grandparents. As yet, not enough attention has been focused, even by social scientists, on implications–positive as well as negative–although the unprecedented sustained growth in number of persons over 65 warrants significant and immediate investment of personnel, time and resources.

Consider the baby boomers. As they advance in years, they will remain by virtue of sheer numbers the predominant age group. In contrast to their parents, they grew up in relative affluence. As their addiction to fads of all kinds attests, they respond positively to the lures and mores advertisers in print and on television so seductively picture. Undeterred by fears engendered in parents and grandparents during the Great Depression, they spend fast and borrow more despite the downsizing in industry, loss of jobs, and continuing decrease in *real* income. Purses and wallets bulge with credit cards, allowing them to spend what they do not have. Who can doubt that the baby boomers will not change their ways as they grow older and change society? There are definite links between demography and economics. What will ensue when 76,000,000 baby boomers retire and cash in IRA's, pensions and stocks to pay not only for trips to theme parks with children and grandchildren but also for visits to the periodontist and the geriatrician?

There is no doubt that demographic change must and will soon alter American life and culture profoundly. Ramifications will permeate every area of society, and the quality of life for everyone will be affected. Although consequences now unanticipated will become known later on, it is already obvious that building design will be modified in regard to lighting and number of steps and staircases, that typeface in books such as this will be larger. The entire highway and transportation systems will be redesigned with regard to abilities and limitations of late-life pedestrians as well as drivers: traffic lights will have longer intervals, road signs will be brighter, midstreet traffic islands will be placed in crossings for slow walkers to await light changes. Bus closing doors and subway escalators will be slower. Not so obvious and much more difficult will be adjusting pensions, Social Security and Medicare amid shifting moral, personal, political and social issues. Will the traditional marriage pledge, "till death do us part," have to be revised for an era in which death may come 70 years after the marriage date?

Obviously, there is as yet little knowledge or experience of maintaining the quality of life of old persons. Could taxes become so burdensome, as the few try to pay for the many, that they act as a disincentive to work? Will the orientation of schools change to fit the needs and desires of old would-be students? What will the emphasis be of TV programs, with a large percentage of the audience 65+? Will the coming bifocal generation give up its love affair with sports and its emphasis on youthful prowess? How will couturiers revamp clothing? Will attitudes toward aging and the aged change? Will there be enough doctors? Out of more than 150,000 medical students in 1996, fewer than 200 chose geriatrics as a specialty. There are so many unanswered questions, answers to which will inevitably be forthcoming whether or not American society is prepared.

Conceptions of stages in the life cycle have changed over the centuries. The ancients thought of the life span as consisting of infancy, maturity, old age. In the 18th century, childhood with its special characteristics was recognized as a separate phase. The idea of adolescence developed in the 19th century, when the period of formal education began to lengthen. In the 20th century, youth had come to be considered a period of transition between adolescence and adulthood; middle age, the time after children grow up and leave home. Until recently old age was thought of as beginning with retirement, usually at 65, although there is no fixed set chronological point at which old age begins. A proposed alternate demarcation is the age at which life expectancy is an additional 10 years, which today would be 75. Applied to persons 75+ the term *old age* at present encompasses an age range of approximately 25 years.

With the coming of extended longevity, early retirement and second careers, phases of the life cycle are no longer clear-cut. Age norms have changed, and boundaries between life stages are blurring. Age is not an accurate indicator as to when a stage begins and ends, such as marriage and education. Americans used to spend close to 1/3 of their lives preparing for the last 2/3, but the time span has changed. They can now expect at least 60 years of adulthood. Gerontologists use the chronology below, not for exact phases of the life cycle, but as an approximation for convenience of classification:

The young-old are those 65-74;
the old-old are those 75-84; and
the oldest-old are those 85+ .

The young-old exhibit none of the stereotypic changes usually coupled with the label *old*. If scientists through genetic manipulation, use of antioxidants, hormone therapy and other measures unknown as of now increase longevity and decrease chronic illness, what new stages in the later years will be recognized, or will the term *old age* fail to survive as a conceptual roof for all phases of later life, from the year 65 on? Will an age-irrelevant society result in which the old are treated as a resource, not a burden?

As in any revolution, this one involving demographic change is impossible to comprehend in its entirety for those in the middle of it. Projections are not immutable although demographic shifts appear certain. A reversal of present trends may occur. Halfway through the 21st century the baby boomers–senior boomers by then–will be replaced by less numerous successors. Though longevity will remain high if new diseases do not break out, the proportion of old people will decline and the population will be younger. What will have to be done then about adaptations made previously for an aging society?

Evidence from study of cultures in the laboratory almost certainly indicates that even without disease numerous human cells are limited to some 50 doublings, meaning that death is inevitable. Much deterioration, including changes in enzyme activity, fat, DNA occurs over time in cultured normal human cells, leading some researchers to think that one day scientists may be able to lessen or eliminate degenerative aspects of aging. Caloric restriction in certain laboratory animals to achieve undernutrition without malnutrition prolongs and in some cases prevents disease-related decline.

Noted researcher Leonard Hayflick takes another tack in *How and Why We Age*. Implicit in his account is the warning that, while researchers have had some success in bettering the health of older persons, progress of significance in the struggle to understand aging is unlikely to occur unless scientists come to grip hard the molecular bases of aging.

By reaching deep within the microworld of the cell, scientists may yet discover the ultimate causes of aging as well as the primary pacemakers and the intricate correlations among the body's aging controls. Availability of molecular biological tools now allows probing of cell structure and components with precision.

Almost every part of the body declines with age, suggesting that a key process is responsible. An *aging clock* may be located in the nucleus of every cell, perhaps in genes. In support of this theory, biologists have recently discovered that life span can be manipulated in laboratory organisms, if not in human beings. Already scientists have found eight genes in the roundworm C elegans that they can manage to lengthen the creature's life span.

But the end of the quest is not in sight. Research into effects of caloric restriction on cells of laboratory animals has resulted in a hypothesis currently intriguing biogerontologists: diet restriction reduces generation of free radicals (molecules which destructively oxidize cellular components), retarding aging by enabling cells to avoid progressive injury and increasing loss of efficiency.

There is as yet no hard evidence for the exact causes of aging, and no one theory can adequately account for all the phenomena observed. Cells which appear so simple to lay people are structures of awesome complexity to scientists. Gaps in knowledge of what occurs match breaks in awareness of how to test theories. Differences of opinion and even controversy are evident although researchers do agree that the specific biomarkers of aging have not yet been discovered and that a unifying hypothesis which elucidates the aging process *in toto* has not yet emerged.

One of the principal enigmas in biology, aging may be not one thing but many. There may be different *aging clocks*, hormone regulators and environmental factors among them, which may lodge indirect constraints on the life span and which are not synchronized, so that rates of aging vary in cells, tissues and organs.

Throughout history people have feared and disliked old age. Although the commonly accepted stereotype that views the elderly as dying a little more every day is inaccurate, most age changes do seem to be characterized by decay and deterioration of structure and function. Abuse, disease and disuse intensify effects. As hair thins and skin mottles and wrinkles, muscles lose strength and joints stiffen, movements slow and hand-eye coordination declines, vision dims and deafness increases, and memory–like old lace–develops holes. But creativity and intellect are not an exclusive province of the young.

Many elderly come to accept and understand themselves and others better. They lead productive lives of immense value to society, enriching and inspiring us all. Chaucer at 60 completed *The Canterbury Tales*. At 69 Mother Teresa won the Nobel Prize for her work with the poor on several continents. At 71 Cecil B. De Mille produced and directed an Academy Award-winning film. Mahatma Ghandi in his 60's and 70's gave spiritual and moral power to the quest for an Indian nation. Francisco de Goya produced famous lithographs in his 70's. Henri Matisse between the ages of 75 and 80 designed the famous Chapelle du Rosaire.

Still others like Benjamin Franklin, who invented bifocals when 78, make important contributions to societal welfare. Martin Buber at 80 brought out *I and Thou*, deeply influencing twentieth-century theology. Frank Lloyd Wright produced about 1/3 of his total output from 82-91. Vladimir Horowitz gave scintillating concerts well into his 80's. At 89 Sophocles wrote a splendid tragedy of old age, *Oedipus at Colonus*. Albert Schweitzer lived in the jungle of darkest Africa and ran a hospital until his death at 90. Georgia O'Keefe and Pablo Picasso continued to paint magnificently at 90. In 1960, the year she was 100, Grandma Moses illustrated '*Twas the Night Before Christmas* for publication. When 102 years old, chemist Joel Hildebrand had the lead article in the *Annual Review of Physical Chemistry*, and Henri Chevreul–also a chemist–changed careers in his nineties to become a pioneer in old-age research, publishing until he was 103 years old. Many Americans in their nineties remained at the top of their professions: George Abbot, director-producer; Irving Berlin, composer; Martha Graham, choreographer; Arnold Hammer, businessman; Bob Hope, comedian; Claude Pepper, politician.

Some gerontologists postulate that old age as we know it (65 years +) may be an artifact of technological society rather than a product of genetics because senescence begins before reproduction and ends far after it. Progress in technology, such as transportation, bettered the diet even as it reduced vulnerability to local crop failure and eliminated famine in the Western world. Medicine and public health practices, such as vaccination and use of antibiotics plus sanitation, government inspection of food, and pasteurization, contained epidemics and mark-edly decreased incidence of disease. Conditions in the workplace were improved as regards occupational health, and lifestyles in general were bettered with reductions in urban crowding and the advent of appli-ances such as air conditioning. Industrialization increased income and made possible retirement communities. In the distant past, the aging mechanism favored early reproductive capability, say at 13 years, fol-lowed within 30 years by full senescence and death–the pattern of living now of Australian aborigines in the bush, few of whom attain old age. Is it farfetched to consider the long-life expectancy of today part of some grand evolutionary design, to regard old age as a landmark in the evolution of *Homo sapiens*? Or is it fantastic to postulate that biological destiny is not beyond control of humankind? The elderly bring much good to society, providing leadership and communicating cultural and behavioral values, which contribute to the advance as well as to the survival of the human species.

Questions abound, for conducting aging research is extremely dif-ficult. Results of aging research are easily compromised, and clear, unequivocal interpretation is not always attainable. Among the vari-ables that cannot be equated is stress. Surveys are notoriously prone to error because they depend on responses of subjects to item wording which may be leading or too general. Still used in surveys of the health of the aged is substitution of proxy responses for those of missing subjects despite the considerable error such use may introduce.

Employing human beings as subjects of experiments has many other impediments. Genetic backgrounds are usually unknown, expo-sure to environment differs, disease records vary, habits are idiosyn-cratic. Repetition and practice can be important variables accounting for differences in performance. Unaccounted for variables may signifi-cantly alter interpretation. A stable environment is impossible to main-tain, even for one individual–let alone the numbers needed for large studies. People tend to drop out if requirements become burdensome. No single researcher lives long enough to completely study lifecycles. Animals make for better subjects in some respects, but researchers need to be positive that results are applicable to human beings.

Characteristics of the setting, whether structural or interpersonal, can influence conclusions. Performance of isolated tasks in a laboratory may be different from how a person acts in real-life situations. This is especially apparent if the way an individual perceives a problem is taken into consideration. In contrast to the young, the elderly tend to examine and evaluate information before producing a response. Late-life adults have learned that too often speed-accuracy trade-off is low: payment for a hasty response is exceeded by cost of error. Mature adults are somewhat cautious, with a previous mind-set, when making judgments, behavioral traits of survival value in real-life situations, but in an experimental setting such characteristics may make the old look slow and uncertain as they hesitate to answer test items.

The two major types of study are subject to serious flaws. A researcher can unwittingly cue in subjects to give what is wanted, and subjects, learning from one test, may on succeeding occasions perform better and better.

Cross-sectional tests generally compare and contrast two or more different age groups at a single point in time to obtain a measure or set of measures. Such comparisons may reflect effects on a cohort, not on individuals therein. Even successive generations may have been exposed to different physical, psychological, historical and social environments, so that differences revealed need not be a consequence of aging. A researcher might try to compare the reaction time to changes in light of twenty-year-olds with those of sixty-year-olds by studying behavior as light flashes in and out. Unless the observer knows the disease background of each group, results will be tainted. More subtle but equally invalidating to an experiment is the tendency of the old to remember better concrete than abstract test items, a reflection of long experience dealing with facts in the practical world in contrast to the school-oriented world of ideas and ideologies of the young.

Longitudinal studies, which attempt to follow a specific group throughout the life span (a long and therefore hardly feasible process) and compare behavior at different times, can be invalid if the test population does not include a stable, broad age range of subjects with a low drop-out rate and if the test environment changes. Even so, results may lack validity because surviving subjects are more representative of a long-lived and geographically stationary population. If a test is given in the winter and a follow-up administered in the summer, weather may account for differences in response. Over the years and decades of the life cycle, cultural and societal change, which affect performance, should be taken into account lest age-related changes be confused with those resulting from passage of time. This is especially important in time-lag studies in which each group is assessed at the same age. To test short-term memory in 70-year-olds, for example, the 1900 cohort is examined in 1970, the 1910 in 1980, the 1920 in 1990 and so on.

When pointing out difficulties with research studies, Leonard Hayflick likes to tell of the Miami population cross-sectional study, apocryphal no doubt, the conclusion of which is that Miami residents are born Hispanic and die Jewish. Not apocryphal are the studies of Terminal Drop, the theory first elucidated in the early 1960's, that a definite decrease in intellectual performance occurs within a few years of death. If tenable, the theory conceivably would make possible early prediction of mortality. Many studies, all in support, began to appear. Then questions about methodology and procedure were raised: the number of subjects involved was small, some were institutionalized for different kinds of medical problems and the age spread was wide. The concept of Terminal Drop, although plausible to many researchers, became moot; and everyone involved perceived that much more work needed to be done before the idea received general acceptance.

What is the moral of these tales? American critic Malcolm Cowley put it well in *The View from 80* : "To enter the country of age is a new experience, different from what you supposed it to be. Nobody, man or woman, knows the country until he has lived in it and taken out citizenship papers." In agreement, B.F. Skinner, famed psychologist, advises: "Old age is rather like another country. You will enjoy it more if you have prepared yourself before you go." The language is different, the inhabitants are strangers and you do not know how to behave until you arrive. The old know what it is to be young, but the young do not know what it is to be old.

The author of *Aging: An Encyclopedia* has taken out senior citizenship papers. In accord with Cowley, he believes it pays to be wary but not cynical and to make use of one's own experience when learning and interpreting what researchers and authorities on aging have to offer. Then it will be possible for the elderly and their children to make informed judgments about medical, legal, financial or other professional advice.

Consider, ever so briefly, the recent formal history of aid to the old. Problems of the aged became more prominent with the Townsend Movement of 1934, and programs of alleviation were soon initiated. Passage of the Social Security Act in 1935 began federal intervention on behalf of the elderly. Regard to concerns of the aged intensified with the First National Conference on Aging in 1950, followed by establishment of a Federal Committee on Aging and Geriatrics in 1951. A dramatic increase in social welfare programs for the elderly occurred in the 1960's and early 1970's, with passage in 1965 of the Older Americans Act to set up the Administration on Aging, Medicare and Medicaid (1966) and Supplemental Security Income (1972). The Nutrition Act became law in 1972 and arranged food programs nationwide for the elderly. In 1973 the Federal Council on Aging was created, and in 1974 the National Institute on Aging was established within the National Institutes of Health. Various congressional committees and private and public councils studied needs of the elderly in ensuing years. More laws were passed, more departments and bureaus were created, including almost 700 area agencies under the federal Administration on Aging. More agencies and organizations appeared in the private sector.

By nature, gerontology and geriatrics are interdisciplinary. As plans and provisions for the elderly increased each year, not just politicians became involved, but also medical personnel, lawyers, administrators, social planners, representatives of private industry, consumer groups, lobbyists, government agencies, associations of every kind, until the present system has become so complicated that with its many legislative acts, directives, and provisos it resembles a maze, if not mazes within a maze. Labyrinthine codes and regulations diminish value of some services. Rivalry and duplication create further complications, fragmenting and confusing lines of responsibility. To help citizens overcome just such a situation, Great Britain created the Citizens' Advice

Bureau with offices generally in main-street shop fronts, to which any-one can take requests for information.

Regard the sharing of information, which in the United States takes many forms.

Responsibilities at the federal level are assigned to the Administration on Aging, the Social Security Administration and the Community Services Administration with their various bureaus and departments. Social service agencies in every county and state make up a second network. At the community level, numerous small and large public and private groups are available to those elderly and their caregivers who can deal with set after set of gatekeepers and ferret out eligibility, type and scope of benefit, means of access and transportation. Some health-care providers cover only what they consider medical problems and not health disorders that might result in impairment or illness. Foot care, except for major surgery, is often not covered. Neither are dentures nor eye glasses nor hearing aids. Yet capability to eat, hear, see, talk and walk properly are essential to physical and mental well-being. The Travelers Insurance Company has reported that almost 40% of late-life adults do not know how to find out about community resources, treatment of different illnesses, public or private insurance, professional home care. No wonder that there are now private-for-profit companies that guide elderly and caregivers through the bureaucratic maze. In addition, there are about 1,000 advocacy groups at national, state and local levels urging that society act to fulfill needs of the aging.

How is the lay person to ask the right questions, get correct answers and obtain directions? Calendar years bring natural and man-made complications, problems, restrictions. Both young and old need knowledge of the true nature of aging and of ways to find help so as to maintain independence and cope successfully with daily activities in later life. *Aging: An Encyclopedia,* by providing explanatory descriptions, enables readers of all ages to thread the maze and find those publications, associations and agencies of most use to them. The most powerful source of power is information.

On the verge of a new era, at the dawn of the Age of Longevity, we are pioneers, you and I, the first generation to enjoy lengthy retirement, make full use of leisure, reeducate ourselves and prepare for multiple careers. "Old men," writes T.S. Eliot, "ought to be explorers." Emily Dickinson adds:

> Down Time's quaint stream
> Without an oar
> We are forced to sail
> Our Port a secret
> Or Perchance a gale
>
> What Skipper would
> Incur the Risk
> What Buccaneer would ride
> Without surety from the Wind
> Or schedule of the Tide

We are the first on a path untrodden, with many new thresholds to cross in a continuing journey of exploration, discovery and change. Old age is a frontier, largely unreconnoitered. The prospect before us is a tremendous challenge. What are the features as yet unmarked on the map of aging?

I hope that this volume occupies a middle ground between the difficult to understand and the simplistic that distorts. The attempt is not to substitute for professional medical care and advice but to help people to help themselves. May the information obtained from *Aging: An Encyclopedia for Adding Years to Your Life and Life to Your Years* enable you to forge ahead through a vigorous, healthy, productive and fulfilling period in the cycle of growing old.

In the oft quoted words of Robert Browning:

> Grow old along with me!
> The best is yet to be,
> The last of life, for which the first was made.

IMPORTANT GOVERNMENT AND PRIVATE ACTS
PERTAINING TO AGING AND THE ELDERLY

1935 Social Security Act

1939 Old Age and Survivors Insurance

1942 American Geriatrics Society

1943 First Senior Center (New York City)

1945 Gerontological Society of America

1946 Friendly Visitors Program

1947 National Retired Teachers Association

1949 Framingham Survey; International Society of Gerontology

1950 National Council on Aging

1956 Social Security benefits reduced for women at age 62

1958 American Association of Retired Persons Baltimore Study on Aging

1959 National Housing Act

1961 Social Security benefits reduced for men at age 62
　　　National Council of Senior Citizens
　　　United States Senate Special Committee on Aging
　　　White House Conference on Aging

1964 Civil Rights Act
　　　National Association of State Units on Aging
　　　Urban Mass Transportation Act

1965 Foster Grandparent Program
　　　Green Thumb
　　　Medicare and Medicaid +OAA funding for meals on wheels and senior centers+
　　　Older Americans Act establishes Administration on Aging
　　　Service Corps of Retired Executives

1967 Age Discrimination in Employment Act

1970 Gray Panthers

1971 Action, an independent agency, to provide funds for volunteer programs
　　　White House Conference on Aging

1972 Adult Day-Care Centers
　　　National Nutrition Program for the Elderly
　　　Supplemental Security Income Program

1973 Area Agencies on Aging
Equal Employment Opportunity Act
Federal Council on Aging
Older Americans Comprehensive Services Amendments (to
strengthen the Older Americans Act)

1974 Association for Gerontology in Higher Education
Employee Retirement Income Security Act
Research on Aging Act establishes the National Institute on
Aging
National Mass Transit Act
Senior Companions Program
Supplemental Security Income

1975 Age Discrimination Act
Ombudsman program for long-term care institutions

1976 First United States hospice

1978 Age Discrimination Act of 1967 amended to raise age limit to 70

1979 Eurage, a consortium of government agencies in Europe to coordinate research on aging

1981 White House Conference on Aging

1983 Social Security Amendments raise the age of eligibility for full
retirement benefits from 65 to 66, beginning in 2009 and to 67,
beginning in 2027

1986 Age Discrimination in Employment Act amended to remove upper age limit
Consolidated Omnibus Budget Reconciliation Act

1988 Medicare Catastrophic Coverage Act

1989 Repeal of Medicare Catastrophic Coverage Act

1990 Americans with Disabilities Act

1991 Civil Rights Act increases funding for the Older Americans Act
Older Workers Benefit Protection Act

1993 Family and Medical Leave Act

PART ONE

IN GENERAL

ACCIDENTS

Accidents fill the world with woe.

Mother Shipton

Older people (65+) make up about 15% of the total population but suffer some 25% of all accidental deaths. The oldest-old (85+) are at greatest risk, experiencing 4 times as many death-causing accidents as the young-old (75-84).

Falls, the most frequent type of accident among older people, are a major threat to independence and a leading cause of loss of life in those elderly 65+, resulting in at least 10,000 deaths annually. The actual number is probably higher. Like suicides, death-related falls are not listed consistently on death certificates. Accurate information concerning incidence, circumstance and cause of falls among the elderly is almost impossible to obtain because too often the faller cannot give an accurate account and there is no witness.

Although falls are generally considered the result of debility, impairment and age-related deterioration in balance and gait function, research studies consistently indicate that a large percentage of persons 65+ are within the range of healthy younger adults on various parameters, including reaction time and muscle strength. Falls are usually caused by multiple converging circumstances: activity-related, behavioral, environmental, pharmacological, psychosocial. Tripping during normal household activity is the commonest cause of falls, turning suddenly the next. Underlying medical conditions, such as arthritis, impaired vision and use of bifocal eyeglasses, osteoporosis and Parkinson's cause many falls among the aged. Medications, particularly long-acting sedatives and anti-depressants, increase the danger.

But even prolonged, detailed investigation does not always reveal the cause of a fall. Such is the case with so-called drop attacks affecting many persons 75+. The fall while walking or standing apparently results from a sudden loss of strength and muscle tone in the legs. Is the sudden loss cardiovascular or neurological in nature or both? Admitting that causes of falling are not well understood, many physical therapists think it probably true that exercise may help older persons prevent falls. They argue that even walking, which may be considered controlled falling, requires coordinated interaction among multiple organ systems. This, they say, can be obtained through simple and easily performed exercises.

The number of falls in apparently healthy elderly persons is not known, but it is substantial although not all falls produce injury. Older people often try to hide frequency of falls, but at least 1 in 4 admit to continual fear of falling. Rates for women are higher than for men. The oldest-old are at greatest risk. About 1/3 of the elderly residing in the community report suffering at least 1 fall a year, and nearly half report enduring multiple falls. Approximately 1/2 of the residents in long-term care facilities, where risks are supposedly minimized, admit to at least 1 fall during their stay. In hospitals, where a patient's stay is generally short-term, falls are frequent, perhaps because of medications. Falls may be even more common in nursing homes.

More than 6,000,000 acute injuries of all types come from falls every year. Results of a fall can be physical (as a bruise, a bone fracture, a restriction of activity) or psychological (postfall syndrome, which includes fear of falling and lack of confidence in ability to maintain balance). Falls forward occur most frequently, but falls to the side and rear are not uncommon. Fractures of upper limbs tend to occur when arms are thrown ahead to reduce the impact. Hip fractures, numbering over 200,000 and generating enormous medical and social costs, are likely to occur from falls to the side. As a result of immobility, many patients develop such serious medical problems as pneumonia. Within a year at least 1 in 4 hip-fracture patients dies. Of the rest, at least 2 in 3 need help from crutches or a wheel-chair.

Falls in the home, especially in the bedroom and bathroom, are the most common cause of trauma to the aged. Generally, such falls are the result of health problems or of environmental obstacles like scatter rugs or a slippery floor. About 1 in 10 of falls among the elderly occur on stairs, head injuries resulting many times. It is wise to learn the side effects of prescription drugs. Older persons, especially those taking diuretic medications, should get up slowly from a lying or sitting position to avoid dizziness from a drop in blood pressure. Fainting or feeling faint after stooping or bending over is different, apparently resulting from a temporary blockage of a carotid artery in the neck and a momentary cutoff of blood to part of the brain. In many cases, causes of dizziness are unknown.

Physical therapists advise older persons not to try to stand suddenly on awakening. When getting up from a chair or bed an elderly person should sit as close to the edge as possible, place feet flat on the floor, lean slightly forward and push with arms and legs until standing upright. Avoid sitting in a low chair. Alcohol, which can affect balance and is related to about half the falls causing head injuries, should be avoided. Anyone with arthritis or Parkinson's should not climb ladders or stretch to reach an object high up. Such persons need to be especially careful when walking downstairs. Anyone with a hearing difficulty should always be aware that she/he may not hear footfalls or a door opening or closing, and should move accordingly.

Research indicates that anyone lacking a strong sense of balance is about twice as likely to fall as a stable person. Exercises should address essential components of balance. They will strengthen feet, hips and legs, help with posture and toughen abdominal muscles. To reduce the risk of falls, the exercises should be performed at least 3 times a week.

Elderly pedestrians are less likely than the young to be struck by an automobile, but once they are injured in an accident they are more likely to die. Motor vehicle-to-vehicle accidents are also a common cause of death among more mature persons, who are heavily dependent on private rather than public transportation. The elderly consider relinquishing a driver's license as a loss of independence and the end of their active lifestyle, this despite the fact that crash risk begins to rise among those 55+ until drivers 80+ have a higher crash rate than any other age group. Even so, chronological age is not an effective predictor of an elderly individual's performance.

To reduce their crash risk, the elderly are strongly advised to avoid speeding at all times, driving during inclement weather, using interstate highways and freeways and driving during rush hour and at dawn, dusk or night. The elderly should avoid unfamiliar routes and traveling long distances. They are warned that medications can induce drowsiness. Vision problems in both daytime and at night can cause accidents because of glare from sunlight or oncoming headlights combined with slowness of reaction time of elderly drivers. Both older pedestrians and drivers for whom arthritis is a problem, knowing that it is sometimes difficult to turn one's head quickly, need to be particularly careful at highway entrance and exit ramps and at street corners when turning across the stream of oncoming traffic. The elderly have difficulty with quick determination of right of way, observing signs and with maneuvering at cross-traffic turnarounds. Since many communities provide free bus service to shopping malls for seniors, it is possible to reduce driving and walking to necessary minimums.

Because they contain corrosive, flammable or poisonous chemicals, many common household products are potentially dangerous not only to one's personal health but also to the environment. After use, they should be stored carefully or disposed of in accord with the manufacturer's directions. Non-toxic cleansers and pesticides are available at food co-ops, health food stores, some supermarkets and through mail-order catalogs. Any merchandise containing chemical bleaches, petroleum detergents, phosphates and synthetic perfumes should be avoided. Alkaline batteries should be mercury-free. Persons using a hearing aid should inquire as to the feasibility of using zinc-air rather than mercuric-oxide batteries.

There are many ways to increase safety in the home. Smoke and radon detectors should be checked continually to ensure that they are in good working order Fireplaces and chimneys should be cleaned at regular intervals. Fuel-burning applianxces should be checked often for efficiency. Easy escape routes should be decided on in case of fire. To prevent flames and shocks, all electric outlets should not be overloaded and should contain circuit interrupters. To prevent scalding, the hot water heater should be set so that temperature does not rise above 120°. A flashlight at bedside and one on a kitchen table are invaluable in case of blackout, and they are much safer than candles. Ladders are taboo, as is stretching to reach a high shelf or plant hanging from the ceiling.

The elderly and those who care for them should keep in mind

Southey's warning made 200 years ago: "The Chapter of Accidents is the longest chapter in the book."

SAFETY

1. The Person
    a. Avoid sitting in a low chair.
    b. Do not get up suddenly from a lying or sitting position.
    c. Avoid alcohol.
    d. Do not climb ladders; stand only on a sturdy footstool, never on a chair.
    e. Do not try to reach for an object high up on a wall or shelf.
    f. Decide on easy escape routes in case of fire.
    g. Utilize a reassurance service, such as the Carrier Alert Program administered by the Post Office.
    h. Keep the home orderly as, for example, never storing items even temporarily on stairs.
2. The Home
    a. Do not use scatter rugs.
    b. Do not use household products containing toxic chemicals or pesticides.
    c. Install and check smoke and radon detectors regularly.
    d. Electric outlets should not be overloaded and should contain circuit interrupters.
    e. Hot water heater temperature should be set below below 120° to prevent scalding.
    f. A flashlight should be kept at bedside and on a kitchen table.
    g. Have fireplaces and chimneys cleaned regularly.
    h. Have sturdy rails installed next to stairways.
    i. Place non-skid mats and grab bars in the bathtub and on the floor.
    j. Utilize a portable telephone.
    k. Have night lights on stairs.
    l. Telephone numbers of a helpful neighbor, doctor, police and fire departments should be posted next to each telephone.
    m. Keep a fire extinguisher handy.

TESTS FOR BALANCE, FLEXIBILITY AND STRENGTH*

BALANCE

1. Stand on your right foot next next to a chair for a count of 10. If unable to keep your balance, grasp the chair with your right hand. If able to keep your balance, stand on the right foot with eyes closed. Repeat with the left foot.

2. Stand with your right shoulder to a wall. Reach forward with your right arm. Measure the number of inches your fingertips move forward before you must take a step to prevent yourself from falling. If you cannot reach from 12-15 inches, you are at risk of falling in everyday activities.

FLEXIBILILTY

1. Can you bend over to touch your toes, put on stockings, tie shoe laces?

2. Is your range of motion limited when you try to turn your head to look right, left or behind you?

3. Is it difficult to raise your arms high enough to comb your hair or to put on an overhead blouse?

4. Women—Do your wear dresses that button in the front or bras that hook in front because they are easier to fasten?

5. Men—Do you have difficulty removing a sweater by placing hands behind you to slip off sleeves?

STRENGTH

1. Can you lift a 10-pound bag of groceries and place it on a kitchen counter?

2. Can you pick up a small child or move a piece of heavy furniture?

3. Do you have difficulty rising from a chair or sofa without using your arms?

4. Do you have difficulty climbing a flight or flights of stairs?

5. Can you open a jar of pickles without difficulty?

ACTIVITIES of DAILY LIVING

Let us then be up and doing,
With a heart for any fate:
Still achieving, still pursuing. . . .

Henry Wadsworth Longfellow

Social scientists use the term *lifestyle* in reference to the totality of ways in which people organize their lives. Lifestyle depends on activities, competence, preferences, time–chance, too, for what is available as well as costs and rewards are determining factors.

Activities help promote feelings of well-being and a sense of identity. A person can be a spectator or a participant. Some activities can be performed alone, as reading, sewing and woodworking. Other activities can be performed in a group, as going to a concert, playing cards, or watching TV. A person is herself or himself and yet many others: child, kin-group member, spouse, parent, grandparent, citizen, friend, neighbor, club member, churchgoer. All these selves with their associated activities lead to life satisfaction, which itself results to a large extent from engagement.

Sociologists assess the ability of the elderly to maintain an independent lifestyle in terms of Basic Activities of Daily Living (ADL) and of Instrumental Activities of Daily Living (IADL). ADL include simple activities associated with self-care, such as bathing, dressing, feeding oneself, moving between bed and chair, using the toilet. IADL include more complex activities, such as getting around in the community, housework and laundry, meal preparation, handling personal finances, shopping. Basic activities–such as bathing, dressing and picking something up from the floor–are not always easy for the elderly, more than half of whom are afflicted to some degree by arthritis. Ability to perform ADL is negatively affected by anxiety, depression, impaired cognition, lack of sleep, malnutrition. In turn, a vicious circle, these lead to low energy, fatigue, withdrawal and–at last–social isolation.

By 75, a majority of the old-old report some limitation in ADL.

The proportion of oldest old is larger. Estimates are that about 30% are unable to carry on one or more major activities of daily living and about 20% are disabled. Probably, from 10-15% of all the elderly find getting around in the community troublesome. Studies show that many more than that percentage indicates have difficulty negotiating a 20" step without help of a hand-rail. Because driving is difficult for many, public transportation is needed, especially in rural areas where roads are not always well maintained.

Almost all late-life adults prefer to remain in their own homes or apartments, not only because of their desire for privacy and independence, but also because they spend much more time there than do the young working population. Security is a major concern. Reassurance services are available for home-dwelling aged, such as a telephone service that calls several times a day or an alarm system utilizing a necklace or bracelet with a button to press for help. Not enough older persons utilize many helpful services, even those without cost. The Carrier Alert Program, administered by the post office, will arrange for the carrier to check on an oldster's well-being if the mail is not picked up. If reading small print is difficult, the post office will have large-print material sent free of charge. To take part, an older person must enroll voluntarily.

Because he perceived that both private and government agencies did not always find many older persons who need assistance, Ray Rascho, director of Spokane's Elder Service, created the Gatekeeper Program, which recruits volunteers, such as bank personnel, bus drivers, deliverers of fuel, grocery store clerks, newspaper deliverers, pharmacists, receptionists, taxi drivers and others to let service agencies know that elderly need help. Gatekeepers are neither spies nor snoops who force assistance on the old. Highly successful in enabling the aged to remain in the community and stay relatively independent, there are more than 200 Gatekeeper programs in the United States. Other such programs are coming into being, usually supported at the start by Area Agencies on Aging. They go under such names as Elder Watch, Elder Link, Neighbors Helping Neighbors. But ongoing funding actually comes from many sources, including federal and state agencies, non-profit organizations and private contributors.

For the elderly with ADL difficulties, formal home-care programs have been developing–not without problems. Varying in intensity and duration, caregiving may be administered from 1 hour to 24 hours a day for as long as is deemed necessary. Demand far exceeds supply. Of the nearly 33 million elderly in the United States, probably 7,000,000 need help with personal care or activities of daily living.

Researchers estimate that approximately 15,000,000 adults in this country are caregivers to an impaired family member. Only about 15% of caregiving in the home is rendered by professionals. In-home care by a relative is the kind of help preferred by every ethnic group. Women, spouses and adult daughters, are more likely than men to become caregivers.

Eligibility for caregiving assistance by a paid professional depends on degree of impairment of the elderly, which is not always easy to determine. Services are generally coordinated by a social worker. Sometimes full-day service is authorized when what is needed is temporary care for a short interval, perhaps an hour or two daily of nursing care or speech or physical therapy or a somewhat more extended period of time of a nurse's aid to help with chores and personal grooming. Although federal, state, local and private moneys are available, funding restrictions apply. Administration is difficult because social services have to be integrated in a cooperative network often composed of people and organizations with differing agenda. Sharing some of the same difficulties are day-care centers which provide counseling, health education, nursing and physician care, therapy and transportation.

Because government agencies may be of little or no help except for the indigent, a number of private services have come into being that find and coordinate services for those elderly who want to remain at home but who cannot fully care for themselves. Such services are expensive and not always easy to find. Aging Network Services, Wsiconsin Ave. West, Bethesda, MD 20814, a national consulting agency, does make referrals.

Anthropometry (study of human body measurements) and ergonomics (study of how people adjust to the environment, especially in regard to machines) are aspects of technology which, if properly applied to needs of the elderly, give prospects of longer and improved quality of life. Such modifications support independence of older persons and reduce burdens of caregivers. The purposes are both positive and negative: health promotion and disability prevention.

Appropriate design of familiar objects that necessitate manipulation lessens the need for assistance by the elderly, in this way reducing health-care costs and preventing institutionalization in many cases. A simple mechanism, such as a lever, can be exchanged for a doorknob, a bed-table that swings over the bed for a tray. A more complicated device, the TV, can be operated from a distance by remote control. An even more complicated utensil utilizing high-energy physics is the microwave, which has made meal preparation much easier. Health care devices, such as blood pressure meters and diagnostic tests, are inexpensive and easy to administer.

Medicare reimburses somewhat for rental or purchase of home-care equipment, so long as a physician certifies necessity. For the seriously impaired, many aids are readily obtainable, including canes, crutches, hearing aids, electric-powered stairlifts and motorized wheelchairs. Bathroom electrical outlets can have ground fault interrupters installed to prevent shock. Clutter should be avoided by storing loose objects promptly and always in the same place. Lower shelves in closets and pantries should be utilized. Cracked sidewalks outside the home and extension cords and shag carpets inside are dangerous. All carpeting should be securely fixed to the floor. Loose linoleum should be picked up or repaired promptly. All floors should be non-slip. A rubberized runner should be placed between bed and toilet. Escape routes in case of fire should be clearly marked or planned for in advance.

There are many helpful devices. Watching TV can be relaxing, but continuous viewing can lead to isolation and atrophy of interpersonal skills. In contrast, the personal computer (PC) is excellent for encouraging independent living, lifelong learning, keeping track of finances, playing games and communicating inexpensively with family and others on an informal basis all over the world. (High school students are delighted to be hired to teach use of the computer, which can be quickly mastered with a little patience and persistence.) A PC can be an audio recorder, calculator, collection of games, fax machine, filing cabinet, library, repository of research on any area known to mankind, travel agent, typewriter, warehouse index (for shopping), word processor. But quacks quack, even on the Internet, which offers inexpensive access to millions of people. It is wise to be wary of advertisers marketing dietary supplements or untested products of alternative medicine.

In the kitchen a high stool, rolling cart, long-handled reacher (to avoid use of a step stool or ladder), finger-glove pot holders, plastic-lipped and divided plates with non-skid bottoms, large-handled cutlery, sink overflow alarm increase safety. An electric toaster-broiler makes meal preparation easier and safer, as do easily read heat controls on the stove and the use of cooking timers. A powerful jar opener and an electric can opener are essential. Handles on cooking utensils should be welded to the body of the appliance and knurled to prevent slippage. In the bathroom non-skid surface on the floor and in the bathtub a tub bench, a raised toilet seat, grab rails at the proper angle and height for tub and toilet, hand-held shower hose, bath-caddy, grounded electrical outlets to prevent shocks, long-handled tooth brush, comb and hairbrush, shower valves that automatically adjust water temperature, a wall-mounted liquid soap dispenser and tempered glass increase both safety and comfort. Chairs with arms make it easier to stand or to sit. Curtain rods, soap holders and towel bars should be sturdy enough to withstand a sudden pull of body weight. Light timers make moving around safer.

Intercoms, detectors (of smoke, carbon monoxide, natural gas and radon), signals (of water leaks), fire and burglar alarm systems are relatively inexpensive. Night lights on stairs help prevent falls, as do lamps that can be turned on and off by touch or a clap of the hands. Crank-operated windows are easier to open and close than are double-hung. Wide doorways and ramps instead of stairways make a building wheelchair accessible. Air conditioning and central heating with individual thermostats in major rooms make life comfortable, reducing stress and the chance of hyperthermia and hypothermia. Key extenders and slower opening and closing doors on elevators facilitate access and egress. Telephones should be conveniently placed, as at bedside, and supplemented by portable devices. Near every telephone should be posted the number of a helpful neighbor, personal physician, local pharmacy, police and fire departments, the nearest poison center. The medicine cabinet should contain only up-to-date drugs, as per the label on each container. Velcro fasteners should be used instead of buttons on clothing, shoes and slippers should have non-skid soles with broad, low heels and women's zippers with large pulls should be placed in front rather than in back. Only prescription eyeglasses should be worn.

Planning ahead and preparing for emergencies help prevent crises and avoid injuries. After needs and risks are identified, necessary changes should be made at once.

Keep an apartment orderly as, for example, not storing items even temporarily on stairs. Place working flashlights in several accessible places to guarantee lighting. To avoid slipping and falling, clean up spills immediately. Have the heating system checked regularly by a professional. Stand only on a sturdy stepstool, never on a chair. Keep a fire extinguisher handy. Outside, make sure walkways are clean and unobstructed.

Even elderly invalids can easily have a safe and attractive home. The simple suggestions, changes and improvements mentioned above will reduce, if not eliminate, risks—making a relatively full and independent life possible. The scientist Thomas Henry Huxley reminds us that "The great end of life is . . . action."

AGE

Who well lives, long lives; for this age of ours
Should not be remembered by years, days and hours.

Du Bartas

Popular assumptions about age too often are based on misconception and stereotype. Asked during an AARP survey to indicate onset of old age, Americans under 30 said 63; those 40-49 said 70; those 50-59 said 71; those 60-64 said 73; and those 65+ said 75. Perceptions about aging and longevity, a mixture of aspiration and dread, are reflected in a 1996 poll of the Alliance for Aging Research. More than 60% of respondents say they would like to live to be 100, but an even larger percentage worry about living for years in a nursing home because of frailty and illness.

Because of the extreme plasticity of aging in human beings, it is impossible to tell at which precise point in life a person becomes old. Except in science fiction and wishful thinking, life is not a staircase, one sharply defined step succeeding another. With a sigh, Benjamin Franklin once confessed that he would have preferred to divide his life into intervals, so that he might live 1 year in every 100.

Despite designations by Social Security and other such programs, a person does not become old at 65. There is no distinct beginning for the senescent period. Nor does age in years equate with decrepitude. Anyone chronologically old need not be biologically, cognitively, psychologically, socially infirm. In the words of Saint-John Perse:

> *Old age, you lied. . . .*
> *Time measured by the years*
> *Is in no way the measure of our days.*

Choice of 65 as the marker of old age is a historical accident, an arbitrary tag, due to influence of Prussian Chancellor Bismarck, who in the 1800's set the retirement age at 65. So, too, the Social Security Act of 1935 defined elderly as people 65+. Even today for convenience sake, gerontologists generally classify the elderly by chronology:

65-75 years: the young-old
76-84 years: the old-old
85+ years: the oldest-old

At the turn of the 20th century, numerical markers for old age were advanced considerably. But age is more than a biologic statistic. Nothing magical inside the body happens at 65 to make a person old instantaneously. George Burns put the absurdity of mere numbers well: "If you live to the age of a hundred, you have it made," he said, "because very few people die past the age of a hundred."

The rate of aging does not change for a cohort (a group of persons born in the same year or same time period) as the members advance in years. Yes, a 70-year-old is more aged than a 40-year-old, but he or she is not losing bodily functions at a faster rate. Nor are changes in one organ of an individual absolutely predictive of changes in other organs of the same person. If pulmonary functions decline rapidly, this does not necessarily indicate that kidney decline will also speed up.

A person ages in widely varying ways at different chronological stages with disparate rates. Diversity increases with age. The older one is the more individualized because of many years of experience of all kinds. Between 21 and 75, reductions of as much as 60% in efficacy of bodily functions have been noted, but the declines are relatively modest because of the considerable physiologic reserve of most organs.

Biologic and chronologic age are not identical. Satchel Paige was correct in asking, "How old would you be if you didn't know how old you was?" Hair may turn gray and skin wrinkle, all the while a person is experiencing excellent heart and kidney function. Almost always there are elderly individuals who are at or above the level of the average younger individual.

No one has detected an exact time-limited typical pattern for the evolving of age. Personal recognition that one is old comes almost always not from within but from the reactions of others. Very few persons accept old age without a struggle. Most people are not eager to be ranked with the old. Witness the popularity of cosmetics and cosmetic surgery for men as well as women.

Conceptions of age change as social structure and environment change. The old of today are growing older in ways markedly different from the old of yesterday. A 75-year-old of today easily has the vigor and appearance of a 50-year-old of yesterday. People tend to forget that in the eighteenth century the poet Robert Burns, along with his peers, had a morbid fear of immediate senescence–at age 45!

Throughout recorded history women had a shorter or the same life expectancy as men. Longevity in the modern era has increased for both sexes, but women today live longer than men. Although females and males age at about the same rates and there is no difference in maximum lifespan, at 85+ there are at least 2 women for every man.

The United States Public Health Service asserts that as many as half the deaths in the entire country may be due to unhealthy life-styles. Men smoke and drink more than women, seek medical attention less, engage in dangerous occupations more and have accidents to a greater extent. These so-called external causes of death are for males more than 3 times the number than for women. Among the Amish of Pennsylvania, where no one smokes, consumes alcohol, drives an automobile, men live about as long as women. Scientists do not know why women elsewhere in the nation live longer than men although diet (thin is in) and fashion (svelte is wealth) may be factors. Paradoxically, elderly women have a higher incidence of short-term disease and chronic illness than do elderly men. Although equalization of life expectancy for the sexes is not anticipated in the foreseeable future, perhaps a reduction in risks of the American male's life style will extend his longevity. If women continue to engage in high-stress occupations, they may die at earlier ages. The sex ratio may shift toward equalization.

In traditional societies of the past, age was defined in terms of function. Among the Eskimos, the aged who could no longer contribute materially to society were put to death or encouraged to commit suicide. In modern technologically-oriented societies, where the elderly can be free of such previously demanding roles as parent, worker, taxpayer, there are many ways to successful aging. Bernard Baruch, who perceived that the judgment that someone is old comes from the reactions of others rather than from an inner sense of the relentless advance of years, said, "To me, old age is always fifteen years older than I am." He was correct: old people rarely feel old. For those who do, realization can be traumatic. Surveys indicate that the majority of persons who do perceive themselves as old are significantly impaired, ill or maladjusted.

Despite age-determined changes, whether complicated or not by disease, most elderly do not feel a significant reduction in quality of life or a need to substantially change their life-style. They are aware of losses, as in vision, income and autonomy; but the slide down is neither steep nor unbearable. Picasso said: "Age only matters when one is aging. Now that I have arrived at a great age, I might just as well be twenty," and Casals at the same stage wrote of his "awareness of the wonder of life and of the incredible marvel of being a human being."

Several rare disorders seem to mimic aspects of aging in human beings. Victims of progeria appear to grow old while quite young, and they die before reaching maturity—usually well before the 20th year. Young persons with Werner's syndrome experience cataracts, hardening of the arteries and osteoporosis. In contrast, sponges, bacteria and various yeasts show no signs of age.

Scientists believe that almost all species have each a characteristic life span. In the case of human beings, life span has not changed in thousands and thousands of years. But life expectancy, which is the number of years on average that a person can expect to live, increased dramatically in the last century for industrialized countries. In the United States of 1900 a person at birth could expect to live about 50 years; today, life expectancy at birth is well over 75 for females, over 70 for males. As of today and on average, anyone 65 has an expectancy of at least 15 years, anyone 75 has some ten years, anyone 85 has about 5 years.

What does the future hold? No one knows for sure, but scientists estimate that eliminating cardiovascular disease, the foremost cause of death in this country, might add 3 years or more to life expectancy.

Researchers have found no single cellular or organismal cause of aging. Genes do exert a powerful effect on life span and biological pattern of aging, but lifestyle and environment profoundly impact on aspects of aging. There is at present no known diet, pill, remedy, vitamin to prevent aging and increase longevity.

At the 100th celebration of the founding of the National Institutes of Health, Dora Zins, age 104, was asked about a formula for longevity. "I can't give you a recipe to live long," she said. "Life is how you live, how you sleep, how you eat, how you drink, how you work. Life is what you are."

Because no exact biomarkers of age have been discovered, life span, which is not directly observable, remains a theoretical construct which can only be estimated. Actuarial data indicate that persons whose parents live to an old, old age have a greater life expectancy than persons whose parents died young. The Bible (Genesis 6:3) tells of God's limitation of the human life span to 120 years, a number which gerontologists think is accurate. Moses, the Bible states, died at 120 years. Elsewhere (Psalms 90:10), the Bible gives the typical life span of ordinary people as 70-80 years: "The days of our lives are threescore and ten; and if by reason of strength they be fourscore years, yet is their strength labor and sorrow, for it is soon cut off, and we fly away."

Most extended longevity claims are preposterous. Maximum life span for the human species is rarely approached. There is a strong tendency, worldwide, to exaggerate age of the elderly—probably in many cases to avoid military conscription or tax collection. Careful interviews with villagers and officials coupled with painstaking scholarly investigation of civil and church records—particularly in South America and the Caucasus, where many amazing longevity numbers have been put forth—do not substantiate any of the claims beyond the age of 96. Nor should one be more trustful of claims emanating from Europe. Supposedly, the age of a Frenchwoman, Jeanne Calment, who died in 1997 at 127 years, has been confirmed. But certification is difficult. Census data in all civilized countries are taken from verbal statements. Written documents offered in support of claims of those purporting to be 100 or older are often unreliable, for birth certificates and passports can be altered and even continuity of identity by having a son assume his father's name. In the future, fingerprints or footprints will appear on birth certificates and thus allow authentication of birth and death dates and continuity of identity.

For a government, calculation of age and estimation of life expectancy are of crucial financial importance. Biomedical researchers are not in agreement as to limits of human longevity attainable in the not-so-distant future, some arguing for an expectancy of about 85 years, others for 95-100 years. The question of who is correct is far from academic. Underestimating numbers of elderly baby boomers who will become eligible for old-age benefits could significantly contribute to bankrupting the nation early in the next century. At present, Social Security, Medicare and Medicaid benefits to the elderly account for more than 1/3 of all federal expenditures. Added to interest on the national debt, sums for entitlement programs will consume the entire federal budget by 2012 warned a bipartisan congressional commission in 1994 unless remedial measures are taken soon.

Life expectancy for them, the elderly recognize, is measured in months rather than in decades. The old have more life behind them than ahead. Prospect of death is a daily reality. There are striking changes in perception of time. To the young, time seems to limp by ever so slowly. To older persons, time always seems to go faster. At the age of 7, one year is 1/7 of a child's life. At the age of 70, a year is 1/70. On an ancient wall of Chester Cathedral, England, the following inscription can still be read:

> Time crept
> When I was a boy and laughed and talked, Time walked
> Then when the years saw me a man, Time ran
> But as I older grew, Time flew.

There are also reverses in direction. Where the young count back to birth, the old count ahead to death. The young think of time in terms of the future, regard the present as moving too slowly, and reckon their existence from a distant point in the past. The middle-aged think of time much as if it were a river where at any one point of their existence the past, present and future flow into each other. But the old are aware not only of different ways for regarding passage of the days but also of the extent to which our lives are governed by time, internal and external, subjective and objective.

Human beings live in accord with internal biological timers, some of which scientists refer to as circadian rhythms, like the one that determines when people go to sleep each night and for how long. Clock time is external, objectively measurable and irreversible, moving inexorably to the future. Deeply personal, internal time, moving back and forth, cannot be measured since it includes thoughts, dreams and a subjective sense of self that can be 17 and 70 years old in the same instant, as the past superimposes itself on the present.

Whether in clock time or in internal time, the elderly tend to consider time and themselves as in the past. Is this why they think of themselves as younger than their chronological age indicates? The present as a marker of old age is not accepted without a struggle, with the future thought of as liable to be worse. The old are more concerned with quality of life than with quantity of years left. For them the future is in the lives of their children and grandchildren. In accord is Browning's Rabbi Ben Ezra, who said:

> I summon age
> To grant youth's heritage.

LESSONS FROM THE LONG-LIVED
RECIPES FOR EXTENDING LIFE NATURALLY

Nobody grows old by merely living a number of years. . . .
Years may wrinkle the skin, but to give up interest wrinkles
the soul.

Douglas MacArthur

1. Engage in an activity like gardening for pleasure; avoid passivity like that of a couch potato before the TV.
2. Enjoy people and develop friendships; refrain from carping at minor flaws and holding grudges.
3. Live in the present by looking forward; do not dwell in the past by looking backward.
4. Actively search for solutions to problems and work hard to achieve success; do not set goals unreasonably high.
5. Have a healthy self-esteem and be proud of what you accomplish; do not take excessive pride in yourself.
6. Be moderate in habits; shun extremes, whether of emotion or diet.
7. Seek an organized lifestyle; avoid becoming inflexible.
8. Cultivate a sense of humor; do not prefer the sad over the comic.
9. Maintain enthusiasm for the joys of life; refrain from such characterizations as boring and dull.
10. Put the body through workouts for pleasure; do not let anxiety about health be a compulsion to exercise.
11. Accept inevitable losses, adapt and move on; do not give way to worry and stress.
12. Be curious and stimulate the mind; do not let the brain idle into deterioration.
13. Enjoy the beauty inherent in the day; do not let your perceptions dull.
14. Be cheerful and optimistic; do not be sad and pessimistic.
15. Remain socially involved, as by volunteering; do not become useless, without purpose.

Accentuate the positive. Eliminate the negative.

FACTORS INFLUENCING LONGEVITY

Accidents
Adjustment: biological and social
Blood pressure
Chance
Cholesterol level
Culture
Diet
Disease
Economic well-being
Education
Environment
Ethnicity
Gender
Genetic inheritance
Lifestyle
Marital status
Medical care
Obesity
Occupation
Social status
Stress
Worry

AGEISM

An aged man is but a paltry thing
A tattered coat upon a stick, unless
Soul clap its hands and sing, and louder sing
For every tatter in its mortal dress.

William Butler Yeats

Robert Butler, MD, introduced the term ageism to designate devaluation of old people solely on account of their age. Sometimes referred to as gerontophobia, irrational fear of and revulsion of old age by an individual, ageism ends as discrimination against the elderly as a group, turning a natural biologic chronological process into an artificially induced social problem. In a real sense, ageism penalizes not just the old but the young and the middle aged as well. Ageism results in job discrimination, media stereotyping and intergenerational avoidance and hostility. Euphemisms like *golden agers* do not help. Ageism threatens self-esteem because most people, young as well as old, value themselves in terms of work involvement and social activity. Denial of access to both results in devaluation that puts elderly people at risk for health-related problems, physical and social.

Popular culture is rife with ageism. Many Americans, glorifying youth and judging human worth in terms of economic utility, view aging with fear and denial. Resulting characteristics of so-called aging imposed on the elderly are spurious. Prejudice and stereotype, which portray the elderly negatively as messengers of death, disease and disability, flourish everywhere. The facts are otherwise, but stereotypes die slowly–if at all. Even social scientists did not until recently consider the unprecedented emergence in the 20th century of an elderly stage in human life as abounding in positive possibilities. Instead, gerontologists along with their colleagues in other disciplines regarded the development solely as bringing with it many problems.

"To the philosopher," said the 18th century French naturalist Georges Buffon, "old age must be considered a prejudice."

Many thoughtful Americans are fearful of becoming hopelessly and irreversibly senile, losing memory, mind and self-control, a dreadful condition which they believe no one can escape, including humanity's greatest figures who succumbed, such as the philosopher Immanuel Kant, writer Ralph Waldo Emerson and statesman Winston Churchill.

Americans are not alone in their fear and revulsion of old age. Past and present generations all over the world have expressed the same phobia, as can be seen in the works of great authors who described old age as repugnant: Aristophanes, Balzac, Coleridge, Dante, Dickens, Hesiod, Moliere, Shakespeare, Sophocles, Turgenev, Yeats. Shakespeare pictured King Lear in old age as a "ruin'd piece of nature," and Samuel Beckett in *End Game* has the characters liken senescence to a garbage can and equate themselves with garbage. Paradoxically, longevity has been sought after in societies throughout recorded history. Ironically, in literature as in life the elderly have been admired for their experience and wisdom while they were sniggered at for forgetfulness and general mental decline.

In popular culture, reflected in the bestselling 1995 Grisham novel, *The Rainmaker*, the aged as a group are viewed as frail and senile incompetents, useless and burdensome, slovenly dressed, wrinkled and stoop-shouldered, shaking and unclean, rigid and inflexible, stuck in the past with desexed and worn-out bodies rotting away with disease after disease, sniveling and crawling around nursing homes in which they wait to die after having lost all vitality. Because of stereotyping, the elderly in the aggregate are considered to be complainers, depressed and withdrawn, preoccupied with their miseries, uninteresting and hopeless, second-class citizens existing on the fringes of society. Yet, as we shall see in the pages immediately following and in "The Family" (pp. 161-165), individual old persons are respected and loved and are as a group given many unrequested favors.

Older persons often bear the brunt of opprobrious jokes, even when told by the elderly themselves. Jack Benny, probably the most famous comedian in the United States of the 20th century, thrived on portrayal of the elderly as tight-wads and eccentrics always lying about their age. In his comedic persona, Benny was 39 even when he was obviously in his 60's and 70's. More slyly disparaging, if less funny, are the greeting cards so popular a short time ago, the cover of which displaying a cartoon of a decrepit old man or woman might have a remark like: "Don't be unhappy that you've finally arrived at 40"—only to be capped on the inside page with: "Even if you'll never have fun any more." Worst of all, were the tasteless "Granny" jokes in the magazine, *Playboy*.

Language is also used to demean the elderly, sometimes unintentionally, sometimes intentionally. Euphemisms like *golden* and *mature* are pejorative. In the world of business, *senior* refers to an executive and connotes authority and prestige. In the world of every day, *senior* refers to an older person dependent on others because over-the-hill and out of the loop of authority. In the sociopolitical arena, the phrase *over-aging of the population* implies a negative view. Some derogatory terms refer to one sex, others to both sexes. Older persons are alluded to as *codger, coot* and *geezer* or as *biddy, hag, witch*. They are characterized as *decrepit, grumpy, miserly, overly cautious*. Such verbal stigmata after a lifetime of use indoctrinate all age groups so that, as Alex Comfort pointed out, "on reaching old age we may be prejudiced against ourselves."

There is irony in young people's holding stereotypical beliefs about an age cohort they will necessarily soon join. But the elderly themselves subscribe to stereotype and prejudice, which determine age-appropriate behavior and create the role they are expected to act out. In her 80's, Floria Schott-Maxwell, an influential Jungian analyst, wrote: "My kitchen linoleum is so black and shiny that I waltz while I wait for the kettle to boil. This pleasure is for the old who live alone." Also revealing how ageism infects the old is the title of Lise Maclay's poem, "I Hate the Way I Look." Yet self-esteem, referred to by sociologists as self-efficacy, is important in meeting challenges and influencing events.

The United States is what sociologists term an age-graded society. Time and again the elderly are told, indirectly as well as directly, to act their age: there is a time to retire, a time for a woman *not* to wear a bikini, a time for a male no longer young to repress sexual desire if he is not to be labeled by the socially poisonous phrase, *a dirty old man*. Adult children asked to consider the sexuality of parents by the director of a home for the aged who was thinking of privacy, found the idea repulsive.

The elderly accept without dispute the public tendency to lump them all together as a homogeneous group when, in reality, they are all individuals, each significantly different from the others. Some, seriously ill, await death. Many others, physically fit and mentally alert, are active participants in rugged trips and challenging college-level courses in various areas of knowledge offered under the auspices of Elderhostel. Some elderly are conservative; others, as the Studs Terkel books show, are radical in both politics and lifestyle. Recognizing these and other facts, gerontologists conclude that the 65+ age group are more diverse in physical ability, intellectual activity, social and political lifestyle, pro-ductivity, creativity, taste and desire than any other section of the Ameri-can population.

Many older people, continuing to hold jobs, are valued members of the work force because they account for fewer accidents, absences and mistakes. While they are slower than the young in some work-related tasks, the difference is more than offset by their use of experi-ence to make wise decisions.

In contrast to acceptance of graying older men who are generally perceived as mature and distinguished-looking, ageism continues to oppress and depress old women. There is a double standard, even in aging. Having lost the freshness of youth, older women are often pic-tured as less attractive as erotic objects, so that, following the dictates of a youth-oriented culture, men prefer the company of young females. Age changes should be thought of not as beauty departing but as beauty evolving. John Donne, famed Elizabethan poet, put the matter well:

> *No spring nor summer beauty hath such grace*
> *As I have seen in one autumnal face.*

As the continuing popularity of Angie Dickinson, Lena Horne, Paul Newman and John Forsythe–all 60+–attest, the old need not be unattractive. Nor are they sexless nor uninterested in sex although the sex drive is but one of several viewed as acceptable for the young but unacceptable for the old.

The strengths of older people are grossly underestimated. Contrary to popular belief, deterioration as a concomitant of aging is neither inevitable nor universal. The process of aging for healthy younger adults has slowed as lifetimes have grown longer, so that the years gained have been added to mid-life and not to old age. Middle age, the prime of adulthood, is now for increasing numbers of men and women the period between 50 and 75. What this means is a gift of 20 to 30 years full of vim and vigor.

Still, for many—bankers, legislators and politicians among them—the new-found longevity of the old is a clear and present danger to society. With the intention of minimizing or denying existing government programs and services for the elderly, they cry out for cost-containment. Seemingly unaware that they are scapegoating and pitting the generations against each other, they complain that the elderly in this period of ruinous deficits are *greedy geezers*, budget busters, who demand too much through *graying* of government outlays—federal, state and county. A *Time* cover of February 1988 reinforced this idea with a picture of a vigorous couple on the way to tennis and with the caption: "Americans are living longer and enjoying it more—but who will foot the bill?" An op-ed article in *The New York Times* of January 1998 asked: "Why do seniors get all the breaks?"

The generation that reached adulthood during and just after WW II, critics assert, benefited from government treating issues involving old age as a subject of social policy (disease and disability, health care, pensions, poverty, retirement) with unprecedented development of services and schemes for transfer of wealth while failing to guarantee similar advantages to succeeding generations. A better approach, critics say, would be for the government to serve as coordinator of funds and services rather than as direct provider.

Projections made before the United States Senate are that by the year 2025 federal expenditure on the aging will reach 40% of the entire budget. Worse, the critics point out, is that today the aged receive at least 30% of all national expenditures but contribute less than 15% in taxes. What such critics omit is that a considerable amount of the 30% is Social Security payment, to which the elderly contributed substantially. More than 3/4 of all elderly never seek help from local Area Agencies on Aging; nor do they seek help from private organizations in their communities. Less than 50% of qualified elderly receive Supplemental Security Income benefits or Food Stamps. At the present time, the percentage of federal income tax revenues coming from the elderly is close to their proportion of the entire population. If runaway health care costs on the national level can be brought under control, many economists and politicians insist that the percentage of the Gross National Product needed to finance benefits to the aged will not increase but may even decrease. Using such material, organizations such as Generations United have been trying to defuse conflicts, real or perceived.

Nevertheless, the hue and cry persists that American society cannot afford the economic burdens of an aging population—until even such seemingly responsible people as Richard Lamm, former governor of Colorado, recommended sharply diminishing health care to many of the ailing aged, going so far as to say the terminally ill "had a duty to die." Such people refuse to recognize the truism that all age groups in the United States have similar responsibilities as well as rights and that all face common problems. Age is not an index of the worth of human beings.

Surveys in the 1990s reveal that generational conflict does not enter any picture of public attitudes toward government mandated benefits. Just the opposite. Widespread support is well established among all age groups. Ironically, when less support of benefits is expressed, it is often by older persons rather than young.

Labor unions and the young have not protested against rising Social Security taxes, for they know that almost always public policy benefits the young as well as the old. In general, there is deep sympathy among the public for needs of the aged. They recognize that security and support, in addition to health, are what promote a good old age. Although Social Security comprises the most important single source of financial support for the elderly, approximately 1 in 18 recipients of benefits is under 18 years. Obviously, both young and old age groups want a secure Social Security system in preference to placing financial responsibility for the needy back on the family alone.

Ageism also makes for a double standard, even in medicine. The elderly themselves subscribe to it. Unaware that usually ill health results from cumulative exposure to risk and bodily insult rather than from biological senescence, they blame aches and pains on old age. Regarding treatment of a chronically ill patient as a no-win undertaking, a number of physicians do not perform well when caring for the elderly. Some doctors follow a policy of benign neglect, as regards hypertension, the chief risk factor for cardiovascular disease in the old, even though it can be controlled. They give as reasons that blood pressure, no matter what, tends to rise with the years and that cardiovascular disease often appears in the elderly without recognizable risk factors. Intervening in such a situation is a gamble, they say, and what there is to lose is at worst a severely limited life span. This although for thousands of years the goals of medicine have remained the same: to relieve suffering and to cure. Age is not mentioned in the Hippocratic oath.

Freud himself in 1924 voiced objection to the elderly as patients. "Near and above the fifties," he said incorrectly, "the elasticity of the mental processes on which the treatment depends is as a rule lacking—old people are no longer educable. . . ." There is a large body of incontrovertible evidence demonstrating that age is not a barrier to learning, that with training older adults can improve performance on intelligence tests and other problem solving tasks. Today, to take another example, if tests of a young person reveal an elevated level of blood sugar, a physician would insist on changes in diet and exercise and probably prescribe medication. If a similar situation were to occur with an old patient, some doctors would consider it the process of aging and do nothing. Abnormality and possible danger in one case, routine and harmlessness in the other.

Admittedly, evaluating the real state of an elderly person's health may be difficult. The multiple diseases to which the old are subject can lead to confusing diagnoses. Nevertheless, a double standard does exist. Too many physicians, perceiving problems of the elderly in terms of negative diagnosis, view old people as "incurable" and think that sickness is a necessary aspect of old age. Even today it is often assumed that the elderly with complaints of chronic pain(s) are not susceptible to treatment because of diminished sensitivity to pain. No contemporary physician would react to a youth the way some doctors continue to treat the old:

> Patient: Doctor, my left arm hurts.
> Doctor: You know as well as I you have to get used to it.
>   What do you expect at your age? You're 82 years old!
> Patient: But my right arm's that old, and it doesn't hurt.
>   OR
> Patient: Doctor, I don't feel well.
> Doctor: You've got to remember you're not getting any younger.
> Patient: I know that, Doctor. I just want to keep getting older.

Probably not apocryphal, the story is told of Conrad Adenauer, who when Chancellor of Germany was bedridden because of the flu. He scolded his doctor and said he had to get better so as to make a scheduled trip overseas. "I'm no magician," said the doctor. "I can't make you young again." Adenauer is reported to have answered: "I'm not asking for that. I don't want to be young again. I just want to go on getting older."

An old person who has not yet adjusted to changes in hearing and vision may be inaccurately diagnosed as eccentric or, in extreme cases, as senile. Doctors, trained to provide immediate curative care rather than to help someone adapt to combinations of chronic illnesses, may lack interest in geriatric procedures, an attitude reinforced by society's negative attitude toward aging and the aged. Samuel Johnson warned: "A common prejudice should not be found in one whose trade it is to rectify error."

Old age as a developmental phase in the life cycle has never been accepted. The old are still seen in popular culture as complainers, uninteresting and hopeless. Maggie Kuhn, founder of the Gray Panthers, accused professionals–social workers and physicians among them–of treating the elderly as "wrinkled babies." Despite such ageism, older persons, vastly increased in numbers and highly skilled by virtue of experience in organizational tactics, have become a powerful economic, social and political force to be reckoned with. Some politicians, fearful of competition for what they deem increasingly scarce resources, talk of generational conflict.

But the generations are interdependent. Long-term goals of the young and the old are identical. There can be no justification for separating the elderly from the rest of the human race. The aged are the link between generations that helps to achieve those goals.

Gerontology and geriatrics have added years to the life and life to the years of the old, giving them time and energy and the opportunity to return much to the very society that derides them, enriching their children and children's children with the wisdom that comes from deep perspective and long experience. The old should be valued for accumulated knowledge, on the basis of which come expertise in living, maturity of judgment, inclusive understanding, a combinatorial faculty that to develop takes years of experience modified by perception.

It is obvious that not every old person is wise. But living into old age may be the only way to achieve wisdom. The aged have for many years been coping with events and people, with tasks and problems, with series after series of changes and transitions requiring flexibility to adjust and meet new challenges. From experience, they have learned that much of life is a tangle of contradiction, irony and paradox, a mixture of the good and the bad, with truth frequently compromised by circumstance. Drawing more on years of social and business intercourse and relying less on speed of response, the elderly have the ability to take the long view and place problems in proper context. Older persons have learned how to evaluate choices, set priorities and determine what realistic responses a complex situation requires despite the ambiguity and uncertainty inherent in so many personal, business and civic problems.

John Boyle O'Reilly would remind the young about the old:

The wealth of mankind is the wisdom they leave.

Cicero would remind the old:

> *Old age is honored only on condition that it defends itself,*
> *maintains its rights, is subservient to no one, and to its last*
> *breath rules over its domain.*

AGENCIES

How widely its agencies vary,–
To save–to ruin–to curse–to bless,–
As even its minted coins express. . . .

Thomas Hood

At the federal level, aging activities generally focus on research and delivery of ser-vices. As a result of passage of the Research on Aging Act, the National Institute on Aging (NIA) was created in May 1974 to be the chief federal agency responsible for pro-motion, coordination and support of basic research and training pertinent to aging and diseases and problems of the aged. As a section of the National Institutes of Health (NIH), the National Institute of Aging conducts and sponsors research, not only in biological and biomedical sciences, but also in behavioral and social sciences, to improve the quality of life for elderly. Some research is carried out by NIA itself in its extensive laboratories and its 500+ bed Clinical Center and Ambulatory Care Research Facility as well as in the Gerontological Research Center in Baltimore, Maryland, which conducts the Baltimore Longitudinal Study of Aging. About 80% of the agency's funds are awarded through grants and contracts to universities, scientific foundations and hospitals in the United States and abroad for carrying out approved research plans.

Delivery of services to older persons using funds appropriated under the Older Americans Act and other legislation is the responsibility of the Administration on Aging within the Department of Health and Human Services. Funds are usually delegated to the state agencies on aging, which administer programs at state and local levels. There are 670 Area Agencies on Aging throughout the nation, each serving a single locality. Names of the Agencies vary from state to state. Each state's Office or Commission on Aging can furnish addresses and telephone numbers of the various Agencies on Aging within its jurisdic

The Older Americans Act, Title XX of the Social Security act, and other legislation seek through provision without charge of services such as meals-on-wheels and senior centers to help the elderly stay out of nursing homes. Programs include: nutrition services, transportation services, development of senior centers, assistance in obtaining employment, housing development and maintenance.

Only a small proportion of the elderly make use of the agencies and their many services. The Federal Information Center has toll-free telephone numbers to call for the facts about government programs and agencies. Numbers can be obtained from the local telephone directory or from the telephone operator. The Administration on Aging, United States Department of Health and Human Services, also supplies information on the numerous services available to the elderly, most of which are free.

AGENCIES AND ORGANIZATIONS
SERVING THE ELDERLY
(For a list keyed to subjects in
Aging: An Encyclopedia, see "Resources," pp. 443-457)

Federal Government

Action
806 Connecticut Ave.NW,
Washington, DC 20525

Administration on Aging
230 Independence Ave. SW
Washington, DC 20201

Department of Agriculture
14 St. and Independence Ave. SW
Washington, D.C. 20250

Department of Veterans Affairs
810 Vermont Ave. NW
Washington, DC 20420

National Institute on Aging
9000 Rockville Pike
Bethesda, MD 20892

Select Committee on Aging
House of Representatives
Washington, DC 20515

Social Security Administration
6401 Security Blvd.
Baltimore, MD 21235

Special Committee on Aging
United States Senate
Washington, D.C. 20510

Private Organizations

American Aging Association
2129 Providence Ave.
Chester, PA 1901

Association for Gerontology
in Higher Education
1001 Connecticut Ave. NW
Washington, DC 20036

Center for Social Gerontology
2307 Shelby Avenue.
Ann Arbor, MI 48103

Gerontological Society of America
1275 K St.
Washington, DC 20005

National Retired Teachers Assn.
601 E St. NW
Washington, DC 20049

International Federation
on Aging
380 St. Antoine St. W.
Montreal, Canada H2Y3X7

National Caucus and Center
on Black Aged
1424 K St. NW
Washington, DC 20005

National Council on the Aging
409 3rd St. SW
Washington, DC 20024

National Interfaith Coalition
409 Third St. SW
Washington, DC 20049

National Senior Citizens Law
777 S. Figueroa
Los Angeles, CA 90017

Advocacy Groups

American Association of Retired
Persons
601 E St. NW
Washington, DC 20049

Gray Panthers
P.O.Box 21477
Washington, DC 20009

International Senior Citizens
Association
255 S. Hill St.
Los Angeles, CA 90012

National Alliance of Senior
Citizens
1700 18th St. NW
Washington, DC, 20009

National Council of Senior
Citizens
1511 K St. NW
Washington, DC 20005

Social Services

American Association of Homes
and Services for the Aging
901 E St. NW
Washington, DC 20004

Legal Services for the Elderly
130 W. 42nd St.
New York, NY 10036

National Association of Meal
Programs
1414 Prince St.,
Alexandria, VA 22314

National Asssociation of Area
Agencies on Aging
1112 16th St. NW
Washington, DC 200036

National Home Caring Council
235 Park Ave. S.
N.Y., NY 10003

National Institute of Senior Centers
c/o National Council on the Aging
409 3rd St. SW
Washington, DC 20024

Health

American Geriatrics Society
770 Lexington Ave.
New York, NY 10021

American Society for Geriatric
Dentistry
211 E. Chicago Ave.
Chicago, IL 60143

Committee on Aging,
American Medical Association
515 N. State St.
Chicago, IL 60610

National Rehabilitation Associa
633 S. Washington St.
Alexandria, VA 22314

Society for Nutrition Education
2001 Killebrew Dr.
Minneapolis, MN 55425

ALTERNATIVE MEDICINE

Hast Thou . . . medicine for case like mine?
Walt Whitman

The current health care crisis is in part a result of conventional medicine's inability to effectively and economically treat chronic diseases and disorders. About 35 million persons in the United States are limited in daily activities by allergies, arthritis, cancer, cardiovascular disease, depression, digestive difficulties, hypertension. But mainstream medicine (also called allopathy and biomedicine), so effective in treating acute infection and trauma, is not as yet prepared or equipped to deal effectively with chronic conditions, especially of many of the elderly who view physicians and medical organizations as impersonal, remote, uncaring. More and more late-life persons trying to conquer disease, disability and chronic pain are seeking nonconventional therapies to complement today's managed health care system.

Congress established the Office of Alternative Medicine in 1992 "to more adequately explore unconventional medical practices." The report of the sponsoring Senate committee states: "many routine and effective medical procedures now considered commonplace were once considered unconventional and counterindicated. Cancer radiation therapy is such a procedure that is now commonplace but once was considered to be quackery." The National Institutes of Health adds that much of alternative medicine is cost-effective and does work. Practitioners insist that alternative therapy (variously referred to as holistic or integrated) is without the potential for harm inherent in the strong drugs and surgery of conventional medicine. The result: alternative medicine is not so alternative anymore. More than 30 medical schools—including Columbia, Harvard and Stanford—offer courses in alternative medicine. Many major medical centers have created clinics offering alternative treatment. Some physicians prefer the term *complementary medicine*, which suggests a merger of the conventional with the unconventional.

NIH, of which OAM is a part, cautions: do not seek alternative therapy (also referred to as mind-body medicine) without first consulting a knowledgeable MD. Ask the alternative-medicine practitioner specific, detailed questions about recommended treatment. Shy away or be suspicious if the practitioner refuses to work with your regular doctor or claims ability to cure all your ailments or insists that a total cure of a specific ailment will result if you sign up for a "complete" series of treatments.

Neither an art nor a science, conventional medicine is a profession, an organized, empirical discipline of diagnostic and therapeutic skills. Like conventional medicine, alternative medicine employs technology But the relationship ends there. Unlike conventional medicine, alternative medicine is not built on a coherent and established foundation of evidence which has passed the rigorous tests of modern-day science. Alternative medicine appeals mainly to those elderly with chronic and incurable diseases or to those with annoying symptoms which doctors cannot explain explain and eradicate.

Many alternative therapies have not been subjected to rigorous scientific investigation. (The federal government is now funding research into various alternative therapies to determine efficacy and safety.) Some are applied by nonspecialists in medicine. Not all elderly adapt easily to all alternative procedures, a number of which, like cell therapy and chelation, come perilously close to quackery and are not discussed here.

For many years, researchers have been trying to find answers to questions concerning the complex interactions between mind and body. How and to what extent is the mind capable of influencing the body, especially as regards cause, course and cure (partial and complete healing) of disorders and diseases? How can patients be helped to obtain techniques and abilities to act on their own behalf? It has long been known that the placebo response (improvement in condition of an ill person as a result of treatment with an innocuous substance, such as a sugar-coated pill administered as if a real medication) often helps patients with lessening of pain and perhaps of other symptoms. Does alternative therapy "heal" because patients believe in the process?

Mind-body procedures are generally considered helpful in treating arthritis, chronic pain, some gastrointestinal disorders, high blood pressure and stress. Patients find mind-body therapies especially attractive because, rather than passively relying on pills and a doctor to effect a cure, they themselves actively play a role in solution of their problem.

Familiar to the general public are art, dance and music therapy, biofeedback, chiropractic, hypnosis, imagery, meditation, mental healing, prayer, psychophysiological therapy, support groups, yoga. More unusual, even strange to the point sometimes of being considered magical, other mind-body approaches like acupuncture, bioelectromagnetics, homeopathy, naturopathy, nutritional and herbal medicine and prayerful healing are based on religion and tradition as well as on science.

Art therapy is a way for patients to express unconscious concern about disorders, including even such varied disturbances as burns and eating irregularities. Dance therapy is effective in decreasing anxiety, body tension, depression and in heightening circulation and respiratory functioning. Adults who have been in a dentist's office recognize the value of music therapy as a relaxant and pain-reducer. Music therapy also works well with cancer and Parkinson's patients.

Biofeedback utilizes electrical and other instruments to enable patients to see or feel or hear information about bodily processes of which they are normally unaware. The resulting "picture" provides feedback and stimulates increased sensitivity by means of which patients can learn through trial and error to control body functions previously considered involuntary, such as blood pressure and temperature. Although conditions where there is severe sensory loss, as from head trauma or radiation injury to skin, do not respond well to biofeedback, additional applications of the treatment are still being discovered.

Hypnosis for curative purposes was utilized in ancient times. The Greeks employed trance states in their temples for healing. In the modern era, Freud used hypnosis in treatment of hysteria but had so much difficulty with the technique that he gave it up. Today, hypnosis is practiced extensively for addictions, such as smoking, for phobias, such as fear of flying, and for control of reactions to such allergies as that caused by poison ivy. Dentists, physicians and psychologists utilize hypnosis, either independently or in conjunction with other forms of treatment, to help patients control pain.

Imagery is a popular technique for influencing the subconscious mind. Patients concentrate on creation of images, sometimes at the suggestion of a facilitator, that will help relieve stress and bring about states of mind and behavior changes favorable to well-being. Often used in concert with hypnosis, meditation and relaxation, guided imagery helps cancer patients to focus on visualizing pleasant scenes or on destruction of malignant cells, in this way replacing fear and pessimism with positive emotions. Supposedly, attitudes change and the will to live strengthens. Tests indicate successful use of imagery in control of chronic pain and in helping geriatric patients enhance immunity.

Meditation is a self-directed way of reducing stress on body and mind. Although its original purpose, primarily religious, was to raise spiritual awareness, meditation today is employed for purposes of self-regulation to achieve relaxation and healing. There are many approaches to meditation, such as concentrating on a repeated word or on one's breathing, but there is one goal common to all: to periodically reach a temporary state absent as much as possible from thought and emotion. Some research studies find that meditation can significantly reduce anxiety, depression and high blood pressure.

Psychotherapy aims at treatment of the sick by psychological or psychophysiological methods such that patients reach a state of health, both mental and physical, no matter how difficult the illness or disorder. Psychology deals with the mind in any of its aspects. Psychophysiology, narrower in range, concentrates on the interrelationship of mental and bodily processes. Once the exclusive territory of psychiatrists and psychoanalysts, psychophysiological therapy today is practiced by clergymen, nurses, social workers, psychologists and even by former patients who argue that they are qualified to do so by virtue of alleviation of their distress. There are more than 100 modes of treatment. Looked at another way, psychophysiological therapy is like a medical traffic circle through which all the health-purveying professions pass and interact. There is much overlap.

Traditionally, psychotherapy utilized psychoanalysis with suggestion, persuasion and reeducation, but today hypnosis, imagery, meditation and other modalities including use of community-oriented support groups can play a role in psychophysiological treatment. Some psychophysiologists claim a direct anticancer effect. Research regarded as valid by all parties indicates that psychophysiological therapy can quicken recovery from certain lesser kinds of medical crises, particularly from illnesses called psychosomatic in which symptoms apparently have no medical cause.

There are many kinds of support groups, some hospital-based, others independent, still others sponsored by various organizations, such as the American Cancer Society. Almost all groups offer support at low or no monetary cost to both patients and their families. Group members form bonds with each other and gain strength from becoming actively involved in the struggle against disease. Generally, the function of a group is viewed as complementary to ongoing mainstream medical care with the hope that psychosocial support will help patients improve the quality of their lives and perhaps contribute to recovery. Research literature is replete with examples of the strong beneficial effect support groups exert on patients with such physical illnesses as asthma, cancer, stroke.

Yoga, a Hindu philosophy originally based on belief that life consists of divinely inspired sequences, has practices that include dietary prescriptions, ethical rules of behavior and routines of physical exercise to obtain control over bodily and mental processes contributing to wellness. Studies show that correct adaptation and sustained practice of Yoga reduce anxiety, lower blood pressure and make respiration more efficient.

Other approaches of alternative medicine may seem strange because they are based on ancient religious practices, old traditions and— a paradox—the latest developments in science.

Traditional oriental medicine employs acupuncture, herbal preparations (discussed below) and massage (kneading outer layers of flesh to stimulate circulation and help muscles become supple). The customary acupuncture method involves puncturing the skin with needles so fine at the tip that there is little or no blood in evidence. Relief from pain and a sense of well-being may result immediately after treatment. Needles are inserted at energy points and channels along a network of meridians that acupuncturists maintain connects with and influences not only surface and structural areas but also organs deep within the body. Sometimes electricity is applied to the needles to further stimulatepoints. When fingertips are used to exert direct physical pressure on the energy points, the method is called acupressure and is supposedly effective in emergency first aid.

There is much scientific evidence for beneficial effects of acupuncture in management of chronic pain—even to analgesia effective enough for surgical procedures—and in treatment of asthma and migraine headaches although exactly how and why acupuncture works is not known save that pain-relieving chemicals (called endorphins in conventional medicine) are released during the procedure.

Still in its beginnings, bioelectromagnetics seems like a story out of science fiction based on the idea that living organisms interact with electromagnetic fields. Electrical currents within a human being can and do produce magnetic fields that spread outside the body, where in turn they may be influenced by electrical phenomena emanating from the earth's own geomagnetic field and from power lines and other manmade objects. Certain bioelectromagnetic frequencies have direct effects on body tissue, even as prescription drugs do. There is much proof that exposure to specific frequencies and to low-level nonthermal magnetic fields can have beneficial effects on the body, such as in bone repair, nerve stimulation and wound healing.

Study of bioelectromagnetics may help scientists discover the mechanisms by which acupuncture and other seemingly esoteric therapies practiced elsewhere in the world for centuries produce their effects on body and mind. None of these is more mystifying than therapeutic touch, which Jean Withers, RN, director of the Haven Hospice Program at JFK Medical Center in Edison, New Jersey, calls magical. To relax a person, the therapist places her hands about 1 inch from the body and moves them slowly from the head to the feet, smoothing out (in theory) the energy field surrounding the physique.

Chiropractic is a form of healing concerned with the relationship between structure (primarily of the spine) and function (primarily of the nervous system). Chiropractors manipulate body structures, especially the spinal column, to overcome dysfunction, reduce pain and restore and preserve good health. Their goal is to prevent disease and to make vital energy throughout the body. By law as well as by training, chiropractors use only manual procedures, relying neither on surgery nor on chemotherapy. Conventional medicine accepts chiropractic as pertinent to orthopedic and neurologic specialties. Studies indicate effectiveness of chiropractic manipulation in situations of lower back pain without major neurological involvement.

Homeopathy is utilized throughout the world, especially in Europe, South America and India. In England, homeopathy is sponsored by the Royal Family. In France, as many as 1 in 4 licensed physicians prescribe homeopathic remedies. Although the theory of homeopathic medicine is diametrically opposed to that of conventional medicine, the market in the United States for homeopathic prescriptions is a multi-million-dollar industry. At the core of homeopathy's pharmacopoeia are materials made from naturally occurring animal, mineral or plant substances—all recognized and regulated by the Food and Drug Administration. Selection of homeopathic pharmaceuticals is based on the idea that *like cures like,* that materials which produce in a healthy person a set of symptoms will prove to be therapeutically beneficial in a sick person with the same syndrome.

The term *homeopathy* is from the Greek *homeo* (similar) and *pathes* (suffering from a disorder). Homeopathic practice is individualized, so that two persons with an identical diagnosis may be given different medicines. Homeopaths theorize that their pharmaceutic materials do not produce a cure in and of themselves but contain enough electromagnetism to stimulate the body's own healing response or vital energy. Clinical trials imply beneficial effects of homeopathic therapy on allergic rhinitis, fibrositis and influenza.

Both homeopathy and naturopathy consider disease processes as symptoms revelatory of but not indistinguishable from underlying problems. Founded in the United States at the turn of the century by a group of physicians from various therapeutic disciplines, naturopathy integrates acupuncture, botany, homeopathy, hydrotherapy, nutrition and manipulative therapy with the practices of conventional medicine. Naturopathic physicians emphasize the inherent healing ability of the human organism. Attempting to individualize treatment according to needs of each patient, they rely on nutrition and establishment of a healthy lifestyle to prevent and to cure disease. Significant benefits have been reliably reported from reliance on a naturopathic botanical formula as an alternative to estrogen replacement therapy.

Nutritional and herbal medicine remain popular in both Western and Eastern traditions, especially because of their insistence that medical conditions are affected by what people eat and drink. Recommended dietary strategies include reduction of consumption of saturated fats, limitation of alcoholic drinks, eating fiber-rich foods and all kinds of fruits and vegetables. Certain nutrients, particularly Vitamins A, C, E, beta-carotene and selenium, are believed by nutritionalists and herbalists to contain antioxidants helpful in dealing with cancer. Herbalists hold that chamomile can help a person relax at bedtime, that peppermint may improve digestion. But herbs, they caution, often take longer to work than traditional Western medications, months rather than days. It is advisable to stop using a herbal preparation which does not help or which produces unpleasant side effects. Because herbs are often self-administered, it is important to consult an authoritative guide (also called herbal) like Michael Castleman's *The Healing Herbs: The Ultimate Guide to the Curative Power of Nature's Medicines.*

Alternative practitioners insist they have many natural substances that behave as do conventional medications but without danger of side effects. Choose, they caution, products with labels specifying concentration of active ingredients and use only under medical supervision. For a full discussion, see M.T. Murray, ND, *Natural Alternatives to Over-the-Counter and Prescription Drugs* (NY: Morrow, 1994).

Almost all varieties of mental healing are similar to those of prayerful healing in that they involve a state of spirituality accompanied by feelings of love and empathy. There are 2 major types of prayerful healing. The healer enters an altered state of consciousness with the desire to be united with God (or the universe) and without contact other than the spiritual to become "one" with the person to be healed. Or the healer physically touches the healee and conveys a "flow of cosmic energy" to the site of illness, as manifested by feelings of heat in both persons. Many published reports, but not scientific studies, insist that healers have been able to affect eye and muscular movement, respiration and even brain rhythms of target persons.

To be trusted as reliable, alternative medicine theories and practices need to be investigated by impartial researchers for validation of effectiveness and safety. Unfortunately, alternative therapies do not lend themselves easily to testing and verification by use of scientific methods, such as double-blind studies. For skeptics among health professionals, the key to perceived usage of alternative medicine is the possibility of tolerance of conjoint therapy with acceptance of cultural variation and without negative judgment until such time that scientific research can reach definitive answers. At present there is a severe lack of facilities for research into alternative therapies, not to mention inadequate funding with consequent deficiencies in training, grants-in-aid and the handing on of newly discovered information. Yet consumers, particularly the elderly suffering from chronic diseases, are turning to alternative medicine because they believe it is less expensive than traditional therapies and can either supplement or go beyond mainstream medicine in alleviation and possible cure. On a worldwide basis, 70-90% of health care derives from folk principles or from alternative medical traditions rather than from mainstream biomedicine.

There is increasing acceptance of some forms of alternative medicine in the United States. More than 60,000,000 Americans in the course of 1 year use an alternative therapy and pay more visits to alternative care practitioners than to mainstream primary care physicians, spending well over $10,000,000,000 of their own money each year because the visits are not covered by insurance. Is it any wonder that responsible leaders in conventional medicine are calling for all the therapies of alternative medicine to be carefully studied to determine their potential for improving both health and health care of the young as well as of the old? In accord are the editors of the prestigious *Journal of the American Medical Association*, who devoted their entire November 11, 1998 issue (Vol. 280, No. 18) to alternative medicine and problems associated with it.

In the meantime, doctors at Columbia Presbyterian Medical Center in New York City, generally acknowledged as one of the best hospital-research complexes in the United States, are trying to develop what they term *complementary care*, by merging the 2 seemingly incompatible systems of therapy, alternative and biomedicine. At Columbia, a patient while receiving treatment from a physician licensed in traditional medicine may engage the services of practitioners of alternative medicine in hypnosis, massage, yoga and even reflexology (rubbing of spots on the foot to stimulate specific organs in the body).

The goal is health. More than 2,500 years ago, Pericles put the matter well. "Health," he said, "is that state of moral, mental and physical well-being, which enables man to face any crisis in life with utmost facility and grace." In modern times, the American Ralph Waldo Emerson, ever pragmatic, said simply: "Health is wealth."

BEATING THE COLD
and THE HEAT

While the earth remaineth, seedtime and
harvest and cold and heat, and summer
and winter, and day and night shall not cease.

Genesis. VIII. 111

The elderly 65+ are more susceptible to all kinds of heat and cold disorders than any younger age group. During the summer–whether in a hot, humid locale like Florida's Miami or a dry, arid place like Arizona's Santa Fe–the possibility of potentially fatal heatstroke among those 65+ is about 10 times that of 30-year olds. During the winter–whether in a damp, cold city like New York in January with temperatures hovering around freezing or in a dry, cold ski area like Vail, Colorado–incidence of the elderly to dangerous hypothermia is much higher than that of the young.

Heat and cold disorders can occur everywhere and at almost any time. They are insidious; that is, they may ambush the unwary or anyone who does not pay attention to symptoms giving prior warning. Heat exhaustion can occur after a stint of gardening under the summer sun; hypothermia, after a walk along winter-windy streets. Ironically, too many elderly persons succumb to temperature-based illness because they are not heating or cooling their dwellings adequately. Effective air-conditioning and heating systems bring mental and physical comfort during the day by giving the body an opportunity to return to normal temperature, and they reduce danger, especially at night, because in an overly hot or cold bedroom an elderly sleeper can lose consciousness and expire without chance of rescue since no one knows what is happening.

As with everything else, there is a price to pay for comfort–this time not only in coin but also in adaptation. Once a person relies on air-conditioning and central heating to beat the weather, the body's ability to adapt to extremes of temperature is diminished for about a week. It takes that long to get used to new temperatures. In the summer, the body attempts to acclimate by raising pulse rate and amount of sweating. In the winter, the body relies on increased pulse rate and shivering. Even after a week, the body may not be fully acclimatized because people work, shop and relax in artificially cooled or heated homes, businesses, malls and automobiles. It is not wise to leave an air-conditioned home to exercise vigorously outdoors on a hot, muggy day; nor is it smart to leave a heated house on a cold, wintry day to go bareheaded for a long walk. No elderly person should try to beat the heat and the cold without using every aid possible.

There are ways to beat heat and cold besides relying on air-conditioning and central heating. "Some are weather-wise, some are otherwise," said Benjamin Franklin. Getting fit is of prime importance. A person who is out of condition responds to extremes in temperature by getting hotter faster on a torrid day, by getting colder on a frigid day. A couch potato with layers of fat suffers sharp declines in reserves of body water, thereby increasing vulnerability to dehydration—a condition equally dangerous in summer as in winter. Anyone taking medications should check with a doctor to make sure that drugs such as antihistamines, beta blockers and diuretics, whether prescribed or over-the-counter, do not unduly affect blood pressure, heart rate, sweating and urination.

Dress for the weather: in summer or in winter, wear a hat and clothing that "breathes." In summer, cover up with lightweight and light-colored clothing. Salt beverages and foods slightly. Wear prescription sun glasses. In winter, use layers of fabrics designed for cold weather. Wool retains heat despite getting wet.

Try to drink more water than usual to avoid dehydration. Avoid caffeine and alcohol, which may increase dehydration. Thirst is not a good indicator because as one ages there is a tendency to drink less. A reliable but not infallible guide to need for water is urine color: if urine is dark yellow, the body is not getting enough water. Sports drinks are not necessary but water is.

Hyperthermia is a term physicians use to designate certain kinds of artificially induced fever. The true form of heat disorder most often encountered is heat exhaustion, whose name is misleading. Rarely is there anything like absolute exhaustion. Onset is usually preceded by anxiety, fatigue, excessive sweating. Chills, headache and upset stomach may occur. Cause may be excessive loss of fluid and/or standing relatively still in a hot area. The pulse slows, the skin becomes cold and pale and unconsciousness may follow. Treatment includes placing the victim flat in a shady place and giving lightly salted cool drinks in small amounts at brief intervals. In contrast, heatstroke is a grave medical emergency caused by inability of the body to cool itself as a result of failure of its heat-loss mechanisms in an environment of high temperature. Onset is often preceded by dizziness, headache and fatigue. Pulse rate and body temperature increase rapidly, and the skin becomes hot and dry to the touch. Heatstroke can cause convulsions, brain damage, heart attack, death. Prompt treatment is essential. An ambulance should be summoned immediately. Until its arrival, the victim should be wrapped in wet clothing or immersed in cold water. After recovery, bedrest for several days is advisable.

Even those fit elderly who think that they can take the heat ought to recognize that they cannot beat it without adequate prior preparation. Similarly, one should be aware of the potential danger in wintry weather. Severe cold can injure blood vessels, nerves and skin while lowering body temperature below life-sustaining levels. Susceptibility to damage from the cold is markedly increased by excessive alcohol intake, dehydration, fatigue, heart condition, hunger. Preventive measures include wearing layers of warm, dry clothing that "breathe" and do not interfere with circulation. Shoes or boots should be insulated but not so tightly that they hinder circulation. Above all (pun intended), one's hat should be of especially warm material because about 1/3 of total heat loss is from the head. Hot drinks and physical exertion do help in beating the cold.

Remaining for a fairly long period of time in near-freezing temperatures can result in frostnip. Parts of the face, ears and other exposed areas appear white and become cold and firm to the touch. Injury is usually superficial. Recommended treatment is reheating by placing an unaffected hand or warm, not hot, object next to the hurt body part. The skin should not be rubbed. Peeling and blistering may follow in a day or two. Sometimes, lasting hypersensitivity to cold temperatures results. More serious is frostbite, a result of excessive exposure to dry cold in below-freezing temperatures. The longer a body part is frozen, the more severe the injury. Immediate action should be taken. Extremities should be immersed as soon as possible in hot but not scalding water. Tolerably hot drinks and warmed, dry clothing will help body temperature to rise and provide some heat to the frozen extremities until medical personnel arrive.

Accidental hypothermia, a grave emergency, ensues when the body cannot maintain normal temperature. Predisposing factors involve alcohol abuse, diminished perception of cold, heart disease, inadequate or wet clothing, diminished central heating, physical weakness, sedatives and tranquilizers, underfeeding, windchill. Accidental hypothermia may occur in a home as warm as 65°, generally taking many days to develop. Especially among the elderly, the condition is potentially fatal. Medical help should be summoned immediately. Meanwhile, rather than attempt to warm the victim too quickly, do get him/her into a sweater and hat and between blankets.

Body temperature, having fallen below 95°, will continue to fall slowly and without the victim's notice. Apathy, drowsiness, fatigue, incoordination and weakness culminate in a state of confusion. Because shivering stops, the body is incapable of warming itself. Core temperature falls even further. Stupor and then coma may follow. Death results if treatment is not begun in time. After summoning medical help, do not let the victim go to sleep. Do not try to warm the victim too quickly. Slow rewarming, so as to permit body temperature to gradually return to normal, begins the treatment of choice. Get the victim into blankets, a sweater and a hat. The doctor will follow up by careful monitoring of the victim, with medical care administered as needed.

Mark Twain was correct in saying that everyone complains about the weather but no one does anything about it. But, as is seen immediately above, the elderly need have no chronic anxiety about extremes of the weather. There are easy and effective ways to beat the cold and the heat.

CRIME

The world abounds with laws, and teems with crimes.
The Pennsylvania Gazette, Feb. 8, 1775

Although data on crimes are imprecise, law enforcement authorities estimate that the elderly have a lower violent-crime victimization rate than that of any other adult age group. Yet many, if not most, elderly worry about crime. Fearing that they are especially vulnerable because of diminished strength and agility, they tend to stay at home especially at night. Women are more afraid than men, blacks more than whites. But police in urban, suburban and rural areas insist that older people are less likely than young to become victims of violent crimes except for purse snatching and pickpocketing, the rates for which are similar for all cohorts of the population.

Many low-income elderly live in high-crime areas. To help them, the Federal Government has created the Federal Crime Insurance Program, which subsidizes in high-crime areas home and business insurance against burglary and robbery that can almost never be canceled or non-renewed because of reported loss. The program is administered by the Federal Insurance Administration, an organ of the Federal Emergency Management Agency.

Because late-life adults are thought to have assets readily available like a bank account and cash set aside for a rainy day, swindlers and thieves find them tempting targets. Older women, in particular, are vulnerable. Many a widow relied on her spouse to handle finances. Traditionally, females, taught to be courteous, consider it impolite to end a conversation abruptly. Given time, quick-tongued tricksters can spin almost irresistible tales.

Confidence men attempt to prey on the elderly with home-repair schemes, real estate swindles, fake hearing aids, unneeded health insurance, expensive funeral arrangements and the like. The problem is national. Roving bands of criminal groups crisscross the United States, committing scams, flimflams or distraction-type crimes whose main target is the elderly. Such groups are usually referred to, not always accurately, as gypsies. They tend to follow warm weather and live in motels off proceeds of their crimes.

Estimates are that more than 30% of victims of telemarketing fraud are elderly. No one knows for sure because many elderly remain silent and do not report the crime. Chuck Owens of the FBI's Financial Crime Section states: "Telemarketing Fraud is a multi-billion dollar criminal enterprise that threatens the economic security of Americans in every state." The National Consumers League's National Fraud Information Center (NFIC) points out ways to avoid telemarketing scams. Consumers should allow time to make a decision. Fraudulent telemarketers try to convey a sense of urgency. Beware of high-pressure tactics, such as insistance that you say yes *now*. Never send money at once or use your credit card to pay for a prize or to enter a sweepstakes. When in doubt, check it out. Evelyn McCoy, a counselor at NFIC, advises investigating legitimacy by telephoning her agency at 1-800-0876-7600. It is better to avoid telemarketing completely. If a marketer calls, just say: "I make no such decisions over the telephone. Write me." Anyone can cut telemarketing calls by writing to the Direct Marketing Association, Box 9014, Farmingdale NY 11735 and asking to be put on its *don't call list.*

Even then, the elderly should be careful. Mail fraud is big business. Some conmen rely on misleading stationery which looks as though it comes from the government. The National Council of Senior Citizens warns against indiscriminate giving to fundraising groups. Private organizations labeled fraudulent because in business for their own personal profit include The Seniors Coalition, The United Seniors Association, 60 Plus and the American Council for Health Care Reform. Using fear tactics in regard to health care and Social Security, these outfits attempt to fleece the elderly through direct mail asking for dues to help them in their supposed struggle to solve problems plaguing those 65+.

As with health, so with crime. The best protection is prevention. A wide-angle peephole viewer should be installed in the front door. All valuable items, as a TV, should be marked with a code number. Recording the make, model and manufacturer's serial number will enable police to enter the items in the national computer network for identification when stolen articles are recovered. An apartment or home and garage should be locked securely after entering or leaving. After purchasing a house or apartment, the tenant or owner should have the locks changed. Use of timers to turn radios and lights on and off will give the impression that someone is at home. Each sliding door and window should have a sturdy lock; each exterior wood door, a deadbolt lock. A security alarm system with panic buttons installed in strategic places and with placarded notice of installation is an effective deterrent, especially if the property is well lighted at night. When outside the home, women should grip a purse tightly rather than let it dangle from a strap, and men should carry a wallet in an inside pocket, not the back pocket. Credit cards or traveler's checks should be used instead of cash. On the street, it is advisable to stay away from a parked car and shrubbery. When approaching one's own car, the key should be kept ready for insertion into the lock. When driving, the windows should be up and the doors locked.

A victim of a crime should notify the police as soon as possible. The National Organization for Victim Assistance, 717 D Street, NW, Washington, DC, 20004, will answer queries by mail, and the NFIC provides advice through a free telephone number: 1-800-876-7060.

As might be expected, there is far less criminality and physical misbehavior among the elderly than among persons in younger cohorts. But there is elder abuse, not by the old, but of the old. The public at large, despite recent accounts in the mass media, remain unaware of elder abuse and consequently about its victims. The various Agencies on Aging are attempting to promote local community awareness of elder abuse and to provide programs for helping victims but without great success. The Subcommittee on Health and Long-Term Care of Congress estimates that more than 1,000,000 older persons are annually subjected to chronic abuse although there is a paucity of reliable, accurate statistics. Such abuse is intimately tied to the family and inability of feminine members to act as caregivers due to changing lifestyles.

Criminologists are reluctant to incorporate abuse as a separate category of unlawful behavior. Their disinclination reduces data available to criminal justice agencies and thus public awareness of the problem. Is elder abuse a criminal act, a psychological problem, or a symptom of society's lack of preparation for dealing with the old?

Racine, famed French playwright, reminds us that "Crime like virtue has its degrees."

DEATH

*It was interesting . . . the way in which death had replaced
sex as the great unmentionable, to be denied in prospect,
endured in decent privacy, preferably behind drawn cur-
tains of a hospital bed, followed by discreet, embarrassed,
uncomforted mourning.*

P.D. James

*I don't want to achieve immortality through my work: I
want to achieve it through not dying. It's not that I'm afraid
to die. I just don't want to be around when it happens.*

Woody Allen

Except in fiction and the theater, people today find death too uncomfortable to think about, too embarrassing to talk about and too painful
to witness. Yet death is the one universal human experience that throughout the centuries has inspired architects, composers, novelists, orators,
painters, philosophers, playwrights, poets, sculptors and theologians to
the heights of achievement.

Long ago, Confucius asked: "If we do not understand life, how can
we understand death?" Decisions about death are no longer clear-cut
because of technological advance like cardiopulmonary resuscitation.
There is as yet no commonly accepted definition of death, perhaps
because dying consists of several stages, from some of which recovery
is achievable. Scientists accept flat electroencephalograph tracings, repeated after six hours, as a sure sign of death, especially if breathing
and heartbeat are absent. An attempt at a formal statement in a lay
person's terms and comprehensive from clinical, ethical and legal points
of view is that death is the immediate result of irreversible cessation of
all functions of the brain and the circulatory and respiratory systems.

But these defining conditions do not deal completely with the end
of life, for hair may continue to grow and cells in skin and bone may
live on. Paradoxically, loss of cells and structures occurs first, not in old

age, but in the fetus before birth. In childhood, baby teeth loosen and fall out. The thymus, which is a glandular structure functioning in development of the body's immune system, tends to wither away in adulthood. Are these to be taken as instances of programmed death?

What is the precise point at which life stops if technological intervention, such as a life-support system, is disconnected? This unanswerable question is why lawyers strongly advise the elderly to have an Advance Directive prepared if they do not wish the dying process to be prolonged by artificial means for whatever reason or if they do not wish to be preserved without rational brainpower but with vegetative functions only.

Persons interested in organ transplantation and persons desirous of prolonging life even of a nonresponsive patient have intensified the debate over how death is defined and determined. Should harvesting organs for transplant from a body whose heartbeat and respiration are sustained by mechanical means even though there is no brain activity be considered murder because the body is still alive? Those interested in successful organ transplantation prefer including in the definition of death a provision as to the earliest possible time for determination so as to maximize harvesting of viable organs. Those interested in preserving life of a patient, as well as hoping for recovery, prefer a more constrained approach to definition.

At the beginning of the last century, the killer diseases were infectious in type. Because of antibiotics, higher standards of living and measures taken to reduce contagion, they are no longer so threatening to large numbers of people. Today, many elderly die as a result of chronic conditions caused by smoking, drinking, air pollution. The three leading causes of death are cancer, heart disease and stroke. Mortality rates from these diseases increase markedly with age, so that death is more closely associated with old age than ever before. Influenza and pneumonia also have a heavy impact. Although still high, the death rate from accidents is declining. Of these principal causes of death, accidents, heart attack and stroke usually require immediate emergency medical care.

Circulatory disorders make up the great affliction of men, whereas women suffer increasingly from stroke and heart attacks. At every age level from 65 on, however, the death rate for elderly men is higher than that for elderly women One explanation offered and not generally accepted is that because women use health services much more frquently than men they receive earlier and more effective treatment, particularly for cancer. Geneticists point out that racial differences in death rates often reflect, not incapacity to survive, but inability to gain access to high quality medical care, as with black males.

From 1950-1985 mortality rates among the young-old declined about 40%; among the old-old, 30%; among the oldest-old, 200%. About 90% of the decline among the young-old was in cardiovascular and cerebrovascular disease, 85% among the old-old and 65% among the oldest-old. Researchers are convinced that death rates are falling and will continue to fall, spectacularly so if a dramatic breakthrough in heart and related diseases should occur. They add that longevity for everyone will be considerably extended if advances in genetic engineering continue at the present pace.

Why even under the best of conditions human beings should develop steadily from birth to maturity and then deteriorate just as steadily until extinction is not known–but speculations abound. The true cause of death, scientists theorize, is not aging per se but vulnerability to disease and such environmental factors as pollution and stress. Precisely what causes vulnerability is not known although actuarial data reveal the rate of dying to double every 7 years beyond the age of 30.

There are specific, accurate and reliable predictors of the end of life. One of the strongest indications of impending death in the elderly of either gender is low vital capacity, that is, inadequate breathing power of the lungs. Generally, those persons 65+ who are unable to perform basic activities of daily living (bathing, dressing, feeding oneself, using the toilet, moving between bed and chair) die within one year. For the elderly 75+, there is a substantially increased risk of both hypothermic and hyperthermic death. During the heat wave of 1995 in Chicago, to take a recent tragic example, many elderly collapsed and died.

Legal determination of death in the United States rests solely on the decision made by a licensed physician. Of the more than 2,000,000 Americans who die every year, at least 800,000 are late-life adults.

Unfortunately, data on their death certificates is often flawed, even seriously inaccurate, although entries are supposedly standardized according to the *International Classification of Diseases,* 9th edition. The physician filling out the death certificate states his relationship to the case, gives the immediate cause of death and may record symptoms or unusual circumstances. There is a category for uncertainty, but it is not often used. Many a certificate is filled out in haste, only to be completed by the funeral director. Research indicates that about 25% of causes of death specified on death certificates are not in accord with autopsy findings. Interestingly, the *International Classification of Diseases* has no category for classification of old age as a cause of death.

Like almost everyone else, the aged know very little about dying. They find it excruciatingly painful to live on while friends and family die. Death of a child is particularly hard to bear. The historian Arnold Toynbee writes in *Man's Concern with Death* that "There are always two parties to a death; the person who dies and the survivors who are bereaved . . . and in the proportionment of suffering, the survivor takes the brunt." Each bereavement is additive, making recovery more difficult. Yet death remains a taboo topic despite the death education movement with establishment of courses in colleges and recruitment of counselors trained to help the bereaved. The word *death* has been replaced by euphemisms like *passed on* and *departed.* Bereaved persons find that their conversation makes others so anxious that even friends find excuses to walk away rather than listen. The process of dying involves care away from society, out of sight in hospitals, hospices, nursing homes.

Because death is hidden from society, Americans are exceptionally vulnerable to shock when they encounter it. They must learn every time how to cope with anticipated or immediate loss. Dying is a trauma, not just for the person whose days are about to end, but for those who go on living, too. Heartache afflicts both. Coping with death demands the almost impossible: practical judgment and emotional involvement. But the world's business goes on.

Sociologists recommend that the elderly discuss with people close to them end-of-life issues even if this means overcoming stiff resistance. Once younger adults are assured that parents and/or grandparents, needing to express feelings and concerns that their affairs are in order and dependents cared for, are not depressed but are desirous of making necessary choices, they overcome feelings that such discussion is morbid.

Many physicians today support telling family and patient the truth in a case of terminal illness, for the dying need to be helped to control pain and bodily functions such as excretion, so that they can pass on with dignity and conquer their fear of the unknown and the end of being alive. The dying need to be able to give and to receive love. Unfortunately, family and friends feel awkward and in the way of the professionals whose job it is to deal with the terminally ill. Except in the case of a hospice, the institutional setting is cold, even forbidding, and visitors do not know how to accomplish a proper leave-taking.

Hospice, an old word with a new meaning, originally referred during the Middle Ages to a place of shelter at which pilgrims could stop for refreshment on long journeys. Today, hospice–the only medical institution in America solely for the dying–refers to a place of shelter for the terminally ill, their families and friends, where palliative, supportive care by an interdisciplinary team is emphasized. Services are available 24 hours a day, 7 days a week. The purpose is not to attempt to prolong life of the terminally ill through aggressive medical intervention but to make dying persons and their families as comfortable as possible while enhancing quality of life. Focus is on management of pain and control of symptoms without loss of dignity and feelings of self-worth. Because for the most part the decision to abandon active curative treatment for patients with advanced malignant disease is straightforward, many hospices will take only cancer victims in the last weeks or months of life or other patients with a prognosis no longer than 6 months to 1 year. Medicare covers some services, and private insurance companies have begun to cover specific facets of hospice care.

Management of those last days matters much. The hospice setting may be a separate facility or part of a hospital or even a home or apartment. Emphasis is on providing a familiar, pleasant atmosphere, as homelike as possible, even in some cases to the point of allowing pets. Every effort is made to ease patient discomfort and embarrassment through control of symptoms, especially pain, both physical and psychological, and through programs encouraging active patient participation. Hospices try to meet the spiritual needs of patients. Scheduling is designed to fit the requirements of each patient, not of the institution. An interdisciplinary team of volunteers and professionals (clergy, counselors, dietitians, nurses, pharmacists, physical therapists, physicians, psychologists, social workers) provides the care necessary to alleviate distress, worry and awkwardness of family and friends during the hospice stay and sometimes for a year or more after the patient's death.

Contrary to myth, hospices do not encourage or engage in active euthanasia although many hospices probably permit passive euthanasia. Passive euthanasia pertains to allowing a patient to die naturally without resorting to extraordinary means to sustain life when the result will be vegetative existence, as for elderly in an irreversible coma or mortally ill with excruciating pain. Active euthanasia pertains either to the killing of a person assumed to be hopelessly ill or to the helping such a person to commit suicide.

In the question of euthanasia, there is much debate for and against. Even among supporters of the right to die, there is no unanimity—some favoring passive means; others, active. Americans who consider active euthanasia immoral and illegal have not been able to solve several dilemmas, as discussed below. Proponents find irony in putting a sick dog to death *humanely,* the while forcing a mortally ill person to live on although chance of such an acutely ill elderly person ever leaving the hospital is 0-5%. Claims to a right to die have been based on constitutional grounds of a right to privacy and common law rights to refuse treatment. Passive euthanasia is now legally supported when informed consent is given by the dying person, the attending physician or close family member.

What safeguards are necessary if suicide, so-called mercy killing or passive euthanasia are to be permitted? Should doctors utilizing new technology continue to keep dying patients alive beyond what was only a short time ago considered to be the point of death? Protracted dying is a new phenomenon with many issues still moot. Who is to decide and on what basis when further medical care is not in the best interest of the patient? Who will be held responsible for ending the days of incapacitated, incompetent, incontinent elderly? Even for doctors who encounter much irremediable suffering, euthanasia does not pose an intractable problem because of their orientation toward maintaining and prolonging life. Death is viewed by many physicians as failure. The public, despite the stand of the American Medical Association against "intentional termination of the life of one human being by another," exhibits more tolerance for euthanasia, especially as regards physician-assisted suicide. In 1991, more than 60% of persons polled supported euthanasia if both patient and family requested it.

The elderly think often about being condemned to impending death. Confronted by the inevitability of death, they tend to review their life and wonder about the meaning of existence. Yet surveys indicate that many elderly aver decreased death anxiety. Of all the age cohorts, the old fear extinction the least. Far worse, they are sure, would be chronic ill health and their transformation into a burden on children. Death, no longer an abstraction, becomes personal and is regarded as preferable to pain and disability.

Once having passed the biblical threescore and ten, the elderly undergo striking changes in perspective of time, with a reversal in direction and an immediate awareness that the calendar is finite—as if every additional day were a bonus. With life foreshortened, the old think continually of the time they have left, and they estimate their age-to-be at death by comparing themselves with their parents. There is, for many, a not unpleasant sense of the appropriateness of closure. For others, observing deaths of friends and family, it is excruciatingly painful to feel more and more a sense of their own mortality.

Older persons know that they must adapt to role changes, one of which is widowhood, probably the most stressful change that can occur in the life of most persons. For the elderly who do not understand the process of grieving, widowhood is extremely difficult, especially if the bereaved do not take advantage of a counseling program. Even then, needed help may not be forthcoming. Little research has been devoted to issues specific to elderly widowed persons. Social programs on a wide scale have yet to be developed.

Grief is an intensely personal experience influenced by biological, psychological and sociocultural factors affecting every aspect of a person's life. Death of a spouse strikes a doubly savage blow, eliminating a trusted companion and ending a familiar way of life. Relationship patterns and rituals disappear. Even anticipatory grief of a survivor whose spouse had been ill for some time does not markedly decrease the suffering although many bereaved persons turn to religion for comfort and guidance.

There is no one way to work through the period of grief. Each survivor grieves at an individual pace and in a unique style. Generally, shock destroys equilibrium, and the immediate behavior of the bereaved may be strange indeed. Refusing to accept the death, the survivor persists in believing that he/she is seeing the departed. Often the widowed is angry with the person for dying. It is not uncommon for the survivor to have a sense of relief mixed, paradoxically, with an intense emotion compounded of feelings of guilt and desolation. Because such sensations are not generally talked about or even admitted, they can do serious damage. In contrast, for someone whose marriage was difficult, death of the spouse may bring anticipation of freedom and a pleasant change of lifestyle.

Unable to accept the reality that the world goes on, preoccupied with thoughts of the deceased, a survivor is out of touch with ordinary activities and falls into periods of despair, loneliness and apathy. Crying and tired, the bereaved withdraws from usual pursuits. The widowed older person has difficulty sleeping, and desire for food all but disappears. Practical matters, such as cooking for one, seem overwhelming hurdles.

For a while people are in and out. Visiting stops suddenly. Despite importance to health and well-being of the grief-stricken, friends, neighbors and relatives often shun the widowed because they have been tainted by death. (Funeral directors advise that Americans prefer services that are brief, quick and with the least fuss.) A period of loneliness ensues although a widow is more likely than a widower to have a close friend to confide in.

Shakespeare's warning should not be taken in vain:

> Give sorrow words; the grief that does not speak
> Whispers the oe'rfraught heart, and bids it break.

Talking about one's grief and widowhood with others tends to lessen and to prevent emotional difficulties. Memorial services help. While a widow is usually free to express her sorrow openly, a grieving husband is uncertain how to express emotions. Neighbors and friends are uncomfortable with conversations based on mourning and are embarrassed by displays of grief. Although there is no boycott, they do tend to stay away just when the bereaved needs them most. There are no social guidelines.

Needing support during the long days and weeks and months after callers have stopped coming, the widowed turns further inward and unrealistically idealizes the departed. Time anesthtizes, and the healing process begins. Recovery may start at any time from 6 months to a year or more. Gradually, past events with the deceased spouse are recalled with pleasure. New contacts are initiated and the bereaved becomes socially active despite recurring but brief periods of depression. Finally, the bereaved resumes social intercourse, along with much relearning of behavior and activities, and regains interest in life. This is under the best of circumstances.

Even today a woman's identity is often determined through her caring for others. When a wife loses her spouse, she to a degree loses a sense of self. Her grief intensifies. Yet older women appear able to cope successfully despite their intense emotional suffering and severe financial deprivation, perhaps because women have strong networks of peer and family relationships. Not so the men even though they remain financially robust.

Becoming a widower in old age brings wide behavioral change and a marked increase in risk factors at the very time the bereaved is confronted with such age-related stresses as chronic illness and physical debility. Widowers, after overcoming grief, need to reconstruct old ties and try to build anew–not an easy task since loss of a wife usually means loss of social affiliations and ties. Single men have much to learn about taking care of home and self–not to mention dating, romance, sex–as though they have to develop a new identity. For too many, as the death rate attests, demise of a wife with all that such bereavement entails is overwhelming. Men expect to die first, and so death of a wife is especially traumatic. Unable to deal with widowhood, men die within a year or two. The highest suicide rate in the United States occurs among the elderly, particularly among white males recently widowed.

But bereavement is an especially trying time for both sexes although not everyone needs help with the adjustment process. There is so much to do despite shock and the disbelief that the loved one will never return. Notwithstanding shortness of breath, tightness in the throat, loss of appetite and even visions of the deceased as if alive, the surviving spouse must see to it that the body is disposed of in accord with religious and cultural traditions, as a wake or a week of visiting at home, then funeral services followed by rites at the cemetery.

Planning in advance for death makes sense although at first thought the idea may seem macabre, even painful, a rehearsal for extinction. Bereavement cannot be made painless, but the bereaved can be helped to bear the burden and to find new resources for living. A program set up in advance, perhaps with the aid of an attorney, accountant or social worker, will provide needed support during the mourning period–particularly for women who, generally younger than their husbands, face the strong likelihood of becoming widows. How can the widow achieve financial independence? Where are deeds to family property, insurance policy, social security card, legal wills? To avoid loss, what should be done with an inheritance? What are the names of the attorney, insurance agent, stockbroker and others dealing with family finances? Have financial arrangements been made for the funeral? Who will transport the body and obtain a death certificate? Has a cemetery plot been chosen? What arrangements are to be made for a monument at the grave site? Should the coffin be of wood or metal? Plain or decorated? Which is more appropriate, home or a room in the funeral parlor for meeting friends and relatives? How many cars in the funeral procession? A grieving spouse is in no mood to arrive at answers calmly and rationally, let alone sift through a list of mortuary services and options presented by a funeral director.

Americans are not used to dealing with the disruptive effects of death. By having the dying removed from the home to the hospital, they minimize exposure to death and sustain the illusion that it is not part of life. Death has become a disagreeable experience managed in secret in an institutional setting. Ironically, the hospital where all personnel and every piece of equipment is geared to saving life, has become the institution where almost every old person is taken to die. The bereaved must rely on strangers to deny the denial of death so widespread in society. Professional counseling and discussion groups, such as the Widowed Persons Service of the American Association of Retired Persons, provide avenues of release from what has been called the most severe psychological trauma in all of human existence.

Cremation is gradually becoming the disposition of choice as the United States death rate rises and religious barriers fall. Far less expensive than ground burial, cremation is also much simpler. There is no casket to buy, no burial plot to obtain and maintain, no cemetery marker to commission. Cremation is appealing to families whose relatives retire and die far away: remains can be shipped without difficulty, and memorial services can be held at any time. In California, where environmental concerns are becoming paramount, more than 40% of the dead are cremated.

Psychologists aver that elderly mourners who attempt to stay active mentally and physically, encourage a network of relatives and friends and remain alert to changes around them are most likely to accept death as a normal, inevitable part of life, so that along with the dying they can be ready to say in the words of the Psalmist, IV, 8: *I will lay me down in peace and take my rest.*

Charles Mackay poeticizes the scientific view:

> There is no such thing as death.
> In Nature nothing dies.
> From each sad remnant of decay
> Some forms of life arise.

WHAT TO DO WHEN DEATH OCCURS

1. Enlist the aid of associates, family, friends, religious leaders. Consider their advice carefully. Make no hasty decisions.

2. Fill out forms for an autopsy (if required) and for donation of body parts.

3. Make arrangements with a funeral director for removal of the body. If the deceased was a veteran, inform the regional office of the Veterans Administration and apply for survivor and burial benefits.

4. Obtain from the hospital or funeral director at least 10 copies of the official death certificate. Copies will be needed for banks, employer, insurance companies, lawyers, pension fund distribution, Social Security benefits.

5. Send obituary notice to employer, friends, newspapers, relatives.

6. Make funeral arrangements: choice of funeral parlor (type of service, date and time, transportation of mourners), selection of cemetery or place of cremation, choice of casket.

7. Meet with the family lawyer for help with the will (or for advice as to what to do in the event a will does not exist), executors, probate, retirement accounts, debts, loans, and other matters regarding settlement of the estate.

8. Locate the birth certificate, Social Security and Medicare numbers, keys to safe-deposit and post office boxes, deeds of ownership (home, land, vehicle), bank accounts, certificates of deposit, stocks and bonds, state and federal tax returns for at least the last 3 years, list of bills to be paid routinely.

9. Notify the insurance company and request payment of life insurance.

10. Cancel credit cards and alert banks. Ask for statements of balance.

DECLINES AND LOSSES

Will you still need me, will you still feed me,
when I'm 64?

Beetles' Song

It is generally accepted that past a certain age, what is
worthwhile in life is gone. . . . Make the mistake of growing
old and all the world will tell you . . . that you can do noth-
ing more useful than remain out of the way.

Isaac Asimov

Current knowledge of prevention and postponement of aging losses and declines is equivocal. Which changes are caused by aging? Which changes are age-related? Which changes are caused by disease? No one as yet can make sharp distinctions in all areas. The National Research Council points out that with but a few exceptions research in health promotion and disease and aging prevention in the past did not focus on the elderly. Instead, researchers generalized findings from the middle-aged. There are scientists performing aging research today, but health promotion and disease prevention for those persons 65+ remain more a slogan than a reality.

For all that hundreds of functional declines and physiological losses accompany the aging process, the rate rising with the years, there is no consistent pattern throughout the aging population. Individual differences in functional capacity of the old are more considerable than those of the young. Rates vary among organs as well as among individuals. There is no single optimum model for aging. Losses are gradual and incremental, in general, but dimensions are multiple. As people age, there is an increasingly constricted capacity to respond to stress. Because of decreases in muscle mass and increases in reaction time, an old person cannot race to a hard-hit ball in tennis as can a young man or woman. Various hormones, as estrogen and testosterone, decline in quantity, and changes in bodily synthesis and secretion of many hormones reduce the efficacy of regulatormechanisms. An example of such a hormone is melatonin, which is under investigation by researchers interested in effects on sleep, among other things.

Many functions deteriorate with age. Physiologic reserves lessen but remain sufficient for effective performance unless diminished by sickness. Scientists agree that some declines, as cardiac output and musculature, are related to lifestyle, mainly to a sedentary way of life. But researchers cannot as yet fully distinguish such declines and losses from diseases underlying the aging process.

Declines are larger in complex than in simple activities. There is a sharper drop in breathing capacity than in nerve conduction: nerve conduction involves only the nervous system whereas breathing involves coordination of responses in lungs, muscles, nerves. Nevertheless, it is a fact that losses in some areas can be overcome and behavior, skill and competence can be improved. even among the oldest-old.

Researchers have proved conclusively that people can learn at any age. Both physical and psychological improvement are possible. Memory can be restored and enhanced. Physical exercise has a beneficial effect on muscles and bones of people 80+. Aerobic exercise helps in achieving faster reaction time and may aid in improving cognitive performance. The converse is true: the more active mentally, the less likely a person is to deteriorate physically. An active approach to preserving functions and overcoming declines includes changing for the positive negative attitudes about aging held by those old people who passively accept the stereotype that deterioration is an immediate, inevitable, normal part of the aging process once a person reaches 65. Psychologists know that the ability to overcome a loss is deeply influenced by belief in having the ability to overcome the loss. The old folk saying is accurate: we are what we do, and we do what we are. Intellectual ability may decline for lack of exertion, both in learning and in entertaining new ideas.

Consider what accrual of years and mistreatment of self do to appearance of the elderly. Physiological changes are gradual, many imperceptible, until attention is called to them when cumulative effects take a heavy toll. On the face skin discolors and wrinkles and sags, lines cross the forehead and surround the mouth, fat pouches hang beneath the eyes. On hands and arms skin has fewer active oil and sweat glands, so that it feels dry and cold to someone touching it. Nose droop at the tip increases, and there is frequent involuntary nasal discharge of phlegm. While men lose hair on the scalp, women's hair thins in the pubic area and in other parts of the body. But hair grows in and on the ears, which themselves seem to lengthen. After decades of the pull of gravity, the abdomen and other anatomic structures sag.

Body proportions change, so that standard sizes no longer fit older people. Height declines as much as 2" for men, somewhat less for women. Posture deteriorates as the head tends to extend forward, the shoulders to be rounded and the upper back to have a hump (referred to as kyphosis by doctors). Standing up and sitting down are no longer effortless because dexterity decreases.

Some of the senses are blunted. Odors may seem less intense and harder to identify. Visual and hearing declines may cause a person to stand closer than is normal and approved of in American society. There are other changes in appearance, as with skeletal muscle mass, fingernails, varicose veins. But the point is that unless countered by diet, exercise and other reworkings in lifestyle such developments diminish feelings of attractiveness, competence and physical ability–producing overall a loss of self-esteem.

As did past generations, the elderly of today have learned to compensate for losses. They adapt to changes in functioning: cognitive, physical, sensory and to circumstances: chance, economic, political, social. They do not go out alone at night; to hear better, they stand close to people; they hold a book farther away; they join organizations that lobby for them; and they live well within their financial means. Such modification is a continual, natural process throughout the life cycle. Learning and change cease only with death. Behavior, competence and skills can be improved in the elderly. They know that practice and experience can alter performance. In tennis, aware that a 75-year-old cannot race as well as a 25-year-old to a hard-hit ball, the elderly player becomes wily and relies on drop shots, lobs and changes of pace

Although comedians joke that shortivity rather than longevity becomes the rule, there is tragedy in the penultimate transformations of the human body. The elderly make up the only age cohort in which decline is inevitable and for which there are almost no guidelines to give structure and direction to their lives. Most adults up to late middle years, disregarding the fact that there is an old person evolving inside even the youngest of us, the young of today becoming the old of tomorrow, harbor a secret conviction that somehow they have prevailed over the physical aspects of aging. But everyone is compelled to face the truth brought by a period of diminishing powers and increasing losses that time escapes no one. Sooner or later, almost every human being faces a period of incapacity before quietus.

Depending on genetics and circumstance, decline—cardiopulmonary, cognitive, neuromuscular, sensory—is either gradual or swift. Performance of activities of daily living at last becomes increasingly challenging or even impossible. Starting at age 20, intensity of illumination needs to be doubled for every increase of 13 years or so if the aging eye is to see. Rheumatoid arthritis in adults has a peak onset from 35 years of age on. Near 50, physical signs of aging are obvious, among them fatigue after brief exertion, graying of hair, slowed growth of fingernails, accumulation of skin spots As the urinary system loses efficiency, the elderly need the restroom more often, sometimes urgently. At 60 the prospect of retirement dismays many, with coronary disease and cancer looming large and close. Hearing deteriorates as sounds higher in pitch become difficult to distinguish. Patterns of speech include vocal tremors and imprecise articulation of sounds. Awareness of the quick passage of time becomes acute. Relationships change over the course of a lifetime, sometimes drastically, through assimilation, attrition, dislocation, migration and a host of other factors. Informal support-networks weaken and disappear. In the 70's death has overtaken more, among them friends and relatives, even the rich and famous, with progressive loss of intimate relationships among peers and out-of-home activities. By 80 most intimates are gone. Survivors perusing the obituary pages learn that they know more dead persons than living, and they speculate as to who will go next. Loneliness is a distinct challenge, as isolation becomes inevitable due to increasing physical handicaps. Loss of mobility results in frustration. Self-esteem drops. Declines in hearing, smell, taste, touch and vision lessen customary sensory pleasures. Life may seem not worth living.

Yet even those most advanced in age remain young persons inhabiting old bodies. Capacity for relationships, intellectual and physical activity, memory and sexuality last as long as life does except in the case of severely debilitating illness.

A complete listing of declines and losses that appear with old age presents a horrendous view unless one keeps in mind that as research advances more and more of the declines and losses are likely to be overcome. Because *Homo sapiens* is a species unlike those of other animals in that it can anticipate its own decadence, it can eliminate retrogression or mitigate its consequences. Some aspects of what was once considered natural mental and physical decline due to aging have now proved to be delayable, preventable and even in some cases reversible. Already researchers have been able to help the elderly improve their memory ability and lessen reaction time.

Much deterioration can be avoided by maintaining an active lifestyle rather than by succumbing to the cultural stereotype of the aged as sedentary weaklings. One can take comfort in the knowledge that the body grows old but the mind stays young. Just as George Bernard Shaw's dictum, "Youth is wasted on the young," may be too harsh, so Richard Henry Stoddard's assurance, "There are gains for all our losses," is too optimistic at the present time. The immune system still loses power wiith age. Tennyson's *Ulysses* is nearer the mark:

> Old age hath yet his honor and his toil;
> Death closes all: but something ere the end,
> Some work of noble note may be done,
> Not unbecoming men that strove with gods. . . .
> Tho' much is taken, much abides; and tho'
> We are not now that strength which in old days
> Moved earth and heaven; that which we are, we are,
> One equal temper of heroic hearts,
> Made weak by time and fate, but strong in will
> To strive, to seek, to find, and not to yield!

DIET and NUTRITION

In these days of indigestion
It is oftentimes a question
As to what to eat and what to leave alone.

Roy Atwell

Diet and nutrition contribute markedly to the quality of life, for they are critical in causation and control of numerous health disorders. Because the effects of diet tend to be cumulative, an inadequate diet begun early in life may contribute to development of colon cancer, heart disease, osteoporosis and other disabling and degenerative ailments. Malnutrition at any age can lead to infection, cognitive impairment and death. On the positive side, favorable nutritional status over the years can enhance prospects for good health and even increase life expectancy.

Brillat-Savarin, quintessential epicure, maintained that physical, psychological and social gratifications of the table outlast those of all other experiences. Food and drink bring such strong emotions and memories at the very time they titillate the senses through color, odor, taste and texture that sitting down to the table with family and/or friends is the highpoint of daily existence for many older adults despite sensory impairments, particularly diminution of the sense of smell.

Convenience of food shopping and ease of preparation are important. Reading labels, storage of heavy cans and cleanup of greasy concoctions can be trying chores. Some grocery chains are experimenting with packaging in small quantities, permitting the cost of food to be lowered at the same time waste is decreased and variety of servings is increased. Especially helpful technological innovations, such as the microwave oven, cut preparation and cooking time.

At 60, husband and wife become eligible for services in government nutrition programs under the auspices of the Older Americans Act. While emphasis is on helping the elderly poor and disabled by locating senior centers in low-income areas where possible, there is no means test and no one of age is excluded. To encourage socialization, congregate meals which contain at least 1/3 of the recommended daily allowance (RDA) of nutrients are provided. For the home-bound aged, the Meals-on-Wheels Program provides meals of similar nutritive value.

But nutritional and energy requirements of the aging have not been established precisely. Based on formulations by boards of nutritionists, there is an RDA for nutritive intake published periodically by the National Academy of Sciences, which furnishes estimates of essential nutrients for healthy persons of both sexes in the different age cohorts. Medical professionals use the RDA as an approximate indication of dietary adequacy. Chronic diseases and medications, as does the state of bodily activity, can affect nutritional status and needs. RDAs do not reflect nutrient-drug interactions. Medications taken frequently may affect nutrient absorption, excretion and utilization.

With age there usually is a gradual decrease in lean body mass and in basal metabolism rate, so that combined with a lessening of activity these changes result in a diminution of energy needs. Is the decrease in lean body mass an inevitable aspect of aging or is it an artifact of inactivity? No one knows. There are no norms for body composition in the elderly. During their 70's many people tend to reduce caloric intake and, in consequence, to lose weight. In contrast, those elderly with an overdistribution of upper body fat, what physicians call an apple profile, a predisposing factor to serious disease, should rely more, if possible, on increased physical activity than on lowering number of calories. (Some studies imply that older persons a little overweight fare better in illness and surgery.)

Despite the aging process, nutritional needs remain basically the same for the elderly as for the young. Essential to nourishment of the older body are 44 nutrients, which consist of macronutrients and micronutrients, preferably from food low in fat and cholesterol and high in essential vitamins, minerals and fiber.

Carbohydrates, fats, and proteins make up the macronutrients. The major function of carbohydrates, which should compose 50-60% of most diets, is to provide energy. Nutritionists recommend as sources of carbohydrates cereals, vegetables and fruits.

Swiftly transformed to glucose or blood sugar, the body's major fuel, simple carbohydrates can give a quick burst of energy. Starches, complex carbohydrates, provide a steadier supply of energy. Fat, the largest immediately available energy reserve stored in the body, provides more than twice the energy per gram weight of other macronutrients. Important for satiety and flavor, fat in the diet should not be reduced drastically below what are considered normal levels in an attempt at quick weight loss. Better is exercise to help maintain an optimally healthful weight, which some nutritionists suggest for those 55+ might be about the same as at age 25. Others argue that differences exist for older persons 65-70 and 85-90. (Standard height and weight tables are not valid for the elderly.) Vegetable fats, as in olive and corn oil, are healthful, but saturated fats, as in meat and coconut oil, should be kept to a minimum, for they tend to raise cholesterol levels.

Proteins, which are not stored in the body, ensure synthesis of constituents needed by the various tissues for maintenance, replacement or growth. Although the typical American diet provides more than enough protein, ability to digest protein apparently decreases with age, so that a doctor may recommend for some individuals extra consumption.

Vitamins and minerals (also called trace elements), which make up the micronutrients, are ordinarily consumed in tiny amounts from food and drink. Except for D, the body does not manufacture vitamins, which can be obtained only from food, drink and supplements. Unlike carbohydrates, fats and proteins, they are not fuels, not interchangeable sources of energy. Vitamins do participate in regulation of numerous bodily processes, but all functions of many vitamins are not known. Usually absorbed unchanged in structure, many function as coenzymes which are essential to catalysts that speed up metabolic chemical actions within the body. Minerals are inorganic substances necessary for tooth and bone formation, blood coagulation, muscle contractility and other processes.

There has been of late an increasing and somewhat alarming incidence of mineral metabolism disorders in persons 55 years and older, especially among those who use laxatives to excess. Calcium metabolism disorders are implicated in osteoporosis. Many elderly men and women do not eat enough dairy products and so do not get enough calcium. Phosphorus intake is excessive among the aged who eat large amounts of meat. For late-life adults on diuretics, potassium deficiency can become a problem. Chromium, essential for maintenance of normal glucose tolerance, is marginally deficient in many 55+. But deficiency of other trace elements is usually not a problem for older persons on normal diets.

Folklore, myth and advertising hype surround use of vitamins and minerals. As a result, many older Americans in search of overall well-being and longer life have unwittingly subjected themselves to the role of guinea pigs in a wide-ranging, ill defined and unregulated *experiment.* utilizing substances that in the long run may prove helpful, harmful or just plain worthless. The elderly are especially vulnerable to vitamin/mineral hype because of their intense desire to reduce the risk and impact of chronic diseases. Unfortunately, vitamin/mineral pills are for the most part exempt from FDA regulation since Congress in 1994 passed the Dietary Supplement Health and Education Act.

Nutritionists state that the best way to ensure adequate amounts of vitamins and minerals is not to go around popping pills but to eat a well-balanced diet with a variety of foods. Vitamin E, for example, is so abundant in such a diet that deficiencies almost never occur. All functions of many vitamins are unknown. Exact requirements of the elderly remain largely undetermined. Assessing precise needs is not easy. Measurement of some of the vitamins is technically difficult, and supplementation may upset dynamic balances of nutrients.

In the case of vitamins, more is not necessarily better. Megadose supplementation can lead to adverse reactions and side effects potentially dangerous. Symptoms, such as loss of appetite and general malaise, are often thought by lay people to be evidence of vitamin deficiency, but there is no proof.

If food habits are basically sound, little change in diet is usually necessary in later years. Although dietary habits and ideas are long standing and difficult to change, even persons with illnesses requiring specific diets or others with allergic reactions, so that they cannot eat or drink certain foodstuffs, soon learn that that with a little thought they can get all the nutrients they need from the many different foods available. Variation and moderation are the guidelines, supplemented by recommendations of the family physician. Sad to say, too many American elderly have a relatively monotonous diet, coffee, margarine and white bread remaining as the core foods. Many of those elderly living alone or in reduced economic circumstances have a total diet poor in quality and quantity.

Vitamins are classed as water-soluble (B group and C) or fat-soluble (A,D,E,K). Because fat-soluble vitamins along with B_{12} tend to be stored in the body, megadoses may prove toxic. Water-soluble vitamins can be destroyed in cooking. Supplementation, when deemed necessary by a physician, should be individualized because people do not all react the same way. Megadose supplements of vitamins and minerals should be taken by only those persons whose doctors through suitable tests have determined the need. Use of vitamin C to prevent the common cold remains a subject of controversy.

Caloric needs diminish with age, but overall nutritive requirements for protein, vitamins and minerals remain fairly constant. Late-life diet should therefore be of higher nutrient density, more nutrients per calorie, to make up for reduced intake: lower in saturated fat and cholesterol, higher in complex carbohydrates and fiber, limited in amounts of meat (5-6 ounces daily), restricted in quantities of salt and simple sugars, with plenty of fresh, raw fruit and vegetables, suitable quantity of Vitamin D, as from fortified skim milk, and moderate in volume of alcoholic beverages.

There is an easy way for the elderly to approximately assess caloric needs. If sedentary, multiply weight by 10; if active, by 12or 13. A totally inactive person of 140 pouinds needs about 1400 calories a day; a vigorously busy person of about 140 pounds, about 1700 calories a day.

Processed foods, such as boxed meals, TV dinners and canned vegetables, which are low in fiber and high in sugar and salt, should be avoided. Not a nutrient because it passes through the body undigested, fiber is important to health of the bowel and other body parts. Immoderate alcohol consumption can cause nutritional deficiencies. Tooth loss may impair chewing ability and contribute to problems in nutrition. It is better to eat several light meals rather than one heavy, a schedule to stave off frayed nerves and supply energy boosts. Many good foods are conveniently portable: apples, bagels, broccoli.

Water is absolutely essential. A person can survive without food for more than 2 months but not even for 2 weeks without water. Some 65% of adult body weight is water. Although necessary to almost all body functions (among them: digestion, composition of the bloodstream, regulation of body temperature), water cannot be stored or manufactured in the body. It must be replaced.

Not drinking enough water can be dangerous. Medical researchers regard dehydration, a fairly common occurrence among the elderly, as associated with a serious increase in mortality. About half the older persons admitted to hospital with dehydration die within a year. Coffee, tea and medications which are diuretics, reduce water content of the body—as do infections and diarrhea. Because iatrogenic fluid imbalance is not unusual, side effects of all prescribed drugs should be checked.

Unless contraindicated by a medical problem such as edema or congestive heart failure, the elderly should include sufficient fluid in the daily diet, usually about 8 glasses (2 quarts) other than alcohol, to maintain normalcy of bowel movements, help regulate temperature and prevent dehydration. Fruit juice and even ice pops help meet the need for water. Because the vast majority of late-life adults do not seem to get thirsty even when in physiologic need, they should make a deliberate effort daily to have a proper fluid intake by drinking at regular intervals throughout the day and at mealtimes.

Despite the fact that many nutritionists think RDAs are too low, Vitamin C and folic acid for example, supplementation of nutrients should not exceed the RDA unless prescribed by a physician. Safety of some over-the-counter supplements is moot, and their nutritional benefits are dubious at best. Vitamin D and calcium taken in megadoses can be toxic. Dolomite and bone meal often include environmental contaminants, such as lead and arsenic, and should not take the place of inexpensive acceptable calcium supplements as in generic oyster-shell calcium or calcium-containing ant-acids.

The war over supplements has not been decided although the 10 billion dollar supplement industry continues to grow briskly. Despite advertising claims, there is no guarantee that absorption of supplements is occurring where it should, in the digestive tract. In 1998 tests at Tufts University, 2 of 5 supplements were not absorbed, and so are probably a waste of money.

Some researchers recommend vitamins C, E and A to reinforce antioxidant defense systems in the body. Anti-oxidants are thought to limit free-radical formation as well as destroy free radicals, thus reducing the risk of some forms of cancer, heart disease and stroke. (Free radicals are deleterious byproducts formed in the crucial process of burning of oxygen by the body's cells.) But several important health groups, including the American Cancer Society, have not yet recommended antioxidant supplements pending completion of further research. A June 2000 report from the prestigious Institute of Medicine concludes that there is insufficient evidence for the taking of more antioxidants than the tiny amounts easily available in a balanced diet. In accord are many scientists who consider it unwise to take megadoses of any nutrient. Beta carotene, for instance, is but 1 of some 500 similar substances called carotenoids. Beta-carotene pills may inhibit absorption of other carotenoids, some of which could be important. Everyone agrees, however, that eating a balanced diet which is also rich in antioxidants can be only healthful. The Roman poet Horace was right. "Learn what and how great benefits a temperate diet will bring along with it," he said, adding, "You will enjoy good health."

Nutritionists point out that a good diet in later years helps decrease risk of disease and increases ability to manage signs and symptoms of disease. Poor nutrition may prolong recovery from disease and increase incidence of institutionalization. Eating fast can lead to overeating because the brain may not have time to signal you are full. People often eat fast because they are hungry. Keeping a food diary will help you control number of calories and types of food Instead of three large meals, eat small portions at intervals throughout the day. Check for hidden salt and fat. Sugar is an appetite stimulant. Dieting does not enable a person to lose weight from a specific part of body. You tend to lose all over the body but not at the same rate at each site. Calory ranges purporting to tell how much to eat each day can be vastly inaccurate.

Diet and nutrition are not synonyms. Diet refers to food and drink in general or to a special regimen of food and drink. Nutrition refers to processes by which a person takes in and utilizes diet for growth, repair and well-being of body tissues. Dietary status is a record or measurement of what a person is eating and drinking; nutritional status is a reckoning of health as influenced by what is being eaten and drunk. Lifelong favorable nutritional status can increase life expectancy; unfavorable can be a risk factor for high blood pressure and certain cancers. A person can have in regard to nutritional status an imbalance or a deficit or an excess because of improper dietary intake or faulty utilization of nutrients by the body. An obese person has an excess; an anorexic, a deficit; a diabetic, an imbalance. Paradoxically, all three instances of such malnutrition may be present at one time in an individual.

Nutrition is a balancing act. Requirements depend on height, sex, weight, health status and activity (metabolic, physical, psychological). Personal opinion of adequacy rather than scientific data is frequently relied on by physicians because measurement of diet and nutrition is imprecise. Recommendations for adequate daily intake of some nutrients are based on guesstimates. Optimal dietary requirements for most vitamins and minerals have not been determined. There is for the elderly no Recommended Dietary Allowance (RDA) of many specific nutrients. Not even residence in a licensed health-care facility is a guarantee of adequate nutritional intake. Though only an approximation, body mass index (BMI) is often used by health professionals to express nutritional status. BMI is determined by dividing weight by double the height, as given in meters and kilograms. A person 2 meters tall and 80 kilograms in weight has an index of 20. Above 30 indicates obesity; from 25-30, overweight; somewhat less than 25, normal.

In spite of the fact that many elderly are malnourished, life-threatening deficiencies of nutrients are unusual save for persons who eat little, have a serious disease or who are eccentric in choice of food as with fad diets. Many older people, especially those living alone, do not bother much with cooking, subsisting on coffee, toast, pastry and the like. Any sharp change in eating habits or drop in nutritional status, not just weight loss, may signal in the aged onslaught of disease in a major organ system and should be investigated promptly. Since nutrient deficiencies are often unaccompanied by immediately recognizable symptoms, physicians recommend that every elderly person who experiences long-term weight loss without an obvious cause should undergo examination for cancer and take tests for thyroid dysfunction.

Dietary reactions of old people have not been well established, so that intake of a nutrient may seem adequate while the actual biochemical benefit to the body falls below standard. Iron absorption may be decreased in persons 65+ because of a deficiency in Vitamin B12 as a result of a drop in hydrochloric acid. Accordingly in 1998, the National Academy of Sciences, which advises the federal government on nutrition, recommended for the first time that a major population group take a vitamin supplement—in this case the elderly and B12. Some aged—especially the poor, the chronically ill and those living alone and housebound—are deficient in calcium, vitamin B_6, vitamin D and overall caloric intake. A more common form of malnourishment is obesity, a body weight 20% or more above standard actuarial height-weight tables, a significant health risk for persons with diabetes, heart disease, hypertension or metabolic disorders. (Validity of these so-called norms has been challenged by researchers who recommend a weight from 3-5% higher. At the periodic physical examination, the doctor should be queried about desirable weight.) With age-related changes and the tendency toward a sedentary lifestyle, the body inclines to fat accumulation, so much so that the prevalence of obesity increases more than twofold between ages 20 and 50.

Perhaps because of pervasive advertising, American culture is drug oriented. Seemingly, there is a quick fix for everything, from headaches to constipation, almost always without regard to consequences. The elderly, particularly, are at increased risk of malnutrition through their routine use of medications, both prescription and over-the-counter, on a daily basis. Because a medication has a therapeutic effect on a young family member does not mean that it will not have a harmful effect on an older person. In general, the fewer the drugs an elderly individual takes the better. Drugs can affect appetite, bring on impotence, alter metabolism, induce lethargy. Conflicting demands of drugs for chronic diseases to which the elderly are prone may complicate drug-nutrient interaction, as in cases of constipation, heart failure, hypertension, osteoporosis. Drug choice and regimen should be carefully individualized by a physician familiar with the patient.

The situation is similar in regard to diet and nutrition. Nutrition and diet began as a discipline some 60 years ago, when the American Institute of Nutrition was founded. But for too many years research priorities focused on livestock, not on human beings. Even today guesswork rather than data prevails among many health professionals. As a consesequence of lack of knowledge, less sophisticated elderly tend to become converts to food fads. While adequate fiber intake may play a part in preventing colon cancer, it is not a cure-all. Lifelong consumption of fluorine in the water supply may help prevent caries in the young, but there is no guarantee that the chemical in large amounts will decrease the risk of osteoporosis in the old although it can easily reach toxic levels. Eating grapefruit, even in large quantities, will not of itself cause weight loss. There is much misinformation and confusion about chemical additives used in processing food to inhibit growth of bacteria and rancidity and discoloration. The Food and Drug Administration monitors these for safety.

In the United States an untold number of instances of food poisoning, probably well over 2,000,000 cases, occur each year. Impact on elderly people can be serious, even fatal. A mild case produces temporary diarrhea and vomiting. Origin of seafood, in particular, should be checked to be sure the items come from clean waters. Meat should be cooked per directions for the proper time period and to the recommended temperature. A refrigerator kept at less than 40° will hold food free of harmful bacteria action for several days. Freezer temperature below 10° will keep food on the safe side for about a year. Frozen meat should be thawed in the refrigerator. Raw meat, especially chicken, should be rinsed well. Everything it has touched should be cleaned thoroughly before the cook turns to the next stage of meal preparation. A wooden cutting board is preferable because bacteria do not survive as well on wood as on plastic. Hands should be washed often. Kitchen sponges and dish towels should be tossed into the washing machine every few days—at the outside.

There is also much false and misleading information being promoted in the media and elsewhere. Diet-related nostrums and so-called nutritional therapies can seem especially attractive to those elderly with chronic degenerative disorders, such as arthritis, digestive disturbances and heart disease. Aside from the waste of money, more than $10,000,000 a year, reliance on such putative remedies as megadoses of vitamins may mean that a disorder, disease or impairment that might have been prevented or lessened in impact by medical means will worsen. The Food and Drug Administration, the United States Postal Service and organizations serving the elderly like the American Association of Retired Persons (AARP) are all trying to educate the public about such health fraud.

The individual food consumer needs to exercise care in several directions. Human beings throughout their early history adapted gradually to a broad range of naturally occurring foods. But the types and mix of nutrients remained relatively constant. Recent technological innovations affecting the type and quantity of available foods have been so extensive and rapid that human beings have had almost no time to adapt biologically to energy-dense foods rich in fats and refined carbohydrates, with one result a rapid rise in chronic diseases. As the encyclopedist Diderot wrote: "Doctors are always working to preserve our health and the cooks to destroy it, but the latter are more often successful."

It is the better part of wisdom to pay close attention to diet and nutrition with their potential for enhancement of life. When, what and how a person eats do have mood-altering effects. Because the body's ability to break down and utilize large quantities of fat apparently lessens with age, fat consumed at meals becomes additional weight instead of being burned as energy. Breaking up the day with 4-6 small healthful snacks rather than stuffing oneself with 3 bulky meals will aid in staving off frayed nerves and produce boosts in energy. Some foods are much more filling than others. Oat meal, more filling than cornflakes, eggs and white bread, satisfies a person longer and helps manage diet by staving off hunger pains. Because eating carbohydrates alone may bring on lethargy, it is advisable to have some protein with them.

Ecclesiastes pointed out more than 2,000 years ago: "A man hath no better thing under the sun than to eat, and to drink and to be merry."

PLEASE NOTE: In late 1997 the National Academy of Sciences' Food and Nutrition Board began to release Dietary Reference Intakes (DRIs) to replace Recommended Dietary Allowances. The aim behind the RDAs is to prevent disorders owing to nutritional deficiency. The goal underlying RDIs is to establish levels for nutrient intake that optimize health, in addition to setting upper as well as lower limits. Unlike RDAs, RDIs will be based on nutritional research with specific age groups—including the elderly. Hopefully, all the new levels set by RDIs will be available soon.

In the meantime, the new recommendations for vitamins and minerals published so far are listed below.

	RDA	DRI
CALCIUM:	For men and women 51+, 800mg.	For men and women 51+, 1200 mg.
FLUORIDE:	No level for those 51+.	For adult men, 4 mg. For adult women, 3 mg.
MAGNESIUM:	For men 51+, 350 mg. For women 51+, 280 mg.	For men 51+, 420 mg. For women 51+ 320 mg.
PHOSPHORUS:	For men and women 51+, 800mg.	For men and women 51+, 700 mg.
VITAMIN D:	For men and women 51+, 200 IU.	For men and women 51-69, 400 IU. For those 70 +, 600 IU.

CHANGES CONTRIBUTING TO NUTRITIONAL
PROBLEMS IN THE ELDERLY:

Oral:
Ability to chew

Taste and Smell

Dryness of mouth

Physical:
Ability to absorb, metabolize and utilize nutrients

Energy requirements

Activities

Appetite

Medications

Functional:
Vision and/or hearing

Disability, as from arthritis

Inability to shop and carry groceries

Psychosocial:
Social relations, as from isolation

Interest in eating, as from being alone

Outlook, as from depression

Financial:
Lessened income, as from inflation

Abundance of income, resulting in dining out where portions are huge and high in fat and calories

Sample Menu: Female

Breakfast
> 1 oz cereal
> 1/2 banana
> 1 c milk
> 1 slice toast
> 1 tsp margarine

Lunch
> 1 small roll
> 2 oz turkey
> sliced tomato
> 1-2 tsp avocado or mayonnaise
> 1 oz pretzels
> 1/2 c applesauce

Snack:
> 2 small cookies

Dinner:
> 1.2 c spaghetti
> 1.8 oz sauce
> 3 1 oz meatballs
> 1/2 c wax beans
> 12/2 c spinach
> 1 slice garlic bread
> 1 tsp margarine
> 1/2 c plums

Snack:
> 1 c skim milk with 2 cups ice, 1 tsp instant coffee, 1 tasp sugar or
> substitute. Mix well in blender to make shake.

Sample Menu: Male

Breakfast
> 1/2 c oatmeal
> 1/2 c skim milk
> 1 slice toast
> 2 tsp margarine
> 1/2 c orange juice

Snack
> 6 crackers

Lunch
> 2 slices bread or small roll
> 3 oz tuna fish
> 1/2 T low-fat mayonnaise plus 1 tsp margarine
> 1/2 c cooked vegetable (can be cold and/or left over from day before)
> 1/2 c sliced peaches 1/2 c skim milk

Snack
> 2 small cookies

Dinner
> 3 oz lean meat
> 1/2 c rice
> 1/2 c broccoli
> 1/2 c cooked carrots
> 1 small dinner roll
> 2 tsp margarine
> 1 small fruit parfait

Snack
> 8 oz skim milk with 2 cups ice mixed in blender. Add 1 tsp instant coffee and 1- 2 tsp sugar or substitute
> 1 oz pretzels

DISCOUNTS

And those who save a little
Shall get a plenty more.

Thackeray

Discounts are the easiest means of saving money available to older Americans. Discounts can be significant, from 5 to 50%, in some cases much more. Golden opportunities for the golden years!

The business community now recognizes that late-life adults make up the fastest-growing sector of the population, in effect an enormous market of potential consumers. As a result, hundreds of discounts, perks and privileges are available and easily obtainable from organizations courting the trade of mature adults.

The United States government offers discounts to seniors who utilize federally owned facilities. A free lifetime-admission permit, the Golden Age Passport, which can be obtained at almost all federally-operated monuments, parks and recreation areas, admits at no charge not only the holder but in addition all companions in a private vehicle. There is a 50% discount for use fees of facilities and services, such as campsites, cave tours and parking lots.

Among the states, official discount programs vary. Some states offer free hunting and fishing licenses to older adults. Almost all the states have discount programs akin to those of the federal government but for state facilities only.

Discounts are not given automatically, not even by the government. Nor are discounted rates always advertised or apparent at first glance. Restrictions may apply. Older adults must ask for discounts and be prepared to offer proof of age by showing a birth certificate, driver's license, Medicare card, or membership ID in a 50+ club like AARP. While many companies accept the AARP designation of 50 years for qualification, some organizations place the minimum age at 55, 60 or even 65. The request for discount should be made before a purchase because most stores and organizations will not make a deduction after the bill has been filled out. Check the regular price to find out if a sale is going on at lower than normal rates. At the discretion of the supplier, a discount may be subject to space availability and be applicable only on certain days of the week or periods of the year.

WHERE DISCOUNTS ARE AVAILABLE

AAA, AARP and other organizations have discount programs for hotel, motel and automobile rental chains.

Airlines offer reduced fares for single round-trips and low-price coupon booklets.

Arboretums.

Banks waive service fees on checking accounts, safe deposit boxes and notary service.

Botanical gardens.

Breweries, as the Miller Brewing Company in Milwaukee, Wisconsin.

Computer clubs and networkings.

Department stores have weekly discount days.

Drug stores reduce prices on prescription drugs.

Education courses.

Fairs.

Health programs, usually preventive, as inoculations. HMOs offer educational materials, lectures and exercise sessions.

Historical Sites.

Home repair services.

Motion picture theaters offer discounts for almost all showings.

Museums lower ticket prices.

National parks and other federal recreation areas.

Newsletters. Consult the *Oxbridge Directory of Newsletters* (available at the library).

Planetariums.

Professional performances, as ballet, circus, concert, drama.

Prescription drugs.

Recreation facilities, such as golf courses and tennis courts, lower membership fees.

Restaurants have early bird specials and menus aimed at senior citizens.

Schools and colleges provide discounts for adult classes.

Shows of all kinds, such as those for autos and gardening.

Ski areas.

Spectator sports events.

Stations for public transportation, such as buses and trains, have discount tickets.

Tax advice.

Television programs and studios.

Theme parks.

Tourist attractions, as Colonial Williamsburg and the Empire State Building.

Travel agents, tour companies and travel clubs.

Ys and other organizations devoted to fitness.

Zoos.

DOCTORS:
CRITERIA FOR CHOOSING

*A well trained sensible family doctor is one
of the most valuable assets in a community.*

Sir William Osler

Availability:

Regular office hours.

Accepts brief telephone inquiries or consultations.

For homebound elderly, makes house calls or will arrange for
same.

Contingency Plans:

Has associates available for temporarily transferring care during
vacations.

Has arrangements in case of illness or retirement.

Costs:

Makes costs clearly understood before scheduling medications,
procedures, tests, treatment.

Prescribes inexpensive generic as well brand-name drugs.

Willing to accept insurance, especially Medicare.

Hospital affiliation:

Has admitting privileges to an accredited hospital, especially to
one associated with a medical school.

Location:

Office should be convenient to bus and other public transportation.

Office should be on ground floor of building in well-lighted area.

Management of care:

Keeps careful records for each patient.

Coordinates care with specialists, keeping track of medications
and treatment.

Sends patient records if patient for whatever reason selects a new
doctor.

Openness:

> Communicates well.
>
> Willingness to discuss treatment alternatives, as recommendation of exercise, stress reduction and weight loss for such a disorder as hypertension.
>
> Answers patient's questions regarding drugs and therapy.
>
> Perceptive of emotional as well as physical state of patient.
>
> Sensitive to such needs of patient as the desire to maintain dignity.

Philosophy

> By considering the physician's function to be that of a partner in healing, the doctor tries to help patients participate in making health-care decisions.

Prejudice:

> Listens to and investigates complaints without attributing them to age.
>
> Recommends appropriate treatment, such as cataract surgery, regardless of age of patient.

Prevention:

> Believer in preventive medicine.
>
> Keeps track of and administers such regularly scheduled immunizations as flu shots.
>
> Gives suggestions about diet, exercise, self-care.

Thoroughness:

> Devotes enough time to eliminate hurrying and to answer patient questions.
>
> Administers a complete examination at regular intervals.
>
> Explains possible side effects of medications.

PLEASE NOTE: It is not easy to determine a doctor's standing. Compiled by the Federal Government, the *National Practitioner Data Bank*, the most accurate and thorough listing of questionable physicians, is off-limits to the general public. Put out by the Public Citizen Health Research Group and available at some libraries, *13,012 Questionable Doctors* catalogs disciplinary records from medical boards in all 50 states, but the information is 3 years old or more. Medi-Net, an internet company, claims to present up-to-date information on every doctor licensed in the United States. Unfortunately, discovering whether or not charges have ever been filed against a doctor is usually impossible unless the case has resulted in disciplinary action.

SPECIALTY PHYSICIANS OFTEN
CONSULTED BY THE ELDERLY

*A rash of dermatologists, a hive of allergists, a scrub of
interns,a chest of phthisiologists, a flood of urologists,
a pride of proctologists, an eyeful of opthalmalmologists,
or a whiff of anesthesiologists, a staff of bacteriologists,
a cast of orthopedic rheumatologists, a gaggle of
laryngologists.*

Anonymous

Doctor's Title	Specialty
Anesthesiologist	Loss of sensation of pain
Cardiologist	Blood vessels, heart and heart valves
Dermatologist	Skin disorders
Endocrinologist	Diabetes, metabolism, thyroid
Gastroenterologist	Colon, liver and stomach
Geriatrician	Ailments of the elderly
Gynecologist	Female diseases, hygiene, sex organs
Hematologist	Blood and lymph system
Nephrologist	Kidneys
Neurologist	Brain and nerves
Oncologist	Tumors and cancer
Ophthalmologist	Eyes
Orthopedist	Bones and joints
Otolaryngologist	Ears, nose and throat
Otologist	Ears
Physiatrist	Movement
Podiatrist	Feet
Proctologist	Colon, rectum, anal canal
Psychiatrist	Mental and emotional
Pulmonologist	Lungs
Rheumatologist	Joints, connective tissue
Surgeon (General)	Operates on various parts of the body
Surgeon (Specific)	Operates within the specialty
Urologist	Bladder, kidneys, male sex organs

PLEASE NOTE: In the United States, an MD can term himself/herself by any of the specialities listed above, including Surgeon. It is almost always better to consult an MD who has passed the "boards;" that is, an MD with the requisite training who has passed an examination given by a licensing agency recognized by the American Medical Association and consisting of an examining board of his/her peers. In general, a board-certified specialist displays the diploma in a prominent place. Most libraries have a copy of *The Official ABMS Directory of Medical Specialists* by the American Board of Medical Specialties Staff and Marquis Who's Who Staff (New Providence, NJ: Marquis, 1997), which describes the degrees and certifications of physicians.

EDUCATION

On one occasion Aristotle was asked how much educated men were superior to those uneducated: "As much," said he, "as the living are to the dead." Another of his sayings was, that education is the best viaticum of old age.

Diogenes Laertius

No longer ending with teenagers, education today is treated as a process of continuous lifelong learning necessary on 2 counts: American society is aging, and advancing technology is rapidly changing virtually all areas of life and work. Retraining of older workers is essential in overcoming skill obsolescence, just as courses in the arts and sciences are important for the elderly in avoiding intellectual obsolescence. Already, say some employers, an electronic engineer's education becomes outdated just 5 years after graduation from university.

Adult-education programs are available today not just in colleges and universities but also in adult day-care centers, churches and synagogues, department stores, libraries, nursing homes, public schools and senior centers. Retirement planning programs are popular along with courses aimed at helping late-life adults develop coping skills and competency in areas such as estate planning, health care, money management. Short-term courses free from the pressures of exams and grades are in favor. The result? Mature adults have returned to school in record numbers.

The Age Discrimination Act of 1975, which made age prejudice illegal in any program receiving federal funds, applied to places of learning. Many states by law permitted a reduction or waiver of tuition fees for elderly enrolled at a government institution of higher education. Private and public educational institutions promptly began adjusting to needs and interests of older learners. Institutions of higher learning soon perceived the benefits of having elderly on campus. Life experience for credit toward a degree became available at many schools. College-level courses could now be taken for credit or non-credit by older persons, usually with a reduction in tuition. Community colleges, especially, became active in developing off-campus programs in such local sites as senior centers and hospitals, providing in addition counseling and remedial support.

Several organizations, among them the American Association of Retired Persons and the National Council of Senior Citizens, are geared to presenting short-term programs designed for older persons. New York University offers to persons 65+ two free courses each semester and biweekly luncheon discussions on subjects of current interest. The University of North Carolina at its Center for Creative Retirement has programs in history, social structure, wellness, with the purpose of helping seniors to become active leaders in their communities. Throughout the United States programs similar to those at NYU and UNC are available at almost every institution of higher learning.

Elderhostel, a separate administration utilizing a network of institutions of higher learning, provides low-cost opportunities for elderly to live on campus and take college-level courses for self-enrichment and intellectual growth from regular faculty members. Famous as a vacation school, it sponsors one-week courses during summer months—with more than 200,000 students and 700 educational institutions participating throughout the world. Elderhostel sponsors travel-learning experiences abroad, such as a trip to China, during which participants study the language and culture. The Discovery through the Humanities Program, sponsored by the National Council on Aging, funded by the National Endowment for the Humanities and led by volunteers, consists of nationwide discussion groups meeting in local churches, housing complexes and senior centers with programs on themes in history, literature, philosophy and the visual arts. The University without Walls, which utilizes radio and/or TV, is a program tailored to individuals by schools involved.

Community colleges, colleges and universities welcome seniors, who are good role models and make use of facilities and instructors that otherwise might be idle. Many institutions have programs with no degree requirements and relaxed regulations for attendance because relatively few older persons enroll in formal education programs. Public libraries, senior centers and offices of local Areas on Aging have information on continuing education courses and programs virtually in every community. It is now possible for older learners, probably for the first time in their lives, to learn about the things they really want to know.

Although the various electronic media, including interactive television, increased opportunities for home learning, the computer has made practicable a wider variety of learning experiences than anything else outside the traditional classroom. With their many Web sites and audio feed, Internet courses–termed asynchronous because they can be accessed at any time–have further facilitated distance learning. Led by a faculty member with whom they can communicate by e-mail, students utilize study guides as well as the customary textbooks, even taking examinations at assessment centers on or off campus. It is now possible that someone can earn a degree without ever setting foot in a classroom.

Education does not cease when work ends and retirement begins. Intellectual stimulation and development as well as maintaining contact with others are as necessary to a 70-year-old as to a 17-year-old. Given normal aging, the elderly can remain or become highly active learners. School authorities have found that late-life adults, even after 4 or more decades away from the classroom, more than hold their own with younger students in courses of every kind.

19th century novelist George Eliot stressed the power of education: "It's never too late to be what you might have been."

ETHICS: MEDICAL

Two things fill me with awe: the starry heavens and the
sense of moral responsibility in man.

Immanuel Kant

It is easy to give advice, not so easy to accept it, exceedingly difficult to act on it. Health care practitioners are continually reminded that the elderly have the same fundamental right as other age cohorts to adequate health care. Physicians are told that they should continually examine their attitudes, if not prejudices and stereotypes, toward the aged who are chronically ill and unattractive by current standards. Rather than patronize, the physician should offer compassion and kindness to all patients. Just as one purpose of medical school is to motivate doctors to regard every sick person as a unique individual in a unique situation, so these are goals, recommendations as to how members of the medical profession should behave rather than how they do behave.

Psychiatry traditionally avoids treating late-life adults, not just because Freud declared that they are uneducable, but also because they are judged as having their best years behind them. Similarly, at health centers the elderly too often receive short shrift because of the perception that their time left is severely limited and because their difficulties and crises are considered inevitable results of growing old. Hospitals, which are prepared for patients with acute illness, are not receptive to chronically ill elderly who stay for extended periods and run up enormous costs. Nursing homes prefer not to treat the sick so much as they want only to accommodate those elderly who for whatever reason cannot survive in the community.

Ethics are standards of conduct and judgment necessary to determination of right and wrong courses of action. Ethics and legalities often need to be considered together because they intertwine as authorities attempt to deal with rights and responsibilities of patients and medical personnel involved in health care delivery. Medical technology, including artificial organs, such as hip replacements, and new drug therapies, which may not have been tested, present ethical issues of safety as well as of access.

Many doctors insist that the legal mandates of Medicare conflict with ethical standards accepted by society for elderly patients. Some analysts agree, stating flatly that age-based rationing of health care is inevitable, arguing that it already exists under Medicare, which through its fee system encourages hospitals to discharge patients early. They argue that because Medicare guidelines do not meet decent standards of medical practice, as in the case of cataract treatment, rationing is being practiced now. They warn that chronic illness and disability are year-round companions of the aged and that 30% of Medicare cost is for treatment in the last year of life. They predict that the baby boomers who vastly outnumber the previous generation and who will undoubtedly live longer will need more financial resources than the succeeding generation will be able to provide. They ask: should life support, organ transplant, replacement surgery, resuscitation be automatic or rationed? They want to know who is to make the determination in each case and on what grounds.

Medical treatment of the elderly can be difficult, especially for practitioners accustomed to providing acute care to young or middle-aged patients. Frequently, the geriatric patient is unique in lacking classic signs and symptoms of a specific illness and in having atypical manifestations of disease. There may be pain, generalized or local, but there are no specific clues as to what is wrong. A chronic disease may coexist with one or more others, complicating diagnosis and treatment. Preoperative care may have to deal with malnutrition, ingestion of drugs as for hypertension, urinary incontinence, arthritis and other disorders commonly found in the elderly. Amelioration before surgery of all serious medical conditions is important. The elderly themselves may not be helpful or cooperative in that, accepting the common stereotype of old age as a period of sickness, they may tend either to refrain from complaints or to lose interest in regaining health.

Competent late-life patients today have the right to informed consent, that is the right to decide what kind of medical care they are to receive. They have the prerogative of refusing treatment or of ordering cessation of treatment, whether for sound or what a physician may consider unsound reasons. The European Code of Medical Ethics of the World Medical Association states: "A doctor engaging in medical practice must refrain from imposing on a patient his personal philosophical, moral or political wisdom."

Traditionally in the last century, medical judgments were made, not by the patient, but by physician and concerned family, who evaded allowing the elderly to act in their own interest and desires although freedom from invasion of one's body is a fundamental tenet of law and medical ethics. Doctors sought to shield patients from bad news, such as a fatal prognosis, for fear that they would give up hope and the will to live.

In the 19th century, physicians were considered consultants who provided opinions and medications while patients made the final judgment. There are physicians today who, believing that medicine is too technically advanced for a lay person to make a sensible decision, impose their own assessment based on professional knowledge and experience, if not benevolence. Too often they forget that technology can lead to more and more data without bringing wisdom. This is one reason it is sensible for a patient to get a second opinion and to seek active collaboration with the doctor from the very beginning.

Increasingly, even highly technical medical decisions are challenged by patients in the courts. In some cases, there have been and probably will continue to be charges of malpractice. The situation is not always clear-cut. Depending on the medication, an elderly person's level of competency may vary with time and amount taken. Who is to make decisions and on what basis? Lawyers and physicians are not agreed on a definition of competency. Unless able to come together with the patient and the family in reasonable discussion, a physician making ethical decisions needs sensitivity and courage–and good insurance. Charges are continually being leveled against physicians and institutions, sometimes rightly so, for controlling the behavior of older people by means of tranquilizers and sedatives as chemical "straitjackets".

Different are situations where the new technology will extend life but not preclude vegetative existence. Patients no longer simply die at home. Many can linger near death for weeks or months, kept alive by machines. Both medical practice and case law have established that cardiopulmonary resuscitation may be rightfully stopped if there is no indication that it will help. But—trained to save life, not end it, to heal the sick, not abandon them—many doctors and nurses are unwilling to recommend disconnecting a life-support system for a comatose patient even at the request of a family, as happened in the Karen Ann Quinlan case of 1976. Few stories in the media have attracted so much intense public attention, as if everyone empathized with the doctors as well as with the family. To avoid such a situation, lawyers recommend that an elderly person make a Living Will and obtain a power of attorney to guarantee that wishes are carried out; hospital administrators advise that the patient decide before treatment and after discussion with the doctor on use of extraordinary means to achieve either resuscitation or extension of life beyond sentient existence and so indicate on hospital records; social workers recommend that family members discuss the situation with the patient and that a surrogate be chosen so as to prevent action being taken without proper permission.

While not applicable to geriatric patients alone, practices of Health Maintenance Organizations under attack across the country, certainly apply to the aged. Concern is that HMOs limit a doctor's judgment as to what is best for patients. Labeling some typical care-plan practices unethical, Kevin Earle, executive director of the New Jersey State Board of Examiners, says: "We can't regulate managed care, but we can regulate doctors." The Board hopes to ban "gag" clauses in HMO contracts that prevent doctors from telling patients that they do not agree with a managed-care company's decisions as to which treatments should be given. The Board also hopes to forbid financial incentives rewarding doctors who prevent patients from visiting specialists or emergency rooms outside jurisdiction of an HMO. Financial incentives of this kind says Dr. Fred Palace, past president of the Medical Society of New Jersey, "amount to a bribe." Should the Board rule that an HMO practice considered by a doctor to compromise patient care is unethical, the HMO will be forbidden to bind physicians to contracts containing such a provision. Cautious optimism is expressed by former United States

Surgeon General C. Everett Koop: "It may take 5 or 10 years to find the right balance of managed care, physician autonomy and patient rights."

Issues of confidentiality are important to the elderly. Laws vary from state to state, but medical ethical behavior is standard. Without written or oral permission from a client/patient, neither a social worker nor a physician should reveal information regarding the individual save that the person is a client/patient. Exceptions regarding the old include elder abuse, danger that the client/patient will harm herself /himself and cases of dementia where the sick person cannot make a rational decision.

Another ethical issue mattering much to the elderly concerns pets. Pets are important to late-life adults. They help dispel feelings of loneliness by fulfilling human needs for love and sharing. They provide a focus of activity, and they give owners feelings of responsibility. Age-blind, they respond to kindness with nonjudgmental loyalty. Large pets, such as Collies, provide security. Despite objections of many elderly, animal models are used in the testing of drugs, in experimentation for analysis of diseases and symptoms and in study of aging processes which certainly occur in all mammals and probably in almost all living things. Congress as well as local authorities have passed legislation placing constraints on pharmaceutical and other organizations doing such research, with the result that researchers make every effort to avoid maiming, killing or inducing pain in test animals.

One of the cardinal doctrines in medicine, of application to animals as well as to people, is the ages-old behest of *Primum non nocere, First, do no harm.*

ETHNIC and MINORITY ELDERLY

And learning other tongues, you'll learn
All times are one; all men, one race.

Rupert Hughes

Classification as an *ethnic* refers to a person belonging to a group differing from society at large in such characteristics as customs, language, nationality of origin, race, religion or social views. Technically, a *minority group* is an ethnic group subject to prejudice and discrimination. In common usage, the terms are interchangeable.

Statistics on minority elderly should be treated with caution. There is often little or no scientific data. In the past, information about ethnic groups was sometimes based on only a few unrepresentative cases and presented as definitive. Data need to be obtained from large studies within each minority population group. Such an undertaking is expensive. But it is safe to say that among minorities the elderly population has been growing faster than among whites, so much so that the projection for the year 2050 is that at least 20% of the aged will be minority in background. Since 1965, when repeal of the quota system for immigrants opened United States borders, large numbers of Asians and Hispanics have been coming as well as immigrants from a wide variety of nations–with visas or without. As a result, the elderly population of the United States is growing increasingly diverse.

Although not identical, aging experiences and feelings are similar in all cultures. Some ethnic groups are more disconnected from the host society, others less, in terms of beliefs, dealings with family and friends, language and values. As generations succeed one another, traditional roles, customs and life-style–accepted and practiced by the first elderly to arrive–deteriorate. This is not to imply that the ideal of an ethnic melting pot is still held. Instead, the popularity of ethnic festivals suggests that ethnicity is widely regarded by Americans as a valuable part of individual identity. Nor is this to deny that great diversity exists within each ethnic population. Among the Hispanics, for instance, there are Central Americans, Cubans, Mexicans, Puerto Ricans, South Americans and others–who differ in regard to economic status, educational level, cultural background. Such diversity often makes generalizations inapplicable. Data gathered about elderly Mexicans in the Southwest are not applicable to Cubans in Florida, Puerto Ricans in New York, Costa Ricans in New Jersey.

Because they are physically different from Europeans, blacks make up a visible minority group–one of the most victimized in American history–subject especially to ethnocentric bias and negative stereotyping. Many black elderly are grandchildren of former slaves. Theirs is a mixed heritage, including Africans, Caribbeans, Europeans, Indians. The black community, Senator Moynihan has written, is characterized by broken families, crime, delinquency, illegitimacy, low income, matriarchal lifestyle. Although there is little reliable data about patterns of interaction between black elderly and their families, sociologists hold that black families are often unstable and disorganized. The church to some extent takes their place, for it is viewed by older blacks as a kind of extended family. There are about 3,000,000 black elderly, almost 15% of the total population of persons 65+. The old-old are likely to be women of limited economic resources. The poverty rate for older blacks is about 30%. They have lower incomes and less education than their elderly white counterparts; about 25% have a high school education. More than half reside in the South, at least 40% with a spouse. But about 1/3 live alone. As of the 1991 census, life expectancy for black women is 74 and 68 for black men. Although life expectancy for blacks below the age of 65 is lower than that of whites, for blacks from age 75 on life expectancy is greater than that of other elderly ethnic groups.

The second largest minority group is Hispanic. Information on Hispanics is not so readily available as it is for blacks. Much of what is known has been gleaned from census data. The number of Hispanics is increasing rapidly. About 25,000,000, they comprise some 9% of the population, their elderly making up more than 10% of all persons 65+. Hispanics come from a variety of cultures and nationalities exhibiting huge differences. About 15% are Puerto Rican. An even smaller percentage are Cuban. More and more are coming from South America. The majority, concentrated in the Southwest, are Mexican. They preserve their language and live in closed communities called *barrios*. Relationships with family and friends are clearly defined and strictly observed. Relatives are usually a person's closest friends. Age and sex essentially determine position and status. Less than 1/3 of elderly Hispanics have at least 5 years of schooling. Retirement from work is viewed as the beginning of old age. Because for Hispanics in general incomes are low and poverty rates high, with at least 20% of the elderly below the official poverty line, many families are unable fully to care for their elders although more than 50% of widows live with their family and remain a focus for much family activity. Mexican elderly have high rates of diabetes.

Unlike other ethnic groups that have tried to accommodate to the prevailing ways of life in the United States, Native Americans for the most part exist in cultural enclaves on reservations isolated from the rest of the population. Information about older Native Americans (Indians, Aleuts and Eskimos) is meager, and much of it is probably inaccurate. Research is sparse. There are only age stratification estimates. About 80,000 or 5% of Native Americans are 65+. About 1/4 of Native American elderly live on reservations or in Alaskan native villages although the proportion has been declining. Because of diversity–several hundred tribal or cultural groups still exist in North America–generalizations are not always valid. Although tradition has been waning, the elderly apparently still hold an honored place. The poorest of the poor, usually without Social Security, many Indians live in substandard and overcrowded conditions although establishment of gambling casinos on Indian reservations is bringing some tribes considerable wealth. The incidence of disease, especially tuberculosis, is so high that American Indians have the shortest life expectancy of all the minority groups.

Most Asian and Near-East elderly are relatively recent immigrants. Their number is increasing, but statistics concerning them are inadequate. Asians make up a number of diverse cultural and national groups: Chinese, Filipinos, Hmong, Indians, Japanese, Koreans, Vietnamese.

About 7% of Chinese are 65+. The sex ratio is unusual: almost 60% of males are elderly. The poverty rate of older Chinese is high. More than half live alone.

Their holding to a value system which considers filial piety central to a normal way of life results in conflict with western culture and its emphasis on independence of the individual. Language is a barrier for the elderly, not only from American society and from other Chinese speaking different dialects, but from access to education, work, institutions of all kinds.

The Japanese, in contrast, have achieved one of the highest socio-economic levels of all the minority elderly in the United States. Their level of education is rather high. The old-old are called Issei (first generation),and the young-old are called Nisei (2nd generation). Filipinos and Indians have also achieved high occupational levels. Except for the Vietnamese, whose recent wave of immigration from Indochina brought a fairly large number of elderly, a smaller percentage of older Asians than Blacks or Hispanics are below the poverty level. Culture shock and intergenerational strain remain serious problems for many Asian elderly.

Until such time as extensive valid research has been undertaken among ethnic elderly, the lack of firm knowledge will hinder attempts to furnish them with support. At the moment, authorities believe that most elderly ethnics live with one or more of their children, but no one knows for sure. One study of aging ethnics, utilizing material from the United States General Accounting Office in 1992, refers to 33% of whites as poor, about 70% of Hispanics, and almost 100% of Blacks.

Some researchers have erroneously regarded increasing age as a leveling force straightening out differences among the elderly. Ironically, ethnic groups themselves have long resisted becoming the objects of study, fearing prejudicial treatment and discrimination. Both attitudes prevent acquisition of sufficient knowledge as a suitable base for planning and implementing programs servicing minority elderly.

Perhaps the best attitude will result from remembering that "God hath made of one blood all nations of men." (Acts, XVII, 26.)

EXERCISE

By chase, our long-lived fathers earned their food,
Toil strung the nerves and purified the blood.
But we, their sons, a pampered race of men,
Are dwindled down to three score years and ten.
Better to use your muscles for health unbought,
Than fee the doctor for a nauseous draught.
The wise for cure on exercise depend. . . .

John Dryden

If exercise could be packed into a pill, it would be the single
most prescribed and beneficial medicine in the nation.

National Institute on Aging

Exercise is of utmost importance to those elderly who would keep their health. Inactivity is lethal. Exercise should be routine, as basic a habit as brushing one's teeth. Among the sedentary elderly, much physiologic decline parallels changes often attributed to aging. As muscles and bones shrink and tendons and ligaments fail to extend, an older person may hunch over, encounter difficulty with balance and suffer back pain. Yet well-controlled longitudinal studies reveal that even in the old-old, strength, flexibility and coordination can be reasonably maintained and improved through training and exercise.

Twentieth-century lifestyles, largely a result of technological advance, required little physical exertion. It is easy for an adult to get used to relaxing after a day at the job by becoming a *couch potato,* forgetting that the rate of deconditioning significantly exceeds that of conditioning. Among the many dangerous potential consequences of a period of inertia, immobility and inactivity are pneumonia and thrombosis (formation of a clot within a blood vessel). A *couch potato* who suddenly races for a bus faces the risk of an immediate heart attack. A sedentary post-menopausal woman, the heart-protecting effects of estrogen having been lost, also faces increased risk of a heart attack. In contrast, stretching, bending, strength training, aerobics and the like not only contribute to muscle tone and joint flexibility but also to organic and cerebral functioning, while making possible full performance of the Activities of Daily Living and permitting a lively social life.

Exercise has beneficial effects on limiting or even reversing some physiologic changes associated with so-called normal aging. It is possible to achieve fitness well into the 90's. Physical activity makes it easier to control nutrient needs and body composition. Exercise can help reduce risk of high blood pressure and stroke, increase cardiac output, intensify bone density, improve sugar metabolism, diminish harmful effects of fat in the blood. Agility, a byproduct of exercise, lessens the chance of falling and permits quick movement in an emergency. Research performed under the auspices of the National Institute on Aging at Atlanta's Emory University of Medicine and at the University of Farmington in Connecticut found that Tai Chi, a graceful form of Chinese martial arts, helps people 70+ improve strength and balance and maintain gains from other exercise programs designed to make falls less likely.

Fitness enhances respiration by increasing oxygen capacity and inducing better sleep patterns, but it is unwise to exercise late at night because intensive activity stimulates bodily systems. Physical training programs speed up reaction time, increase attention and improve memory. Work capacity, well-being, self-image and self-esteem improve as a person gains a sense of self-empowerment and control. Exercise is a natural mood elevator. Physical exertion produces endorphins, chemicals in the brain responsible for creating good moods. Exercise can supply even the busiest of businessmen with the stamina to make it through the busiest day. Exercise is important in preventing and treating such a disorder as varicose veins, especially common among older women who have had several children. Exercise can even help in predicting one's physiologic future, for stress testing has prognostic significance. Obviously, physical training can help add years to the life and life to the years. While Jack Lalanne may be exceptionally endowed, he is an example of what can be accomplished. But a warning against over-optimism: although fitness cuts the risk of dying, there is no proof that exercise will increase human longevity beyond the maximal life span of 120 years.

Exercise is more than haphazard physical activity. There is a high degree of specificity in response to physical training. Exercise should be carefully planned and designed, with not just physical fitness in mind. It is not true that there is no gain without pain. Some exertion may be good, but more need not be better. As everyone else, the elderly tend to attempt too much when motivated. They need to be taught when to stop and rest and how to recognize signs of overuse or of distress. Interval training (intermittent periods of high and low demand) is easily adaptable to these purposes. Also recommended is an exercise program of moderate intensity, such as walking for distance, which research indicates is nearly as protective as vigorous exertion.

Properly constructed and performed, an exercise regimen reduces risk for certain diseases common to the elderly—colon cancer, hypertension and osteoporosis among them.

It is never too late to start an exercise program. But anyone 65+ desirous of beginning a vigorous exercise program should first have a thorough medical examination, including stress tests that utilize a treadmill or bicycle to monitor blood pressure, electrocardiac activity and heart rate. The American College of Sports Medicine endorses use of stress tests for anyone 65+ with a background of medical problems, including risk factors for heart disease.

Even as the young, the elderly respond well to exercise, particularly in regard to balance, coordination, endurance, flexibility and strength. Most body organs function almost as well in active healthy elderly as in the young. Aerobically conditioned elderly perform physical activities with reduced heart rate and blood pressure. Levels of oxygen consumption can even be higher in aerobically trained elderly than in many young adults. Most exercisers, young or old, after a few months of regular activity feel better, look better and have more energy—so much so that they do not feel up to par if they miss a session or two.

Exercise does have a negative side. There is no denying that certain types of exercise, such as riding a stationary bicycle, can be boring. To make an exercise period interesting, time to do it with an interesting

TV show. If working out at home, get inexpensive equipment that can easily be put away, and make sure that there is room for full movement on all four sides. Weight lifting, which demands continual repetition, can also be dull unless done with a like-minded group in which participants encourage each other.

Many exercise regimens act upon more than one physiological system and can have harmful as well as beneficial effects. Although relatively common, most injuries are minor–resulting from falls and overuse. It is inadvisable to exercise during an acute illness. Extended periods of jogging and aerobic dancing, even when carefully engaged in, can be dangerous to knees and other parts of the body. The most serious adverse effect of aerobic exercise is fatal heart attack; but such an occurrence is rare, usually occurring in a person with some prior form of ischemia (obstruction of blood flow). Signs warning that exercise should be stopped at once include chest pain, nausea, loss of muscle control, dizziness or lightheadedness. If the symptoms persist, a doctor should be consulted. Specific goals of exercise vary according to the subgroup of elderly and the individual within the group. An exercise program should be tailored, preferably by a physician and a physical therapist, to the capability, need and desire of each individual. Precisely how much physical activity to recommend for the average late-life adult is unknown although the potential for endurance training and moderate aerobic activity seems present into the 70's at least. Type of exercise–bicycling, calisthenics, dancing, sports, swimming, water aerobics–should fit a person's lifestyle. (A frequently neglected aspect of fitness, especially by lay persons, is balance.) Walking, the most popular form of exercise in the United States, is virtually injury-free and burns almost the same number of calories per mile as jogging. Not only that, it can be done in the safety and comfort of a mall.

It is wise to move into an exercise program slowly and gradually, building up over months, not weeks. Most injuries occur because people try to progress rapidly. No exercise can overcome effects of years of sedentary living overnight. Different kinds of exercise do not all work the same sets of muscles.

There are three fundamental types of exercise. Stretching readies muscles for movement and prevents tight muscles from injury when they are contracted quickly. Stretching maintains and promotes flexibility. Of particular value in treatment of arthritis and bursitis, stretching helps prevent loss of mobility and injury to the joints. Endurance training utilizes repeated rhythmic movements to increase heart and breathing rates, improving coronary and lung efficiency as well as their capacity to do work. Strength building increases muscle mass and the ability to deal with heavy and bulky weights.

Many organizations offer exercise guidance at a reasonable fee. Well-trained instructors at the local Y will help beginners achieve a healthful balance of activity. A sensible home video can provide a worthwhile introduction to simpler exercises and exercise machines. There are athletic contests for late-life adults who compete by sex and age group.

For the young-old (65-74), exercise should include moderate aerobic conditioning, breaking into a mild sweat and raising the pulse to about 75% of the highest heart rate safely reached during previous exercise testing under the supervision of a qualified physician–which can be computed approximately for the healthy as follows: 220-age X .75=desired rate of heartbeats per minute. For example: 220-70=150. 150X.75=112.5. The exerciser should check pulse rate before exercising and about 15 minutes after ceasing activity to be sure that heart beats are in the target range and that they return to normal in a relatively short time.

For the old-old (75-84), exercise is concentrated on flexibility and strength. For the oldest old (85+), coordination and balance are emphasized. A training schedule of 30 minute sessions 3 times a week, or an approximation thereof, will result in maintenance as well as in some improvement, depending on intensity and type of activity.

Physical trainers recommend a day of rest following each session of strenuous exercise. Some exercises, as walking and the rotating of joints to prevent stiffness and preserve range of motion, can be done on a daily basis. Cool-down and flexibility exercises should be executed at the end of every session, warm-up and stretching at the beginning.

Clothing should be loose and comfortable and in layers, not plasticized, so as to permit as the body warms up circulation of air and evaporation of perspiration, which are necessary to regulation of temperature. Good shoes, shock-absorbing and arch-supporting, clothing that does not impede movement and a program providing gradual increase in intensity and duration of exercise as well as instruction in the techniques of the various activities will almost always prevent injury.

Especially for the sedentary, at 75 or thereabouts distinct losses in functional reserve occur although not the same way or to the same extent in all organs and in all individuals. Exercise at this stage is of significant benefit in maintaining optimum functioning. Many elderly face impairment from heart disease, arthritis or stroke, but the profile of physiological decline is not universal. Much interindividual variability exists although strength typically declines as about 1/3 of muscle mass is lost. The remedy is light weight work or resistance exercises. It is also important to move each of the major joints through its full range of motion at least once a day, an activity that can be accomplished by doing household chores.

There is a gender gap which is diminishing somewhat in regard to exercise. In general, by approaching any exercise or sport intensely men have been more likely to remain active than women. With the advent of aerobic dancing and exercise classes for women, female participation in exercise has reached new heights. Unfortunately, neither men nor women are attracted to those activities of most benefit. Men have more muscle; women are more flexible. Men tend to work out with weights; women take classes in which stretching, relaxation and yoga are emphasized. Both sexes would be better advised to incorporate different types of activity—such as weight-lifting, stretching, endurance, agility-balance-coordination training and aerobics—into their exercise programs. A good way to remain fit, in addition to a formal program, is to integrate exercise into one's life-style by doing jobs, such as gardening. Studies of energy cost equivalents have shown that a housewife when thoroughly cleaning her home can often use more physical energy than her husband who works in industry.

The admonition of Edward Stanley, Earl of Derby, should not be taken in vain: "Those who think they have not time for bodily exercise will sooner or later have to find time for illness." Rest and rot. Move and improve.

BENEFITS OF REGULAR HIGH-FREQUENCY
AND ADJUSTED-INTENSITY EXERCISE FOR THE ELDERLY

Helps to improve Quality of Life by:

> Enabling performance of activities of daily living
> Encouraging social contact
> Bolstering confidence in ability to maintain an independent lifestyle
> Imparting overall feelings of well-being
> Improving dexterity, flexibility and sense of balance
> Increasing endurance, strength and work capacity
> Speeding up quickness of response

Helps to Improve Physical Health by:

> Controlling nutrient needs
> Improving heart and blood vessel fitness
> Increasing oxygen capacity
> Intensifying bone density
> Modifying symptoms of chronic disease, such as arthritis
> Tending to normalize blood pressure

Helps to Cultivate Mental Health by

> Inducing beneficial sleep patterns and overcoming insomnia
> Assuaging feelings of anxiety
> Overcoming or preventing depression by elevating moods

EXERCISE ERRORS, SYMPTOMS, REMEDIES

Errors	Warning Signs	Remedies
Not setting up a program under guidance	Injuries	Conult a physical trainer
Beginning without a warm-up	Pain	Do calisthenics or other easy activities first
Not maintaining good posture	Soreness, injuries	Consult a physiatrist
Holding breath	Dizziness	Exhale as you lift weights; otherwise, breathe evenly
Exercising in pain	Soreness	Stop or ease off intensity
Bouncing while stretching	Muscle tightness	Stretch gradually
Touching toes with locked legs	Back pain	Bend knees slightly
Too quick a pace	Raised pulse that does not return to "normal"	Find a comfortable pace and/or level of exertion
Not drinking enough water	Malaise, headache, nausea	Sip water between events
Exercising late in the day	Insomnia	Exercise earlier

PROBLEMS AND SOLUTIONS WHEN INITIATING AN AEROBICS-BASED EXERCISE PROGRAM

(Adapted from L. Zohrman MD, Beyond Diet . . . Exercise Your Way to Fitness and Health, Published as a public service by Mazola Corn Oil. No date.)

Sign	Cause	Action to Take
Breathlessness after exercise	Heart and lungs not conditioned	Exercise less vigorously.
Calf pain	Strained muscle or faulty circulation	If occurs repeatedly, consult a physiatrist
Cramp at side (side stitch)	Diaphragm muscle is in spasm	Sit and lean forward
Dizziness or lightheadedness	Perhaps not enough blood arriving at brain	Place head between knees or lie supine with feet higher than head
Heart beat irregularity or palpitations	Disorder in cardiac rhythm	Consult a physician
Insomnia	Exercising late in the day	Exercise in morning or afternoon
Nausea and/or vomiting	Insufficient oxygen reaching body tissues	Exercise more slowly and/or less vigorously

FAMILY

The family is more sacred than the state.

Pope Pius XI

The family is a great institution, but who wants to live in an institution?

Anonymous

The American family plays a decisive role in the well-being of the elderly who as the years pass become more and more dependent upon others, particularly in regard to finances, health, housing and mobility.

People establish a family by marriage. A family may be nuclear, extended, "step," intergenerational–each with its own particular configuration. A nuclear family, which has characterized society in the United States for centuries, consists of wife, husband, children. When several nuclear families are joined through marriage, an extended family results. But many kinds of ties other than the biological develop and bind people to one another, functional, legal, social and psychological among them–a tangle of arrangements with potential conflicts. More and more often today, a family becomes a network which includes friends and even neighbors as well as relatives, with consequent diminution of traditional obligations of kinship. Census data suggest that by the end of the century a majority of Americans will belong to a family including at least 1 stepparent. Already, 1 of every 2 marriages ends in divorce and 1 of every 3 children resides with a stepfamily.

Individual families differ considerably in ability to cope with challenge and threat. Some become stronger; others recover partially or break down completely. By a disruption, such as divorce, nuclear family structure changes to single-parented or fractured. With remarriage, two or more family structures may blend, creating unanticipated problems. Increasing longevity and decreasing fertility rates are changing the traditional family structure from a pyramid with a few elderly and many children and grandchildren to a narrow structure with few children and grandchildren. Caregiving is becoming a regular experience for members of multigenerational families. Since women outlive men, aging families include more grandmothers and great-grandmothers than grandfathers. Of the approximately 95% of older adults who reside in the community, many are part of what sociologists call a later-life family; that is, the family has decreased in size because of the "empty nest" phenomenon. Most such persons, preferring independence, do not move into the home of a relative even after death of a spouse.

In so pluralistic a nation as the United States, cultural expectations of traditional behavior may be difficult to achieve in new social situations. Contingent on the type of family, members may enjoy non-traditional roles and expectations and act under loyalties and lines of authority unusual in the past. However, important beliefs, norms and values transmitted by the family persist even if traditional bonds show signs of weakening.

No matter what the family structure and the social milieu, in general parents and children continue being of concern to one another, creating a feeling of involvement especially important to aging individuals who have a strong need for love and respect from their offspring. Although the parent-child relationship is dynamic, undergoing continual change, lines of communication are kept open. Many aging parents manage to sustain the family setting despite widowhood. About 80% of the elderly live within 1/2 an hour's distance from children. Contrary to stereotypical belief, aging parents are in frequent communication with family members, at least semi-weekly or weekly, by telephone, E-mail or in person. Although contacts may be short, even hasty at times, they serve not only as a way for parent and child to monitor each other's welfare but also as a means of conveying advice and providing assistance. It is not the number of meetings but the fit between generations that counts. The black family, a matriarchy characterized by instability and illegitimacy, is an exception.

Not that all is well. Parent-child relationships are filled with misunderstanding and guilt. Parents and children come from different age cohorts whose separate experiences because of the quickening pace of social change do not make it easy for either generation to empathize fully with the other. The lifestyle of one generation may distress the other. Parents are often reluctant to grant grown children equal footing with them as adults.

Society offers no specific guidelines for adult children of elderly parents; grown children are not legally enjoined to do anything for mothers and fathers. Why is it, then, that adult children continue to meet filial responsibilities? The Fourth Commandment states: "Honor thy father and thy mother." The Judeo-Christian tradition roots familial obligations in moral values that are still so powerful that family alienation from the elderly does not endure.

The family remains, and is likely to remain, the primary support system of the aged for sustenance and well-being. Both politicians and sociologists warned that in the final years of the last century a serious shrinkage of economic resources has become apparent, so much so that there will be a definite expansion of demands for elder care placed on family members. At present, Medicare pays for some 30% of short-term, acute health-care expense whereas family and friends assume the total financial and other burdens of long-term care. Will HMOs with their concept of managed care help control rising health-care costs of the present generation of elderly?

Rather than resort to institutionalism, many families undergo serious hardship to keep parents in their own home and in the community. Nor does help from the older people to the younger cease, for besides advice many parents provide financial support and assistance of whatever kind is needed, such as child care and performing errands. Traditional patterns of mutual aid persist amid the interchange of resources, even as the balance of power shifts from the care recipient to the caregiver. But old people in America move into their children's homes only when so poor or sick that they cannot care for themselves. And middle-aged women, once the chief source of family support for the old, have entered or are entering the labor force and are no longer so available despite what sociologists call the family's matrifocal tilt: sons tend to separate; daughters, to stay close. Hopefully, medical advances will make up for the absence of women who work outside the home. .

Because people are living longer, there is a marked increase in 3-,

4- and even 5-generation families, which at the beginning of the last century were virtually nonexistent. At least 40% of all 65+ are members of a 4-generation family. By the year 2020 the typical family is expected to consist of 4 generations. Today, many elderly have children 65 +, who may be in need of help and health care. The obverse is true: this is the first time in history that the average married couple has more living parents and grandparents than children. It is not unusual to meet a couple with 4 parents and 8 grandparents. In this situation, it is not possible for parents and children to assume caretaking responsibilities for all members of the family. Almost 1 in 3 persons 50-70 in age are taking care of older relatives. In the year 2050 the baby boomers will be older than 85 and have relatively few children to support them. Families will be forced to rely on such formal private and public systems of service as day-care centers and support groups.

As stressful events that accompany old age increase in number and severity, elder abuse may occur, whether in the form of chronic verbal attack, physical injury, neglect, violation of rights or misuse of money and property. Not a problem separate to itself, elder abuse is one of the family conflicts appearing during later life that need to be put into proper perspective, not the least concern of which is the matter of degree. Otherwise, the problem cannot be defined, its extent not known, its causes obscure.

There have always been conflictual relationships between the elderly and their offspring. The old may act or be helpless, and the caregiver may be unable to cope. Financial expenses may increase. Career goals and plans for the future, such as travel, may be disrupted. Physical and mental stress may be exhausting, as caregivers find themselves immersed in the role. Adult children, somewhat resentful, in addition to providing care try to maintain their roles at work and in society. At which precise point do the negative manifestations of caregiving go beyond the restraints of propriety? There is much diversity in types of elder abuse, whether by children or other relatives. Neglect and maltreatment, whether emotional or physical, can take many forms.

Although the National Aging Resource Center on Elder Abuse in the United States provides only estimates of the number of cases of mistreatment, social workers think the rate of elder abuse is rising. Even loosely defined, old-age abuse in the United States by a family member probably affects some 1,000,000 persons a year. The actual number may be higher. Mandatory reporting of elder abuse is legally imposed on social workers and physicians in most states. But authorities think that they often choose to ignore it in order to avoid involvement. Isolation of old persons as a result of retirement may also act as a barrier to detection and reporting of maltreatment. Relatively few older persons reside in nursing homes, about 5%, and so there is much less information obtained about institutional abuse than about domestic. Undoubtedly, some elderly victims do not report abuse because of shame, fear of retaliation, inability to live elsewhere. Some reports, contrary to popular belief, imply that females of advanced age are likely victims of abuse by their middle-aged daughters.

It is not uncommon for adult children to make decisions for parents without consultation, irritating the elders or compelling them to behave as dependents–in either case endangering a good family relationship. Even so, the vast majority of elderly parents report satisfaction with their family, adding that when help is needed their children can be relied on for sensible, responsible action. When tallied, the reports indicate that about 80% of health care to the elderly is provided now by family members, responsibility for which is almost always assumed by adult daughters and daughters-in-law. Unless the cure rate of medicine advances at a phenomenal pace or the elderly learn how to stay healthy, who will assume that responsibility in the year 2020, when because of the number of baby boomers the need of the aged for home health care could conceivably increase by at least 50%?

Certainly, despite the warnings of some that the family is a declining institution, parents and children are continuing to try to take care of their own: "God setteth the solitary in families." (Psalms, 68,6)

FINANCIAL MATTERS

How pleasant it is to have money!

Arthur Hugh Clough

Lack of money is the root of all evil.

G.B. Shaw

Most people think that the elderly need less income than the young. With age, buying patterns do change. While the old spend much less on clothing, entertainment and transportation than the young, costs for food, shelter and energy are frequently similar. But medical expenses undoubtedly are greater. Surveys indicate, strange as it may seem, that older persons spend a larger share of income on health-care today than before enactment of Medicare. No wonder polls of the elderly indicate that at the top of their financial concerns are medical expenses.

Social Security is the major source of income for most elderly. Since 1935, the date of inauguration of Social Security, their economic status has steadily improved due in large part to governmental wage and price indexing. Numerous elderly married couples received about a 50% boost in retirement income. In addition, those who owned their homes gained a tidy nest egg as housing prices jumped well ahead of the government's price index for commodities. But as private pension plans in business and industry became widespread, so did mismanagement and abuses, a situation Congress tried to correct with the Employment Retirement Income Security Act (ERISA) of 1974.

In general, say many financial advisers, the old are not hurt by inflation, for most of their sources of income rise with prices. Others think that the apocryphal story of the man who on recovery from a coma lasting several years, called his bank soon after release from the hospital and was informed that his bank balance had grown to more than $1,000,000, provides a sensible warning. The operator came on the line and he heard: "Please deposit $75,000 for the next three minutes."

Although there appeared to be a sustained diminution of poverty among older persons, for those elderly accustomed to low wage levels, depressed economic circumstance has been a lifelong condition worsened by loss of employment in old age. The poverty rate for elderly blacks and Hispanics is about 3 times that for whites. For others, reduction of income is a new condition resulting from retirement or widowhood. As a result, the percentage of elderly householders near or below the poverty line has increased: The United States General Accounting Office estimates that about 1/2 of elderly homeowners, many of whom are women without much earning power, exhaust about 1/2 of their income on electricity, gas, water, maintenance and taxes.

There are two sides to this story. Sociologists who have studied poverty rates among the elderly state flatly that the United States has the highest index of countries analyzed and that percentage of income support for the elderly is distinctly below that of other nations in the industrialized nations. At least 8,000,000 persons 65+ are living near or below the federal government's determination of poverty level. In addition, there is another "hidden" poor population among the elderly because census figures do not include the aged who live with others, generally family members, and those in institutions.

Poverty varies according to age, race, sex. The oldest-old have about double the number of poor persons as the young-old. Indeed, the best off of all the elderly cohorts are those young-old who are married, in good health and with pensions and other assets. Older females living alone have a higher percentage of poverty than older males in similar circumstances. The highest percentage of poverty of elderly persons is among minority women living alone.

While the median income of elderly families remains below that of younger families, the economic lot of many older persons has steadily improved since the Great Depression. Bonds and stocks have become more and more important as sources of income. Millions of elderly entered the bond and stock markets by way of mutual funds, reaping gains year after year. But distribution of assets other than home equity is more unequal than in the other age cohorts, with the bulk of property and other holdings concentrated among the wealthy elderly.

Financial advisers strongly urge the elderly to keep a budget and accurate financial records, not just for tax purposes, but to insure that they live within limits. Advisers warn that credit cards invite over-use. Such temptations must be overcome early in the game. They add that at least 3 months' income, enough to cover ordinary expenditures, be kept in a separate bank account for emergencies. It is wise to have a pension plan checked by an accountant or a lawyer before retirement to be sure that the contract is for life and that a spouse or other loved ones are protected. Advisers also point out that while most elderly do not need life insurance, those who think they do should read the policy carefully, especially the fine print, because benefits may be much smaller than the impression created by the sales pitch. Nursing home insurance should be bought only from a company with assurance of an excellent reputation by a state oversight agency. Such insurance ought to be guaranteed renewable, with pay for all levels of care and with minimum requirement of prior hospital confinement.

Many organizations offer discounts to the elderly. One of the best is the Golden Age Passport provided free by the federal government to persons beyond the age of 62, and which entitles the recipient and companions in an automobile free access to all national parks and monuments. Members of both the AARP and the National Council of Senior Citizens are eligible for discounts from airlines, hotels, rental car companies. Almost all motion picture theaters offer discounts to people 65+. (For a detailed discussion, see pp. 132-134).

Financial planning is important. But engagement of a professional financial adviser is not necessary for most elderly. To benefit from the services of a financial planner, an elderly person's annual income should be at least $50,000. Otherwise, the costs will in all probability exceed the benefits. Financial planners may charge a flat fee or hourly rate, receive a commission on all transactions or utilize a combination of fee and commission. Financial planners who receive a flat fee or hourly rate are considered to be the least biased in recommending bonds, insurance and stocks. Before deciding on a financial planner, it is wise to interview several. Every reputable financial planner will welcome being interviewed by a prospective client. (See the checklist below.) It is wise to be alert to anyone who says, Trust me," and to anyone who offers equities with barely true sales points.

Determination of finances is relatively easy. Compute the total monthly income from Social Security, pension or salary, dividends from investments, interest on savings. Then subtract from that sum monthly expenditures for essentials (food, medical bills), insurance, housing, recreation, taxes, utilities. What is left over is called Discretionary Income, money that can be spent as one wishes. If the number is negative, a person can withdraw money from savings accounts or investments or obtain one of the new mortgages designed to provide monthly income to elderly house owners. If such be the case, it is important to know approximately how long it will be possible to obtain money. Simply divide the total amount of money that can be withdrawn by multiples of 12: for 1 year divide by 12, for 2 years by 24, etc. Any bank manager will help without charge in making the figure exact.

While purchase of life insurance by most elderly is foolish, drawing up a will is wise. Yet 2 out of 3 persons die without having made a valid will, with the result that in an expensive and slow process government determines what happens to all assets left—without regard to impact on one's family. Unfortunately, a will is subject to probate, a probably slow and expensive procedure of government for validating the document. Fortunately, a husband and wife can avoid probate by placing property, including bank accounts, in joint ownership. There are other ways to avoid probate, such as by setting up a living trust, but this should be done by an expert in estate planning law and procedures. Current law allows a person to leave any amount to a spouse free of federal estate taxes and to leave to one's other heirs an estate of up to $700,000 (a number that will increase gradually in succeeding years) free of federal taxes.

Many oldsters do not know about federal, state and local tax deductions and exemptions, information available at the library or in one of the programs from communities and organizations (even the IRS).

The American Association of Retired Persons has an excellent program staffed entirely by volunteers who have been commended again and again for the accuracy of returns they have helped older adults prepare.

"In this world," said Benjamin Franklin, "nothing is certain but death and taxes."

CHOOSING A FINANCIAL PLANNER

Finding a Financial Planner:

Ask friends, relatives, business associates for recommendations.

Interview a few financial planners: bring written questions; jot down answers.

Questions to Ask a Financial Planner:

What type of client do you prefer?

What is your business philosophy, especially in regard to buying and selling securities?

Can you furnish a list of referrals from satisfied clients?

What is your business experience?

How do you get information on financial developments?

At my request, will you work with other professional advisers such as an accountant, attorney, banker?

Exactly what do you provide: a general plan, recommendations with pros and cons, periodic review?

What information from me will you require?

How much time after I agree to be your client will you need to present a plan?

With whom will I have contact on a regular basis, with you or with associates?

Do you monitor the plan? How and how often?

How long must I remain your client?

What happens if I reject part or all of your plan for me?

Precisely what is your fee structure?

How do I pay you?

Aspects to Investigate:

>Complaints registered with the Better Business Bureau.
>Credentials.
>Professional Affiliations.
>Registration with the Securities and Exchange Commission.
>Under supervision of a government agency.

FRIENDLY ENVIRONMENT

There's many a life of sweet content
Whose virtue is environment.

Walter Learned

Creation of an aging-friendly environment enables even disabled elderly to maintain independence. Based on study of aging and preferences of the elderly, gerontechnology, sometimes referred to as gerodesign, is a relatively new multidisciplinary field that combines art and technology, psychology and physiology, with the aim of mitigating age-related losses and of achieving for the elderly attractiveness, comfort, new opportunities, privacy and safety at relatively little expense through optimal design of products and systems requiring low physical effort and with a tolerance for error.

The first international conference on gerontechnology was held in 1991, taking into account advances in anthropometry (study of human body measurements) and ergonomics (study of how people adjust to the environment, especially in regard to machines), aspects of technology which emphasize ease of access, economy of movement, flexibility, safety and wellness.

Sociologists assess the ability of the disabled elderly to maintain an independent lifestyle in terms of Basic Activities of Daily Living (ADL) and of Instrumental Activities of Basic Living (IADL). ADL include simple activities associated with self-care, such as bathing, dressing, feeding oneself, moving between bed and chair, using the toilet. IADL include more complex activities, such as housework and laundry, meal preparation, handling personal finance.

Almost all houses are built for young persons who seemingly never grow old or disabled. If properly applied, the findings of gerontechnologists, engineers, and social workers are certain to result in appropriate redesign of familiar objects to ensure a longer and improved quality of life by taking account of cognitive, mobility and perceptual limitations that often accompany aging. Actually, the special features will be beneficial for everybody at every age level. The building will not look odd nor institutional. Every house will have a first-floor master bedroom with unobtrusive access to the outside. Special attention will be given to needs and desires of women because they comprise a distinct majority at the higher ages.

Optimum design is to create safe, uncluttered halls and rooms. When entering a dwelling, people should be able to quickly identify the specific function of each room and the objects in it, including foyer and entrance hall. Both the walkway leading to the front door and hall floors are textured to make them slip-proof. Lighting is automatic by means of a pressure- or motion-activated 2-way switch at the top and bottom of hallways. Levels of light are uniform, so as to eliminate dark, shadowy areas. Wide doorways in halls and rooms and on ramps instead of stairways make a building wheelchair accessible. If a stairway is present, it should be wide with no step higher than 18" and a handrail should be clearly marked. Light bulbs should be powerful enough to show step height for ascending and step width for descending. Thermostats controlling heating and cooling should be large enough to be read easily. A lever should be used instead of a doorknob. Windows are crank operated because easier to open and close.

Gerontechnology considers the floor carefully. Obstacles like raised door sills are eliminated; tacked-down carpeting is installed where possible to decrease risk of injury to self and crockery from falls. Textured, non-skid, non-glare tiles are installed in bathroom and kitchen. The floor and walls in every room have contrasting colors. Abrupt transitions, as from carpet to polished tiles, are minimized.

Material of all furniture is fire-resistant. Chairs with arms make it easier to sit and to rise to a standing position. Chairs are light in weight, padded and supported by legs directly under them in front and rear. Instead of a long couch, chairs and seats are angled toward each other because older persons frequently need face-to-face contact for visual clues, such as facial expressions, if they are to hear clearly. Table-tops are wide and have rounded corners. Rather than legs, a pedestal supports the table so as not to interfere with placement of a cane or wheelchair.

Communication between older adults is enhanced in quiet surroundings. Through use of acoustic tiles, carpeting and window cover-
ings, background noises can be eliminated. Isolating heating and air-
conditioning systems will minimize distracting sounds. The colors blue
and green, which have a soothing and restful effect, are reserved for the
bedroom whereas pastels appear in the other rooms and over windows
to add a livelier quality.

At all entrances and exits to an apartment or house, lights triggered
by motion detectors should be installed. Within a room, lighting can be
evenly distributed to avoid shadows by aiming lights at ceilings and
walls. Windows and skylights with tinted or polarized glass should be
placed to prevent glare. Blinds should be used at windows that fill with
bright sunlight. Night lights should be placed in hallways, bedrooms,
bathrooms.

There are many helpful devices. In the kitchen a high, comfortable
stool, rolling cart, long-handled reacher (to avoid use of a step stool or
ladder), finger-glove pot-holders, lipped and divided plates with non-
skid bottoms, large-handled cutlery and an electric toaster-broiler make
meal preparation easier and safer. Handles on cooking utensils should
be welded to the body of the appliance and knurled (ridged or beaded)
to prevent slippage. All work surfaces should be at the same level, so
that heavy items can be slid, not carried. The countertops should have
colored accents, so that edges can be readily seen. Counters should
have space open enough to accommodate a wheel chair. Shelves should
be at or near chest height or be able to be lowered by levers to avoid
difficulty in reaching for objects like canned food. To minimize bending, the dishwasher should be installed about a foot above floor level. A
foot pedal should be conveniently placed to operate faucets. The wall
oven should have a side-swinging door. Because most house fires start
in the kitchen, an extinguisher should be within easy reach.

In the bathroom, which should be next to the bedroom, non-skid
surfaces on the floor and in the bathtub a tub bench, a raised toilet seat,
grab rails at the proper angle and height for tub and toilet, hand-held
shower hose, bath-caddy, grounded electrical outlets, long-handled tooth
brush, comb and hairbrush, antiscald bathtub and shower valves that

automatically adjust water temperature, single-lever faucets that do not require twisting, toilet paper holder with serrated edges for one-handed tearing, soap-on-a-rope and tempered glass increase both safety and comfort. Curtain rods, soap holders and towel bars should be able to withstand a sudden pull of body weight. Sensor-activated lights should be installed to turn on automatically when someone enters.

The disabled prefer to remain in their own homes or apartments, not only because of their desire for privacy and independence, but also because they spend much more time there than does the rest of the population. There are many safety and home care devices. Motorized wheelchairs aid in lifting and transportation of impaired elderly. A significant recent development is widespread use of medical equipment, such as different kinds of monitoring equipment, by nonprofessionals. Security of another kind is a major concern. Intercoms, detectors (of heat, smoke, carbon monoxide, natural gas and radon), signals (of water leaks), fire and burglar alarm systems are relatively inexpensive. Night lights on stairs help prevent falls, as do lamps that can be turned off by touch. Slower opening and closing doors on elevators facilitate access and egress.

It is easy to make a dwelling safer. Telephones should be conveniently placed (one at bedside) and supplemented by portable devices. Close to every telephone should be posted the number of a helpful neighbor, personal physician, local pharmacy, police and fire departments, the nearest poison center. The medicine cabinet should contain only up-to-date drugs, as per the label on each container. A fire extinguisher should be kept handy. Household combustion appliances, such as a gas range, are vented to the outside.

The suggestions, changes and improvements of gerontechnology will reduce, if not eliminate, risks–making a relatively full and independent lifestyle possible. John Ruskin, famous for his lectures on architecture, wrote: "This is the true nature of home–it is the place of peace; the shelter, not only from injury, but from all terror, doubt and division."

GENDER ROLES

All the world's a stage,
And all the men and women merely players.

William Shakespeare

In a society dominated by the elderly, as may be the case starting in 2020, when the baby boomers come of age, mores will probably no longer be masculine in tone. Some sociologists maintain that there will be no reason for feminism since a female majority and the blurring and reversal of behavior and social differences that often occur in the last third of life may occasion deep changes in behavior, values and institutions.

There is a need for more research on aging to address the changing psychological and/or cultural differences between men and women, for while continuity and tradition persist change does occur. Boys were reared to be assertive and independent and girls to be passive and dependent—with the result that men and women differed in aggression, dependence, expressiveness, social behavior. The vast majority of women did not exercise real power either within the family or outside. Men made important decisions. Not today. Other views of women's place in society are coming to the fore as more and more women obtain economic independence. Yet a focal message for most women remains the same: the primary role of females in American society is that of family nurturers who supply the home with offspring and care for kin, both children and adults. Any other role is secondary. An unmarried woman of today is expected to provide nurturing care even at the cost of a career. In this era of multiple-generation families, a 45-year-old married older woman still in the work force may supervise a teenager at home at the same time that she accepts responsibility for care of an elderly mother and even older grandmother.

Despite disparities in training and experience, women and men grow more alike as they age, particularly from the year 65 on. Such gender-role convergence occurs more in females than in men. Reasons? Feistiness makes aging easier. A majority of elderly women live alone, a situation unprecedented historically, and one that demands psychological assertiveness to promote independence. With the advent of women into the work force, the relative power in marriage given the male breadwinner has been diminished. In addition, because of retirement and the passage of years, older persons are no longer directly involved in either industrial production or familial reproduction. Among the married young, work options at home and in industry help cause gender inequality since occupations and family responsibilities to a large extent are sex-segregated, whereas retirement and the years after menopause apparently contribute to the leveling of sex-role differences.

A period of redirection of personality occurs among the elderly, a major turning point in the life cycle, as both sexes move toward androgyny. Many older women become more dominant and egocentric, more independent and assertive, even as many men become more passive and affiliative, more caring and nurturing While the tendency toward same-sex friendship persists, both men and women are likely to have women as confidantes. Traditional domestic divisions of labor into male and feminine are no longer sharp. Elderly women outspokenly make decisions for the household. Elderly men perform household chores. In the Baltimore Study of Aging, begun in 1958, elderly men listed housework as one of the physical activities they had increased considerably.

Ironically, the double standard pertaining to aging persists even here. Older men see themselves and are seen by others as admirable for performing cross-gender tasks in the home whereas older women see themselves and are seen by others as not gaining esteem for performing such tasks.

Although more males are born than females, male mortality is higher than that of females. Is that because the female of the species is hardier than the male? Has the improvement of modern standards of living, including public sanitation and medical care, benefited women more than men? In partial answer to these questions, it is instructive to remember that a woman has been schooled from early life to a nurturing role, first as mother, then as nurse to an aging husband older than she and who will probably leave her a widow. Actuaries work on the assumption that male risks for mortality are higher than those for the female since males engage in more dangerous activities. Males are more likely to commit suicide than female counterparts. Is part of the reason that single men are more likely to be social isolates than single women? There is much evidence that people with little social support are more likely to die earlier than those with a large social network. By age 65, almost 70% of women are widowed in contrast to about 20% of men, with the result that many older women live alone while the majority of men live with a spouse.

But mortality rates become more similar in old age, especially among those 85+.

Female longevity increases chances for a woman to be ill. Ironically, males have a higher death rate, but females seemingly have a poorer state of health. Men have more physical strength than women although both sexes weaken in old age as muscle mass is lost. Old men are more likely to succumb to lethal diseases; women are more likely to suffer from chronic ailments. Men have higher rates of hospitalization but fewer bed days; women have higher use of physician services and incline to longer hospital stays. 75% of older men are married, a much smaller percentage of females. Older women have poorer nutritional status than men, for they consume less calcium, iron, protein. Older women have a higher urinary incontinence rate than men, with a ratio of about 2:1. Hearing difficulties are more common and more severe in men In general, the sensitivity of touch remains the same in both sexes save that pressure-touch threshold on the index finger and the big toe declines more in men than in women. While hypochondriasis is more common among women than among men, self-esteem of men is more vulnerable to images of masculinity, so that they are more likely to deny even obvious symptoms that suggest declines in health and activity levels. Real health differences between the sexes, some gerontologists assert, may not be quite what they seem.

Elderly men and women are victims of ageism, but women in particular suffer devaluation. Women, generally perceived as becoming old much before men, are disparaged for signs of old age. While an older man prefers the company of younger women and will marry a younger woman without fear of opprobrium, an older woman will not marry a young man for fear of public ridicule and censure. Most women, if they live long enough, will be poor: wages are lower than those of men. With no one willing or able to care for them, women beyond the age of 75 make up about 3/4 of nursing home residents.

Women, because they live into advanced old age and become housebound with chronic ailments, are potential victims of neglect and abuse by their adult family members. Nevertheless, there is consensus among gerontological researchers that women age with less difficulty than men, perhaps because they gain freedom and authority with the years.

In art and literature of previous eras, perspectives were almost always male. The situation is slowly changing as evidenced by a novel such as *The First Wives' Club* and the appearance of older women in magazines modeling Armani suits as well as intimate apparel and thinking about adventurous retirement plans. Because the elderly have more discretionary income than the young, the trend is likely to persist. But on TV, women appear much less than men and they disappear when they move too far beyond the age of 30. More than 90% of TV characters over age 65 are males. Older women are depicted as eccentric, silly and stubborn—increasingly sexless; older men as smarter and with sexual allure. The exception is daytime soap operas, for there older women are portrayed sympathetically. In commercials, old men with graying temples lend an air of authority to claims for medications while older women sell dentures and leak-proof undergarments. Newscast anchor persons usually are older males accompanied, perhaps, by pretty young women.

Although advertising agencies remain vehemently devoted to the targeting of youthful and youth-loving consumers, Michael Eisenberg, founder of *Prime Life Network*, a cable channel established in 1997, is determined to break the TV stereotype of what it means to age in America today. Other cable companies with the same aim include *Our Time Television* and *Act III*. The times they are achanging.

Not just on TV but everywhere says Kate Field:

They talk about a woman's sphere as though it had a limit;
There's not a place in earth or heaven,
There's not a task to mankind given,
There's not a blessing or a woe,
There's not a whispered "yes" or "no,"
That has a feather's weight of worth
Without a woman in it.

GERIATRICS, ANYONE?

When one's all right, he's prone to spite
The doctor's peaceful mission.
But when he's sick, it's loud and quick
He bawls out for a physician.

Eugene Field

Amazing benefits can be realized from disease and disability prevention as well as from care of the aging and the aged. The Alliance for Aging Research, a highly respected research group based in Washington, DC, has calculated that if doctors specializing in diseases and problems of old age could enable elderly Americans by just one month to stave off physical dependency (inability to perform necessary activities of daily living, such as marketing and cooking) monetary savings to the nation would be enormous–probably at least $5,000,000,000. But, just as probably, it is not going to happen.

Not that matters started badly. In 1983, the Public Health Service began the Geriatric Education Center (GEC) initiative to overcome the shortage of personnel with training in treatment and care of the elderly. By 1989, more than 35 centers had been created and some 3,000 health care professionals had participated in the program. Networks were created, academic courses developed, resources for doctors made available. Then funding for the GEC initiative was decreased, and momentum slowed.

Although physicians committed to a career in geriatrics are critical to providing health care for the aging, there are now scarcely 2 certified geriatricians for every 10,000 Americans. "Already," states David Reuben, MD, head of the Department of Geriatrics at UCLA's School of Medicine., "there are areas of the country with high concentrations of older persons where you can't find a geriatrician." According to studies by the Rand Corp., California think tank, there is need in the United States right now for more than 20,000 geriatricians, almost triple the number available.

Yet of the 125 medical schools nationwide fewer than 1/10 have as requirements for graduation courses and clinical experience in geriatrics. One result is that not even 1% of the 16,000 doctors graduated in the United States each year become geriatricians. In 1992 the Alliance for Aging Research reported that 18 states have 1 or no board-certified geriatricians and that 9 states have 2 for every 1,000 persons 65+. What will happen when many of the 76,000,000 baby boomers begin to reach age 65 within 2 short decades?

What will happen? What will happen when there are hordes of elderly with few doctors trained to treat them? What will happen when doctors with no experience in geriatrics are called upon to treat 76,000,000 aged Americans? Symptoms of diseases among the aged are atypical. Prevalent diseases of the elderly, while not life-threatening, are almost all chronic. Elderly people 65+ do not respond necessarily to medications the way persons in other age groups of the population do.

But almost all doctors are now trained to deal with acute diseases in which symptoms are usually recognizable and results of drugs relatively easy to predict. Misdiagnosis of the elderly will undoubtedly occur, and many will be shunted unnecessarily into nursing homes. Instead of staving off physical dependency for one month, doctors may help in creating it, perhaps for years.

Physicians themselves will be in trouble, for they are quite uncomfortable dealing with the death of patients, an inevitable contingency when working with the oldest-old. The cost to the nation of geriatric ignorance will be far beyond the $5,000,000,000 that could have been saved were there available enough physicians trained in treatment of the elderly.

Why is there such a shortage of geriatricians? For a doctor, dealing with the elderly is neither financially profitable nor socially rewarding. Incomes are below those of other specialties, even those of pediatricians. Cures of chronic diseases are almost always impossible, so that a physician may not be able to determine how he has benefited a patient. Treating bed-ridden elderly is not especially rewarding to a doctor who keeps in the front of his mind that such patients have a severely limited lifespan. Nor is working with the chronically ill aged so attractive in the eyes of medical practitioners as helping a seriously ill young person quickly to overcome a malady and go back to work and family. The sick elderly, whether you are a doctor or not, are hardly considered desirable company in our society.

But the number of geriatricians can be increased dramatically— with almost no effort. All that need be done is to require high-level courses and experience in geriatrics for graduation from medical school. Unfortunately, as Linda Barondess, executive vice-president of the American Geriatrics Society, points out: "There isn't time." Robert N. Butler, MD, editor-in-chief of *Geriatrics* and chairman of the Department of Geriatrics and Adult Development, Mount Sinai Medical Center, New York, warns: "You can't create geriatricians overnight. It takes some time to train them." It is tempting to add: trainers will have to be trained before they can train trainees.

Nevertheless, the endeavor can and should be made, supplemented by private and federal awards in support of the immediate training of geriatric nurse practitioners and creation of geriatric centers in addition to those administered now by the Veterans' Administration. Otherwise, a countrywide disaster is in the making with broad deleterious implications, social and financial and medical.

"Life," Jane Ellen Harrison would remind the young, "does not cease when you are old."

GRANDPARENTHOOD

Grandchildren and grandparents have a very special relationship.

Emory Petrack, MD

Grandparenting is a uniquely human role, an indication that Homo sapiens bears the greatest parental burden in the animal world. For human children to survive, the father needs to help the mother. But young parents have such time-consuming workloads today, when two-incomes are necessary to so many families, that parental burdens become increasingly difficult to bear. As a result, children benefit more than ever before from the protection and care of grandparents.

Unlike the parenting role, however, grandparenthood in the United States is an ambivalent, if not anomalous, kinship position. The relationship used to be trifold in nature, for it involved the needs and desires of grandparents, parents and grandchildren. Today the bond of union is fourfold: almost 50% of married older adults are great-grandparents. What can be said of tomorrow if the tendency for couples to divorce and remarry increases? Already many men in their 50's and 60's who have remarried are discovering that they have children and grandchildren of approximately the same age. A child may have 8 grandparents and 16 great-grandparents, more if step-grandparents and step-great-grand-parents are counted. If grandparents and great-grandparents compete, how do mothers and children decide who gets the attention? Research by sociologists on such intergenerational conflict is inconclusive.

Reliable and valid research on grandparents is scanty; on great-grandparents, virtually non-existent. Much of available material is based on self-report questionnaires. Yet this is the first era in recorded history that so many human beings have not only lived long enough to become grandparents but can reasonably expect to spend as much as 4 decades in the role. In the last decade of the 20th century, more than 90% of mature adults with grown children were grandparents.

Being a grandparent has different meanings for different people.

Grandparenthood is a relationship, a role and a status. While there are no well defined norms and clearly articulated guidelines, there is a central core of feeling and idea. A small minority of grandparents find the role uncomfortable and unrewarding, while others who enjoy grandparenting nevertheless experience emotional, financial and physical stress—especially if they assume parental responsibility and become the sole caregivers of their grandchildren.

Most grandparents enjoy a delicious sense of timelessness, continuity and identification in reliving their own early experiences, as well as a feeling that a part of them will live on, as they play with and watch over grandchildren. Satisfaction, pride and pleasure are evident. Grandchildren give meaning, substance and direction to life. Grandparents harbor a sense of personal worth when they act as helpmate to parents through baby and house sitting. Removed from functional authority, they relish the freedom from the responsibility of disciplining and criticizing when giving children toys and candies and, more important, opportunities to be themselves and grow, loving and loved. Grandparents today generally have more money and time to spend on grandchildren than did their own grandparents. No wonder the grandparent-grandchild relationship in America is warm, indulgent.

Grandparents spend the most time with the grandchild during preschool and elementary years. The relationship broadens and deepens. Grandparents serve as role models and repositories of living history. During adolescence, the relationship narrows and the time spent together is negligible. But the grandparent is always present as a source whom the grandchild can tap for advice, if not for substantive help. After grandchildren become adults, grandparents learn that as with their own children they have to let go.

Traditionally, grandparents had neither legal rights nor obligations. Rules and priorities of an earlier time no longer apply. Today, all 50 states have adopted statutory provisions for grandparents' rights. Even so, grandparents sometimes have to petition courts of law for whatever privileges, such as visitation, they seek. With the coming of adulthood to children in an era so permissive as this, kinship lines of authority and obligation blur, and a number of unexplored issues dangerous to family existence come to the fore.

Divorce presents many problems. When a marriage dissolves, one spouse frequently divorces the other's family, too. In such a situation, can a grandmother fill a mother's shoes, as when harboring a divorced son's children? What can and should be done when step-grandparents are given responsibility for rearing your grandchildren and you fear that they are weaning the young ones' affection away from you? A different sort of conflict occurs when, as is often the case, grandparents who are better off financially than the divorced parent given custody of the children persist in buying youngsters expensive items. Prickly problems involving intergenerational competition and family bonding result.

Grandparents view themselves as what psychologists and social workers call *resource persons*. Most are careful not to encroach on the autonomy of their children; they delight in being valued for easing burdens in the raising of the grandchildren. Equally, they take pleasure in being valued by grandchildren, whom they indulge in many ways, loving without demanding anything in return. Distance does not appear to lessen closeness of ties, for it is easy to maintain contact by telephone. Grandparents relish the situation, for they have all the joys of parenthood with almost none of the anxieties and responsibilities. This is not to imply that grandparents as family members do not themselves have personal problems and difficulties, so that they may object to being pressed frequently for financial or some other kind of support. Many of today's aged grandparents have elderly children who themselves are in need of care. They must balance desires to help with their own needs and aspirations, so that they do not end as surrogate parents and nothing else. The grandparents' egos, social and power needs have not changed. If they are not met, serious family friction may ensue.

Although outside the ordinary intimate family situation, the Foster Grandparent Program confirms the worth of grandchild-grandparent relationships. *ACTION,* a federal volunteer agency, administers the program, which provides part-time employment at a small stipend for low-income persons 60+. The elderly work on a one-to-one basis with disadvantaged children in both residential and community settings, providing support, companionship and love. Many children soon show social and psychological improvement, and many foster grandparents affirm the program's value for the elderly who feel useful and needed in their community.

Some aspects of the grandchild-grandparent relationship have remained the same over the centuries. Simeon Strunsky points out: "The people whom young sons and daughters find it hardest to understand are the fathers and mothers, but young people can get on very well with the grandfathers and grandmothers." Those grandparents who have enjoyed several grandchildren know that the bonds are closest until the children are about 10 years of age. Although it is time to let go, the influence remains. Years ago, Victor Hugo wrote, wisely: "If you want to reform a man, start with his grandmother."

HEALTH-CARE COSTS

It is past all controversy, that what costs dearest,
is, and ought most to be valued.

Cervantes

Having risen sharply in the last few decades, health care costs are a major problem for all age cohorts except, perhaps, for the ultra rich. The elderly 65+ are the most concerned, fearing that both private and public sectors of the health-care system are financially out of control.

Surveys indicate that despite the fact older persons make up the only age cohort with ready access to universal health coverage under government sponsorship, more than 30% of the income of many is spent annually for health care. Chronic illnesses dog them with risks of serious illness and disability requiring special facilities and services. No longer employed, they have less private insurance than the young. Out-of-pocket expenses for medical care are often more than 3 times that of the rest of the adult population.

Taking the lead in financing health services, Congress in 1965 enacted Medicare, an insurance program emphasizing acute care, and Medicaid, a welfare program with a means test, to help the elderly poor deal with a serious illness. The government's annual expenditure for health care via Medicare and Medicaid is near 50-65 % of all medical costs.

Enacted in 1965 as Part of President Lyndon Johnson's Great Society, Medicare (Chapter 18 of the Social Security Act, Health Insurance for the Aged) is a federal program to reimburse health care providers for certain services to the elderly. Everyone 65+ and eligible for Social Security is also eligible for Medicare, regardless of assets and income. But coverage is automatic only for retirees on Social Security. Others must apply once 65. Part A (Hospital Insurance Benefits), supported by the payroll tax for Social Security, is insurance that without additional costs assists enrollees in paying for hospital stays, therapy in a nursing facility, home health services, hospice regimen and short-term acute care in a nursing home. Part B (Supplementary Medical Insurance Benefits), a voluntary program sustained by premiums of enrollees and by general revenues, is medical insurance that pays for *some* of the cost of physician services, outpatient care, home health care and needed supplies. Unless coverage is refused, enrollment in Part A includes the opportunity to enroll also in Part B. Because Part B is heavily subsidized, elderly enrollees pay about 1/4 of the program's cost.

Medicare pays for a little more than 1/3 of actual medical costs for most enrollees. For this reason and because Medicare does not cover all health-care expenses, including those of mental health, dental needs, most kinds of long-term care and preventive services except immunization and mammograms to a limited extent, more than 2/3 of enrollees have private insurance to bridge the gap. Before purchase of a private insurance company's Medigap policy, an enrollee should check to be sure it does not duplicate or overlap Medicare provisos. The AARP, the National Council of Senior Citizens and other associations offer members supplemental group health insurance programs.

Preventive inoculations and tests are not always easily affordable. But there are associations and pharmaceutical companies as well as local governmental health departments which offer free tests, inoculations and the like at stated times throughout the year. September is National Breast Cancer Month, with mobile units offering testing services at shopping malls, health expositions and other convenient locations. During Adult Immunization Week in October local pharmacies, senior centers and supermarkets make their facilities available for inoculation against the flu.

In the past, sick people went to their family doctor who, if necessary, made referrals to specialists. Today, millions of the elderly belong to a Health Maintenance Organization (HMO), a health-care provider that emphasizes prevention the while it offers medical services usually referred to as managed care for a fixed, prepaid monthly fee. Most Medicare enrollees who participate in PARTS A and B are eligible to join an HMO if they do not have an end-of-stage disease. Medicare pays for membership. HMOs provide at least the minimum package of benefits available under Medicare, usually without deductibles or copayments, in this way seemingly combining Medicare and Medigap insurance and providing the elderly with protection from excess expenditure. But an HMO requires members to choose a doctor on its staff, so that a family doctor becomes a thing of the past and a feeling of depersonalization by patients can result. Since fewer than 5% of enrollees are 75+, HMOs in general have not assumed any specific responsibility for geriatrically oriented health care.

There are two main types of HMO. One of the ideas governing both besides creation of an efficient cost-cutting medical organization is prevention of illness, until now more of a slogan than a reality. A group-practice HMO has a panel of salaried or contracted doctors who meet patients in offices at a centrally located building. A member has as a personal physician a primary-care doctor, usually an internist. When the internist thinks that a visit to a specialist is needed, arrangements are made for the HMO member to see a specialist on the panel. In an independent-practice HMO, doctors under contract provide medical services in their individual offices. Members of both kinds of HMO may use affiliated hospitals and skilled nursing facilities at the decision of their doctor. Some HMO's have been accused of trying to cut their own maintenance costs by forcing doctors to restrict services and to make it difficult to see specialists in timely fashion.

Congress in 1965 enacted Medicaid as Title 19 of the Social Security Act, Grants to States for Medical Assistance Programs, jointly financed by the federal government and the states, designed as an extension of the public welfare system to furnish health care to low-income persons of any age. Harder to understand than Medicare, Medicaid is not so much a national program as a grant-in aid to the states, which are responsible in large part for administration and supervision. Each state in the program is required to pay for doctor services not covered by Part A and for tests, x-rays and outpatient services. There is a means test. Medicaid, because of its provision for long-term nursing-home care, has become for the eligible general public the main source of financing such a stay. To be eligible, prospective nursing home patients must deplete assets and income, a situation some families are calling "eligibility spend-down."

In an attempt to help the elderly avoid financial disaster, Congress in 1988 passed the Medicare Catastrophic Act, which provided for unlimited hospitalization and hospice stays as well as for improved home health services. But the monthly premiums and the annual supplemental premium were so costly, as angered elderly complained, that the potential benefit was clearly not worth the expense to the average old person. In response, Congress repealed the Act.

Concerned that hospital costs were rising too quickly, Congress in 1984, by setting fixed rates for hospital lengths of stay, changed the way Medicare paid hospitals. One result was that hospitals began discharging patients as soon as possible. Another was the rise of nursing homes and home health programs to furnish posthospital care. Although there have been many complaints that hospitals were discharging patients "quicker and sicker," studies show that the change in method of hospital payment by Medicare did not result in harm to patients in regard to mortality or to increased rate of readmissions.

Perhaps 30% of Medicare-Medicaid payment is for elderly in nursing homes, whereas less than 1% is usually allotted to programs directed at maintaining them outside such institutions. But there are other government programs for geriatric care in the community. Title XX of the Social Security Act countenances state reimbursement for home health-care services to weak and frail elderly. The Veterans Administration gives priority to veterans with service-connected disabilities, but veterans may obtain non-service connected health-care services free of charge on a space-available basis.

As with health care costs in general, the expense of operating Medicare since its introduction in 1965 has increased hugely. Critics asserted that Part A by providing incentives to institutionalize the sick was financially seductive not only to patients but also to hospitals and physicians. The elderly had to pay for medical care unless hospitalized, and doctors and hospitals were reimbursed for each day a patient remained in the hospital. To cut costs, administrators from the Health Care Financing Administration in the federal Department of Health and Human Services instituted in 1985 a different method of payment. Medicare patients are categorized into one of some 475 diagnosis-related groups

(DRG), for each of which there is a fixed dollar amount paid to hospitals. If a hospital at discharge of a patient has spent less than the DRG amount it can keep the difference, but if a hospital has spent more it must absorb the loss. Ideally, the DRG system discourages overtreatment and overuse of hospital services. In practice, say critics, hospitals are discharging the elderly much too soon.

Every state has a Peer Review Organization (PRO), an association of doctors under contract to the federal government to make certain that Medicare patients receive fitting care. Medicare patients (or someone acting on their behalf) who think that coverage is denied unfairly or that in the hospital they received improper treatment, either inadequate or inappropriate, or that they were discharged too soon should appeal immediately to the local PRO. For the address, consult the telephone directory, the nearest social security office, the state agency on aging, or the Office of Medical Review in Baltimore, MD (410-966-6851).

The subject of medical insurance is still being hotly debated by all age groups throughout the United States. There is private insurance, purchased by employers for workers or bought out-of-pocket by individuals despite the expense. Long-term insurance, covering nursing home stays, is still being perfected by private companies. It is obvious that as the population ages the need for medical care will grow although the majority of elderly are relatively independent and need only some medical support. Less than 30% of eligible older Americans receive help from Medicaid. More than 40% eligible for the Qualified Medicare Beneficiary Program do not use it for assistance. Ironically, the medical requirements of the oldest-old, the fastest growing age cohort, are not large for two reasons: 1. the oldest-old, perhaps because they represent the survival of the fittest, are generally robust; and 2. when the oldest-old die, they do so quickly and without costly lingering. In confirmation is a study by the Health Care Administration published in 1993 that concludes: "There is no evidence that increased costs for persons in the final year of life are a special problem, different in magnitude from the overall growth of Medicare expenditures." The actual pressure that will push health-care costs up, way up, is the sheer number of baby boomers, all 76,000,000 of them, who will be retiring at almost the same time.

The financial prospect is both daunting and appalling. Neither sociological nor policy issues have been worked out although many kinds of plans have been proposed, including deferred payment, HMO's with prepaid plans and some form of medical savings account. Undoubtedly, Congress will be pressured to take action in the near future. But it is not easy to solve politically problems inherent in complex issues, as the Clinton Administration learned when it presented for reforming Medicare-Medicaid a program so ungainly that even proponents admitted its impracticality.

To Luke's admonition, "Physician, heal thyself," might be added, "and thy ways of doing business."

PLEASE NOTE

The Tax Payer/Relief/Balanced Budget Act of August 1997 contains provisions designed to prevent projected insolvency of Medicare until 2007. To be careful, Congress included a provision that a commission report in 1999 on success of the revisions and on other changes recommended for maintaining solvency.

The bad news for elderly individuals is twofold. By 2007 the monthly premium will increase to $105.40, in contrast to the current $59.70. As of 2002 a person may switch back to Medicare from an HMO only once a year.

The good news is that the new law includes not only a home health-care benefit of up to 100 visits after hospitalization but also a list of more options, including choice of savings accounts and health-care providers. In addition, preventive-care services include the cost of mammograms, pap smears, screening for some cancers and for osteoporosis. The new provisions of the Tax Payer Relief/Balanced Budget Act should be checked against the medicare coverage charts on p. 194 below.

Arthur F. Beringause

MEDICARE–MEDICAID:
ESSENTIALS AND DIFFERENCES AT A GLANCE

Features	Medicare	Medicaid
1. Type of Plan	An insurance program, partially paid for by members, which emphasizes acute care.	A welfare program for the indigent.
2. Eligibility	Everyone 65+ and on Social Security.	Based on a means test, which differs from state to state, for income and financial assets.
3. Sponsorship	Founded and funded by the federal government.	Federal-state copartnership
4. Oversight	The Social Security Administration supervises, deducting premiums from the monthly Social Security check.	Each state welfare office.
5. Entitlements	Part A is an automatic insurance program that assists in paying for hospital costs. Part B is a voluntary program, sustained by premiums, that pays partially for physician services, home health care and some supplies.	Qualifications vary from state to to state. Generally, pays for most prescribed medications and nursing home expenses. A number of states permit the elderly to qualify by "spending down" income and assets.

HORMONES and AGING: BREAKTHROUGH?

A tiny paper, tightly rolled . . .
Contains within its magic fold
A mighty panacea.

Henry Sambrooke Leigh

Vitamins, antioxidants and now hormones. Has the time come for hormones to be considered the wondrous elements, found at last, that will slow aging, lessen the impact of debilitating ailments on the elderly and contribute to their well-being?

The word hormone is from the Greek *hormone*, meaning to stir up, stimulate. Scientists refer to a hormone as a substance produced by the endocrine glands and circulated in body fluid to an organ or tissue at a distance where it influences cellular activity. Today, many hormones are prepared synthetically in a laboratory.

More and more researchers are exploring the effects of replacement of hormones that either decline significantly with age or cease to be produced in the body. As yet no one has been able to make clear the mechanism(s) underlying age-related declines in hormone levels of the elderly or to demonstrate convincingly how a substance such as the hormone precursor DHEA (dehydroepiandrosterone) exerts biologic influence. Signs and symptoms of hormone deficiency may not be present. If present, their interpretation may be difficult because of coexisting chronic disease(s).

But studies even so preliminary as those now taking place in laboratories all over the world give reason to believe that hormone replacement therapy will one day play a significant role among the elderly by helping physicians deal with cancer, diabetes, heart disease and obesity, perhaps by intensifying the immune system. Hoping that the promise of these early studies can be sustained, perhaps even to the finding of an antidote to disabilities associated with old age, officials of the National Institute of Aging have recently made available some $2,000,000 for further research on people 60+. Much is at stake. Will hormone therapy arrive in time to help make healthy the more than 7,000,000 of the present generation of elderly, who because they cannot perform activities necessary to daily living, need long-term care costing billions of dollars?

Women for some years have been receiving hormone therapy to counter effects of osteoporosis after menopause. Such hormone replacement in older women has been well documented, and the results widely studied and acknowledged in many cases as beneficial. The story is not the same with older men. Much less is known about effects and replacement in older men of hormone levels that have declined or cease to be produced.

Deciding to investigate, the late Dr. Daniel Rudman and colleagues at the North Chicago VA Hospital accepted a grant from the American Federation for Aging Research. In 1990, they published a study which concluded tentatively that growth hormone replacement therapy in older men increases lean body mass and decreases fat mass. Dr. Rudman recommended caution, for his study did not show that supplementation necessarily increased muscle strength and enhanced physical fitness. He also recommended heedfulness and further study of testosterone treatments because adverse reactions had been reported in elderly patients. Nevertheless, his work electrified researchers who wondered whether or not women could also benefit from growth hormone replacement therapy.

Since 1990 there have been other studies confirming changes of body composition as a result of hormone treatment. The most recent, reported in the April 15, 1996 *Annals of Internal Medicine,* concludes that while hormone replacement therapy does increase lean tissue mass and decrease fat mass it does not significantly improve muscle strength and endurance or cognitive performance in elderly men.

But hope springs eternal. Researchers continue to consider that supplementation of hormones may have beneficial effects on both men and women. DHEA, among other hormones, is being seriously studied. Risk of breast cancer is highest in women with lowest concentration of DHEA, which declines markedly with age. Can DHEA supplementation reduce that risk? Will growth hormone replacement therapy help to reduce old-age disability and increase general feelings of well-being? No one knows. But there is much optimism even though at present the results of increasing blood hormone levels in the elderly to those found in younger adults have not consistently proved safe and beneficial. Notwithstanding, among graying baby boomers there appears to be a growing mystique of growth hormone as an anti-aging quick-fix.

Monetary costs for would-be supplementers of synthetic growth hormone are extremely high, about $12,000 for a year's supply. Because of the prospect of huge profits, several major pharmaceutical companies are in hot pursuit of inexpensive surrogate chemicals to restore by means of pills or skin patches hormone levels that with age have declined or ceased to be. There is also a growing number of physicians, many of them members of the American Academy of Medicine (established in 1993 and in 1998 not yet recognized by the federal government's American Board of Medial Specialties), who practice growth-hormone-replacement therapy now despite the 1997 warning of the National Institute of Aging at the National Institutes of Health concerning potential dangerous and freakish side effects.

There are cautionary voices. Dr. Robert N. Butler, the highly respected doyen of geriatricians, is one. He takes as an example melatonin, a hormone produced by the pineal gland whose secretion declines with aging. Claims have been made for melatonin's age-reversing, disease-fighting, sex-enhancing capabilities. Writing in *Geriatrics* (Feb. 1996, vol. 51, No.2, p.10, Dr. Butler warns people to be aware that optimum dosage and delineation of side effects for human hormones have not yet been determined. Drugs such as DHEA and growth hormones. should be carefully studied. He adds that "Some may prove to have important physiologic functions and offer therapeutic possibilities. But until we have clear indications that this is so, doctors should exercise caution and encourage their patients to do the same."

Before regarding a hormone supplement as safe, people should be aware that adverse side effects may take decades to show up. In the past, the synthetic estrogen, DES (diethylstilbestrol), was given to expectant mothers to prevent pregnancy complications. After some time, it was discovered that children born to mothers who took DES had much higher cancer rates than normal. Result? The hormone is now banned in the United States.

Research projects involving hormones seem promising. Their goals are tantalizing. But many aspects of hormone- replacement strategies remain controversial. There is no confirmation in large-scale, properly controlled double-blind trials. Until then, it is wisest to heed with Dr. Butler medicine's basic maxim, *Primum non nocere*: First, do no harm.

HOSPITALS: CLASSIFICATION and FUNCTION

How many desolate creatures on the earth
Have learnt the simple dues of fellowship
And social comfort, in a hospital.

Elizabeth Barrett Browning

General (also called Community) Hospitals:

Most common hospital in the United States.

May be for profit or nonprofit.

Differ in size, the larger hospitals having more equipment and more types of specialists on the staff.

Try to provide personalized care.

Public Hospitals:

Owned and operated by a government agency.

Usually quite large and located in cities.

Generally lacking in amenities.

May be affiliated with a medical school or schools.

Primary aim is to care for low-income patients.

Teaching Hospitals:

Affiliated with a medical school.

A major purpose is to train medical students.

Quite large, with highly qualified personnel and excellent equipment.

Staff doctors customarily are instructors and/or researchers in the affiliated medical school.

Accustomed to treating uncommon as well as common medical problems.

Patients are examined, not only by specialists, but also by interns and residents, so that privacy may be invaded time and again by different groups of students and instructors.

Some treatment may be done by newly graduated physicians who do not have much experience.

Has social workers available to explain community services.

Specialized Hospitals:

There are different kinds:

Access only to particular groups or organizations, as the Veterans Administration Hospitals.

Treat one type of disease, as cancer, or one section of the body, as eyes and ears.

N.B. Neither nursing homes nor rehabilitation centers are hospitals.

PERSONNEL

Medical

Attending Physician: A doctor in charge of care of an individual patient.

Consulting Physician: A specialist asked by the Attending Physician for an opinion.

Fellow: A doctor who is working toward a specialty.

Intern: A doctor serving an apprenticeship after graduation from medical school.

Medical Student: A student who performs simple medical procedures.

Resident: Having completed an internship, a doctor receiving advanced training.

Nursing

Nurse: A registered nurse (RN) who has passed a licensing examination qualifying her to administer medications, take blood, check a patient's vital signs, alert doctors.

Practical Nurse: A nurse with less training and responsibility than an RN.

Orderly or Nurse's Aide: A person hired by the hospital who helps with custodial tasks, such as cleaning up after a medical procedure.

Staff

Social Worker: A person trained to aid patients in many ways, such as solving medical financing problems and obtaining post-hospital health-care services.

Technologist: An aide trained to administer medical tests.

Therapist: A physical or speech rehabilitative specialist who helps a patient regain skills.

HOUSING

Home is the place where, when you have to go there
They have to take you in.

Robert Frost

Rather than talk of housing per se, sociologists who study the aged speak of the *living environment and the dwelling*, that is of shopping facilities, medical installations social services (churches, clubs, senior centers), neighborhood safety and transportation as well as of living quarters. While the home as the chief site for daily living is important to the elderly because in contrast to other age groups they spend an increasingly large proportion of time there, availability of foodstuffs and friends and the clustering of services also matter much. If transportation is not readily accessible, a home, no matter how attractive, can become a virtual prison and deny feelings of independence and of being in control of one's life so important to older Americans.

Many types of housing are open to the elderly. Desire to remain in a particular kind of residence may alter in response to availability of assistance, nearness of friends and relatives, condition of the building, health problems, declining income, neighborhood changes, retirement and widowhood. Solutions to the problem of housing are almost as diverse as the life-styles of the elderly themselves, varying from the "snowbirds" who migrate to a warmer climate during winter months each year to the daily habitués of the local community's senior center. Some elderly rely on themselves to reach a decision; others depend on help from the family. Very few pack up and leave permanently, not even to a home a short distance away. Only about 1% move to another state. Among those who migrate, two moves are typical: at retirement and after a disability, whether minor or major. A tiny percentage of the elderly are homeless; the very few research studies on them concentrate on their trials and tribulations.

Almost every sector of society offers solutions in regard to housing older persons.

The vast majority of late-life adults live in conventional housing, single-family houses and apartments. Private for-profit companies build so-called adult (that is, retirement) communities, some of which are self-contained small towns with a safe, ordered and predictable leisure-oriented lifestyle like Sun City in Arizona. Private non-profit groups (charities, churches, foundations, fraternal orders) sponsor or build various kinds of living facilities, such as old-age homes. Assisted living and continuing-care communities require an entrance fee or initial lump sum payment, sometimes quite large, and subsequent monthly maintenance fees possibly subject to periodic increase. They care for elderly who cannot live on their own but who do not need the higher level of care supposedly provided in nursing homes. They should be licensed by the local department of health and services to senior citizens. Public organizations (local, state and federal governments) usually offer units in housing previously erected for the poor and the physically handicapped.

Although home ownership does decline in those elderly 80+, about 3/4 of persons 65+ own their own home, with near to 4/5 of those homes mortgage-free. About 1/2 the elderly live in houses erected before WWII. Home owners are usually advised to keep the house so as to maintain one's roots, avoid the stress of moving and preserve their independence. Giving up a house with its possessions accumulated over the years is like discarding important parts of a person's life, such as courtship, marriage and parenthood.

Usually the most valuable economic asset of the elderly, their home generates feelings of security for the future. Maintaining a home is important to protect the investment as well as to enjoy it. Federal tax incentives for home ownership are helpful. But there are home repair, insurance and utility (lighting, heating, air-conditioning) payments to make. Even slight upturns in inflation can make upkeep and maintenance burdensome. Not quite 10% of homes of the elderly have serious problems such as a leaky roof or faulty heating equipment. Although free from indoor and outdoor maintenance, apartment dwellers, too, cannot escape such trends, for they continually find rent increases and rising utility bills in their mailboxes. Worse, most elderly renters live close to the poverty level. To help the elderly who spend a high percentage of income on property taxes, all the states have established some kind of tax relief program.

Houses of the elderly are usually older and of poorer quality than dwellings owned by younger persons. Realtors feel that in general the elderly are overhoused in regard to number of rooms and square footage since the buildings were selected for their appropriateness in midlife and the children left long ago for their own dwellings. About 1 in 3 homes owned by the elderly have at least 1 extra bedroom and 2 or more extra nonsleeping rooms. But to many older persons a house is not just a home. Savings from years of mortgage payments are stored there. From appreciation of house prices, it has become a nest egg to be used for emergencies and sold only as a last resort. They know that today it is easy to obtain a reverse mortgage or home equity loan using the dwelling as collateral; in some instances the loan may be advantageous since interest charged by the bank is deductible for tax purposes.

Some elderly who live in a large home engage in what today is called home-sharing, renting a room or rooms for money and/or assistance with such chores as yardwork and grocery shopping. Feelings of companionship and security are byproducts of home-sharing. Among persons over age 75, particularly African-American men, this is becoming a popular living style. Not quite the same is shared group housing, which resembles a commune. Usually, 4 or 5 unrelated women over age 80 occupy a house or large apartment, sharing the kitchen, bathroom and living room but each having her own bedroom. Sponsored by a government agency or nonprofit organization, shared group living arrangements are relatively inexpensive.

Families which have a large enough dwelling lot, particularly in the South, often allow elderly parents to live on the property in a mobile home. Other families do the same but with a free-standing removable housing unit often called an ECHO house (an acronym for Elder Cottage Housing Opportunity). In either case, while the family and the elderly can obtain privacy by shutting doors, working out a stressless modus vivendi may take time and patience.

Unable to compete with the young for choice apartments, elderly renters tend to live in older buildings in poorer areas of cities. Housing is the major item in the budget of most older people. The United States Senate Special Committee on Aging has estimated that this kind of renter, more likely than not a female 75+ and living alone, spends about 50% of income on rent. Referred to as part of an "invisible population" by sociologists, other elderly live in single rooms of inner-city hotels (SROs) where baths are shared and kitchen units are unavailable. Although such housing, slum housing really, is undesirable to many, elderly loners, mainly men, prefer it to an institution. Their eagerness to remain independent despite poverty and old age has locked them into a situation where isolation and alienation are the rule.

Many late-life adults reject congregate housing even when it is low-rent because of the rules and regulations that come with subsidization by state and federal governments. Others capable of living independently like the idea of living in a multiunit apartment building where the management provides some supportive services, such as furnishing one meal a day in a central dining room and arranging for residents to meet socially in group facilities. In some congregate housing buildings, a section called "assisted living" is set off to provide help with activities of daily living for those people with chronic health problems that make it impossible for them to live independently.

A person entering a continuing-care retirement community (CCRC) signs a lifetime contract which guarantees shelter and health care within the facility, usually a high-rise building or physically adjacent buildings. Although most CCRCs are owned or sponsored by private nonprofit organizations, fees can be sizable, both entrance and monthly, but service is total and for a lifetime. An elderly person might begin by occupying an apartment in the equivalent of a congregate housing facility, move in subsequent years to a room for the semi-independent in an assisted living center, end by withdrawing to a nursing home. Continuing care communities appeal most to single, white females over age 80. Drawbacks to CCRCs include possibility of declining quality of services, changes in management and risk of financial insolvency of the owner. Horror stories abound, whether accurate or not, and there is an obvious need for government investigation and possible regulation.

Increasingly attractive to working-class retirees in states with a mild climate like Florida is housing in a mobile-home-park where companionship, low-cost and security are part of the setting. But many parks rule that the age of a mobile home to be admitted must be under 5 years, so that retirees in their 70s and 80s who cannot replace the unit they bought in their 60s have trouble finding a park willing to take them. And some parks where land has increased in value raise rents sharply. The oldest parks, without many amenities, cater to retirees trying to stay independent on small incomes supplemented by Social Security payments.

Federally assisted housing programs for the elderly began in 1956 when Congress amended the Housing Act of 1937. The first program exclusively for the aged came in Section 2302 of the 1959 Housing Act, which still makes low-interest loans to non-profit persons and organizations building housing for low-income elderly. Congress created with passage of the 1974 Housing Act the so-called Section 8 program, which subsidizes rent for low-income families, including the elderly. By the late 1980's about 500,000 public housing units were occupied by the elderly.

Passage of the Fair Housing Amendments Act of 1988 makes possible occupation by low-income families of housing projects from which nonelderly were previously excluded. Another negative force is the NIMBY (Not in My Back Yard) phenomenon: the public often object to having low-income housing placed in a particular neighborhood because of the increased need for an infrastructure of parking, sewers, water, or to housing projects for the elderly, whom they regard as so senile and frail that they increase the burden on the police and sanitary departments. Ironically, many older people themselves are part of the NIMBY phenomenon.

It is often difficult to make definitive pronouncements about housing for the elderly. One thing is certain: at least 90% want nothing to interfere with their independent lifestyle. About 25% of these live alone. Surveys reveal that older inhabitants themselves specify fewer flaws in housing designed for them than do sociologists and other investigators. They minimize the difficulties in post-war suburbs for those elderly who have difficulty walking and do not drive. But the same elderly often outspokingly resent having to share living quarters with physically or mentally-impaired aged. Late-life adults also resent housing guaranteeing their comfort and safety but subjecting them to bureaucratic regulation, often interfering with their preferred lifestyles. In the end, though, most recognize the necessity of trade-off–accepting the not-so-good in return for what they deem desirable and affordable.

Peace be to this house. (Luke, X,5.)

HYPE

What is truth?

Pontius Pilate

Professional journals and the mass media are replete almost daily with startling reports of breakthroughs in medical matters—pharmaceutical, prosthetic, surgical—as technological expertise of researchers continues to advance almost by geometric progression. Or so it seems. Dr. Robert N. Butler, head of the Geriatrics Department at Mt. Sinai Medical School, points out that all the clamor about the melatonin "miracle," the drug that is supposed to revive ailing bodies and make the old young, is based on *one* experiment with rats and not humans. Some miracle!

Careful reading of books, newspaper and magazine articles and close investigation of claims made on radio and TV produce results not so sensational as authors and announcers make them out to be. Case in point: in mid-1996 *Parade Magazine,* which is distributed through newspapers to millions of readers all over the country, contained a manufacturer's coupon promising to save purchasers $2 and guaranteeing *Enhanced Physical Endurance* to swallowers of Ginsana and *Improved Memory and Concentration* to swallowers of Ginkoba. Above the coupon was a notice in large type that the claims were based on reliable studies. Nowhere was there a reference to even one particular study. Obviously, advertisers are convinced that people will swallow anything, even unfounded and seeminlgy preposterous claims.

As 76,000,000 baby boomers approach admission to the cohorts of American elderly, albeit unwillingly but inevitably, bookstore windows throughout the nation are featuring colorful volumes which purport to reveal the secrets of eternal youth and reversal of the aging process. It is not uncommon to find an assertion that aging is a disease caused by serious vitamin deficiencies. Nor is it unusual to find tomes that begin in authoritative fashion with accounts of promising areas of cell research but end by treating hypotheses as facts. It is pure speculation, not fact, to state that within a decade telomere researchers will have found ways to reverse aging and to eliminate cancer, heart disease, stroke.

This is the age of hype, a word cut from hypodermic, referring to writing or speech intended to stimulate (as by injecting a drug) and to publicize in a sensational manner for the express purpose of promoting sales. Another term, much older, *Caveat emptor (Let the buyer beware),* has become increasingly relevant.

Cosmetics, always a fertile field for wily marketers aware of the desire of men and women to look young, is filled with pseudoscientific anti-aging claims. In reality, what advertisers trumpet as results of aging–skin spots, wrinkling and loss of elasticity–are almost always the result of exposure to the sun. Prudent consumers consult only reputable physicians with the experience and knowledge to treat skin problems.

Consumers need to be on guard against follow-the-leader mentality, simplistic interpretations, unsubstantiated claims. The public must beware by being aware. But this is not easy for most lay people, whether reporters for newspapers and their readers, whether for TV commentators and their listeners, who are neither scientists nor technicians.

Accurately condensing a complex scientific research study into a short newspaper column or TV sound bite is impossible. Aside from distortion resulting from translation of highly technical vocabulary into common terms, there is the twisting of conclusions because of omissions of fact that take up space and time to explain. Newspaper headlines and introductory phrases on TV broadcasts are designed to be bait, as though readers and listeners are fish waiting to be hooked.

Although the FDA has tried with regulations, "Standards of Identity," to establish criteria for terms used in packaging, it is easy for marketing pitchmen to evade stipulations. Because some words, *organic* for example, have not been defined officially, no federal standard exists and there is no national certification program. *Organic* foods are not necessarily safer nor purer nor more nutritious than conventional foods. *Patented* on a food label does not mean that the product necessarily does what the manufacturer claims. By law, manufacturers when marketing supplements do not have to prove them safe or effective.

Certain terms, *bran* and *wholesome* among them, are not mentioned by the FDA. Other expressions, called *code* or *buzz* words, imply much more than their dictionary meanings, as is the case with *lower in* or with *wholesome.* Some foods are lower in fat than others but still contain much fat. *Wholesome* suggests vim and vigor and general good health. Fiber, whether in grains or in vegetables, is no cure-all; if taken in too large quantities, fiber can rob the body of needed nutrients. "Natural" vitamins are no better than synthetic: both have identical chemical structures. Anti-oxidants do not clean out the body nor prevent death of cells. While growth hormones are banned from use in poultry, drugs are not—with the result that bacitracin, both a growth drug and an antibiotic, is used because the Agriculture Department characterizes it as only an antibiotic.

Even the world of science, dedicated to unvarnished truth, has been infected by hype. Publication and publicity mean promotion and prestige and grants of large sums of money. Claims of importance for research subsequently found to have limited scientific value occur not infrequently although scientists try very hard to police themselves. Administrators and researchers are always checking, ever on the lookout for "doctoring" of records and data as has happened in recent years in the best of laboratories, among them Cornell and Rockefeller Universities.

Studies and surveys are often referred to in the mass media as if they were double-blind, controlled research (that is, both the subjects of the research and the researchers themselves do not know who is receiving a drug, who is receiving a placebo), presenting material collected as scientifically reliable whereas in fact it may be inaccurate or merely suggestive. There are vast differences between a survey in which respondents state opinions or give statements they regard as factual and a research study based on experimentation and verification of every detail, a study that other scientists can replicate accurately.

What can a lay person do to distinguish fact from fiction, truth from hype? On New Year's Day, 1998, a *New York Times* headline reported: "Study Finds Less Connection between Fat and Early Death." On the same day the Associated Press headlined of the same study: "Excess Weight Can Be a Burden on Longevity." Thereupon editors of the *New England Journal of Medicine*, which published the study, stating that in their opinion the results of the study are suggestive but not conclusive, warned: "we should remember that the cure [with ineffectual and sometimes dangerous weight-loss schemes] for obesity may be worse than the condition."

Even when so prestigious a periodical as the *New England Journal of Medicine* publishes a story, the reader should determine whether or not material presented as evidence is preliminary or conclusive, theoretical or factual. A story may come with caveats. To what extent does the author qualify statements? Are pros and cons indicated? Because no single study can provide definitive proof of efficacy of a medication or therapy, it is important to ascertain whether or not the results have been duplicated elsewhere. An additional way of getting at the truth includes finding out who funded the study (a private company can benefit enormously from a favorable attitude toward its product). and determining whether or not it has been reviewed by scientists widely regarded as impartial,. "It is not unusual," *The Wall Street Journal* (March 19, 1998, p. 1) reports, "for influential medical professors to receive honorariums, consulting fees and expense-paid travel from medical companies whose products they write about or even test."

In general, lay people need to remain skeptical. Medical cynics laugh that a miracle drug is a substance which when injected into a rat produces a scientific paper. Initial announcements of "discoveries" are almost always ballyhooed in the popular media. Follow-up stories, whether with confirmation or retractions and corrections, are almost never reported. Anyone looking critically at stories purporting to tell of breakthroughs in science should not jump at conclusions but wait to learn to what extent they are products of truth-seeking or of hype. Has the breakthrough been replicated by other scientists? Has the scientific community accepted the results as reported in the media? Above all, in matters medical, what is the opinion of specialists in whose area of expertise the "discovery" lies?

No matter how effective a drug or treatment appears to be as presented in even the most prestigious of journals, it is best not to make changes in one's lifestyle without consulting the family physician. A medical doctor can help with advice as to efficacy, possible side effects and expense. Wary consumers can consult *The Johns Hopkins Handbook of Drugs Specially Edited and Organized by Disease for People over 50* by S. Margolis (N.Y.: Random House, 1993), which is written expressly for lay persons.

BUZZ WORDS THAT SHOULD RING ALARM BELLS

Food
> All natural, natural flavor, natural ingredients, free range
> Fast food, quick preparation, frozen dinner
> Fat free, reduced fat, health food
> Fulfills all requirements, home style
> Low cholesterol, lower in calories
> Made with (with how much?), organic
> With a touch of (how much is a touch?), lean, lite, light

Medications
> Antioxidant
> Quick weight loss
> Enhances (as awareness or memory)
> Recommended by (a Hollywood personality)
> Erases (as wrinkles)
> More powerful
> Rejuvenating
> Used in Europe for years

LEGAL MATTERS

The law is good, if a man use it lawfully.

I Timothy, I, 8

Many legal documents are available in generic form either as preprinted statements or as computer software products. But some states do not accept generic documents, and others have severe restrictions about their use. If a lay person using a generic form omits a detail or employs language a court does not deem legal, the complete document may be declared invalid.

For the elderly, there are many reasons to obtain advice from a lawyer, not the least of which is making a customized, valid, unbreakable will to ensure the rights of a spouse and children, especially in cases of second marriage. (Even persons with few savings and little property need a will to avoid having state law decide who gets which possessions.) Elder law attorneys can for clients lower, if not eliminate, almost all estate and inheritance taxes. A trust or other device to avoid probate can be expensive to have prepared by a lawyer, but it will then avoid fees, including taxes and payment to executors and court-appointed lawyers, which can be considerable. A skillful lawyer will save the seller or buyer of a condo, co-op or home worry and time as well as money. For anyone who does not want extraordinary measures employed in prolonging life, a lawyer is indispensable in drawing up a document known as a Living Will, which is discussed below. Although the easily filled-out Uniform Donor Card, which states a person's preference for donation of body parts after death, is considered a legal document in most states, a lawyer can guarantee its efficacy everywhere. An attorney can reduce worries about Medicare and Medicaid legalities, which can be quite complicated.

The Legal Services corporation was set up as a private, nonprofit entity by federal legislation enacted in 1974. Funds come from the federal, state and local governments and from private sources. The LSC provides legal services to low-income individuals. Older persons may also receive help from local legal aid offices, especially in regard to public benefit claims.

The Age Discrimination in Employment Act is aimed at protecting older workers against discrimination no matter what their age. Anyone discriminated against can file a charge with the local Equal Employment Opportunity Commission and seek help in instituting suit within the guidelines of the law. But it may be an uphill fight. The implication of several recent federal court decisions is that discrimination suits may become difficult. Federal appeals judges have agreed with management lawyers that companies are not guilty of bias even if hiring, promoting or downsizing policies fall more heavily on older than on younger employees.

As a result of government involvement, today's legal environment is not the same as that of even a short decade ago. Legal ramifications have multiplied. Government programs have created rights and entitlements with unique legal issues. Entitlement rights are obligations of society to provide certain individuals or classes of individuals with concrete goods or services. Medicare, Medicaid and Social Security are entitlement programs, as is Meals on Wheels. Resulting administrative regulations, agency reports, guidelines of all sorts, judicial decisions, and legislative statutes have modified legal relationships.

Medical care pertaining to the elderly is administered through a host of legal considerations. In some ways, the elderly are at increased legal risk. Statutes in several states specify that old age is an acceptable ground for suing to prove incompetence. Many elderly are likely to be alone and isolated. Caregivers, as a result, may incline to act in "the patient's best interest" although the course of action is not one the patient would prefer. To protect such patients, medical law includes confidentiality, informed consent (the right to agree to or to refuse treatment), use of medical students, termination of treatment, determination of disability, negligence, liability, malpractice, powers of attorney, involuntary commitment, discharge of patients, guardianship, elder abuse whether in the family or in an institution.

In general, Social Security and other benefits can be paid on behalf of an older recipient whose physician certifies incapacity to manage such payments. Likewise, guardianship can be obtained when a late-life adult is judged after a court hearing to be unable to manage his/her affairs. Limited guardianship gives stated rights and responsibilities to the guardian. Full guardianship delegates to the guardian all the older person's legal rights.

Medicolegal problems likely to arise in care of the elderly revolve around informed consent, whether implied or expressed; mental competency; confidentiality and use of records, including patient access; financing; conference decisions and range of options;, advance warning and directives; surrogate decision-making; long-term care; competence of patient. Medicolegal problems abound in nursing homes regarding mental capacity, informed consent, use of physical restraints (as side rails of a bed or bars on a wheelchair), right to privacy.

Probably for the elderly the most important aspect of planning ahead concerns what should be done by or for a patient in a health crisis. Yet, according to the American Medical Association, more than 2 of 3 Americans have made no such plans despite the fact that consequences can be dire. If a person is unable to make a medical decision, hospitals and physicians generally will carry out the desires of the immediate family. Sometimes, especially when an elderly patient is frightened, physicians in an attempt at kindness encourage family decisions without the patient's agreement and permission. In cases of disagreement or in situations where there is no immediate family, courts of law make the determination.

Guardianship, sometimes called conservatorship, is a legal device for declaring a person incompetent, so that the courts can appoint a guardian to oversee financial affairs, living arrangements, medical decisions. Elderly persons desirous of warding off guardianship, so that they may act independently and maintain control of their assets can obtain advice and help from the local Area Agency on Aging.

Unless mentally incapable, every adult has the legal right, which lawyers call self-determination, to plan ahead for medical care. To ensure that right, Congress enacted the Patient's Self-Determination Act in 1990, which requires health-care facilities to ask patients if they have made out an Advanced Directive. Perhaps because of recognition that the Act has the paradoxical effect of making an option obligatory, Congress did not spell out penalties for health-care providers who do not honor an Advanced Directive.

The most effective plan for self-determination involves making decisions ahead of time and also choosing someone who will make decisions in the future with you or for you if you are unable. An Advance Directive, which can include an Instruction Directive and/or a Proxy Directive, will do just that. It is wise to review the Advance Directive periodically with the primary care physician because when new therapies become available in the future statements made in the past may be too vague to accurately guide clinical decisions, as the use of new drugs which must be applied immediately in case of a stroke.

An Instruction Directive, which states a person's express wishes, should be documented carefully, expressed in writing and signed and notarized to make sure that it is legal in every State. Because it directs physicians to furnish or to withhold particular medical procedures and it spells out in detail in which situations treatment is to be refused or discontinued, it should be gone over with a doctor familiar with the writer's medical condition.

A Proxy Directive names the person(s) to carry out the wishes in the Instruction Directive. Accordingly, it is wise to discuss desires with the Health Care Proxy, not only to state what to do in specific situations but also to make clear the general attitude and philosophy of the person setting up the Instruction Directive, so that in an unforeseen situation the Proxy does not have to make a life-and-death decision without proper grounding.

There are serious drawbacks to a Living Will, sometimes referred to as a right-to-die will because it directs physicians to cease invasive measures of treatment or to remove life-sustaining equipment in the event of terminal illness or irreversible condition. While Living Wills are legal in almost all the States, it is generally advisable, if not necessary, to consult a lawyer to interpret the law since provisions and requirements vary among the states. Otherwise, it might happen that caregivers who seemingly comply with the provision of a Living Will do not receive legal immunity. Not everyone defines dying, death and terminal illness in the same way.

More flexible than a Living Will but not so comprehensive as an Advanced Directive, a Durable Power of Attorney can be drafted by a lawyer to apply to all medical situations in which a patient is judged incapable of making competent decisions. (A regular Power of Attorney allows a competent person to give over rights to someone else, as to sell stocks, but the right lapses if the person becomes incompetent.) A Durable Power of Attorney permits appointment of a surrogate, whether relative or no, to make medical determinations should the adult subject be incapacitated. As with an Advance Directive, it is wise to explain to the surrogate your general attitude and your preference for specific treatments. Power of Attorney is a contract and as such enjoys full protection of the law, but it does not guarantee fidelity and integrity of those we trust. If you suspect that the surrogate is breaching duty, request an accounting.

With Nietzsche the elderly agree that "it is our future that lays down the law of our to-day."

LEGAL DOCUMENTS IMPORTANT
FOR DECISIONS IN LATE LIFE

1. Advance Directive: States which treatments are acceptable or unacceptable, not only under ordinary circumstances, but also when a condition is irreversible or an illness is terminal. Can include an Instruction Directive and a Proxy Directive (see below).
2. Durable Power of Attorney: Permits appointment of a surrogate, whether a relative or no, to make determinations for a person who has become incapacitated.
3. Guardianship (sometimes called Conservatorship): Is a legal device for declaring a person incompetent. Can be obtained after a court hearing or in case of a medical emergency if a physician certifies incompetency. Limited guardianship assigns specific rights and responsibilities to the guardian. Full guardianship gives to the guardian all a person's legal rights.
4. Instruction Directive: Directs a physician to furnish or withhold particular medical procedures.

5. Living Will (sometimes referred to as a Right-to-Die Will): Directs physicians to cease invasive measures of treatment or to remove life-sustaining equipment in the event of an irreversible condition or terminal illness.

6. Power of Attorney: Allows a competent person to give over rights to someone else. The right lapses if the person becomes incompetent.

7. Proxy Directive: Names the person(s) to carry out the Instruction Directive.

8. Uniform Donor Card: States a person's preference for donation of body parts after death.

9. Will: States a person's desires concerning disposition of estate after death.

THE LIBRARY

How much are we bound to those munificent . . . heroical
patrons, divine spirits, that have provided for us so many
well-furnished libraries.

Robert Burton

Much more today than just lenders of books and periodicals, the more than 15,000 public libraries and branch libraries in the United States are changing with the times in form and content. After years of inadequate funding and general neglect, libraries are experiencing a rebirth of construction and renovation. They have become community cultural centers, offering not only information by way of books but also diverse programs and activities for socialization and entertainment. They are being redesigned in many cases to compete with the large bookstores with their homey seating nooks and easily accessible materials. Many a library will soon have an E-mail bar flanked by banquettes for group studying. Yet almost everything the library offers will remain free of charge.

If the main center or one of its branches is not easily accessible, the library will use its bookmobile service to deliver requested materials to selected neighborhoods and institutions and to present a stock of items for people to choose from. In addition to a circulating collection of thousands of books, even the smallest and poorest community library offers a wide variety of materials and services. There are movies, tapes and records for short-term examination or long-term borrowing. Telecaption adapters and large-print books help the impaired in sight and hearing. Like the other librarians, the most helpful of people, reference librarians conduct a telephone information service on anything and everything.

Libraries are becoming media centers with audio, video and CD-ROM equipment available around the core of book stacks. The latest electronic information technology is being acquired, with much of the cost of installation and training library personnel to use it paid for by private parties or government agencies. Personal computers are hooked up to information suppliers by way of catalog terminals and modems with access to the Internet.

The immediate result is the ability of library patrons to contend successfully with the increasing torrent of data available in this, the age of information. Consider: one issue of many a Sunday newspaper probably contains as much information as a person could obtain during an entire lifetime back in the 1700s.

In today's library, patrons arrive almost as though in shifts. Early on, adults with a special interest such as stocks or current events take advantage of the comfortable quiet sections where they can concentrate without interruption. Discussion groups deal with books and with topics in the news. Instruction in arts and crafts and lessons in first aid are given. During the late afternoon, students do homework and pursue research projects. At night, organizations including those of the elderly utilize the community room.

The library is a never-ending source of enrichment. As Sir William Osler put it: *"Money invested in a library gives much better returns than mining stock."*

MARRIAGE

I am my beloved, and my beloved is mine.

Song of Songs II: 16

*Were he not to marry again, it might be concluded that his
first wife had given him a disgust to marriage; but by taking
a second wife he pays the highest compliment to the first,
by showing that she made him so happy as a married man,
that he wishes to be so a second time.*

Samuel Johnson

Long-term marriages are a new phenomenon. At the beginning of this century, most marriages were terminated after 20-30 years by the death of a spouse. Survival much beyond the Golden Wedding Anniversary occurred for less than 5% of marriages. Even today little is known about marriages 50 years or more in duration. Sociologists, because both male and female longevity have dramatically increased, are now studying marital unions of older people in regard to satisfaction, gender role differences and other behavioral aspects.

Studies of marriage over the life cycle sometimes present varied and inconsistent conclusions. Sociologists have generally assumed that attitudes and behavior established in middle years are likely to persist in late years. But little is known about homemaking wives who have retired from jobs in industry. There has not been enough investigation of the sexual behavior of older couples. Because of the increase in human longevity, new stages of married life appear to be emerging. Will the traditional marriage pledge, *till death do us part,* have to be revised for an era in which death may not occur for 70 years after the marriage ceremony?

Among the elderly, a higher proportion of men than women are married. Studies show that morale of older married couples is higher than that of singles, states of health are better, social integration is on a more secure plane and rates of institutionalization are lower. Battering of elderly married women by their husbands is unusual. Demographers point out that married people live longer than do single. The vast majority of long- wed-people rate their marriage as happy, admitting readily that the partnership is sustained not only by loyalty but also by personal investment in the relationship.

As if that were not enough, the same studies reveal that older married women in contrast to their single peers are less likely to be poor and more likely to reside in their own home. Knowing that marriage is of utmost importance in maintaining resources necessary for independence in later life, many happily married wives fear widowhood. About 1/2 of women 65-74 are widows whereas the majority of men are married. Of the older adults who continue to reside in the community, about 2/5 of the women and 3/4 of the men continue to live with their spouses. Residing with someone other than a spouse is much more common among older Blacks and Hispanics than among Whites.

Older married couples have had an intimate relationship for many years. Now beyond the pressures of earning a living and of rearing children, they can concentrate on activities of personal choice. As might be expected, they have fewer marital problems than young couples. They cooperate on chores, and they share responsibility when making decisions. Despite declines in health and losses in the death of friends and loved ones, older husbands and wives consistently report that marriage enhances the quality of life.

Retirement and the empty nest present problems. Wives are more affected by departure of the offspring; husbands, by loss of the job. After the last child leaves, the average married couple will probably live together for at least 15 years. Husband and wife must learn how to deal with one another on a 24-hour basis after years of seeing one another for an hour or two in the morning and 4 or 5 hours at night. Many a husband, missing his job and previously structured schedule, fears he is in a rut and does not belong anywhere. Many a wife anxiously anticipates what one spouse referred to as "Twice as much husband, half as much pay." Such fears are unfounded, sociologists point out, for husbands after retirement tend to be more helpful with household tasks.

Such variables in the dynamic nature of marriage as role-assuming, communication, decision-making and division of labor have to be readjusted. If the marriage relationship has developed into a time-tested and valued friendship, the older couple will then experience once again the process of loving discovery and marital satisfaction will increase. Many such couples state that their marriage has improved because, free of household responsibilities, they have ample time, opportunity and energy for each other. They are enjoying the "golden years" for which they planned. Research by sociologists indicates that the risk of divorce declines the longer people remain married.

But there are gender differences in perceptions of marriage. Some studies suggest that in regard to sexual relations, social interaction and performance of household tasks, marriage for many older husbands and wives is so different that they seem to be reporting on disparate unions almost as if they are part of 2 distinct marriages. In general, retired husbands indicate more marital satisfaction than do their wives who complain of less discretionary time and more meals to prepare. A major exception occurs in dual-paycheck marriages where wives report that after retirement there are an increase of togetherness and a lessening in pace and number of household chores.

Marriages are more frail than ever. Empathetic communication with patience and good humor is not easy to achieve. The divorce rate continues to rise, so that a continually increasing proportion of the population reaches old age in a state of living alone. For couples after retirement and with an empty nest there are difficulties inherent in reestablishing relationships, especially today when so many women feel a strong need to redefine their identity. Focusing attention on what they perceive as their own needs, they become achievement-oriented and seek self-reliance through employment outside the home. Marriage counseling, if engaged in early enough, can be helpful in this transition period.

Divorce and remarriage present serious problems to the elderly. Children often cause difficulties. Older women after divorce are on an even lower financial level than widows. Former friends find it difficult to sustain a relationship with both parties. Although remarriage rates among the elderly are low, men marry at a higher rate than women, often choosing a much younger marital partner. White males have a higher probability of getting remarried than Hispanics and Chinese, blacks the least probability. Treating the new mate as a replacement for the former spouse and not as an attractive person in his or her own right will make for a troubled marriage. Empathy and patience are essential, as are flexibility and adaptability. When asked, late-life adults say that they re-married chiefly for companionship. Many admit an added inducement is that husbands and wives care for each other in case of ill health.

A large proportion of unmarried older men and women live together without benefit of marriage from fear of financial disadvantage from pension plans and tax laws although a change in Social Security now allows remarried elderly to retain benefits in full.

Ideally, said Goethe, "The sum which two married people owe to one another defies calculation. It is an infinite debt, which can only be discharged through all eternity."

MEDICATIONS

Better use medicines at the outset than at the last moment.

Publilius Syrus

To live by medicine is to live horribly.

Carl Linnaeus

Wisely prescribed and used, medications are safe and effective for the elderly despite the facts that every medicine has side effects and every drug regimen poses potential risks to patients.

Serious concerns with pharmacotherapy of the elderly, who as a group are the largest consumers of medications, involve dosage as well as choice of drug. In trials of new drugs the elderly were usually excluded because of fears that they are likely to experience complications. Only recently have some old people been included in clinical trials of new medications. Drugs are usually designed for and tested by young and middle-aged adults. A result is physicians' ignorance of optimum amounts and extent of possible side effects of drugs on old people. This is one reason doctors prefer to begin drug therapy for the elderly with increased dosage and moderation of dosage and then with careful follow-up, always watching for development of tolerance. Hopefully, projects such as the Baltimore Longitudinal Study of Aging will increasingly provide doctors with indication of proper dosage.

Even so, the elderly should consult the pharmaceutical company's printed instructions before taking a drug. It is frequently forgotten that drugs are chemical compounds made up of substances almost always foreign to the body, with potential for harm as well as good. Instructions about dosage and interactions with alcohol, food and other drugs should be carefully followed. A relatively new field, chronotherapeutics, has introduced a fresh element for older persons to be aware of when taking medications. Because our bodies operate on biochemical rhythms that predispose us to specific conditions at set times, researchers are creating medications that are most effective at those moments. A new high blood pressure drug, for example, has been designed to peak in the morning when elderly people usually experience a surge in vascular pressure. Researchers are working on drugs for asthma, headaches, peptic ulcers and various sleep disorders.

Both pharmacists and doctors can help patients save on costs of medications, especially by use of generic equivalents. Drugs have 2 names. The brand name, protected by patent for at least 17 years, is usually sold by only 1 company. The generic name is generally indicative of a drug's chemical makeup. Any manufacturer approved by the Food and Drug Administration may sell a generic drug under its chemical name or a brand name different from the original. Today, because generic drugs are closely monitored by the FDA for equivalence to the original brand-name medications, they are almost always as safe and effective as their originals.

Drug use increases with age. Self-prescribed medication is a common form of health care among the elderly. Undoubtedly, folk remedies like herbal teas and chicken soup are widely used. The most commonly purchased over-the-counter drugs include analgesics, antacids, laxatives, nutritional supplements. Older persons 65+ comprise about 12% of the population but estimates are that they account for at least 30% of all drugs prescribed by doctors and 40% of all over-the-counter medications. The elderly often swap drugs: reliable estimates are that at least 10% take drugs prescribed for someone else. A large number of elderly patients take a broad range of medications for diverse chronic ailments. Women consume more drugs than men, especially psychoactive medications that affect the mind by way of a calming or sedating effect.

Medical coordination is frequently poor or nonexistent: it is not uncommon for a physician to prescribe a drug without asking about the patient's other prescriptions. Surveys published in the *Journal of the American Medical Association* reveal that almost 1/3 of older adults are taking at least one drug that they should not get, risking such side effects as confusion and heart problems.

Unwise use of drugs, prescribed or not, can lead to severely adverse reactions and to failure of vital functions and death. Such drug reactions may account for more than 10% of all hospital admissions. Statistics from the United States Drug Enforcement Administration (DEA) make clear that about 70,000 emergency room visits each year involve prescription tranquilizers, including sedatives and sleeping pills, drugs attractive to many of the elderly.

Rampant abuse of medications goes virtually unnoticed, obscured by a cloak of respectability. If at a dinner party a guest takes out a vial of heroin, more than instant notice will be paid by everyone else at the table. If that same guest were, instead, to take out a bottle of valium, no one would comment, much less even notice.

If prescription drug abuse is to be prevented, both lay people and health professionals must act. Physicians need to be aware of the pharmacology involved and to make adjustments to fit the needs of elderly patients. Patients need to learn the characteristics of drugs and under what circumstances to take them. As a person ages, responses even to drugs familiar from childhood on may change.

Because drug interactions are not easy to predict, the medicine cabinet can be a disaster in the making. Sir William Osler, one of the world's most highly regarded physicians, warned: "Medicine is a science of uncertainty and an art of probability." Few drugs have a narrow range of effects. Age-related changes, drugs taken with other drugs and consumed with various foodstuffs can affect distribution, concentration and effect to produce negative reactions, some of which are hazardous. Processes of input, movement and elimination are of especial importance in judging onset, duration and potency within the body. So, too, is dosage, consisting of the drug itself plus other ingredients needed to make a utilizable medicine, whether a capsule, pill, solution or tablet taken orally, or an intravenous injection, skin patch or suppository.

With aging, lean body mass decreases and proportion of fat to body weight increases, so that effects of a fat-soluble drug, as one of the benzodiazepines, may last longer in the elderly than in the young. Broccoli and other green, leafy vegetables can reduce effectiveness of Coumadin, a blood-thinner medication prescribed to reduce blood clots. High-fiber cereals may cripple absorption of Lanoxin, a medication used to control irregular heart rhythms. Some antibiotics can raise blood levels of antihistamines to perilous levels. Aspirin can lower the operation of beta blockers prescribed for high blood pressure. Non-prescription drugs may interfere with prescription, as antacids decreasing tetracycline absorption.

There are many other such instances of negative medication reaction, whether over-the-counter or prescribed. Feeling that more than one drug for the same complaint will intensify effect and hasten relief, many elderly swallow multiple medications. NSAIDs taken with aspirin make up a drug cocktail, which may cause internal hemorrhaging. Yet more than 50% of NSAID prescriptions are for individuals 65+. Aspirin itself can lead to toxicity with a wide spectrum of features, such as hyperventilation, that may be mistaken for symptoms of disease. Sedatives can make a patient lethargic, interfere with sleep patterns and introduce confusion. Almost the opposite is true of antidepressant drugs, which may have as side effects undue excitement and postural dizziness. Medications to ease symptoms of a cold may cause urinary retention and give trouble to an older man with an enlarged prostate.

The most frequently encountered side effect of medications is dry mouth (xerostomia), an uncomfortable condition with extreme dryness and/or burning sensation in the mouth. Approximately 400 medications ordinarily used can cause the disorder. There is no known cure. For persons who must continue taking such medication, the National Institute of Dental Research recommends drinking sugarless liquids, sucking on hard candies, avoiding alcohol, coffee, sugar, tea and highly acidic food. Adequate liquid is important to wash down numerous medications to avoid esophageal injury.

It may seem like an exaggeration but it is true that many older persons, relying on more than one physician for help with their chronic ailments, purchase drugs from more than one pharmacy—accumulating as many as 10-15 drugs, each to be taken on a 2-4 times a day schedule. Aware that as the number of drugs and doses goes up, the percentage of elderly who take their medicines correctly goes down, Dr. I. Rossman, former head of the American Geriatrics Society, tells nevertheless of a patient for whom he believed he had justifiably prescribed 19 pills daily: "a pill for diabetes, a female hormone pill, a diuretic for her high blood pressure, another pill three times a day for high blood pressure, a mild tranquilizer three times a day for her jitteriness, an antihistamine for her hay fever, potassium supplements to correct a low potassium level, and a calcium tablet three times a day." Such regimens compel caregivers or patients to administer 50 and more dosages a day. Noncompliance, the term doctors use to indicate that a patient is not taking a medication as prescribed, is almost inevitable. Yet, as Dr. Rossman points out, adherence of the sick older person to the proper regimen is crucial.

To help prevent untoward occurrences, the elderly should have all prescriptions filled at one local pharmacy which will keep tabs on all prescriptions and explain the possibility of interactions and associated side effects. When a doctor prescribes a drug, the patient should have the nurse or the physician write down name, dosage, method of ingestion, possibility of interactions or side effects.

Unfortunately, many elderly do not comply with a prescription and its regimen, especially if removing a bottle cap is difficult or if the regimen requires 3 or more drugs and two or more doses a day. There are many other reasons for noncompliance. Some elderly forget to take a drug at the proper time, others take a drug only when they think they need it, still others stop taking drugs when beginning to feel better. For a symptomless disorder, such as hypertension, many persons gradually stop taking medications. Despite insurance, cost can be a problem. Prices can be high enough to encourage non-compliance either by not filling a prescription or by not completing the full course of medication in order to keep a few precious pills in reserve. Duration of medication therapy for late-life adults is ordinarily long-term. If side effects occur, as is often likely, such a long-lasting drug regimen can lead to a decline in quality of life and increasing noncompliance, which may be of non or partial use, of incorrect dosage or of improper timing.

Noncompliance can be dangerous for the individual and for the public at large. If a sick person does not complete a drug regimen, microorganisms may flourish and a contagious disease spread.

Drug-taking behavior of the elderly is characterized by abuse and misuse as well as nonuse. Frequently, purchase of over-the-counter medications is not necessary. Often the elderly do not tell the doctor which drugs they are using. Sometimes, as in the case of vitamins, they do not know that they are swallowing drugs. Both chronic diseases and disorders of older people are seldom immediately perilous and thus do not require prompt medication. There are nondrug alternatives, such as counseling, dietary modification, relaxation techniques, that may be effective treatment for minor complaints like constipation and tension. Even so, the elderly are notorious for relying primarily on drugs and then stockpiling (sometimes beyond the expiration date) or exchanging medications with friends who appear to have similar symptoms, thereby making a bad situation worse. One friend may give another antacid for what seems to be indigestion when in fact the discomfort is cardiac-related.

A major problem is taking several drugs for the same ailment although in combination the drugs can have severe negative effects: an arthritic may be taking under its brand name ibuprofen prescribed at or near maximum levels and obtain over the counter another medication for pain and discomfort without realizing that it, a generic counterpart, contains ibuprofen. Ignorance of drug action may cause serious problems: a laxative may speed passage of other medications through the gastrointestinal tract, resulting in decreased absorption and ineffectiveness. Another difficulty occurs when an elderly person tries one medication after another in an effort to obtain relief, as in the case of someone complaining of a sleep disorder. The number of drugs purported to assist in obtaining sleep is staggering. Trying drug after drug can result in disaster because the ability of the body to eliminate drugs declines with age.

Too often evaluating the role medications play in the health of the elderly seems like part of an insoluble puzzle. Common adverse effects may be mistaken for complications from the several chronic diseases which almost all elderly experience. Lifestyle factors, such as cigarette smoking and use of alcohol, need to be kept in balance with drug therapy. There are interactions of prescribed with self-prescribed over-the-counter drugs. Effects may never be directly verifiable, as in the absence of a stroke in an older person who for decades has been taking antihypertensive drugs to control high blood pressure. A serious impairment which no one perceives in time, such as kidney damage, may be an inadvertent result of long-term drug use. Unable to make verifiable assessments for many drugs, physicians may estimate risks as well as benefits on the basis of trial and error.

It is a good idea for the buyer of medications to be aware. In 1990, a panel of experts in geriatric medicine and pharmacology issued for concerned physicians a list of medications inappropriate for older patients. Estimates are that about 1 in 4 of the elderly in the late 1980's were taking at least 1 of the contraindicated drugs. The FDA asserts that about half of all prescribed medications are used improperly by patients.

But approach to use of medications should not be negative. It is also a good idea to remember that medicine, as James Bryce MD pointed out, "labors incessantly to destroy the reason for its own existence."

PLEASE NOTE: Unfortunately, sale as a neutraceutical (a dietary supplement) of a compound that may have serious adverse, even life-threatening, side-effects is legal and above-board. The law permits a natural product to be marketed without a prescription providing that the packaging makes no claim for treatment of disease. Although quite clearly the equivalent of a drug, some neutraceuticals are available over-the-counter and without instruction from a licensed medical practitioner in stores that sell vitamins and nutrition products. Perhaps the 1998 brouhaha over the taking of the not yet scientifically proven neutraceutical Androstenedione by home-run king Mark McGwuire will result in changes in the law requiring regulation for efficacy, stability and safety. Until then, anyone taking a dietary supplement that has not been subject to human clinical trials is unknowingly taking a substance that may have powerful and harmful long-term effects.

In 1999 pressure from the drug industry and Congress to get the FDA to approve drugs quickly may have caused lowered standards. Consumers should be wary of new drugs and watch for troublesome side effects. No one should take a drug unless absolutely necessary.

There may be nondrug therapies that can be tried first. Whether prescription or over -the- counter, no medicine is without risk of side effects, allergic reactions, interaction with food, drink and other drugs.

WHAT A PATIENT SHOULD KNOW
ABOUT EACH PRESCRIBED DRUG

Names, both brand and generic.

Purpose and dosage to take.

Time to take the drug: hour(s) of morning, noon or night.

Circumstances: with liquid or solid food before, during or after meals.

Duration of period for taking the drug.

Activities to avoid while taking the drug.

Side effects and what to do about them.

Interactions with alcohol, food and other drugs.

Storage and expiration date.

Do other medications sound like the drug prescribed, so that an error can occur—as Adderal for Inderal or Rimantadine for Amantadine?

FACTORS THAT ALTER DRUG DISPOSITION IN OLD AGE

Absorption

There is a reduction in small bowel surface and in stomach acid. Even so, there is little change in absorption with age.

Distribution

There is increased body fat but a reduction in lean body mass and in total body water. A higher distribution of drugs in body fluids. Often there is prolonged elimination of fat-soluble drugs.

Liver Metabolism

There is a reduction of liver mass and in liver blood flow. Enzyme activity is decreased. Metabolism of some drugs is reduced.

Kidney Elimination

There are reduced blood flow and filtration. Although there is a marked variation in individual cases, there is generally a decreased kidney elimination of drugs.

MEMORY

There are three early signs of old age.
The first is loss of short-term memory
And I don't remember the other two!

Old age occurs when you finally get it all together
and you cannot remember where you put it.

Anonymous

More ill-founded beliefs survive about the minds of older persons than about any other aspect of aging.

Biological decline of the brain is not inevitable. Although disproved by irrefutable evidence, the idea that millions of brain cells are lost daily throughout the aging brain is still widely held. Neuron death in normal aging does not account for so-called age-related impairment of memory. The brain does shrink, and some cells do die. But remaining cells can make new connections and the brain can continue normal functioning. A major basis of learning and memory, the number of connections between cells is crucial if the brain is to continue to process information and use it through adulthood.

Significant memory loss and sharp intellectual decline in older persons almost always are symptoms, not of aging, but of an illness or disorder. The vast majority of older persons are mentally flexible and fully alert. Except in cases of age-related disease like Alzheimer's, mental processes of mature adults do not differ fundamentally from those of the young. Both physical and psychological impairment can cause or masquerade as deterioration of memory. Auditory or vision deficits may block a person from remembering a name because of inability to hear or see clearly. Fatigue and stress can interfere with recall. Research shows conclusively that when the elderly discard the negative stereotypes of aging that dominate our culture, their memory performance improves dramatically. Once the physical or psychological difficulty is taken care of, there is little or no trouble with memory among older people.

The best way to hold onto and improve mental performance is to use it. The brain's neurons perform better and more efficiently with increased activity. Mental stimulation contributes to enhancement of the brain as physical exercise helps to improve the body. Disuse undoubtedly explains much of what appear to be declines. Adults are not required, as are the young, to learn and memorize all kinds of new things every day of their lives. Memory skills do lessen although in daily life even those persons long out of school function within the normal range of remembrance. It is frequently overlooked when contrasting memory ability of the young and the old that because of their orientation toward learning and school the young employ memory aids, such as notes, lists, mnemonic devices. While these are not unavailable to adults, few use them.

Too often memory tests by psychologists who would compare and contrast ability of different age groups are given in a void without the contexts of daily life to provide validity. This may be one reason the old perform more poorly than the young when trying to memorize artificially designed word lists for immediate recall. This is not to deny that with age some degree of short-term memory loss may occur, but researchers caution that such lapses can be due to lack of effort and intellectual stimulation. Although experiments do imply some age-related slowing of the retrieval process in late life, memory need not decline significantly among the elderly.

With older adults, fear of memory loss is often greater than the actual loss itself.

The elderly report more memory problems and have more negative views of current memory ability than the young, probably because of anxiety and perhaps of depression. Older adults find it hard to accept that age-related changes in memory do not occur despite the fact that shifts in storage capacity of long-term memory have not been discovered. They do not believe that occasional brief memory lapses are normal and that for individuals of *all* ages details of remote events in the distant past become increasingly uncertain. For them, admitting to having misplaced an item or to having forgotten something is humiliating. In many aspects, behavior of the aged, as anthropologists have convincingly demonstrated, is a reflection of stereotypes and expectations of the dominant culture. In China, where age does not bear connotations of mental degeneration, elderly perform better on tests of memory than do their American counterparts.

The human brain, the most complex structure the process of evolution has produced, has much unused potential for storage of memory. Insofar as psychologists can ascertain, there is no limit to the amount of information that can be retained. Contrary to folk belief, there is no marked decline in short-term memory of aging adults. Much of what is deemed forgetfulness is actually a result of distraction and/or stress, not paying close attention or of trying to do do several things at the same time. Robert MacNeill, former co-anchor of the prize-winning public television news broadcasts, often forgot "on-camera" names of celebrities he was interviewing. A person may put car keys down on a chair while answering a question from a friend and then not remember where the keys are.

Occasionally, the old may suffer from inability to retrieve a word, the tip-of-the-tongue phenomenon; the word does come later, much the way a person entering a room forgets purpose yet remembers on leaving the room and then returning. Psychologists call this phenomenon benign forgetfulness, and regard it as harmless, supposing that it reflects disuse and a sedentary way of life encouraged for the old by society. When people of advanced age are coming out of electroconvulsive therapy, they frequently and with no hesitation recall accurately and in detail events and factual data of long ago.

Samuel Johnson, the renowned lexicographer, said: "There is a wicked inclination in most people to suppose an old man decayed in his intellect. If a young or middle-aged man, when leaving a company, does not recollect where he laid his hat, it is nothing; but let the same inattention be discovered in an older man and people shrug and say, 'His memory is going.'" Unfortunately, the stereotype that memory fails as the years pass, if accepted by someone growing older, will become a self-fulfilling prophecy.

There are some caveats which, it is important to recognize, apply to people in general regardless of age. Researchers have not learned precisely how the brain integrates and organizes information into categories; that is, as yet, no one knows how memories are established and arranged although there is much evidence that dissimilar kinds of memory involve diverse sectors of the brain, thus making it likely that they are ordered and reconstructed differently. Recall of facts learned in school, such as that 9X4=36, remains accurate throughout life whereas to both the young and the old, memory of personal events or of sequences of public events is often inaccurate.

Because long-term memory is dependent on receiving and then finding the right cue, whether visual or aural, recall may not be exact. Psychologists liken memory to a vast library but without a simple system, such as the Dewey Decimal, for bringing forth information accurately. People who live together know from experience that squabbles occur quite often because of differences in remembrance of how and when things happened. Recollection may even be made to fit preconceptions of what should have happened. Apparently, memory is constructed bit by bit in the brain, so that events that occurred separately may fuse in retrospect. Subsequent experiences may disrupt and distort an original memory and, indeed, even persuade people that they are remembering events that in actuality never occurred. Memory is reconstruction, not replication.

There are other reasons that memory is not always exact. Recall has three aspects: recognizing items to be evoked, searching for information and bringing forth the material. Failure of accurate recall can occur if memory of an old event is closely associated or intertwined with a new one, as one's graduation from school with that of a grandchild. Total failure can occur if an old but brief memory is associated with a new one, as in the case of a name not referred to in a long time with a similar name newly heard. Motivation is important. If people find no relevance in an item, they likely will not remember it.

Memory difficulties may also be caused by emotional stress and preoccupation with solving a problem. Sometimes, in favor of pleasant memories of an idealized past, an older person forgets recent events because the memories are so painful. Is this why in old age recollections of experiences in youth appear to be retained better than memory of incidents in mid-life? Sometimes, immediately after having moved into a strange, new neighborhood, a person forgets the way home. Such forgetting is normal for young and old although with age people may need more time and effort to recollect newly acquired directions.

Long-term memory is dependent on receiving, retaining and then locating cues in the right place in the brain. People may remember relatively accurately an event but not how they acquired the memory. When emotions are involved, distortions may occur. If they subsequently hear or see another version of the event, they may confuse the new account with the original memory, even to the point of regarding the new as correct and substituting it for the first recollection. Apparently, this is what happened a few years ago when psychologists dug out of adults supposed memories of child abuse. Subsequent investigations in courts of law determined that the "memories" were indeed fabrications.

A puzzling mix of complex processes including cognition, integration, perception and the senses, memory is composed of but 3 stages: 1. learning, 2. storing and 3. recalling information. These stages occur in both long and short-term memory, in both the young and the old. If a person remains healthy and keeps active physically and mentally, there are no substantial changes in memory, whether primary, secondary or tertiary–as explained below. In common with the biceps, memory needs exercise. Because with aging there is extremely little diminution of capacity to store information, concerns of aging persons about memory loss are almost always out of proportion to actual or suspected declines.

In fact, reminiscence is often used as the basis of therapy for both alert and confused elderly, whether in an institution or at home in the community. Particularly for persons in early stages of dementia, the therapist concentrates on long-term memories as stimuli somewhat to halt deterioration and improve the quality of life. Some psychologists assume that the elderly benefit when in group sessions they reminisce and engage in feedback with peers. Other therapists insist that results are inconclusive.

Many psychologists classify memory in three different categories. Primary memory is short-lived, as a telephone number just looked up. Since most adults, old as well as young, can recall without difficulty up to 7 items of information, telephone numbers are generally limited to 7 digits. There are minimal age differences in primary memory except in cases of divided attention. When in such a situation a person must hold multiple new items in primary memory while retrieving information from secondary memory, there is some decline in ability of many older persons. Secondary memory is the ability to remember extensive amounts of information over a relatively long period of time, as items in a schedule of social events. Hypothetically, this is "where" conscious and unconscious memories reside. Tertiary memory refers to information held in storage for quite a long time, as the meanings of words learned as far back as early childhood.

There are other ways to categorize memory. Prospective memory, to take one example, refers to a person's recalling in the present a need to perform an action in the future, as buying during the next shopping trip a specific grocery item in the supermarket.

Procedural memory, based on both cognitive and motor skills, is different. A person, having learned how to swim, can automatically and permanently recall and utilize the process without conscious awareness.

If a person remains healthy and keeps active physically and mentally, there are no substantial changes in memory. Two processes are at work. Memory involves retaining and recalling information. Because with aging there is extremely little diminution of capacity to store information, concerns of aging persons about memory loss are almost always out of proportion to actual or suspected levels of decline. Basically, cognitive structures of a healthy 70-year-old do not differ from those of a 7-year-old. Thoughts and memories may increase in number, but the structure encompassing them remains the same. Although the brain is not a computer, the image the machine furnishes is helpful in picturing the situation: the mental "hardware" of young and old human beings is the same and the "software" becomes more sophisticated with age.

There are many physical causes of memory loss, some of which are treatable. But there is no evidence that any drug can improve a healthy person's memory. Particularly when misused, alcohol and some medications, as certain kinds of sleeping pill, can cause memory difficulties. Alcohol taken to excess can result in total forgetfulness lasting a day or more. Poor nutrition, a thyroid deficiency and diabetes may occasion memory problems. A tumor in the brain or liver may result in memory troubles. Many infections, such as those of the urinary tract and bladder, may result in memory difficulties.

In cases of disease, there may be serious memory declines. Anemia in the old can produce confusion and forgetfulness. It is abnormal and a sign of dementia when a person forgets much easily recallable information, as addition of simple numbers and the names of persons in the family. Victims of Alzheimer's disease, the most common form of old-age dementia, suffer disorientation in time and space and encounter difficulty in word finding when trying to communicate. Progressive, irreversible memory loss is the most notorious symptom of this debilitating disorder. More research is needed, not just in the case of Alzheimer's Disease, to determine the impact of disease and medication on memory in the elderly.

To a large extent, memory depends on a person's desire to recall someone or something. Routines help. Place an object, such as a wallet or purse in the same place each night, as in a large bowl near the door, and you will the following morning remember where it is. Always checking the calendar early in the morning makes it unlikely that you will forget appointments or errands. If something is not in its accustomed place, the elderly should go back and look carefully because often the problem is not memory but quickness of perception accompanied by physically overlooking something, perhaps because of vision difficulties. One way of unsticking the memory is to distract the conscious mind. If you misplace house keys, do not become upset. Instead, say the names of the presidents or count by threes. In a moment or two, you should be able to find the keys.

Paradoxically, there are times that forgetting helps remembering. To remember where you left a car in a parking lot, you forget where you parked the last time you were there. Psychologists say that such forgetting is automatic, unconscious–a necessary process if a person is to remember accurately life's myriad facts and details. .

More than 2,000 years ago, Cicero denied that with age the memory is necessarily impaired. "The aged remember everything that interests them," he said, adding: "I certainly never heard of any old man forgetting where he had hidden his money!"

"Remembrance and reflection, how allied!" exclaimed the poet Alexander Pope. He was right. Memory and learning are permanently and inextricably linked. Memory, given effort and thought, can be maintained and even improved at any age.

THE NURSING HOME

All these things, sorrow, misfortune, and suffering, are out-
side my door.

Charles Fletcher Lummis

Milton Berle tells of having checked into a nursing home and becoming
annoyed that no one recognized him. Approaching a resident, he asked:
"Do you know who I am?" "No," she replied, "but if you go to the front
desk the clerk will surely tell you."

Many nursing home administrators and proprietors know that there
are numerous ways to improve the nursing home environment, sometimes without undue effort and expense. The ceiling where bed-fast
patients focus attention can easily be decorated or painted with games.
A room can be set aside for privacy where residents as well as family
and friends can get together. Patients can be made aware of their right
to express grievances without fear of reprisal and with prompt redress
of legitimate complaints. Staff can learn patients' names and address
them as adults, not as children. Adequate pay and bonuses for positive
recognition of service can go a long way toward raising level of commitment and creating enthusiasm in staff. Hopefully, more and more
nursing homes are striving for improvement.

Not really a home, a nursing home is a place of residence, too
often little more than a temporary survival center for those elderly who
cannot fend for themselves in the community, especially for those with
psychological difficulties–although a nursing home is supposedly not
intended for care of the mentally ill. (Estimates are that about 50% of
elderly in a long-term care setting have a dementing illness.) Nursing
homes have yet to display a commitment to rehabilitative therapy aimed
at helping the elderly return to living in their community.

Basically, there are three kinds of nursing homes. A skilled-nursing
facility is supervised by a medical director, has physicians on call and
employs licensed nurses. An intermediate-care nursing home provides

individual care and/or custodial services for patients with difficulty performing such basic activities of daily living as dressing and eating. A non-skilled facility, sometimes referred to as a geriatric facility, which may be licensed by the state or local community rather than the federal government, offers minimal individual attention.

Residence in some nursing homes leaves much to be desired. Management rather than human need is the criterion. Emphasis is on day-to-day routine and "baby-sitting" care of the sick rather than on prevention, treatment and rehabilitation. Deprived of privacy and subject to rigid segregation, many elderly become depersonalized. Deterioration is almost inevitable, so that the elderly in nursing homes are more likely to be depressed than those living in the community. Institutional neurosis (state of apathy and passive acceptance) almost becomes commonplace. Because entrance is too often followed by decline and early death, nursing homes are sometimes characterized as "warehouses for the dying." Some nursing homes do not have even minimal discharge procedures because the assumption is that a move to a nursing home is terminal. No wonder very few individuals want to move to a nursing home or that relatives who place their loved ones in such a facility suffer intense guilt.

Nursing homes provide 24 hour care that is not possible for financial or practical reasons in a person's original residence. When choosing a nursing home, a family should consider location, level of care and condition and treatment of residents. Unannounced visits are an important way of checking. Are patients dressed and active? Does each resident keep his/her own money, possessions and clothing? Are valuables and financial records concealed from strangers? Visitation rights? Access to a telephone? Sanitation? What kinds of food are served? How and where? What provisions have been made in case of fire? Is there an ombudsman?

Every nursing home should be licensed and employ the correct number of licensed personnel as well as a properly qualified medical director who has been trained in treatment of older adults. Ideally, by utilizing skilled nursing care and rehabilitation services the nursing home can develop a regimen for each resident, with the aim of helping the person achieve optimum physical, social and psychological well-being in performance of the basic activities of daily life.

Most nursing homes are operated for profit, with the remainder being run by the government or private, nonprofit organizations. Some hospitals have links to established facilities. The occupants at any one time represent only approximately 5% or so of all elderly, the overwhelming majority of whom vehemently desire to retain residence in the community. Perhaps 40% of the elderly will spend some time in a nursing home during the course of their lifetime, and half of them will die there. Women make up nearly 3/4 of the elderly population of nursing homes, and about 1/2 have no close living relatives. Patients for short stays come usually from hospitals, often for terminal care after a long illness. Patients for long stays are those for whom return home is not possible.

Nursing-home occupancy is so expensive that most elderly cannot afford it. At present, nursing-home charges in the state of Florida, for example, are approaching $40,000 a year. Medicare provides only limited coverage for nursing home residency. Private insurance, often called medigap insurance, is available to help with cost coverage not provided by Medicare, but each policy should be carefully studied to determine how much of a resource it actually is. Medicaid, a joint state-federal benefits program based on financial need, is one of the chief sources of patient funding for nursing homes, paying for more than 1/2 of the number of seniors admitted. Guidelines for qualifying vary from state to state. Information can be obtained from local nursing home licensing agencies or from the state Department of Health. Generally, a person seeking eligibility must expend all resources to the point of impoverishment to obtain coverage, after admission becoming a virtual prisoner unable ever again to set up an apartment. (In most states, Medicare and Medicaid fund home-care and other services to a limited extent for those elderly capable of remaining in the community, and Medicare now includes hospice programs—in this way reducing somewhat the nursing-home population.)

At present, there are about 2,000,000 nursing home beds in the United States, a larger number than that of acute hospital beds. Estimates are that because of the baby boomers the need for beds will rise to nearly 4,000,000 in the year 2020. If the authorities become more efficient and stringent in inspection and regulation of nursing homes, the facilities will improve. This is an area in which organizations of the elderly, such as the AARP, need to take more action. Then with Richard Watson Gilder, people entering a nursing home will be able to say to their family: "This, dear one, is our home, our rest."

CHOOSING A NURSING HOME

Activities:

All activities should be age-related and made available to all.

Professional staff should plan activities for recreation and/or therapy.

Is there a calendar of activities, including religious services?

Appearance:

Residents should be clean and neatly dressed.

The entire building should be immaculate, and hospital odors should be minimal.

Choosing a Nursing Home

Obtain a list of homes from the State and local Office of the Aging.

Get recommendations from clergymen, friends, family physician, relatives.

Before deciding, visit several homes.

Costs:

What does the basic rate cover? Are there extra charges? Are bills itemized?

What provisions are there for patients' spending money?

Is the home eligible for Medicare and Medicaid reimbursement?

Independence and Privacy:

Are residents free to move around in designated areas?

Are lounges available for socializing?

No room should have more than 4 beds.

Each room should have provision for privacy and personal storage space.

Are rooms, corridors and elevators large enough to accommodate wheelchairs?

Hospitalization:

In case of emergency, which hospital is used?

How are nursing home patients transported to and from the hospital?

How long will the bed and room be reserved for a hospitalized resident?

Licensing:

State Nursing Home License

American Association of Homes for the Aging

Nursing Home Administrator License.

American Nursing Home Association.

Joint Committee on Accreditation of Hospital Certificate.

Certified in both Medicare and Medicaid programs.

Location:

Is the home in the community in which the patient lived?

Is the home conveniently situated for regular family visits?

Are there outdoor gardens with benches?

Medical Staff:

There should be enough registered nurses to answer calls of residents promptly.

A qualified geriatrician should be on staff and present or on 24-hour call.

Are provisions made for physiotherapy, dental care and other specialized services?

Nutrition:

A qualified full-time dietitian should plan and post tasteful, balanced menus.

Are diets and snacks arranged for patients with special needs and preferences?

Patient socializing should be encouraged in an attractive communal dining room.

Staff should be regularly assigned to patients who cannot feed themselves.

Procedures:

The staff physician should examine each new resident as soon as possible.

Every patient should have an up-to-date chart of medical status and needs.

All staff should treat residents with kindness and respect for individual dignity.

Patients should be dressed in street clothes and allowed to keep possessions.

Visitors should be permitted to inspect facilities, including kitchens.

A barber and a beautician should be available.

Is the Patient Bill of Rights displayed prominently?

Married couples should not be separated.

Accepting tips should be forbidden to the staff.

Visiting by family and friends of residents should be encouraged.

Rights of Patients

To speak with an Ombudsman.

To utilize services of a personal physician.

To receive advance information as to changes in care and treatment.

To voice grievances without reprisal.

To have privacy in medical treatment, communications (written and oral), personal visits.

To have records remain confidential.

Safety

Does the home meet local and federal fire and building codes?

Is a recent inspection report on display?

Is the neighborhood safe for ambulatory residents?

Is the building accident-proof, with adequate lighting, grab-bars, stairways, tip-proof chairs?

PAIN

Like dull narcotics numbing pain.

Alfred, Lord Tennyson

A paradox. Although pain is the most common complaint for which patients seek medical treatment and although chronic pain has a magnified impact on the older population, incidence of chronic diseases increasing with age, surveys among the elderly consistently reveal age-related decreases in sensation of pain throughout the body except for the joints. Painless acute myocardial infarction (heart attack) occurs much more frequently in late-life adults than in the young. Studies of sales of analgesics (medications that enable fully conscious patients not to feel pain) back up the surveys, for use of pain-killers lessens with age. The comparatively small proportion of pain-clinic admissions among the elderly constitutes further proof.

Despite research, the cause of age-related reductions in pain remains unexplained. Scientists theorize that the nerve apparatus involved in pain perception does not decline with age. Social workers think that a large proportion of older persons surveyed may not admit to pain because they believe it to be a result of aging in general and of deterioration from specific diseases that come with growing old. Many others of the elderly, researchers assume, have learned to be more stoical as time passes.

Experience of pain by older persons is influenced by many years of expectations, emotions, memories. The result, some psychologists hold, is not that the elderly have become indifferent or impervious to harmful sensations. Rather, they have learned to be pragmatic. Continual complaining results in friction and negative attitudes among family and friends. Late-life adults have come to hold the truth of the old adage: laugh and the world laughs with you; cry, and you cry alone. This although their aches and pains may add to the limitations affecting their activities of daily living.

But there is much cause for optimism. Pain management continues to improve. At home, prescription pain reducers can alleviate discomfort; steroids can help erase feelings of intense fatigue. In the hospital, if pain increases toward unbearable levels, morphine in high doses can ease a slide into temporary unconsciousness.

Because pain is easier to counteract before it sets in, preemptive medication should be given, if at all possible, before aching becomes established. Research indicates that pain medicine administered before surgery can have a major impact on recovery. In general, as much medication for pain relief should be administered as to make the elderly person comfortable. More and more hospitals are now permitting Patient Controlled Anesthesia (PCA). Patients themselves take pain medication as they feel they need it by pushing a disc on a pump which delivers a dose via a needle placed previously under the skin. Because the procedure is computer monitored, the patient cannot take an overdose. Pain, it seems, can often be conquered.

Not a simple matter, pain can come from within and without. There are various ways to classify pain, none fully satisfactory. Somatogenic pain can be understood in connection with physical mechanisms. Psychogenic pain can be understood in terms of psychology; that is, pain occurs without bodily injury sufficient to explain the origin of the ache or sting. Acute pain, almost always immediate in onset and short-lived, generally has a readily identifiable cause, such as an endangering injury, and responds well to analgesics. Symptoms include almost instantaneous quickening of heart rate and rise in blood pressure. Chronic pain, generally lasting 1,2,3 months or more, is more difficult to deal with. It may be continuous or recurrent, steady in intensity or variable. It may be due to 1 or to several of the illnesses to which some elderly are prone.

To an observer, reaction of the sufferer may seem out of proportion to the hurt, especially if bodily injury or disease does not appear to account for the degree and duration of pain. Sleep disturbances, decreases in appetite and periods of constipation may occur. Psychological factors become important, and depression can result The consequences of untreated severe chronic pain in older persons may be social isolation and inability to perform activities of daily living, with disablement following quickly.

Because pain may have many causes, it is sometimes difficult to classify and thus to decide on proper therapy. Diagnosis of pain can be subjective, with a high degree of imprecision. Except for anesthetists, most physicians receive little formal training in pain therapy. Chronic pain may follow surgery or, as with headache or low back pain, there may be no bodily injury apparent. In the elderly, pain predominantly psychological in origin is rather rare. Most of their chronic pain is physical in cause at the outset, as from arthritis. Aging persons with arthritis and low-back trouble, indeed anyone with a history of pain, should avoid high-impact aerobics, tennis and jogging. To lessen pain from chronic musculoskeletal conditions physiatrists prescribe moderate exercises performed daily, such as calisthenics, stretching, swimming.

When a pain killer is deemed necessary by a physician, analgesics are prescribed in low doses, the dosage being adjusted upward incrementally. (An analgesic induces a state in which a person does not feel pain although fully conscious. An anesthetic induces a loss of sensation, such as touch, in addition to loss of pain. A local anesthetic's effect is limited to a specific area; a general anesthetic's effect may involve a more general area and a loss of consciousness.)

Luckily, there are many possible approaches to pain management. Traditionally, application of cold, heat and drugs were major means employed. Today, there are specialized clinics for helping people manage intractable pain. People suffering from a terminal malignant disease, such as cancer, generally get some relief from continual application of morphine or another narcotic. A patient undergoing elective surgery may receive analgesics before the operation to lessen postoperative pain. In addition to drugs, nerve-blocking therapy, as injections of local anesthetics, may be appropriate. Narcotic patches, placed on the skin, are effective. Recently approved by the FDA are analgesic lollipops, which come especially wrapped so that children cannot get at them. Sedatives, because they enable the elderly to rest during a good night's sleep, help reduce anxiety and stress. Victims of pain caused by an illness or disorder, such as diabetes mellitus or stroke, do get a sense of ease from anti-depressants or anticonvulsant medications.

Aware of the side effects which medications, such as NSAIDs can produce in older persons, physicians interested in alternative medicine may recommend that acupuncture, biofeedback, humor, hypnosis, massage, physical therapy, relaxation techniques or visualization be used in tandem with medications. Proletherapy, endorsed by C. Everett Koop, former Surgeon General, is an alternative medicine treatment relying on injections of sugar and an anesthetic for chronic pain from sciatica and other musculoskeletal problems.

Also concerned about side effects of drugs, physicians practicing conventional medicine follow the adage: "Start low and go slow."

While there is no proof as yet from research studies, there are indications from athletic trainers that special magnets, called biomagnets, may provide an alternate form of relief from muscle pain. Similarly, despite lack of controlled clinical trials demonstrating efficacy, a biomedical device called TENS (for transcutaneous electrical nerve stimulation) has been in use for several years to reduce muscle pain. Currently, scientists at Abbot Laboratories are working on a painkiller, ABT-594, which in animal studies seems many times more powerful than morphine and without serious side effects, such as those from opioids and NSAIDs.

Researchers in molecular biology have recently confirmed that pain involves multiple neuro-transmitter targets in the central nervous system and spinal cord, as well as various receptors and enzymes. Hopefully, further advances in understanding basic mechanisms of pain will result relatively soon in new medications and approaches to pain management with powerful impact on suffering all the way from ache to agony.

Apparently, Robert Gilfillan's prediction is coming true:

> There's a hope for every woe,
> And a balm for every pain.

PREVENTION

An ounce of prevention is worth a pound of cure.

Folk Saying

*The doctor of the future will give no medicine, but will
interest his patient in the care of the human frame, in diet
and in the cause and prevention of disease.*

Thomas Edison

*We must think of our whole economics in terms of a
preventive pathology instead of a curative pathology.*

Richard Buckminster Fuller

Prevention can be carried to absurd extremes. By remaining indoors, a
driver can avoid death on the roads. Screening an entire population
against the possibility of contracting a rare disease the origin of which
is unknown and for which there is no cure is impractical medically and
monetarily. No matter how efficient, inexpensive or sensitive the test, it
is valuable as a screen for disease only if one intends to act on results.
Properly applied, preventive procedures can save millions of lives and
billions of dollars. Prevention is preferable to therapy. Yet the ravages of
disease today are generally dealt with after incurring rather than before.

The United States expends about $1,000,000,000,000 (one trillion
dollars!) every year on health care, nearly one half of that huge sum to
pay the costs of the elderly 65+. This although savings by an equally
amazing sum, exceeding by far proposed budget cuts in health care,
could be achieved if aging and age-related disorders were staved off
for 5 years. Researchers estimate that a 5-year delay in the onset of
Alzheimer's disease would reduce by half the number of victims of this
dread malady, saving approximately $50,000,000,000 every year—not
to mention the incalculable suffering undergone by the sick and their
families. All this from postponing the outbreak of just one disease afflicting the elderly! Imagine how many more billions of dollars individuals,
family members, employers, and the federal government could avoid spend-

ing if other age-related diseases, such as diabetes, glaucoma and Parkinson's were checked for 5 years.

The figures above are realistic. The *New England Journal of Medicine* reported in 1994 that vaccinating in 1991 older people in Minneapolis against influenza resulted in fewer deaths, fewer hospitalizations, and much lower health costs during the flu seasons of the following 3 years. Average saving in this study of 25,000 people was about $120 for each individual. Extrapolate that number to include all older people in the United States, and the resulting figure is well over $1,000,000,000. All this from one vaccination!

The prestigious National Academy of Sciences Institute of Medicine in 1991 published a research plan on aging to be developed under auspices of the federal government, the product of contributions from outstanding scientists and scholars, entitled *Extending Life, Enhancing Life: A National Research Agenda on Aging.* A summary compiled by the Washington-based Alliance for Aging Research follows:

Research Area	Research Priorities
Basic biomedical research	Abnormal cell proliferation
	The aging brain/Alzheimer's disease
Clinical research	Functional impairment and disability
	Interaction of age-dependent physiologic changes and disease
Behavioral and social research	Interaction of social, psychological, and biological factors in aging
	Changes in population dynamics; the postponement of morbidity
	Changes in societal structures and aging
Health services delivery research	Long-term care and continuity of care
	Costs and financing of long-term care
	Medications and older Persons
	Mental health services
	Disability and disease prevention and health
Biomedical ethics	Dilemmas involving life-sustaining
	Allocation of health care resources
	Participation of older persons in research

The plan has yet to be implemented.

Ironically, politicians continue to bicker over schemes to pay for Medicare and other health-costs of the nation's elderly instead of encouraging scientists to discover means of halting age-related diseases in the first place. Even the National Institute of Aging does not give research on processes of aging priority. Despite public outcry over the huge national debt, politicians ignore the obvious: ever-rising costs of health care can be reversed by helping the elderly 65+ to remain disease free. Proof is in recent history of the elderly.

Since the early 1980's, as a direct result of scientific research, the elderly–including the oldest-old–have been much healthier and with far lower rates of disabilities than demographers had anticipated. Surveys indicate what physicians call a compression of morbidity among those 65+, that is a lessening of disease–especially chronic diseases, including arthritis. Almost 90% of those 65-74 report no disability, and of those 85+ more than 40% state that they are fully functional. In 1982, 1 in 4 persons 65+ was disabled. In 1997, just 15 years later, 1 in 5 persons was disabled. The gain in number is truly large: 1.2 million persons, so state researchers at Duke University. Today's elderly classified as disabled are more able to handle Activities of Daily Living than their predecessors of 1982. During the same time period the proportion of elderly in nursing homes declined from 6.3% to 5.2%. Much of the increase in health and functional status is due to preventive measures, including such changes in lifestyle taken by late-life adults themselves as in bettering nutrition, quitting smoking and engaging in exercise.

Yet of the $1,000,000,000,000 laid out in this country each year for health care, a tiny amount, less than 2%, is allotted to finding methods for prevention. Even smaller amounts are assigned directly by the federal government, for example, the National Institutes of Health allocating well under 10% of its entire budget to scientific research into aging. Except for a guide to clinical preventive services published in 1989 and a program to encourage people to adopt measures designed to reduce preventable disease and disability, both under the auspices of the United States Department of Health and Human Services, not enough has been done to educate the public although preventive action can and should be taken in youth and middle as well as in old age. It must be admitted that the AARP did try. In support of the HHS plan, it launched a *Healthy Older Adults 2000* educational campaign aimed at Americans 50 years and older.

But politicians and the government are not solely at fault. For years it has been obvious both to scientists and the lay public that individuals can safely take prevention and even cure into their own hands. Ever since research on chronic diseases started with initiation of longitudinal studies, such as the Framingham Heart Study in 1949, scientists have identified more and more risk factors and efficient methods of intervention although overall knowledge of health protection in later life is still rudimentary. While nutrition and exercise will not restore youth to 80-year-olds, a dietetic plan and an exercise program properly made out and followed can for many, many elderly eradicate frailty and help produce a state of good health. For those with a familial heritage of a particular disorder, such as breast cancer, heart disease or stroke, finding out what early symptoms are can be a health producer and life saver because it will then be possible for physicians in almost all cases to take preventive measures early enough to prevent disaster.

Everyone should keep copies of records of physicians and dentists. Why physicians and dentists? Because anyone lasting 80 or more years will undoubtedly outlive quite a few dentists and doctors who during the first years of a person's life are undoubtedly older. Keeping records eliminates faulty memory and chasing after facts about events that occurred in the dim past of 30 or so years ago. Because doctors are allowed to destroy patients' records, usually after 7 years, it is a good idea to get annually a copy of your medical file.

Vaccinations remain important. They can and do prevent even virulent diseases. Protection against illness is imperative. Influenza vaccination is recommended each year starting in September, pneumonia revaccination every 6 years after the first dose. Both diseases are 2-3 times more likely to strike older than younger persons. Because tetanus is primarily a disease of older adults, everyone 65+ should receive the full series of tetanus vaccinations. Although incidence of diphtheria has decreased markedly, many elderly should be immunized since they lack protective levels of antibodies. The DT vaccine for adults includes immunization for both tetanus and diphtheria. A booster shot should be administered at least once every 10 years to retain proper levels of immunity.

All elderly should be careful not to make abrupt or drastic changes in lifestyle. There are cases on record of older persons who, worried about high cholesterol levels, stop drinking milk and then develop osteoporosis because they did not think of finding alternative sources of calcium.

Some doctors are taking a different approach from that of traditional medicine, which relies on diagnosis, then on intervention with drugs and/or surgery in expectation of quick cures. As the medical field matures into the health field, prevention becomes more and more important. Physicians have been prescribing permanent lifestyle practices—diet, exercise, physical therapy, psychological help and techniques of alternative medicine like biofeedback—which do not result in quick cures but do help people function better and perhaps prevent disability and illness.

Meanwhile, scientists are going ahead with basic research in fundamental processes of aging research in the hope that it will turn the practice of medicine around from trust in treatment to more reliance on prevention. Promising areas of research into basic cellular and organismal processes include studies of hormones, free radicals and genes and of possible inter-relationships. To take one example, the search for genes influencing life-span and aging and those that cause disease or make a person susceptible has 5 main approaches: identification of genes that predispose to disease; production of tests that determine the presence or absence of given genes; development by the pharmaceutical companies of medications that neutralize potentially threatening genes; creation of a map of genes in the human body; application of findings to live human beings. Already, a gene which regulates life-span has been found in *Caenorhabditis elegans.*

Unfortunately, gene research still does not have the full backing of politicians and government agencies, as indicated by official recommendations that research funded by theNational Institutes of Health be applied only to animals despite reminders by scientists that problems cannot always be solved in laboratory test tubes and testing on animal subjects

Perhaps the baby boomers who have just begun to reach 50 years of age will awaken politicians to the necessity of scientific aging research. This youth-worshipping and age-fearing generation will be increasingly influential in the coming years even as one and all, some 76,000,000 strong, they meet on the most intimate level the potentially marring degenerative diseases of aging. Will they then perceive the need for research into methods and techniques of prevention, shifting emphasis from the medical model of fighting disease to the health model of wellness?

It is a realization devoutly to be wished.

Charles H. Mayo MD, founder of the great clinic that bears his name, said over and again: "The prevention of disease today is one of the most important factors in the line of human endeavor." He would have been delighted with the testing of the drug tamoxifen on 13,000 women judged at high risk for breast cancer. Commenting on the resulting successful reduction of the cancer, almost 50%, Richard D. Klausner MD, director of the National Cancer Institute, said flatly: "The results are remarkable. They tell us that breast cancer can be prevented."

ANNUAL MEDICAL TESTS
RECOMMENDED FOR PERSONS 65+

Blood (including cholesterol and glucose)
Electrocardiagram
Eyes (including vision and glaucoma)
Hypertension
Occult Blood in Stool
Physical Examination
Sigmoidoscopy (at 5 years after 2 annual consecutive negative tests)
Stress
Teeth and Gums
Urinalysis

For Females	For Males
Breast palpation	Prostate
Mammography	
Pap Smear	

RELIGION

*I say the whole earth and all the stars
in the sky are for religion's sake.*

Walt Whitman

Because the spiritual dimension is beyond the scope of direct empirical investigation, the therapeutic potential of spirituality in general and religion in particular has been neglected in the Amerian health-care system, which has become increasingly technologically oriented and impersonally administered. Walter M. Bortz II, MD, the highly respected former head of the American Geriatrics Society, points out "that there is a spiritual, psychologic belief-system component to all human illness. . . . a belief system which is the fundamental wellspring of life." "Physicians," he adds, "see illness as a circumscribed technical event and forget the other."

Yet research indicates that belief in religion and acceptance of its meanings correlate with increased physical and mental health and a lower incidence of disease. "We cannot prove scientifically that God heals, but we can prove that *belief* in God has a beneficial effect," maintains D.A. Matthews, MD, Associate Professor of Medicine, Georgetown University. A recent study by researchers at the University of Dartmouth Medical School discovered that among 232 elderly heart patients, the death rate in the first 6 months after surgery was significantly lower for those finding "strength and comfort" in religion. Epidemiologists at the Public Health Institute, having studied the effects of religious observance on 5,000 persons for over 3 decades, concluded that those who attended service once a week or more had lower death rates than did occasional churchgoers. Researchers also found that regular congregants who had begun attending church service while practicing poor health habits were more likely than infrequent churchgoers to improve their lifestyle by cutting back on alcohol, quitting smoking and engaging in exercise.

In times of stress or crisis, religion is a source of comfort to those who in faith accept its teachings because it gives meaning to life and provides a structure of behavior to follow. Gradually, attention is being drawn to relationships between spiritual belief and physical and mental health. Johns Hopkins University School of Medicine now offers a course in how doctors can make helpful use of patients' religious commitment.

Human beings possess physiological, psychological, social and spiritual aspects, which–interdependent, commingled and interacting–make up the context of the whole person. Even atheists feel that they are part of something infinitely greater than their individual selves Whether in industrialized countries or in third-world nations, people need love and meaning to bring justification to life with its intractable complications, problems, obstacles. Belief in supernatural causation, as magic and taboos, is common in Africa, Asia and Latin America and can mimic disease and lead to death. Somewhat analogous is what in the West is called psychogenic disease, in which a person who feels helpless and hopeless becomes so depressed that illness and even death result.

No longer central to the life of Western society, power of religious institutions has been steadily eroded and replaced in large part by empiricism and scientific "truths." Value systems based on worldly ambition and secular self-concern prevail. As religious symbols of eternity deteriorate, life on earth becomes ever more precious. Religion no longer provides the only framework for understanding life and death. Even rituals, such as mourning rites, are now shaped to a large extent not by religious custom but by norms from the world of business.

Nevertheless, religion remains important, especially to the elderly. Religion takes many forms, but essentially it is a system of belief and ritual by means of which people worship the supernatural and respond to and make sense of what they feel is sacred. Religion with its emphasis on humankind as a family is profoundly social. Belief in life after death provides reassurances of survival and feelings of solace and continuity. Is there any wonder that many elderly for whom time and death make up a daily frame of reference have a heightened religious consciousness in old age?

The great psychoanalyst, Carl G. Jung, said that the majority of religions are complicated systems of education for death, part of a universal quest to make death acceptable by explaining why people die. Some philosophers, maintaining that in the major religions the meaning of existence is found in answers to questions of final causes and ultimate ends of man and the universe, agree that the prevailing purpose of religion is preparation for death. Theologians point out that religion awakens the latent spirituality within many persons who then feel that they are part of something infinitely greater than the individual self: the body may die, but the soul survives as part of the eternal. They add that religion provides a supportive environment especially important for the old whose close awareness of mortality raises ethical and theological issues. Certainly a doctor's attitude toward death, whether the physician is religious or not, determines to a large extent treatment of elderly patients.

Historically, belief in heaven and hell was a way to create security in a largely unstable and unfair world. Religion helped people orient themselves to disaster, disease and death—inevitable experiences of human existence. Today, many late-life adults have not become unbelievers. National studies conducted by such organizations as the Princeton Religion Research Center reveal the extent of religious involvement among America's seniors. More elderly in the United States belong to a church than to any other kind of voluntary agency. About half of all those 65+ attend church in an average week. About the same percentage state that trust and faith in God combined with prayer are coping strategies they rely on when facing major life events. Nearly 1 in 4 older adults prays on a regular basis, and about the same number read parts of the Bible daily.

Surveys reveal that women show a significantly higher level of religious behavior than men. Researchers have also found higher levels of religious involvement among ethnic elderly than among Whites. Blacks affiliate with Protestant churches, and Hispanics remain with Catholic churches.

The attempt to find help in dealing with physical misfortune and to obtain direction and meaning in life is a never-ending spiritual journey. One of the commonest questions of the elderly (Why have I lived?) is essentially a spiritual query. Some old people find relief and consolation in philosophy; others, in religion. Some elderly rely on study, reflection and self-exploration; others, on religious organizations with prayer meetings and retreats. Radio and television have made religious programs available to everyone, so that physical church attendance is not the sole sign of religious activity.

Although few clerics have received pastoral training in dealing with needs of older parishioners, the elderly in religious organizations more than in any other type of social institution, are likely to develop friendships and to find other resources for help in alleviating loneliness, lessening despair, accepting the losses of age, developing compensatory values giving meaning to life and mitigating fear of death. Many elderly tell researchers that religion has become increasingly helpful to them as they age. Church-sponsored service to the elderly, such as visits from youngsters, is commonplace. The disabled can expect to be visited regularly by a member of the clergy. Researchers have consistently found that among many elderly successful personal adjustment is closely related to religious activities and attitudes.

Early Christian tradition going back to St. Augustine regarded aging and death as direct results of original sin, of disobedience to God's ways by Adam and Eve. Protestant theology challenged this view as a corruption and declared it null and void. For Jews, as *Genesis* makes clear, life is good and long life is esteemed. *Deuteronomy* regards long life as a reward for adherence to the Covenant. *Proverbs* considers old age to be a ripening into maturity. Jews have always respected the elderly and early on came to consider care of the aged as a community concern. Islam accepts the Bible but points out that old age is accompanied by losses that destroy human beings. Like the Bible, the Koran directs children to be kind and respectful to aged parents. Unfortunately, as in the Western world, negative images of the elderly are commonplace in Islamic culture. This despite the fact that throughout history and everywhere on the globe religious figures have been depicted in statuary and painting as older persons.

As with so much else in medical treatment of the elderly, two of the more important keys to success are tolerance and acceptance without prejudgment. Doctors often do not listen responsively to spiritual questions from elderly patients—whether from a desire to remain religiously neutral or to avoid imposing their own views and beliefs. Yet the original oath taken by Hippocrates, considered the father of medicine, contains the pledge: "I will keep pure and holy both my life and my art." Permitting an older patient to benefit from orientation and belief in religion and its practices can be therapeutic for the patient as well as an aid to practitioners of mainstream scientific biomedicine.

Religion provides a moral compass for elderly believers to steer by along life's paths. Often, religious custom, behavior and belief support a subjective sense of well-being, a deep feeling that life is meaningful and good, despite an accumulation of chronic health problems. Call it the placebo effect. Call it what you will, say the researchers. Religious elderly seem less vulnerable to the hurt caused by stress. Faith and religious observance attendance enhance a person's sense of well-being.

"There are more things in heaven and earth," said Hamlet, "than are dreamt of in your philosophy." Einstein concurred, insisting that "Science without religion is lame. . . ."

RETIREMENT

We rarely find a man who can say he has lived happy and
who, content with his life, can retire from the world like a
satisfied guest.

Horace

Availability of retirement to masses of people distinguishes old age in
the 21st century from that of any previous era. Retirement today may
last for 20 or more years, a major portion of an older adult's life.

But retirement as it is known today does not appeal to everyone.
There are different ways of looking at retirement. Most people consider retirement as a period of leisure starting with the end of full-time
employment reached through attainment of an age limit and receipt of
a pension, public and/or private. Popular views regard retirement as an
entitlement, an earned right after years of labor, as a well-earned rest,
as an opportunity for self-indulgence. Hostile economists have called it
disguised unemployment; political scientists, creation of an enormous
leisure class. Christian theologians have attacked concepts of retirement as encouraging self-centered values and pastimes. Gerontologists
have referred to it as a roleless role.

A historical accident, specification of 65 as the beginning age for
retirement has been replaced with more flexible policies. Bismarck, by
adding 20 years to the life expectancy of his era, set 65 as the year
workers might begin receiving a pension. Were that specification applied today, retirement would start well after 95! The majority of Social
Security beneficiaries now legally retire before 65, many as early as 62.
Federal Law 98-21, passed in 1983, raises the retirement age to 66 as of
2009, to 67 as of 2027, seemingly judicious choices in view of the
likelihood of increased life expectancy and longevity. Pension plans,
health benefits and legislation influence retirement patterns. Recent Congressional action has outlawed mandatory retirement based on age for
most workers not yet 70 and has increased Social Security benefits for
delayed retirement past 65. In the main, older workers, already eligible

for retirement, do not apply for disability benefits. Social Security disability programs, however, do continue to provide a bridge for younger workers seeking to retire.

Differences in retirement trends of older Americans are dramatic. Blue collar workers tend to retire as soon as possible, not so professionals. The labor force participation rate for full-time work has dropped about 30% for men 60-64; about 40% for men 65-69; about 50% for men 70+. In contrast, women continue to work: for females 60+ the labor participation rate for full-time work has hardly changed. For women the significant predictor of retirement is not pensions but older age. Statistics for part-time work reveal a much different situation. The proportion of men 65+ working part-time has grown from just under 40% in 1970 to just under 50% today. For women the growth is from about 50% to about 60%. Such statistics indicate that the trend toward early retirement may not persist. Will there be a reversal of retirement patterns, with people continuing to work after age 62 or moving into second careers? The answer will become clear as the baby boomers age.

Why the shift to earlier voluntary retirement? Reasons are primarily economic although it is obvious that the quality of retirement years depends to a large degree on a person's state of health and fitness. Because retired persons who fare best have pensions in addition to Social Security, Congress with the Employee Retirement Security Act of 1974 (ERISA) aimed at insuring such extra benefits for all workers. Another innovative step occurred in 1975 with establishment of Individual Retirement Accounts (IRA), which permitted setting aside for retirement a portion of annual income, tax deferred.

The first generation to spend an entire working career under coverage of Social Security arrived at a retirement age in the 1980's, having also benefited from growth of private pensions, from the post WW II boom in real wages and disposable income and from the sharp rise in real estate prices. Each succeeding cohort of workers received higher benefits, even as their assets increased from higher yields in financial markets and perhaps from larger amounts of personal savings. (Although income may decline with age, evidence suggests that older people retain or increase their assets. The overwhelming majority of the elderly hold assets primarily in the form of home equity.)

There has been an enormous growth in private pension programs albeit without enough protection through government supervision. The percentage of total retirement income made available through pensions has been steadily increasing. About 2/3 of the baby boomers approaching 50 years of age are covered by some type of employee benefit plan. In contrast to today's elderly they will on retirement probably receive a higher percentage of income from pensions despite the present-day trend toward shifting away from their employer or union and onto them responsibility for financial risk and future benefits.

Both Social Security and private pension plans contain retirement incentives for many workers, in that they know in advance approximately what their benefits will be. The worker eligible for retirement has a choice between immediate cessation of work with a smaller payout or a delay with a larger annual compensation after retirement. Either situation may mean a pay cut, a definite decrease in net compensation. It is advisable for an individual to consult an accountant to determine which situation is the better.

Although never intended to be the only source of income in retirement, Social Security today constitutes the elderly's single most important source of economic support. This was not the original intention as President Roosevelt pointed out at the signing of the Social Security Act in 1935: "we have tried to frame a law which will give some measure of protection . . . against poverty-ridden old age." Subsequently, Congress introduced in Social Security a critical element of financial stability through automatic increases to parallel rises in cost of the standard of living, so that workers contemplating retirement feel protected against financial disaster, including inflation. They need not worry about financial support for their spouse since Social Security has a survivor benefit.

Even so, workers who desire to maintain their pre-retirement lifestyle would be well advised to consult an accountant or financial planner about beginning personal savings early and continuing saving after retirement. The cost of maintaining a pre-retirement lifestyle in retirement is about 70% of pre-tax income. Retirees can become economically vulnerable. The period of life spent receiving pensions is lengthening. Workers retiring at 62 today have a life expectancy of 20-30 years, with the incidence of disability rising alongside age. As retirees age, income and ability to build additional assets diminish because inflation and other factors remain beyond their control.

Retirees with employer-provided health care benefits should not assume that such aid is absolutely guaranteed for the future. Unless an employer has contracted in writing to continue services, nothing in federal law prevents reducing or eliminating them. In recent years, some major corporations have done just that as a way of containing ever- rising medical costs.

The United States Department of Labor's Pension and Welfare Benefits Administration warns that the legal terminology in a health-benefit document plan is not always easy for lay people to interpret. It is advisable for a worker before retirement to have an attorney experienced and competent in this area go over the contractual provisions to determine whether or not the employer has guaranteed without modification continuation of benefits for the life of the worker. The Labor Department recommends that employees who are retired and are concerned about retirement health benefits or in dispute with employers, consult a union representative and/or an experienced labor attorney.

While there is no reason to assume that current retirement patterns are permanent, there is reason to assume that shortages of workers will develop in the 21st century. Retirement by age 65 has become the rule. The Bureau of the Census estimates that the number of Americans 65+ will increase from about 12% of the total population today to about 22% by the year 2030. The ratio of the number of working age population, 18-64, to those eligible for retirement, 62+, will drop from today's 5:1 to tomorrow's less than 3:1. Since much of the decision to retire is based on financial incentives, older workers may easily be enticed into remaining on the job by employers willing to make work economically attractive. Obviously, retirement and hiring policies of the old will need to be reexamined. Meanwhile, the elderly constitute our greatest unutilized human resource.

The route to retirement for a large minority of workers is not straightforward. There has been much bridge employment, that is, part-time employment in a new line of work at lower pay. Some of this type of job-changing as a result of retirement is voluntary. Some is involuntary, the result of the downsizing of numerous corporations. AT&T in 1996 announced the pending dismissal of more than 40,000 employees. There is no doubt that older workers, displaced through downsizing, face restricted job opportunities.

The nature and meaning of retirement have changed with the years. Polls taken in the late 1950's indicate that many workers, no longer fearing health, social and economic problems after retirement, expected the period following their work years to be on the whole a pleasurable state. They looked forward to engaging in beloved activities for which they previously did not have time. (Contrary to accepted stereotypes, as a visit to a retirement community with its numerous challenging activities will reveal, most retirees do not attempt to while away the days sitting on a bench.) By the early 1960's there was a definite trend toward voluntary retirement. By the 1980's more retirements were voluntary than involuntary. By 1990, only about 15% of males and 7% of females 65+ had not retired from work.

Yet sociologists estimate that 1 in 3 new retirees has trouble adjusting. Many admit to problems with anxiety and depression. The eminent psychologist Erik Erikson noted that "the separation from the work setting often removes the individual from those circumstances in which he or she learned to demonstrate competence and initiative." While retirement planning should begin early, detailed planning ought to begin around age 50. Counseling before and after the date of retirement helps alleviate difficulties.

In an effort to help workers adjust to retirement, many corporations are giving employees the option of phased retirement, allowing them to start reducing their weekly work hours a year or two before permanently leaving the work force. Those workers needing money after retiring face annoying problems of age discrimination, even in looking for part-time jobs. Some dread loss of status and of relationships made at work, which furnished additional benefits by providing a role and somewhere to go with useful things to do and think about. To a large extent, work regulated their activities, providing a sense of identity and social standing in the community. At home, retirement puts additional strains on the marriage relationship: neither wife nor husband any longer has exclusive access to time and territory for much of the day. At retirement, most persons do not relocate. Many of those who do move away suffer from stress of adjusting to a new environment and remaining in control of all aspects of the move, such as purchase of housing and making new friends.

Availability of activities for use of time and of opportunities for socializing are pivotal factors in assuring satisfaction and a high quality of meaningful life during the retirement years despite the inevitable losses of old age occasioned by chronic disease, functional decline and death of friends and loved ones. Both government-operated senior centers and retirement communities furnish a variety of opportunities, as do local organizations in communities throughout the nation. The Commonweath Fund's study in the early 1990s found that more than 80% of those 55+ and more than 50% of those 75+ are involved in volunteer activities, either with organizations or with direct care given to families and neighbors.

The present system of employment is set up for short lifetimes. Longevity increases will certainly prolong the typical period of retirement. Resulting questions have not as yet been answered. At the individual level, retirement marks the end of one stage in the life cycle. But period lines appear to be blurring. What stage will follow? Will second careers become more attractive? At the industrial level, retirement increases the number of people in economically non-productive roles. At the societal level, will retirees be considered drones marking time or as productive persons with definite contributions to make for the welfare of all? In partial recognition of the situation, Congress passed the Amended Age Discrimination Act of 1978 and made mandatory retirement illegal for most workers.

By making use of sabbaticals will those elderly who do not want to stop working be able to enjoy a mix of work and leisure? What provisions can be made for the involvement and participation of the elderly in society? What role will educational institutions play? If the rate of disease rises with age, what will happen to the economic status of those persons 65+? Lifetime savings can easily be depleted by prolonged illness.

Since World War II, increasing numbers of women have joined the labor force. Before the war, husbands retired and their mates continued to regard themselves as housewives. Currently, a clear majority of women 65+ consider themselves retirees rather than housewives. Will married women, usually younger than their mates, continue to work after their husbands have retired?

Relatively little is known of circumstances after retirement today by both husbands and wives. Couples generally apply at or near the same time for retirement. Will women, more likely than men to outlive their spouses, be able to maintain their retirement lifestyle, or will they fall below the poverty line and live in substandard housing?

Because salaries of women are still lower than men's, their incomes after retirement are relatively low, accounting for the poor morale of many single retired women. The situation appears to be changing for the better, but progress is slow. AARP analyst Evelyn Morton maintains that in 1998 "8,000,000 million Americans 65 and older, or 25%, live[d] below or within 150% of the poverty line."

Much more useful information will become available from the federally sponsored Health and Retirement Study, begun in 1992, with its wide-ranging scope and immense sampling size, as economists and demographers track medical and economic conditions of middle-aged Americans so as to gauge private and public resources needed as the last age group born during the Depression enters old age and moves into retirement. Data collected will help political leaders seeking to realistically shape government policies and programs aimed at the rapidly increasing population of the elderly while taking into account the proportionately fewer workers who will be available to pay the costs. Already, Social Security, Medicare and Medicaid benefits to the elderly account for more than 1/3 of federal spending. Added to interest on the national debt, sums expended for such entitlement programs might exhaust the entire federal budget by 2012, so warned a bipartisan congressional commission in 1994. Hopefully, the politicians will act well before then.

What will happen to society if increasing numbers have nothing constructive to do in retirement, if people in succeeding generations who could be producers are dependents instead?

THE SENSES

My heart thanked God for the goodly gift of sight
And all youth's lively senses keen and quick. . . .

Wilfred Wilson Gibson

The senses receive and react to stimuli, as an odor or sound, by means of specific bodily mechanisms or structures called sensory receptors, which make possible communication between human beings and pass information about the physical world necessary to survival on to the central nervous system and thence to the brain, where it is comprehended. The senses are commonly thought of as a group of 5: hearing, sight, smell, taste, touch. But there are other senses, as kinesthesia (awareness of the position and movement of body and limbs in space), temperature discernment and experience of pain.

The senses tend to decline somewhat from the second decade of life although rates of change vary considerably and none of the changes appears to be inevitable. Further research is needed to gain a full understanding of sensory loss in old age. On average, as people age the losses are small but increase in effect with the passing years. The sensory system of a healthy older person remains robust although more intense stimuli may be needed to arouse some sensory receptors: stronger flavors, brighter lights, pungent smells, louder sounds, heavier touch. While perception and recognition of odors do diminish, awareness of alkaline, bitter, metallic, salty, sour and sweet tastes in foods remains relatively strong—with sweet generally the best preserved.

When disorders of taste (gustation) and smell (olfaction) occur among the elderly, inadequate intake of essential nutrients may result, but the disorders are usually not incapacitating or life-threatening. Not so with dysfunction in hearing, kinesthesia, sight, touch. Caused by changes in muscles and the central nervous system, the lessened ability to orient the body in space may result in falls or difficulty in walking. Sensory symptoms should not be disregarded because they may result from serious systemic or intracranial malfunctioning. Whether minor or severe, sensory impairment has a strong impact on quality of life of the elderly.

Losses in vision and hearing are among the most common untoward conditions of the elderly. By age 80, only about 1 in 10 will retain 20/20 visual acuity even with eyeglasses. (Risks and causes of visual impairment are discussed in *Vision,* pp. 416-422). Probably 95% of sensory stimuli reaching the brain come through the eyes, making possible orientation in the 3-dimensional world which surrounds human beings and, in addition, something unique in the animal kingdom: conversion of writing into images, so that communication of thought can take place over time.

Hearing also is important to communication. Yet by age 80, more than 1 in 3 persons suffer from hearing impairment. Authorities agree that periodic screening for impairment may go far in helping to prevent permanent hearing disability but not for people persistently exposed to such noisy environments as high-decibel rock-and-roll concerts. While researchers have not been able to greatly enlarge knowledge of the human auditory system, they have made possible technological advances to help hearing-impaired elderly. (Helpful devices as well as problems with the auditory system are discussed in *Hearing,* pp. 363-367).

Many researchers think that loss in ability to smell is due to age-related physiological changes, while for loss of taste development of medical conditions is more important. Studies of changes in taste and smell are often difficult to interpret, and not all studies are in agreement.

The senses of taste and smell not only provide pleasure; they give warning of danger, as with spoiled food or the ingestion of poisons. While taste declines with age are usually modest at first, olfactory impairment may be severe. By age 80, smell detection ability in most men and women has declined about 50% as contrasted with what it was in young or middle age. Odors are less intense and more difficult to identify. Because taste and smell are physiologically interdependent, trouble in one often affects the other but not necessarily. Olfactory disturbance can involve either loss or reduction of smell or increased sensitivity to pleasant or disagreeable odors.

Oral hygiene, dental health, texture and visual appearance of food may impact on taste, and lifelong dietary preference may influence it. Ordinary foods people eat in India would be considered by Americans too sour to be edible. Loss of dentition and wearing of dentures also play a role in diminishing taste perception. Smoking and some drugs (vicristine is but one example) can alter or impair taste. Scientists do not fully understand the sensory basis of flavor, and they caution that not all findings concerning taste are conclusive. Although the tongue begins to atrophy with age, the number and sensitivity of tastebuds apparently continue unchanged. But it is obvious that declines in taste and smell, which cause old people to complain that food does not taste the way it used to, can result in lack of interest in food and in weight loss and malnutrition. One way of possibly enhancing taste is by taking a mouthful of food, chewing and then exhaling through the nose with the mouth closed, so that vapors enter the nasal cavity and contact olfactory sensors there.

Much more research is needed if changes associated with aging in regard to the senses are to be dealt with adequately. Too often, as in studies of kinesthesia, pain, temperature and touch, findings are inconclusive. In general, the sensation of touch (including feelings of vibration and pressure) diminishes slightly with age, as does realization of pain and temperature. Receptors for touch and pain are located throughout the body but primarily in the skin, whose surface makes up the largest sensory organ in the body. Pain can be caused by cold, heat, pressure, punctures, scratches. Those elderly suffering from an impairment of postural control and with a history of falls often have a higher threshold of tactile perception than what is regarded as normal.

But, as Napoleon remarked of taste and the palate, a person's senses "can, in time, become accustomed to anything."

SEX

*The omnipresent process of sex, as it is woven
into the whole texture of a man's or woman's
body, is the pattern of all the process of our life.*

Havelock Ellis

Contrary to accepted stereotypes, the sexual dimension remains important in old age. Desire for an intimate relationship, physically oriented, with a person of the opposite sex continues throughout the lifespan. The National Council on Aging's 1998 survey that almost half of the elderly report they are sexually active was greeted publicly with surprise. But sex is a basic drive. The fact is: no one had previously surveyed that age group.

Sexual activity is conducive to mental and physical health in later years. More than a source of physical pleasure, performance of sex bonds a marital relationship. Psychologists who have studied long-married couples report that with increasing age much more attention is given to the woman's affectional roles than to her functions as housewife or as manager of the domestic economy. After health, love is the single most important determinant of the outlook on life of elderly married men. Married couples with an intrinsically-valued relationship can enjoy old age as a time of sexual rediscovery.

Single men and women 65+, believing that incidence of sexually transmitted disease is quite low among the elderly, do not have the same fear as the young of contracting herpes or AIDS although the number of AIDS cases is rising–particularly in cities. As the baby boomers enter mid-life, some are paying a price for earlier sexual behavior when promiscuity seemed risk free. Recognizing the danger, the AARP produced in 1996 a video focused on AIDS and the elderly.

There are other and much different problems for the vast majority of older persons. Despite changes in sexual morality for young adults leading to more open sensual behavior, cultural expectations regarding old-age-appropriate behavior have developed into a pervasive system of hurtful restrictrive norms. A generation or two ago sexuality did not create problems for the elderly. With advances in longevity have come fallacies, misconceptions, myths, stereotypes and taboos. Sexual attraction between older men and women does not look ridiculous. It is a fiction that only dirty old men are interested in sex. Men do not naturally lose their capacity for erection. The appeal of sex does not decline in women at the end of their procreative years. Women continue to be interested in sex. Men and women do not tend to become neuter. This side of 100, there is no decade in which sexual interest and activity of men and women is completely absent.

Society has discarded many taboos concerning sexuality of young adults but kept proscriptions against sexuality in old age. The very idea that normal elderly have sexual drives, fantasies and intercourse is anathema. The old are regarded as gender-neutral. Children of widowed parents discourage remarriage. What age prejudice regards as virility at 25 becomes lechery at 65. The humorist Sam Levinson said: "When I first found out how babies were born, I couldn't believe it. To think that my father and mother would do such a thing." Then, after a pause, he added: "My father, maybe, but my mother–never!" What fun Levinson could have had with today's situation, now that the sexual revolution of the 1960s has reached the general population. "Imagine," he might say, "the disapproving clucks of oldest-old parents 85+ about their liberated young-old children 65+ engaging in non-marital sexual adventures, such as *swinging,* amid the eroticization of everyday life!"

Much of the sexual dissatisfaction of the elderly stems from opinions of appropriate behavior held by the young and from health difficulties. Many old people, accepting the negative stereotype of the aged as desiccated, desexed individuals, tend to comply with it. They accept without complaint invasion of privacy, a common infraction, whether within their family or in a nursing home or less formal institution. Numerous medications prescribed for the elderly, such as the anti-hypertensives, have sexual dysfunction side effects not mentioned by too many medical personnel.

Generally, frequency of sexual intercourse depends solely on male desire, older women following the cultural norm by tending to be more concerned with their appearance, as with removing the growth of facial hair, than with sexual capability.

Judith Viorst writes:

> It's hard to be devil-may-care
> When there are pleats in your derriere. . . .
> It's hard to surrender to sin
> While trying to hold your stomach in.

Dryness and thinning of the vaginal wall may be sources of intense discomfort to the female during coital thrusting by the male. Motor symptoms of Parkinson's and joint deformation from arthritis may make intercourse difficult but not impossible. Arthritics, particularly, soon learn how to position themselves, as the woman lying in bed with a pillow under the hips while the man standing faces her. Many older men, unaware that with age the sexual response slows, do not take the time needed for arousal and reaching climax. Resulting anxiety over performance may cause episodes of impotency. So, too, overindulgence in food and alcoholic drinks can interfere with a man's potency, as can marijuana, tranquilizers, diabetes, obesity. At times of erection difficulties, many older couples enjoy mutual stroking of penis and clitoris.

Fear of any kind can make a man temporarily impotent and a woman unable to enjoy intercourse. In the aftermath of a heart attack, fear may keep either or both husband and wife from sexual expression despite the fact that death as a consequence of intercourse is quite rare. Intercourse uses no more energy than that expended climbing a short flight of stairs. Although, barring illness, men are fertile throughout the life span, the husband usually because of ignorance as to how the body works becomes sexually incapacitated first, leaving the wife to act as caregiver, with resentment to follow.

Religious and social proscription against autoeroticism has eroded.

Once considered a perversion and a cause of mental illness, masturbation is now acknowledged by physicians as well as psychologists to be a normal sexual activity throughout life for anyone of either sex. Almost all males have masturbated, and at least 4 of 5 females. Masturbation is now recognized as a healthy act in later life not only because it serves as a substitute for those without partners but also because it is a gentle source of sex for the infirm. Masturbation is particularly beneficial for widowers who would otherwise find it difficult to restart after a period of total abstinence from sexual activity. But masturbation is a supplement to coital intercourse that is of value to women as to men both as sexual outlet and source of pleasure. Chance of an unmarried older woman finding a sex partner is small.

As with so much else in aging, there are physiological and psychological changes in regard to sex. Both sexes retain capacity for pleasure in the role of sexual partner. Biologically, men encounter more drawbacks. Socially, women suffer more disadvantages because of the double standard wherein they are devalued as physically unattractive. Older men tend to marry younger women; older women tend to be widowed and not remarry. Vaginal dryness and urethral inflammation occur in the female. But water-based soluble preparations can help lubricate a dry vagina, and more frequent intercourse encourages production of estrogen that will help moisten female sexual tissue. Apparently, sex is a natural Kegel exercise: women who have regular sex relations have less difficulty with problems of mild urinary incontinence. The male, because of reduced blood flow in the penis, needs more stimulation and time to achieve erection, and he will not be able to have another erection for several hours or days whereas in the past just watching his wife undress was enough to arouse him on a nightly basis. Although capacity for erection is not lost with age, emission of seminal fluid is lessened and the pleasure from ejaculation is diminished. Some men may experience orgasm without ejaculation, a disturbing experience to anyone not prepared for it. Most males have at least one temporary but unexplained period of as much as five days when they cannot perform. If they do not give way to anxiety, there is no cause for concern. Even sexual dysfunctions, such as age-related erectile difficulties generally are susceptible to treatment, especially today with new medications such as Viagra.

There are many successful devices and approaches sex therapists have to offer. When not enjoyable, sex can become so through medical and/or psychological therapy. The major age changes in the healthy male are in amount and character of stimulation needed to produce an erection and in the lengthening of the refractory phase. In contrast, the post-menopausal female, free from concerns with menstruation and possible pregnancy, more easily reaches orgasm than ever before. Unhampered by a refractory phase, she maintains the capacity of orgasmic response typical of her younger years.

Sexuality in both sexes endures better than many other bodily systems. In surveys, about 75% of persons 65+ report being sexually active, about 50% of those 75+, about 10% of those 85+, and some men in their 90s state that they are still sexually active.

Sadly, many women in their 60s and 70s have vital sexual feelings but almost no means for expression.

There is a paucity of reliable information on the sexual activity of elderly single men and women. *The Internet Yellow Pages* lists organizations with up-to-date information about how to reach unmarried late-life adults.

There is little research on aging homosexuals, even less on aging lesbians. A broad study of the impact of aging on homosexuals is R.M. Berger's *Gay and Gray: The Older Homosexual Man* (Ill.: Univ.of Illinois Press, 1982; reprinted, Allyson Pubs., 1984), which reports a relatively high level of satisfaction and acceptance of self growing older. As M. Kehoe reports in *Lesbians Over Sixty Speak for Themselves* (N.Y.: Harrington Park Press, 1989), most lesbian elderly appear to want a steady love relationship with strong friendship ties. There are several dozen organizations formed by and for aging homosexuals and lesbians to help them cope with the challenge of growing older. Senior Action in a Gay Environment in New York City, Legacy in Chicago and the National Association of Lesbian and Gay Gerontologists in San Francisco provide education and counseling services and issue newsletters.

Human sexuality does not begin and end with coition. Love exists on many levels. Knowledge of what to expect physiologically and psychologically makes possible a realistic, continually exciting relationship–emotionally fulfilling and physically satisfying.

Long-married couples enhance their old-age satisfaction with sex through direct communication. Men and women, they have learned, do not experience sexual activity in identical ways. Good sex, they know, requires discovering what pleases your mate and increases desire and passion. They welcome frank discussion of sexual concerns and needs. Aware that the ability of old men to have an erection peaks in the morning hours, they tend to have sexual intercourse early in the day.

Although it can result in mutual gratification for older couples, oral sex should not be insisted on if either partner is definitely averse or fearfully uneasy. Sex therapists advise that husband and wife think of the penis and the vulva as aesthetic as well as functional objects–fascinating in texture and erectility. Couples unaccustomed to oral sex, should shower first, so that pubis, penis and scrotum are not regarded as unclean. Genital kisses can make for pleasure. A woman inexperienced in oral sex should begin by taking only the tip of the penis into her mouth and passing her lips and tongue lightly around the ridge, afterward going on to explore. An inexperienced man should begin by kissimg her vulva, afterward going on to explore.

Over the years, the elderly have learned that the popular conception of love as intense desire characterized by passionate physical activity climaxed in simultaneous orgasm is naive and simplistic. With age, the act of making love invariably changes. But that does not mean sexual activity dies. Nature imposes no age limit on an active sex life.

For healthy couples, the satisfying of sexual desires usually continues into their 70s and 80s, especially if sex made for valuable experiences in their earlier years and they have kept their sense of humor. With Arthur Guiterman they know when not to take life too seriously:

> Amoebas at the start
> Were not complex;
> They tore themselves apart
> And started sex.

Sex in old age is softer, calmer. For mature adults, coitus is not the only condition of sexual activity. The elderly know from experience that if sexuality does not exist between the ears it will not endure between the legs, that intercourse between the sexes consists of shared pleasure, a special kind of intimate, caring, meaningful communication,often achieved through talking and touching and caressing and affirming feelings of attraction to one another. Friendship, a sense of play, respect, tenderness and trust are significant qualities. Sexual enjoyment does not depend solely on genital performance. Quality, not quantity, matters. Emotional and relationship characteristics, as well as sensual, give import to sexual expression.

It is improbable that the baby boomers and succeeding generations of older adults will let themselves be proscribed by socially imposed norms. Free to find their own forms of sexual gratification, they will say with Goethe, the great German poet:

> *So, lively brisk old man [and woman]*
> *Do not let sadness come over you;*
> *For all your white hairs*
> *You can still be a lover!*

SKIN

. . . arm impregnably the skin.

Ralph Waldo Emerson

Appearance of skin is a good general indicator of age. Skin changes by the time of old age, more common in sun-exposed face and hands of Caucasians, include dryness, brown spots, loss of elasticity, roughness, shrinking of the underlying cushion of fat, thinning and wrinkling. (Skin in unexposed areas, such as the buttocks, remains elastic, smooth and soft.) Over the years, continual pulling and pushing of facial skin into such expressions as smiles and frowns result in creases and furrows. A decreased sweating response results in poor heat management; and decreased sensory perception results in poor cold management, especially as regards shivering to create warmth. Ability of the skin to synthesize Vitamin D decreases. Fingernails become fragile and easily torn while longitudinal striations appear. Toenails discolor from fungal infections. Hair changes may cause cosmetic problems, as a genetically linked condition produces a receding hairline in men and thinning hair in women. In men, brittle hair appears in and on ears and nose. In women, there is an increase of fairly dark hair on the upper lip and chin but a decrease in hair on head and pubis.

The skin of older men looks younger than that of older women because testosterone, a key male hormone, assists men's skin in staying elastic, thereby delaying wrinkling on average about a decade after women. Men have a thicker, oilier skin that resists sun damage better than women's skin does. Thin skin is vulnerable to frequent and cumulative injury. Nevertheless, the elderly body can repair, even if only partially, extensively wounded skin but not malignant melanoma.

Elderly men get more malignant melanoma and are more likely to die from the cancer, perhaps because men have more sun-exposed jobs and because they do not detect the disease in early stages as well as women do. It is wise for both sexes to check for quick-growing moles and to have the doctor at the annual physical look for unusual skin spots. Men in particular should have a friend or spouse periodically examine skin on the back, for it is there that the cancer is likely to start in males. Women should inspect legs carefully for rough patches and unusual moles, for it is there that the cancer is likely to start in females.

Even small doses of sunlight repeated a few minutes at a time may contribute to making skin look old. Everyone should avoid unnecessary exposure to the sun, making sure to wear sunscreen of at least SPF 15 on the skin when outdoors. But sunscreens, as is explained below, may provide a false sense of security about how much sun a person can safely get. Safer are physical blockers like white pastes of titanium or zinc oxide.

Federally sponsored studies of more than 20,000 noninstitutionalized elderly indicate that at one time or another about 40% suffer from a skin disorder severe enough to occasion examination by a doctor. As a result, researchers recommend that a **complete** skin inspection be part of the periodical physical examination of everyone 65+. But even common skin disorders are so different in the elderly that diagnosis is frequently difficult and the cause of the disorder often unrecognized. Caucasians develop dozens to hundreds of tan to dark papules (elevations of skin), while blacks develop darker papules early on. Such lesions are benign and rarely require therapy. The most common type of skin cancer is basal cell carcinoma, slow-growing plaques often with ulceration, found most often in fair-skinned men in sunny climates. This cancer is quite rare in blacks and Orientals. Surgical excision is recommended as producing the highest rate of cure. Obviously, prevention involves reduction of exposure to sun.

A large number of skin disorders troubling the elderly are preventable or treatable. Intake of adequate amounts of fluid helps prevent skin deficiencies. By improving blood flow to the skin, exercise helps nourish collagen fibers. But the outer layers of skin are in actuality dead tissue, so that no amount of cosmetics applied can feed them. The ravages of sunlight, a notorious enemy of skin, can be diminished by use of sunscreens. This does not mean that a person can safely increase time in the sun. Sunscreens do not block all rays. If without a sunscreen you can stay in the sun for 10 minutes and with it you can manage to stay 3 hours, you are now getting 3 hours of intense ultraviolet radiation. The resulting color change is in response to skin damage which may be dangerous: there is no such thing as a healthy tan. To prevent serious sunburn, use a sunscreen and try to be outdoors only before 10:00 a.m. and after 3:p.m., for then the sun's rays are least intense.

With age, the skin produces less sebum (a fatty lubricant), leading to fissuring, irritation, itching, and scaling. Fissuring, cracks in the skin that appear usually on fingers, may be painful. They can be controlled with use of lubricating creams and mild corticosteroids. In general, it is wise for the elderly to apply skin ointment or oil liberally, especially in cold weather, and to use an indoor humidifier. Dry skin is the result of a loss of water. Oil helps hold water in. Ulcerated skin of the torso appears in those elderly with vascular disorders which restrict blood flow to the skin and/or those persons who are confined to bed or wheelchair. Frequent turning and use of special air pillows and mattresses reduce the incidence of this painful disorder. Surgical debridement, employment of special dressings and skin grafts may be necessary in severe situations.

Much is unknown about itching, the most common skin complaint of the aged, and a safe, completely effective anti-itch agent has not yet been found. Sudden onset of itching may indicate presence of gallstones, kidney or liver disease, thyroid disorders. Persistent itching may denote scabies. Any such condition should be checked promptly by a physician.

Even as skin tone changes, hair loses pigment. Melanin, the pigment that also colors eyes and skin, is not delivered to hair follicles of older persons. The result is that new hair growth is white or gray. There are fewer hairs, with a 10% decrease in density each decade. Individual hairs are thinner because they squeeze through shrinking follicles. Not much can be done although Rogaine, an FDA-approved treatment for hair loss, available over the counter, may help solve the problem. Dermatologists warn against overbrushing and overwashing.

SLEEP

Sleep that knits up the ravell'd sleeve of care,
The death of each day's life, sore labour's bath,
Balm of hurt minds, great nature's second course,
Chief nourisher in life's feast.

William Shakespeare

Many elderly, if not most persons 65+, have some sleep difficulty. Less than 15% of the total population, they purchase almost 1/2 of all over-the-counter sleep medications. Sometimes family members, believing that 8 hours of sleep are necessary for good health although in reality the amount needed varies from one person to the next, persist in recommending sedatives, inadvertently encouraging long-term psychological dependence of an older relative on drugs because initially the pills help in falling asleep. Most physicians agree that sleeping pills on a temporary basis can be useful if no psychiatric problems are present. If taken over a long period of time, many sleeping pills may perpetuate insomnia by interfering with normal sleep rhythms. Similarly, long-term reliance on alcohol decreases restful sleep and causes early awakening. Sedatives can cause falls. The extent of harm that can come from mixing prescribed medications with unprescribed is not known but the danger is real. With age people often absorb and excrete medications slowly. Most drugs are imprecise and wide in range of effect, aspirin, a common example, having multiple consequences. Almost 10% of hospital admissions of the elderly are due to adverse drug reactions.

While some psychologists state that from maturity to old age the decline of time spent sleeping is small, many elderly report that they sleep fewer than 7 hours a night, and awaken frequently. Very few, less than 2%, grouse that they get too much slumber. Anxiety and tension, which may be symptoms of depression, lessen ability to fall asleep and to stay asleep. Nocturia (urinating during the night), painful leg cramps and involuntary leg jerks are common. Although the mechanisms involved are poorly understood, a physician should be consulted about such disorders in case of complications. Otherwise, what people consider insomnia is usually nothing to worry about because it lasts a night or 2 and then disappears. But it is annoying–especially if after interruption a person is unable to return to deep sleep. In general, brief nightly awakenings do not block feelings of rest when a person awakens in the morning.

While sleep is undoubtedly needed for survival–enabling the body to rest, repair itself and refuel–the exact purpose remains obscure. But no one can do without it for long. Some psychologists postulate that sleep helps people to forget as well as to remember, to sort out the day's events and to discard the unneeded. The precise amount of sleep required by healthy individuals is unknown. Individual needs vary widely, from as little as four hours a night to as much as nine hours and more. Edison slept a little; Einstein, a lot.

Sleep deprivation, if prolonged, can be dangerous for the elderly, psychologically as well as physically. People of any age who routinely miss sleep are more prone to illness. In the case of the elderly, body systems, already under stress from chronic diseases, are adversely affected. Blood pressure may rise and the brain not function properly. Sufferers, unaware of adverse changes within, awaken in the morning sluggish, tired and irritable to the point that they do not think clearly. Stumbling and falls, leading causes of accidental injury and death among the old, can result, as can an unknowing family's decision to institutionalize a seemingly senile older relative.

At one time or another, virtually all the aged suffer from one or more so-called *sleep disorders,* an umbrella term health professionals use when referring to the kinds of sleep difficulty, from inability to fall asleep at night to frequent awakenings to the need for naps during the day. The elderly report sleep difficulties as frequently recurring. Older men sleep more poorly than women, but older women complain more than men of sleep problems. Sleep disturbances are a common side effect of prostate trouble in the male and of menopause in the female. Sleep time lost in this way is minimal, 3 minutes or a bit longer for each occurrence, but the victim after weeks or months of such nightly disturbance tends to need longer and longer periods of time to return to sleep after each interruption. Sometimes breathing during sleep ceases for a short time. Such episodes, called sleep apnea, occur repeatedly, in the old rather than the young. Not dangerous in the healthy elderly, such episodes are still under investigation as to causes.

Aside from the impact of physical and psychological difficulties, changes in sleep patterns and schedules seem to be a consistent and reliable sign of biological aging. There is an increase in number of nightly awakenings and of daytime naps. Generally, older persons prefer an earlier bedtime and a quite early (at least to the young who would sleep late if they were permitted) wake-up time. The various functions of the body are regulated by internal biological clocks called by scientists circadian rhythms. In regard to sleep, the body temperature sequence appears to be the marker for the nightly patterns of slumber. Because the temperature cycle tends to shorten with age, the elderly prefer the aforementioned early to bed and early to rise behavior. If the circadian rhythm is disrupted, so that an individual goes to bed too much before the usual time and wakes up far earlier in the morning, the biological clock can be reset by exposure to bright light, a procedure best performed by a physician specializing in sleep disorders.

One age-related sleep change seems to have predictive value. Statisticians report that elderly men who sleep less than 4 hours a night are some 3 times more likely to die within 6 years than those who sleep 7-8 hours a night. But there are no data documenting other adverse effects of sleep disruption in the elderly.

Physicians warn that any person 65+ having sleep problems for more than a month should have a thorough medical examination. Sleep is essential to emotional in addition to physical well-being. It is wise for the sufferer or someone close, either a relative or a caregiver, to keep if at all possible a log for at least two weeks prior to the checkup. The log should include pattern and hours of sleep, number and length of daytime naps, names of medications, type of nutrition and amount and time of exercise. Generally, the doctor will advise a normal, healthy adult 65+ that what needs to be done to get rid of minor sleep problems is to use the bed only for sleeping and not for reading, to reduce liquid intake at night, particularly caffeine and alcohol, to follow a regular sleep-wake schedule, to exercise early in the day and to avoid heavy meals late at night. If the doctor thinks that the sleep disturbance is related to a medical and/or psychological condition, the older patient may be referred to specialists who can determine proper treatment. Occasionally, the cause is found to be neither physiological nor psychological but mechanical: a lumpy or too hard or too soft or worn-out mattress. And the cure is in a visit to a reliable store.

Dr. William Dement, doyen of the modern field of sleep research, recommends that to sleep better a person should control noise, light, temperature and buy the most suitable bed. Sticking to a regular schedule is helpful: generally, early to bed and early to rise is best for older people. Bright light, especially sunlight, helps to set the "biological clock"-with the result that a person feels sleepy at about the same time every night and tends to wake at the same time every morning. Older persons should be careful about use of cough/cold and headache preparations containing caffeine, for such medications can set off insomnia. It is inadvisable to eat a heavy meal just before bedtime. Studies indicate that bed mates have better patterns of sleep than those who sleep by themselves.

It is important, says Dr. Dement, to recognize that sleeptime cannot be perfect. A few awakenings during the night are normal for older persons. Even inability to go back to sleep immediately after awakening early in the early morning is not harmful if the person feels wide awake and energetic during the daytime.

Studies debunk the notion that the elderly need less sleep than the young. Older persons may delude themselves by thinking that they require less sleep when in actuality they may be sleeping at several times during the day. Almost everyone needs 8-9 hours of sleep out of every 24. Many persons need more when they need to rely on judgment and creativity.

"Now blessings light on him that first invented this same sleep," Cervantes wrote. "It covers a man all over, thoughts and all, like a cloak; 'tis meat for the hungry, drink for the thirsty, heat for the cold, and cold for the hot. 'Tis the current coin that purchases all the pleasures of the world cheap; and the balance that sets the king and the shepherd, the fool and the wise man even."

SLEEP STRATEGIES

1. Avoid alcoholic drinks at night.
2. Avoid caffeine laden drinks (coffee, tea, soda) after 5 pm.
3. Avoid eating in the middle of the night.
4. Avoid a heavy supper.
5. Avoid smoking at bedtime or during the night.
6. Do eliminate daytime naps to prevent wakefulness at night.
7. Do go to another room if awakened and read a book until sleepy. Then go back to bed.
8. Do have a glass of warm milk at bedtime.
9. Do have a light snack before bedtime.
10. Do not go to bed much before your usual time.

SUPPORT GROUPS

What has upheld you on your way?
What has supported you when faint?
On what have you for strength relied?

George Sands Bryan

Although many caregivers are not aware of how unready they are at the time of diagnosis of a serious disease, most soon learn through sad experience that if they are to go on helping their loved one they themselves need the help of a support group. Support groups also aid those persons in distress who are trying to deal with situations as serious as alcohol abuse, death of a spouse, divorce, suicide.

There is little doubt that support groups make up one of the more effective ways of sustaining caregivers by providing opportunities both to find encouragement in their daily efforts and to learn from others facing similar situations how to solve the many problems encountered in dealing with older persons increasingly helpless in functioning. An Alzheimer's victim, for example, may ask the same question over and over again despite its having been answered repeatedly. In the support group the caregiver will find all sorts of suggestions for dealing with this problem, including the writing of a note or the making of a tape recording which the patient can consult. The group will supply caregivers with lists of outside services and professionals. Support groups also have hot lines for members to call for immediate help with any kind of problem.

Support groups do more than provide practical suggestions for treatment of patients. Generally, support groups have trained, experienced leader-conveners who make sure that meetings serve the needs of all members whether social, emotional or educational. Without such help, caregiving can be a lonely, frustrating and depressing experience, wearying in body and spirit. Vice President Al Gore quotes a wife acting as caregiver to her husband, a victim of Alzheimer's disease: "My life can be described as a funeral that never ends."

Since a support group consists of persons all in the same situation, caregivers can find at meetings, not only practical advice for handling daily situations, but also encouragement and emotional comfort so necessary if they are to go on. In the support group a caregiver can relate personal thoughts and emotions socially unacceptable elsewhere and feel empathy from other members who know how distressing it is to be in the position of chief decision-maker for a parent or spouse suffering from cancer, senile dementia or other debilitating illness.

Support groups are usually located in community centers, family agencies, homes for the aged, nursing homes, religious institutions. There are many national societies for specific diseases, each with its local branch and support groups easily locatable through the telephone directory. They sponsor research, educate the general public and inform government and social service agencies about the needs of those affected to whom they give care. The Alzheimer's Association, to take but one example, having received a grant from the United States Justice Department, created in 1992 the Alzheimer's Safe Return Program, which helps identify and locate missing memory-impaired persons.

Also helpful are adult day care centers, which offer a safe haven and a variety of activities not only for those elderly with functional impairment but also for their family caregivers. Professionals are available to answer questions and provide assistance. Help with eating, walking and using the toilet is provided for persons with handicaps. Many centers arrange for transportation and even for coverage during work hours of family caregivers.

TRANSPORTATION

Could I transport myself with a wish. . . .

Joseph Addison

Particularly for the elderly, among whom are a larger proportion of persons with low income than in other age cohorts, difficulty with transportation restricts, if it does not deny, social contacts and activities and acquisition of goods and services. Money alone is not the reason. Transportation problems of the aged have three main causes: cost, design barriers and physical limitations of both buildings and human beings. Staircase steps may be too high, and public address announcements may not be made clearly. Not just lifestyle but the entire quality of life is affected. Even as changes in eating habits result in malnutrition, so impaired mobility compounds feelings of isolation and hopelessness and leads to depression

Transportation systems throughout the United States offer reduced fares to older people, applicable at nonpeak hours when the number of passengers diminishes. Buses and subways, as a result, are generally affordable. But low income makes airplane travel a problem. The cost of buying, operating and maintaining a car has risen dramatically within the life time of those 65+, who remember new cars selling for under $2,000 and gas prices hovering around 27 cents a gallon. Insurance companies sometimes cancel policies of older persons or raise rates despite a long and careful study by the National Research Council showing that drivers 65+ are less likely to have an accident than those under 25.

To a large extent, self-esteem, independence and mobility of most older persons depend on ability to drive. For many, driving is not a luxury but an absolute necessity. On average, the elderly travel nearly 4 miles to the nearest shopping area, 6 miles to a medical facility, about 4 miles to a personal place of worship.

Yet automobile travel for the elderly is not easy. In addition to reading, driving is the most complicated visual undertaking most of the elderly perform. Details must be perceived, recognized and coordinated instantly with other data from knowledge and memory. Per mile, a driver must make nearly 20 decisions, some instantaneously. This although vision alters with age. Going through intersections is hazardous because the driver must watch almost simultaneously cross streets, signs, traffic lights and pedestrians coming from all directions. There is difficulty changing focus from near to far and back again. When moving at speeds beyond 35 mph, many older people find reading signs beyond their ability. Slower reaction time, an accompaniment of age, makes negotiating heavy traffic and merging onto expressway lanes nerve-wracking. . Sudden glares, as from oncoming headlights at night or sun rays between tree branches overhead during the day are disconcerting and present difficulties of adjustment. Bus and train travel can also be trying, what with announcements difficult to decipher, high steps to climb and rapidly closing doors to negotiate nimbly.

Congress has tried to ease the situation by passage of an amendment to the Urban Mass Transportation Act of 1964, which made available some funds for better transportation facilities for the elderly, with the National Mass Transit Act of 1974, which provided for reduced fares, and with the Surface Transportation Assistance Act of 1978, in support of public transportation in non-urban areas. (Today, more elderly live in suburbs than in cities.) Many urban as well as rural communities attempt to meet needs of older persons by providing buses for marketing or for traveling to and from senior centers. Volunteer drivers are often used to supplement such services at holidays and on group outings.

While there are programs administered by the AAA and the AARP which evaluate cognitive and physical skills and show people of any age how to improve driving skills, it is advisable for the elderly, particularly the oldest old, to plan ahead for the day when they may no longer be able to drive safely. It is wise to investigate and actually try alternate means of transportation before giving up a driver's license. To learn which transportation resources and other assistance options in a community are available to the elderly, call toll free 800-677-1116, the Elder Care Locator, which is funded by the US Administration on Aging and operated by the National Association of State Units on Aging.

The elderly are sympathetic to Philip Guedalla's assertion that "The true history of the United States is the history of transportation. . . ."

PUBLIC TRANSIT DIFFICULTIES OF THE ELDERLY

Vehicles

High step required to enter/exit

Difficult to get into or out of seats

Seats not available/forced to stand

Difficult to reach handholds

Cannot see out for landmarks

No place to put packages

Poor information presentation

Poorly visible signs

Infrequent service

Acceleration/deceleration too sudden

Schedules not maintained

Poor driver attitude and assistance

Inadequate or inappropriate routes

Not enough transfers

Terminals

Long stairs

Long walks

Poor fare collection facilities

Information clarity and dissemination inadequate

Poor crowd flow design

Insufficient seating

Poor interface with other modes of transportation

Employee assistance/attitude poor

Crowd flow nondirected

Transit Stops

Insufficient shelter

Platform incompatible with vehicle

Inadequate posting of information

Too many transfers required

Length of stops too short

Not enough stops

Poor location for safety and convenience

TRAVEL

One of the pleasantest things in life is going on a journey.
William Hazlitt

Surveys indicate that travel by singles as well as by couples is the activity most desired by older Americans. According to a survey by the National Tour Association, especially favored are visits to national parks, historical sites and special events. Such a journey can be an adventure, an exploration of something different, a chance to get away and relax, a learning experience, a physical challenge, a visit to the old country and much, much more—whatever the individual considers and wants it to be.

Older adults looking for new travel companions should consider grandchildren. Traveling with grandchildren can be inexpensive and delightful. Several travel organizations, Elderhostel among them, offer tours designed by educators, leisure counselors and psychologists to take advantage of normal school breaks. Youngsters 6-12 years of age travel best. They enjoy the preliminary planning, especially helping choose places to visit and things to see. Trains, planes and cruise lines offer discounts. Hotels usually permit kids to stay in the same room with grandparents at no extra charge. Bonds between the generations strengthen as they share learning experiences mixed with recreation.

Information is the key that opens the door to successful travel. Acquaintance with the culture, health, history, fauna and flora of a region make a trip there more interesting. *Know before you go* should be the motto of elderly travelers. Almost every geographical area in the world has an office of tourism (with quarters in major American cities) that will send on request descriptions of places to visit, schedules of events, weather patterns and much other data—including lists of attractions that offer discounts to mature adults. Supplementing this material with notes from guidebooks and from the book, *Consumer Reports Best Travel Deals,* and their *Travel Newsletter* available at many libraries will make possible a delightful trip for even the most timid and reluctant person getting on in years.

Whether for travel at home or abroad, it is wise to plan ahead for possible medical problems. With some precautions, there is no reason an older person cannot take even a lengthy trip. Telephone the member services department of your HMO and inquire about out-of-area coverage and a toll-free number in case of emergency. On two 3-by-5 cards, write your personal physician's office and beeper number. Do the same for your dentist and a reliable neighbor. Be sure to indicate the digits needed to reach your long-distance telephone company. Clip to each 3-by-5 card a photocopy of the first two pages of your passport, airline and RR tickets, eyeglass prescription, credit card number. Do not carry the cards in your purse or wallet: conceal one on your person, the other in your luggage.

For persons with a serious medical condition, joining the Medic Alert Foundation International will enable health professionals anywhere to quickly determine proper therapy. The International Association for Medical Assistance to Travelers will provide services and doctor recommendations at no charge: membership is free but donations are requested. Within the United States, the American Academy of Family Physicians will send travelers a list of certified family doctors. Both Travel Assistance International and Access America, Inc., sell temporary health and/or trip cancellation insurance. Policies should also cover trip interruption due to accident or illness. TAI, linked to Europ Assistance Worldwide Services, will provide coverage for a medical evacuation. Every local Department of Health has information needed about vaccinations required for trips in the various countries. As of 1977, the Blue Cross and Blue Shield Association in Chicago has been putting together a new and growing network (Blue Card Worldwide) that will permit members traveling abroad to receive medical care at any of 40 participating hospitals located at major destinations throughout the world. Members do not have to pay a hospital upon discharge: Blue Card Worldwide works like a credit card.

Before going on an extended trip, every late-life adult should have a thorough medical and dental checkup. Essential are ample supplies of prescription drugs, toothpaste, aspirin, over-the-counter medications for digestive and bowel upsets. In addition to a prescription for lenses,

eyeglass wearers should carry an extra pair. Include medical documen-
tation giving allergies, blood type and special conditions. Check with
your doctor both about your record of inoculations and need for need
for new and booster shots.

To avoid aches and pains, begin at least two months prior to leaving an exercise regimen for flexibility, strength and stamina. Travel
today includes prolonged sitting, carrying of suitcases and unfamiliarity
with foreign-made beds and other furniture. In the German country-
side, to take but one example, mattress and pillow are arranged almost
as though the guest is to sleep in a sitting position. While traveling
maintain the exercise regimen, and keep to a healthy diet by not overeating and by drinking plenty of fluids. Pace yourself: do not wear
yourself out by scheduling too many events. On a long trip, take a holiday
from your holiday by resting for a full day or an afternoon or evening.

A friend or relative should have a detailed copy of the traveler's
itinerary, so as to be able to communicate in case of emergency. Enlist
the aid of a trusted neighbor to monitor your home, fetch the mail and
hold a spare key. Arrange automatic timers to turn on lights and a radio
or TV. Hire a responsible firm to care for gardens and lawns.

The United States Department of State through its Citizens Emergency Center provides at no charge an excellent booklet about traveling abroad, *Travel Tips for Senior Citizens.* It is wise to make your own
checklist of things needed, such as an alarm clock, sunglasses, sewing
kit, folding umbrella, Scotch tape, Swiss army knife, flashlight. For a
US passport necessary when traveling abroad, apply at least 6 months
in advance to one of the State Department's regional passport agencies
or to one of the numerous post offices or courthouses authorized to
handle passport applications.

Credit cards have largely replaced travelers checks. They have four
advantages. Cards are not bulky, and card holders do not pay until
arrival home. The exchange rate is generally good, and the card's charge-
back provisions offer protection. For emergencies, take along at least
20 $1 bills. Anyone carrying travelers checks should be careful not to
endorse them in advance. Unlike credit cards, travelers checks often

cannot be used unless the holder presents proper identification. Keep an envelope to hold all credit card bills.

If traveling in your own car, have it fully checked and serviced before leaving. Join an automobile club that offers 24-hour roadside assistance. Be sure your insurance policy includes towing, an inexpensive way to avoid huge costs if the car breaks down. If traveling by rental car, use a credit card (with its guarantee of insurance coverage) to avoid paying the expensive daily insurance the rental company offers. Be sure to check beforehand about age restrictions: some companies, especially abroad, do not rent to anyone 70+. To avoid getting lost, arrange to rent a vehicle with a computer navigation system. Find out about driver's licenses abroad from the American Automobile Association. Regardless of age, no one should drive for a long period without frequent rest stops. In Europe, where virtually every destination can be reached by train, rail passes make travel inexpensive and easy.

Whether traveling independently by bus, car, plane or train or booking a trip through a tour company, make reservations early and get a confirmation number in writing (called a printout by travel agents) for protection against a computer glitch or loss of records. Prior to purchase, comparison check prices and special deals for older adults. Discounts usually have restrictions, which should be carefully analyzed. Travel agents have a database for schedules and fares, and they are knowledgeable about other aspects of journeying—including the many clubs and companies sponsoring guided and independent tours for older adults, both married and single. They make reservations and indicate personal preferences, such as for special dietary needs. Generally, services of travel agents are free. It is a good idea to check their reputation with a local agency, such as the Better Business Bureau. Beware of low prices quoted in tiny newspaper ads: they may be an invitation to a bait-and-switch scam

No matter how efficient the travel agent, be sure to reconfirm requests when you check in at the airport, hotel, and car rental agency. Always write confirmation numbers, such as for flight and hotel room or car size in a daily organizer or ticket jacket, so that even if computers are down and your reservations are lost you will still be accommodated.

Anyone with a heart condition or other serious condition should discuss circumstances in advance of a flight: most airlines can make adequate arrangements, including special meals and wheelchairs. If a flight will last less than 4 hours, avoid an enforced fast by taking along food that travels well, tastes good even though cold, and does not spill.

On short, connecting flights there may be no amenities, not even a snack. Prepare for delays at airports and terminals by carrying a back-pack with snacks, reading material and other diversions. Raisins, dried apricots and apples take little room. On long flights, drink plenty of fluids but not alcohol, flex your hands frequently, use an inflatable U-shaped travel pillow for your neck and head, get out of your seat and move around. While seated, loosen shoes or remove them because feet tend to swell on long flights.

There is an art to packing. Pack only what is needed to avoid unnecessary weight when carrying luggage in customs areas. Prepare for different kinds of weather by planning to wear layers, so that clothing can be added or removed according to the day's climate. Put toiletries and a change of clothing in a carry-on bag so as to have basic necessities if the rest of your luggage is misplaced or lost. Also include a sweater, for airplane travel is often cold. So that everything matches and is easy to keep clean, women should build their wardrobe around one color, such as navy or black. Men and women should avoid white, which stains easily. Both sexes should pack combinations of clothing which give the appearance of an expansive wardrobe. Leave space for purchases on the journey.

Use a carry-on for breakables and valuables in small containers. Keep wash and drys and a washcloth in plastic bags. Include enough necessities to last the entire trip plus three days, the period during which most "lost" luggage is returned by airlines to rightful owners. Put an unusual ribbon, such as a print or a combination of colors, on all handles to be sure that both the carry-on and other luggage are easily recognized. Luggage should be light weight and have wheels. Baggage tags should have a flap, so that no one can easily see the address.

To beat jet lag, try to adust to local schedules, especially eating and sleeping times. If arriving in the morning, stay awake until regional bedtime. If arriving at night, go to sleep as soon as feasible. Walking during the day following arrival is helpful because natural light helps the body clock adjust.

Be prepared. Then with diarist Samuel Pepys you, too, can say: "I ended this month with the greatest joy that ever I did any in my life, because I have spent the greatest part of it with abundance of joy, and honour, and pleasant journeys. . . ."

ADDITIONAL TIPS FOR TRAVELERS 65+

Pack old clothes which can be discarded after use and thus gain room for gifts and souuvenirs.

Do not pack fragile, perishable items.

Enclose a copy of your itinerary plus your name, home address and tour group (if any) in each piece of luggage.

Make a list of items packed (with location) and keep it on your person.

Keep a copy of each medical document on your person.

Bring generic versions of all prescription drugs.

Carry antidiarrhea medicine on your person.

Because feet and ankles swell on flights, pack slippers in your carry-on.

Be prepared to counter the unexpected and not get upset.

If you have a cold, take an antihistamine or decongestant 1/2 hour before flight time.

Drink only bottled water, fruit juice or soft drinks.

Get plenty of sleep.

Avoid buying antiquities unless certain purchase is legal.

Find out when the United States Embassy is open. It may be closed at night. During the day, embassy personnel will contact your family and provide a list of lawyers if needed.

Driving customs differ in many countries. Hire only a reputable driver. If you drive yourself, get adequate insurance. In some countries, if someone is hurt in a traffic accident, the police may arrest everyone at the scene.

A HEALTH KIT FOR THE ELDERLY TRAVELER

Adhesive tape bandages

Antifungal cream

Antihistamines

Antinauseant

Anti-inflammatories: aspirin or acetaminophen or ibuprofen for minor aches and pains

Bacitracin or other antibiotic ointments for cuts and scrapes

Bandages: adhesive, elastic, flat

Calamine lotion and steroid creams

Cough medicines and oral decongestants

Diarrhea preventers and remedies

Hydrocortisone cream for allergic skin reactions

Insect repellent containing deet

Medication(s) your doctor recommends for your conditions

Motion sickness patches

Nasal decongestant spray

Nonsteroidal antiinflammatory drug (there are many; take what works for you)

Orabase (an anesthetic for tooth or minor mouth injuries)

Pads of gauze and rolls of first-aid tape

Prescriptions (signed by a doctor for medicines and eyeglasses)

Safety pins

Scissors

Sunscreen lotion or spray with SPF of 15 or higher

Tweezers

Vaseline

Zinc oxide

PLEASE NOTE: Because many drugs and medical supplies common in the United States are difficult to find abroad, carry your own kit. Keep medications in original containers to avoid being charged with possession of illegal substances.

USE IT OR—

Today, people 65+ ski, climb mountains, go camping in the most rugged of wildernesses—enjoy an active and vigorous lifestyle. Theodore Roosevelt would be delighted even though there is a *but*. Despite the publicity given the Senior Olympics, the significance of this remarkable change from the lifestyle of yesterday's elderly has not received the attention it deserves except among small groups of researchers and science reporters. Yet economic and social implications for the general public are profound.

Even though researchers are not in full agreement as to which factors are most responsible for changing the experience of old age in America, all come to the same conclusion: today's elderly are not only more longevous but are more agile, healthy, robust and vigorous than previous generations. Actuaries calculate that a man at age 70 today has a good chance of living another 17 years, while a woman at the same age may expect to live another 20 years.

Can it be, contrary to prevailing views, that chronic, disabling disorders need not increase with age, that old people need not be frail and weak, infirm in mind and body? The National Long Term Care Surveys, which regularly observe almost 20,000 elderly 65+ from ethnic groups at all income levels, find with every year a larger percentage of older persons healthy enough to live independently and to take care of themselves. The number of diseases afflicting the elderly 65+ has declined by more than 10% over the last decade. Indeed, there have been steady annual declines in disability rates since 1982, when the surveys began, to 1994, date of the most recent survey.

Why is it that the annual mortality rate from heart disease and stroke dropped sharply during that period? Why is it that the incidence of painful chronic diseases and debilitating disorders like arthritis, emphysema and high blood pressure is not necessarily increasing with age? Answers may have as much to do with changing attitudes and habits as with medical and technological advances. Late-life adults are willing to respond to sensible advice about modulating longevity and the rate of aging. They can and do change lifestyles to improve fitness and well-being.

Despite the rapid increase in numbers of the elderly, the old-age cohort will not be anywhere near responsible for the terrifying drain on the nation's financial resources forecast by economists just a few years ago. Just the opposite is true! The great majority of older Americans are now reaching 65 in good condition. Fewer than 1 in 20 of those are in nursing homes. Declining disease and disability rates among the elderly from 1982–1995 have already saved Medicare at least $200,000,000,000. That millions of elderly will probably enjoy an active and productive old age is a distinct economic plus in the coming years not only for Medicare but also for Social Security, whose economic solvency seemed in doubt partly because of what was erroneously perceived to be the need of frail and weak elderly workers to retire early.

Why the health changes in favor of coming generations of the elderly? Factors involved in the answer are undoubtedly multiple and intertwined. Consider the effects of the Internet, travel, activity of all kinds. Reliable estimates are that in 1980 more than 60% of elderly 85 + had less than 8 years of school. Already that figure has dropped considerably to as low as 20% or lower. Educated persons are more likely to try to gain control over their life and thus to heed education, not just formal schooling, but informal learning gained from reading, TV and warnings to change diets, cease smoking, adopt an exercise program.

Other factors involve improvements in communication, medicine, public health, technology and transportation. Old people today do not suffer from lifelong difficulties that earlier generations endured as consequences of poor drinking water and lack of hygiene, of marginal nutrition and inadequate medical knowledge and procedures. In addition, coming generations of the elderly will have a high comfort level, what with improved working conditions and ease of transportation, with hip replacements and gene therapy and other medical marvels like cloning techniques. A better way of life, taking the above factors into consideration, will compress disease and disability into a shorter time period and postpone their onset–the oldest-old remaining healthy and vigorous for many years.

Based on recent research, demographers and gerontologists theorize that only some 30% of so-called aging characteristics are genetically founded. The obvious conclusion, not taking luck into account, is that whether people end up in old age sick or healthy depends largely on the way they live and act. Put another way, people themselves are largely responsible for their success in growing old. Those elderly who engage in productive activities like a second career, creative hobbies and volunteer work age well, while those who lessen physical and mental activity suffer declines in mind and body, in memory and physique. Active people gain a network of emotional and social support, have a better self-image and are more likely to be capable of overcoming untoward events and of bouncing back and attaining success in their endeavors.

In this regard, something astonishing is already happening, giving the lie to doomsayers complaining that gerontology is creating a period of "survival of the unfittest." Ponce de Leon would be jealous.

The process of aging for active healthy people has slowed as lifetimes have grown longer by as much as 35%, so that the years gained have been added to mid-life and not to old age. Middle age, the prime of adulthood, for untold numbers of men and women is being postponed to the period between 50 and 75 years, so that old age starts at some point after 75. For the baby boomers, who in 1997 were approaching 50 years of age, what this means is a gift of 20-30 years–a gift of a new stage in adult life full of vim and vigor.

Researchers out of the Massachusetts Institute of Technology study-ing today's cohort of the oldest-old state that they are healthy and active until very near the end when they take sick for a short period of time. The act of dying, usually preceded by a brief period of uncon-sciousness, is normally peaceful.

Staying active mentally, physically and socially contributes mark-edly to successful aging. Theodore Roosevelt was correct. Couch pota-toes, take heed. Rest and you rust. Rest a lot and you rot a lot. "**USE IT OR LOSE IT!**" ought to be the slogan of everyone desirous of growing old while healthy in mind and body.

VETERANS

Ecce quomodo mundus suis servitoribus reddit mercedem.
(See how the world rewards its veterans.)

Alexander Pope

Created in 1930, the Department of Veterans Affairs (VA), oversees federal programs for which some 30,000,000 veterans and their 50,000,000 dependents–nearly 1/3 of the population of the United States–are eligible. With a budget approaching $40,000,000,000 and the number of employees nearing 250,000, the VA is by far the largest government system in the world providing health care and economic and other kinds of benefits to discharged service men and women.

A huge enterprise, the VA knows that it will be even larger as the number of veterans increases and they and their dependents grow older. The VA expects that by the end of this century the number of veterans 65+ will reach at least 35,000,000.

Through 3 Departments (Benefits, Medicine and Memorial Affairs) the VA oversees more than 170 medical centers, 230 outpatient clinics and 125 nursing home-care units. It operates an immense loan guarantee program and an even larger insurance program. For service connected disabilities and pensions, it sends checks totaling about $15,000,000,000 a year. The VA administers more than 110 large national cemeteries, and it provides a flag to drape the casket and reimburse the family of a qualified veteran who is buried elsewhere about $300 for funeral and burial expenses. Since passage of the GI bill in 1944, the VA has helped more than 20,000,000 veterans take part in education and training programs. This is not all. The VA operates a toll-free service for the hearing-impaired, and it furnishes copies of military service records on request.

Veterans Benefits Counselors are stationed in every regional VA office to answer questions about eligibility for specific programs. There is also a toll-free nationwide telephone service (1-800-827-0648) that automatically connects veterans and their dependents to the nearest VA office.

YOGA and TAI CHI

Health is the vital principle of bliss,
And exercise, of health.

James Thomson

More and more HMOs are now trumpeting the benefits of yoga, a
system of exercise that has withstood the test of time for 2,000 years.
While some proponents of yoga make its program seem like a panacea
for the world's ills, the HMOs in their practical approach to prevention
of health disorders recommend yoga for benefits which can easily be
documented and proved. Yoga can be practiced by persons of all ages
(except young children). Practicers of yoga need little equipment and
very little space. Because yoga improves flexibility, joint mobility and
muscle tone, it helps develop and intensify a sense of mental and physical well-being. Yoga increases circulation and therefore the volume of
oxygen to all parts of the body. A yoga session of only 15 minutes a
day is easy to fit into a busy schedule. Separate elements of many
postures called *yoga bits* can be employed at other times during the
day to promote deep breathing and relieve tension. And the benefits
are long-lasting.

In the United States, a yoga session generally starts with a warm-
up period succeeded by breathing exercises. Stretching drills follow.
Full yoga exercises cap the session. Because all the movements are
performed slowly, risk of strain or injury is sharply reduced. Yoga sessions wind down with relaxation techniques.

Of the 7 schools of yoga, Hatha is the most popular in the West.
Hatha yoga utilizes both an external and an internal approach to the
overall goal of balancing and uniting mind, body and spirit. Essentially,
it is a discipline (the literal translation of yoga from Sanscrit) with a
holistic base that views the nature of living as series after series of
interacting wholes which add up to more than the sum of the parts. But
the philosophy behind yoga need not be dealt with. The yoga practicer
moves through a sequence of body postures called *asanas* executed in

association with sets of breathing exercises called *prayamas*. An inner meditative program of self-analysis is arranged to match the external sets of physical movements and postures, in reality a series of stretches that gradually develop into more intricate poses by way of smooth and graceful movement.

As with other exercise programs, yoga must be performed correctly. Unlike jogging, to take but one example, it is almost impossible to perform yoga correctly by studying pictures and following written directions. An experienced, qualified instructor is essential.

Properly performed, yoga's utilization of alignment improves one's carriage and helps develop poise. Yoga works well in tandem with aerobic activities and weight training so as to reduce the likelihood of injury in various sports. For the elderly, yoga is effective in reducing the pain and stress that accompany such chronic ailments as arthritis, and it is a definite aid in alleviating back problems.

Also of particular value to the elderly is the Chinese exercise program *tai chi* (pronounced tie chee), which gained the attention of Americans when during Nixon's trip to China in 1972 TV cameras pictured hundreds and hundreds of people performing the movements in early morning. Recent research corroborates Chinese claims that tai chi has a positive effect on balance and strength. A study under the auspices of the National Institute on Aging completed in 1996 determined that for the elderly practicing tai chi helps prevent falls and reduce depression and other negative mood disturbances, while increasing cardiorespiratory function. There are other benefits. Characterized as moving yoga, tai chi strengthens muscles and improves coordination and stability.

To Americans, the flowing movements of tai chi look like elements in a graceful dance. This may be why tai chi is often referred to as Chinese shadow boxing. Actually, tai chi is based on imitation of calming scenes from nature, as mimicking movements of animals in a slow and graceful choreography. The fluid exercises involve gradual shifts of weight from one leg to the other while smoothly rotating the trunk from side to side and setting arms in precise positions. Because movement is slow and rhythmic, non-jarring and gentle, there is little chance of injury. Throughout a tai chi session, exercisers breathe deeply but gently, and try to concentrate inwardly on the body so as to reduce tension. Tai chi can be performed anywhere, alone or in groups, in informal attire or a business suit at any time of the day, with music or without.

As with yoga, the philosophic principles underlying tai chi need not concern American exercisers. Also as with yoga, a skillful teacher is essential. Although a tai chi session starts with simple breathing exercises followed by several moments of easy stretches, soon movements become more complex and gradually combine into smoothly flowing motions.

Despite esoteric pretensions of some adherents, yoga and tai chi are not so much therapies as disciplines, self-administered forms of athletic training, which utilize principles of exercise physiology for fitness maintenance and improvement. The name *yoga* comes from the Sanskrit word meaning "yoke," referring to the discipline's beneficial linking of the muscular and the emotional, the physical and the mental. When yoga and tai chi are added to aerobics and other aspects of a wellness program, exercisers can feel that they themselves are achieving health protection and augmenting illness prevention.

Truly, as Andrew Lang wrote:

When every "programme's" been gone through
This good old world will wake anew!

PART TWO

DISEASES AND DISORDERS

AILMENTS

How sickness enlarges the dimensio
of a man's self to himself.

Charles Lamb

For what are we all, ultimately, but patients.

John H. Stone, MD

Geriatricians refer to disease as an abnormal condition in the body or mind that interferes with proper functioning. Statisticians estimate that most persons 65+ have no major health problem but about 80% have one or more chronic diseases, at least 30% have 3 or more chronic diseases. (Disease is considered chronic when lasting three months or more.) On the positive side, this means that today about 20% of older persons, at least of those up to 80 years of age, are without symptoms of known serious or chronic diseases. On the negative: about 20% of those elderly 65+ need assistance with such Activities of Daily Living (ADLs) as bathing and dressing, and an equal percentage need help with such Instrumental Activities of Daily Living (IADLs) as meal preparation and house maintenance. Cognitive impairment is unusual. Probably less than 5% of the 65+ group living in the community exhibit difficulty with reasoning and/or orientation to their environment.

In terms of time and the human life span, illnesses apparently develop in clusters, with young adulthood likely to be the healthiest period. The period during which need for medical and social services to deal with illnesses and their results increases most rapidly is 70-79. Multiple ADLs and IADLs are not unusual then. In contrast, having survived into the 80s and 90s, many persons are likely to enjoy a robust old age.

Apparently, one major illness lowers resistance sufficiently to allow others to appear, the so-called cascade phenomenon: treating one disorder without treating those associated with it may hasten decline of an elderly patient. Although occurring infrequently among the elderly, acute episodes of such illnesses as influenza and pneumonia can be seriously debilitating—resulting in slower rates of recovery and higher rates of death than in the young. Perhaps because of declining levels of immune function during the 70s, there are elderly who have become increasingly liable to multidimensional impairment from diseases in increasing numbers, some of which appear almost only during those years, as do Alzheimer's and Parkinson's. The coming increase in large numbers of the elderly, a result of the aging of the baby boomers, is bound to reveal individuals who are severely handicapped and need services of all types.

Contending with more than one disease complicates the job of the physician as well as the life of the patient. Both can agree on the goal: to achieve well-being as soon as possible by restoring ability of the patient to perform necessary activities of daily living. From the point of view of the patient who does not give up, chronic diseases may become tolerable, even accepted as a "normal" part of old age. And a condition may be capable of significant improvement or even of a cure. From the point of view of the physician, an elderly patient frequently presents a diagnostic puzzle. Categories blur. The doctor must be exceedingly careful. Although few diseases are unique to late adult life, great variation in physical, medical and mental condition exists among the older population.

Disease in the elderly may manifest itself differently from the way it does in the young. Perception of pain lessens, and response to treatment is generally slower. Heart attack without pain may occur to a higher degree in the old than in the young. Seriousness of disease can be different for the elderly. Cancer may be less aggressive, as in the prostate. But influenza, which hampers the young, may be lethal in the old.

For the elderly, there is generally no single correct determination or magic bullet to cure a condition. Symptoms of one ailment may camouflage or mask those of another. Confusion may be the result of dehydration; so-called senility, the result of malnutrition. Treatment for one ailment may cause another, what doctors call the iatrogenic effect, as diuretic therapy for hypertension occasioning incontinence. The predictive value of laboratory tests is relatively low because biochemical markers of disease in the elderly infrequently have notable diagnostic importance. The patient must be careful to keep account of the various medications which taken at the wrong time or in incorrect combination can interfere with each other and make matters worse. Physicians know that side effects of medications are a common cause of difficulty.

Illness causes changes of behavior in a person of any age. For the elderly, alterations that apparently come with the advance of years may make some illnesses difficult to recognize. The obverse is true. Clear delineation between health and disease is not always possible. Diagnosis of chest pain is often not easy, since among late-life adults many causes exist for this symptom. Some acute infections can exist with no increase in body temperature. For a number of reasons, disability, impairment and handicaps similar to those caused by disease may accompany advanced age, particularly among those elderly 75+.

The old sometimes tend to minimize or dismiss as signs of age what the young regard as symptoms of disease, so that underdiagnosis is fairly common. But overdiagnosis is not uncommon as, for example, with diabetes and hypertensive disorders. Cultural beliefs and stereotypes may sometimes influence the old to associate what seem to be irreversible pain and discomfort with senility. Such credulity can be dangerous, especially if a physician is not consulted for treatment and accurate, relevant information is not available. Some symptoms may portend serious disease. Rectal bleeding may be mistaken for hemorrhoids.

This is not the time for pessimism. Many a disorder, which occurs because of failure to correct conditions easily under an elderly person's control, can be prevented by education beforehand. Ironically, symptoms may lessen with age, as urinary-tract functioning may improve by the patient's learning bladder control although the doctor may be unable to discover the exact disease underlying the condition. Cancer can be less aggressive, as in the case of the prostate, and cancer rates, in general, begin to drop at about the 85th year. But a cardiac arrhythmia can increase as a result of excessive intake of caffeine and produce symptoms such as lightheadedness and palpitations. Wearing an overly tight collar or sharply turning the neck can put pressure on the carotid arteries and cause what physicians call syncope, a fainting spell.

A complete yearly examination, with tests, vaccinations and immunizations, is imperative. In general, the earlier an illness is diagnosed and treated, the more likely the chance of recovery. Additionally, physicians at the annual examination can encourage regular exercise, a balanced diet, moderate intake of alcohol, discontinuance of smoking. Health, it seems, is the province to a large degree of those seniors with a sensible lifestyle. Good health practices add years to life expectancy and life to those years. .

At the beginning of the 20th century, chief causes of death were acute, fast-acting diseases. At the end of the century, long-lasting diseases such as cancer, heart disease and stroke accounted for more than ¾ of all deaths among those 65+. Neurological disease has become more common among the elderly. Accompanying these diseases are medical problems resulting from arthritis, diabetes, urinary tract infection and vision and hearing difficulties. Such ailments are multi-system and overlapping, chronic and degenerative–at this time receiving palliative rather than curative medical procedures although research for more effective therapy is ongoing and even increasing.

Most chronic illnesses cannot be cured. With no identifiable cause, they tend to develop slowly, worsen progressively and cause permanent pathological change. Because with age pain sensitivity is often decreased and pain location can be capricious, it is possible that unrecognized illness is responsible for some of the pathology. Men are more likely to suffer lethal conditions; women are more likely to experience chronic conditions that are rarely life-threatening. Geriatricians emphasize that because of the shift from acute to chronic disease behavioral, environmental and social factors as well as biological should be taken into account when treating the elderly.

Long ago, Aristotle understood that "in the case of certain maladies a diseased state of the body and shortness of life are interchangeable, while in cases of others, ill-health is perfectly compatible with long life." Diseases of old age, chronic and generally incurable, may be slowed or even controlled to the extent that quality of life does not suffer.

Modifiable factors include diet, habits and environment. Increasing attention should be paid to preventive health care by the individual who in so many ways is his or her own best health-care provider. Advertising campaigns for health promotion and disability prevention, such as those dealing with heart disease and cancer, will help keep the elderly alert.

Knowledge makes for good medicine. For more information about women's health, telephone the National Women's Health Network Information Clearinghouse at 202-628-7814. Free information packets on women's health issues–including fibroids, contraceptives, estrogen replacement therapies–are available. The Office of Research on Women's Health of the National Institutes of Health has a list of free publications: telephone 301-402-1770. For more information on men's health, telephone Men's Health Consulting at 1800-WELL-MEN. For booklets (called Men's Maintenance Manuals). from the founders of Men's Health Week and the Association of American Family Physicians, dial 1-800-955-2002. There is a Men's Hotline available by telephone at 512-472-3237 and on the Internet at www.menhotline.org.

All elderly should have annual vaccinations against influenza, which can be lethal, and periodic vaccinations per recommendation by health professionals against equally dangerous pneumonia and tetanus. Retirees engaging in foreign travel should consult a physician in advance about pertinent immunizations. Along with the yearly checkup, women should have a pap smear and breast examination; men, a prostate examination. Included in the testing program for both sexes should be an examinations for colon and rectal cancer. Early intervention in the form of screening for such vision problems as cataracts and glaucoma may prevent illness and disability later on.

Attention by parents to proper nutrition of children may be useful in stemming development later on of chronic disease in adults.

Care of another kind must be taken. Health quackery is a booming business, particularly among the elderly. Estimates considered reliable are that sums in excess of $10,000,000,000 are wasted on quackery every year! Promises for cures of arthritis, sexual problems and weight control are innumerable and ubiquitous. Advertising makes frauds attractive, with anecdotes by seemingly ordinary but responsible people offered as proof in lieu of hard scientific evidence which can be checked in any responsible medical journal, such as that of the American Medical Association. Guarantees are made that treatment will be painless and permanent if *medications* continue to be bought.

To avoid quackery: unusual degrees, such as DN (Doctor of Naturopathy), should be checked with the local medical society; anyone promoting one treatment for several types of disease should be suspect; treatment in a foreign country, such as Cuba and Mexico, where governmental policy is not so rigorous as in the United States, should be avoided.

Even so, this is a time for optimism. Prospects are bright for further application of new research to the elderly. Health care of the aged is responding to new knowledge and research in geriatrics and gerontology and to the technology of other areas as well. Diseases of the elderly are increasingly being brought under control. Many complaints, thought to be reactions to stress, are responding favorably to meditation and to forms of training the autonomic nervous system. Genetic engineering and gene therapy, it seems certain, will soon be able to curb more than some of the adverse effects inherited along with the family tree.

Delivering immediate medical services to some of the most remote areas is no longer impossible. Telemedicine, a new technology making use of two-way television systems, enables doctors and nurses to examine and treat patients hundreds and hundreds of miles away. Instead of traveling hours, if not days, to consult a specialist, persons in rural areas can obtain an appointment almost at once. Already the entire body of medical knowledge and the history of individual patients are immediately available via the Internet, on which hundreds of government agencies, hospitals, medical organizations, periodicals, physicians, and universities have health-related sites. Soon, all that knowledge combined with actual examination of patients will instantly be accessible everywhere, helping significantly to postpone illness and to minimize its effects—in the process assuring the well-being and improving the quality of life for many 65+.

Traditionally, the thrust of efforts at treatment of chronic diseases has been palliative rather than preventive. Today, identification of environmental, physiological and social modifiers of aging is proceeding apace. As new understanding of the causes and pathophysiology of disorders and disabilities of aging emerges and leads to better diagnostic and therapeutic techniques, the practice of geriatric health care will concentrate more and more on prevention–in this way bettering the quality of life and paving the way for successful aging.

In the 20th century with virtual elimination of acute diseases, such as typhoid fever and diphtheria, one of the most significant advances in the entire history of the health of human beings occurred. But survival from diseases that in previous eras killed early in life allowed illnesses that occur later in life to increase considerably in frequency. In the 21st century the fundamental medical challenge will be to postpone/prevent/cure/ such serious illnesses as cancer, heart disease and osteoarthritis.

This said, a warning is necessary. As with everything else they purchase, elderly medical consumers need to beware and be aware. Despite the aura of omniscience surrounding some doctors, modern medicine is neither all-knowing nor all-powerful. Elderly patients usually expect and want quick diagnosis and immediately successful treatment of ailments. But doctors do not have all the answers to curing diseases. Notwithstanding the achievements of modern medicine, the majority of ailments remain clouded in mystery. Many an illness afflicting the elderly is exceedingly difficult to diagnose. For older patients, medical tests are not always worth the expense and trouble. In general, early diagnosis helps only when effective therapy exists. At the present time, some cancers are especially difficult to treat even if detected early in the elderly. False positives on tests may persuade healthy oldsters that they are ill. Medications may interfere with one another and have dangerous side effects.

> "The number of diseases is a disgrace to mankind," said Fenelon.

FROM THE FEET UP:
WHAT THE ANNUAL CHECKUP SHOULD CHECK

By the Physician:
> Height and weight

Skin from feet to head (including ears) by looking for signs of cancer
> Between toes by looking for abnormalities
> Fungus under toenails
> Ingrown toenails
> Signs of nerve damage by pricking legs
> Reflexes by tapping under knees
> Varicose veins
> Rectal examination by looking for hemorrhoids
> Prostate by digital probing (Men)
> Groin and abdominal areas by probing for abnormal masses
> Breasts by visual examination, palpation and mammogram (Women)

Armpits and neck by massaging for signs of lymph node swelling
> Blood pressure by cuffing an arm
> Heart and lungs by listening with a stethoscope
> Neck by listening for a clogged carotid artery
> Tongue and mouth by looking for signs of oral cancer
> Ears: listening for signs of hearing loss.
> Eyes by examining for loss of acuity and dark spots in the field of vision

By the Lab and/or Technicians (Tests and Screening):
Blood
> Electrocardiogram
> Pap Smear (Women)
> PSA Test (Men)
> Stool
> Urine

COMMON COMPLAINTS OF THE ELDERLY

Angina pains
Arthritic pains
Backache
Constipation
Cold hands and feet
Dyspepsia
Falls
Getting up at night to urinate
Hearing difficulties
Insomnia
Intermittent claudication (pain in calves while walking)
Irregular heartbeat
Itching
Lack of taste in food
Loss of hair
Nasal discharge
Recurrent cough
Sciatica
Spasms and cramps, especially at sleeptime
Swallowing difficulties
Stiffness (that makes difficult an activity such as cutting toenails)

POSSIBLE SYMPTOMS OF ILLNESS AMONG THE ELDERLY

1. Behavior change, as refusal to eat or drink.
2. Breathing difficulty.
3. Bruises
4. Coughing.
5. Diarrhea.
6. Disorientation
7. Falls.
8. Fever.
9. Hallucinations.

10. Headache(s) if persistent.
11. Incontinence
12. Memory loss, especially if general and persistent.
13. Moaning.
14. Mouth sores.
15. Pulse, whether high or low. Physicians consider a pulse of 60-100 beats per minute normal for most persons.
16. Skin changes, such as to dry or quite pale.
17. Stiffness when moving.
18. Swelling, especially of feet.
19. Tremors.
20. Vomiting.

Please Note: The above list is not exhaustive. Taken by itself, any one symptom may not indicate illness. When a cluster occurs, a doctor should be consulted.

SYMPTOMS ASSOCIATED WITH AILMENTS OF THE ELDERLY

Cardiovascular:
> Ankle swelling, chest pain from exertion, difficult or labored breathing, discomfort while lying down so that there is a need to sit up, palpitations (feeling actions of heart).

Central Nervous System:
> Anesthesia, convulsions, dizziness, headache, paralysis, tingling of skin, tremors.

Gastrointestinal and Liver
> Appetite level change, blood in stool, difficulty in swallowing, food intolerance, indigestion, jaundice, nausea and/or vomiting.

Genitourinary:
> Blood in urine, difficult or painful discharge of urine or difficulty starting stream, excessive secretion of urine, malaise, weight loss.

Hematological:
> Anemia, bleeding, bruising.

Musculoskeletal:

Chronic pain, inflammation, stiffness, swelling, weakness.

Pulmonary:

Color or odor or blood in sputum, cough, excessive amounts of sputum, infections, wheezing.

DISEASES AND DISORDERS OCCURRING FREQUENTLY AMONG THE ELDERLY

LOCATION	ILLNESS/DISORDER
Ear	Presbycusis
	Tinnitus
Eye	Decline in Acuity
	Cataract
	Diabetic Retinopathy
	Glaucoma
	Macular Degeneration
	Presbyopia
Genital and Urinary Organs	Incontinence
	Ovarian Cancer
	Prostatism
	Prostate Cancer
Gastrointestinal Tract	Colon and Rectal Cancer
	Hiatus Hernia
Glands Secreting into the Bloodstream	Diabetes Mellitus
Heart and Blood Vessels	Angina
	Arteriosclerosis
	Heart Failure
	Hypertension
Muscles and Bones	Arthritis
	Osteoporosis
Nervous System	Alzheimer's Disease
	Depression
	Parkinson's Disease

BASIC ILLNESSES CAUSING DEATH IN PERSONS 65+
(ARRANGED IN ORDER OF FREQUENCY)

Heart Disease
Cancer
Cerebrovascular Disease (Stroke)
Diseases Affecting Lungs (Asthma, Emphysema)
Pneumonia and Influenza
Diabetes
Cardiovascular (Hardening of Arteries)
Kidney Disease
Blood Poisoning
Liver Disease
Hypertension (High Blood Pressure)
Ulcers of Stomach and Small Intestine

Please Note: Alzheimer's Disease is not included in the list because diagnosing it as the primary cause of death is impossible in many cases. Accidents and suicides, also leading causes of death in the elderly, are not included because they are the results of ailments rather than the causes.

ARTHRITIS

Surgeons . . .

Spend raptures upon perfect specimens
Of indurated veins, distorted joints,
Or beautiful new cases of curved spine.

Elizabeth Barrett Browning

To the extent that it can be identified on X-rays, arthritis is judged to be the most common chronic disease in the elderly, affecting large numbers of those 65+ and causing pain, stiffness, swelling and limitation of movement of the joints of the affected parts. Arthritis (from the Greek *arthron,* joint) is a generic term meaning joint inflammation. A catch-phrase for many conditions, the term arthritis is commonly used today to refer to more than 130 different ailments of such elements of the musculoskeletal system as joints, ligaments and tendons of joints and muscles. (Lay persons generally use the term arthritis to refer to sore or swollen joints.)

There are many hypotheses as to origin of arthritis. Exact causal mechanisms are unknown although trauma to the joints is thought to be important. Arthritis has an insidious onset and a low mortality rate. Unfortunately, there is no simple test to ensure an accurate diagnosis.

Researchers have identified more than 100 kinds of arthritis, which vary in symptom, amount of wearing away, degree of inflammation and extent of disablement. In particular, the most common forms, osteoarthritis, rheumatoid arthritis and gout, which are age-related, can be devastating psychologically as well as physically. In addition to joint pain, eye problems, fatigue, headaches and rashes may be symptoms. Some elderly find it relatively easy to cope after reassurance that they do not have a severe form that will worsen with time. Others may become depressed because of pain, expense incurred for medication, inability to perform activities necessary for daily living and a consequent need to depend on other people. Shopping or visiting neighbors seems impossible. Sex becomes increasingly difficult.

But the outlook is far from hopeless. Under the supervision of a rheumatologist and with proper treatment—diet, medications, physical therapy (vigorous, regular exercise to help with range of motion, muscle weakness and malalignment of joints), and surgery if absolutely necessary—different types of arthritis can be brought under control, slowed down, and lessened in intensity. For example, bursitis, inflammation of a small fluid-filled saclike cavity near a joint, can irritate and even injure shoulders, elbows and knees; but the condition usually responds well, if caught early, to doses of an NSAID, as Ibuprofen.

The effect of NSAID's varies with the individual, so that a person may have to sample several before discovering one that moderates stiffness and reduces pain. In general, elderly patients are given a low dose to prevent adverse reactions, such as gastrointestinal bleeding. If taken over time, the drugs can precipitate asthma symptoms and cause tinnitus and internal bleeding. A major benefit of NSAIDs is that they suppress inflammation but do not lessen significantly the body's capacity to fight infection. Also helpful in relieving pain is Tylenol, which has a low risk of causing side effects such as stomach irritation.

Males are more commonly affected by arthritis earlier on; with the passage of years, the sex ratio is reversed. The usual type that affects late-life adults is osteoarthritis, the oldest and most prevalent chronic disease known to humankind. Also called degenerative arthritis or degenerative joint disease, osteoarthritis is a noninflammatory, progressive disorder caused by breakdown of cartilage and formation of bony growths and fluid-filled sacs in the joint. Eventually, cartilage may dwindle away completely, leaving bone surfaces without a protective buffer. The cardinal symptom is pain worsened usually by physical exertion, subsequently relieved in part by rest. Obesity aggravates the pain. Among men, weight-bearing joints usually affected include knees, hips and discs of the spine. Among women, the extremities—hands, knees, feet—are usually affected.

Onset of osteoarthritis may not be severe, with morning stiffness of weight-bearing joints often the first symptom. Cartilage in joints thickens, cracks, frays and wears away, so that bones no longer glide easily back and forth. As the disease worsens, motion causes pain and sometimes instability. Deformity often results, restricting movement and causing functional impairment, making it difficult to perform household chores, such as bending to retrieve an article from the cupboard under a sink. Those elderly with osteoarthritis associated disability have some trouble with walking, climbing stairs and even standing. Often, pain is not localized: if osteoarthritis reaches the spine, nerves in the neck and back can be affected, with pain, tingling and numbness as far away as the feet.

Treatment of osteoarthritis should be individualized. Major purposes are to relieve symptoms and to limit progression of the disease. There is no cure although with early diagnosis and treatment rheumatologists can generally gain control of the disorder and minimize damage. It is possible to reduce symptoms with drugs, heat and special exercises. Therapy in more painful cases of osteoarthritis may include injection of corticosteroids or surgery. An extremely powerful medication, a corticosteroid can help reduce severe flare-ups. But equally adverse side effects, including heart disease and osteoporosis, can result unless the drug is carefully administered by a concerned rheumatologist. Although several European investigations report beneficial effects of glucosamine and chondroitin, the Food and Drug Administration has not approved their use because as yet large, controlled US studies have not been completed. Replacement with prosthetic joints may be tried as a last resort. If successful, such surgery can change a virtual cripple into a fully active person.

To maintain flexibility, strength and proper posture, victims of osteoarthritis should try to avoid further injury to the joints. Properly done, exercise is beneficial because it helps maintain flexibility and joint mobility. By increasing the amount of fluid in the joints, exercise increases lubrication. Exercise should be designed to develop and maintain full range of motion and to strengthen muscles around arthritic joints so as to reduce strain. Trying to engage in an active aerobics-based program can lead to disaster. One guide to safety: pain should not last more than two hours after a period of exercise. Should pain persist, exercise should be discontinued and a doctor consulted. A physiatrist, without increasing an elderly person's pain and causing fatigue, can adapt an exercise program to the degree of disability and to the joints involved, as exercising in a swimming pool to lessen stress on the knees.

If at all, possible, an elderly person should at the very least engage daily in moderate levels of general physical activity, such as frequently standing tall, raising arms above the head, rotating shoulders, swiveling the torso at the hips, and extending the legs. Whether standing or sitting, good posture (shoulders back and head upright) is important.

Rheumatoid arthritis is a severe chronic inflammatory condition affecting connective tissue throughout the body. At first, fatigue and stiffness occur, followed by pain in swollen joints. As the disease progresses, membranes lining joints overgrow and erode cartilage and bone. More serious than osteoarthritis, it has greater potential for pain and crippling disability. Initial targets sometimes are hands and wrists although in older persons hips and shoulders are quite often affected first. Onset can occur early, even in 20-year-olds, and so elderly victims may have been carrying the disease for a long time. But first occurrence after 60 is not uncommon. Rheumatoid arthritis has periods of relative or complete remission followed by flare-ups. Symptoms include anemia, fatigue, fever and weight loss. Elderly patients with active rheumatoid arthritis usually have significant redness, warmth, swelling and tenderness in at least one joint.

Cause of the disease is unknown although emotional upset can trigger episodes, so that some physicians occasionally refer to it as psychosomatic. Considerable evidence indicates that it is an autoimmune disease, wherein a person's antibodies launch harmful attacks on the body's own tissues. As the condition of joints worsens and the disease progresses, affected tissues undergo changes that can lead to further erosion of cartilage, joint deformation, disability and eventual invalidism. Treatment, similar to that of other forms of arthritis, involves anti-inflammatory medication carefully prescribed by a physician plus exercise. Now available are several disease-modifying antirheumatic drugs (DMARDS), such as gold injections and methotrexate.

Although there is no cure for osteoarthritis or rheumatoid arthritis, considerable progress has been made in therapy and management, so that it is now unusual for many to be bedridden or crippled by the disease. A cervical pillow during sleep will help keep the head in a neutral position and diminish strain on joints in the neck. Several kinds of devices are available to make performing Activities of Daily Living easier. Mechanical devices as well as body mechanics can be employed to great advantage. Bars with wheels to enable sliding a heavy object like a refrigerator will help an older person avoid pushing and lifting. Men should build up the grip on a screwdriver with tape to make twisting easier; women should place the strap of a handbag over a shoulder to take the weight off hand and wrist. Other assistive devices are useful for opening jars and for helping to put on shoes and stockings. There is a gadget to aid in buttoning a blouse, another to fetch items on a shelf above the head, still another to help getting out of a bath tub, and so on. Both arthritis specialists and general surgical supply houses have complete catalogues, as do many therapists who are of great value in helping arthritics master skills needed in daily living. Counselors are available to help people avoid becoming manipulative and complaining, behavior that often results from painful, debilitating chronic diseases.

Gout, a recurrent acute form of arthritis, is a metabolic disease in which excess uric acid precipitates to form sharp crystals in such joints as the ankle, knee and elbow. Appearing without warning, gout may be occasioned by overindulgence in rich food and large amounts of alcohol. Generally, the disorder has a dramatic onset with severe pain in the big toe. Affected joints are hot, reddish and swollen. A physical examination is almost always enough to make an accurate diagnosis.

While gout may emerge in the early 40's, peak age of onset in males occurs in the fifth decade and in the sixth in females. In men 70+, chance of recurrent attacks is small. In women of advanced age, an attack of gout may occur because after menopause and with the passage of years there is a buildup of serum uric acid.

Treatment of gout is directed to relief from inflammation as soon as possible. Although gout is well-controlled by drug therapy, often by an NSAID with serum uric acid-lowering properties, lifelong medication is the norm. Prophylactic medication given daily can prevent re-currence. Also recommended is increased intake of carbohydrates, which are associated with uric acid elimination. Otherwise, attacks can be-come more frequent and the fingers, elbow and knee can be affected.

Unfortunately, arthritis quackery victimizes many elderly, who spend millions of dollars, if not billions, on bogus remedies that are useless and potentially harmful in that they delay fitting treatment. Advertise-ments featuring testimonials from satisfied customers for copper bracelets, macrobiotic diets, and—oddly—training in sexual techniques are pro-moted as certain cures. Unaware that arthritic pain normally comes and goes in recurrent patterns, elderly victims because of the placebo effect may regard fraudulent remedies and sham treatment as effective although temporary.

The best ways to protect oneself from such quackery are simple and readily accessible. If the *cure* offered is for a specific disease, in this case arthritis, there are national organizations that will provide accurate information and advice free of charge. Government and consumer or-ganizations, such as the Food and Drug Administration and the Council of Better Business Bureaus, can also be easily contacted about claims of cures and medical breakthroughs.

In medicine, as in other areas, the buyer must learn to beware of easy and quick fixes.

THE BACK

Oh, my aching back!

GI Complaint, WW II

More than 200,000 elderly Americans have had a back problem, a malady with a strong probability of recovery and, too often, recurrence. As many as 3 in 10 older persons may have a chronic back complaint at this moment. Yet studies suggest that the frequency of the disorder does not increase with age.

As with so many other ailments in the elderly, symptoms, causes and treatment can differ considerably from those in young persons. Orthopedists (physicians whose specialty is treatment of the skeleton) hold that normal wear and tear of aging need not be responsible for back pain although with age and inactivity the spine's discs may begin to dehydrate and lose flexibility. Nor are gynecologic disorders usually the cause of such trouble. Aware that back pain often disappears spontaneously after a time, many physicians characterize the disorder as self-healing. In the absence of malignancy or other medical emergency, physicians generally do not attempt to fit an episode of low back pain into a specific syndrome. They regard it as a symptom rather than as a disorder, and they try as soon as possible to help relieve the pain with an analgesic, such as acetaminophen.

Determining the exact cause of back pain can be difficult. The spine, a complex structure which supports and lets the torso bend, turn and twist, consists of vertebrae (bony or cartilaginous segments) alternating with flexible discs (rounded and flattened structures with gel-like centers). In persons 65+ acute back pain can be caused by poor posture, by a sudden twisting movement, by bending from the waist to push or lift a heavy object, by infections, by weakness of abdominal muscles or by instability of the vertebrae resulting from changes in the discs that separate them.

Pain can occur at the place of difficulty or it may be referred elsewhere. Sciatica, usually caused by nerve compression as a result of disc protrusion, may accompany low back pain or appear alone–with pain radiating along the sciatic nerve and down the buttock and rear of the leg to below the knee. Rheumatoid arthritis involving the hips may appear as low back pain. Osteoporotic fractures of the sacrum (the thick, triangular bone at the bottom of the spine) can cause low back and leg pain.

If the pain worsens over time, the doctor will check for an infection or malignancy and proceed from there. Otherwise, the orthopedist or physician of choice may prescribe rest followed by use of a special corset. Specific movements under supervision of a qualified therapist or physiatrist (a physician whose specialty involves movement) will also be prescribed although as yet there is little scientific evidence as to the extent of exercise efficacy. Caution is needed because improper movement may irritate an arthritic joint or further damage a weakened disc. Many physicians hold that surgery should be avoided if at all possible because the percentage of success is not particularly high, especially in case of a pinched nerve (wherein a tendon or other body part is impinging on a nerve and causing pain).

In general, to avoid and/or prevent back pain, strengthen the abdominal muscles, bend at the knees and not at the waist when lifting a heavy object, try to carry heavy objects close to the body and above waist level. Check out sports carefully. Golf is notorious for injuries to the back. Before engaging in a new sport, an elderly person should consult a sports medicine practitioner, and then follow with coaching, both to develop skills and to avoid injuries.

Otherwise, a late-life adult will, with Edwin Markham's ploughman find "on his back the burden of the world."

CANCER

May cancer rot their herring gut. . . .

W.H. Auden

Risk of cancer and of death from cancer increases significantly with age. Despite media clamor and sympathy for children who are afflicted, cancer is unusual before adulthood. Cancer is mainly a geriatric disease, whose incidence and death rates are highest among America's elderly. Probability of developing a cancer within a 5-year span increases from 1 in 700 at age 25 to 1 in 14 at age 65. More than 50% of all cancers are found in the 65+ age group. Some epidemiologists warn that unless methods of prevention and/or cure are found soon there is possibility of a virtual cancer *epidemic* about the year 2030, when at least 20% of the entire population of the United States will be 65+. Hard hit will be Afro-Americans, among whom cancer mortality is about 30% higher than it is for whites. No wonder the United States with the National Cancer Act declared war in 1971 on this dread scourge.

There is some good news. Many of the elderly respond to treatment as well as the young. Although cancer is generally thought by lay persons to be inevitably fatal, some types are curable. A considerable number of researchers hold that the 1990s will be remembered as the decade when medicine measurably began to turn the tide against cancer. In the last 5 years of the Twentieth Century there was about a 3% drop in the number of deaths from cancer, primarily from earlier and better detection, changes in the American lifestyle and reduction of exposure to noxious chemicals in the workplace.

There is bad news. Research for treatment and a cure is substantial and never-ceasing, and has been going on for a century or more. Despite billions of dollars spent on research, physicians have not found a magic bullet against cancer such as they did with polio. Chemotherapy, radiation and surgery remain the major treatments although the first 2 are sometimes toxic. Origins of many cancers remain unknown. People do not act properly even when causes and preventable action are obvious: 25% or more of America's current crop of teenagers have taken up smoking, and millions of adults refuse to stop.

Incidence of each kind of cancer tends to peak at certain ages in the elderly. Among men 75+, prostatic cancer comprises 25% of all malignancies; GI cancer, 25%. Among women 75 +, breast cancer comprises 25%; GI cancer, 15%. Although largely preventable through cessation of smoking, about 50% of lung cancers occur in those 65+.

The average age at diagnosis of colon and rectal cancer is 60-70 years. Skin and breast cancers seem to occur almost entirely among the elderly. Yet experts state flatly that the majority of cancers can be prevented by avoiding known carcinogens, such as tobacco or excessive exposure to the sun. Obviously, there is need for cancer education.

Although cancer research comes with a vast vocabulary, medical terminology for cancer is straightforward. Cancer is a general term for the more than 200 kinds of abnormal, uncontrolled growth of body tissue. A tissue is a group of cells that compose one of the structural materials of the body, as muscle tissue. A neoplasm, a new growth of tissue that seemingly has no physiologic function, is termed benign if it does not spread from one part of the body to others even though it damages somewhat the material in which it is growing. The word tumor is also used to refer to a growth with no discernible physiologic function, and it may be new or old. A neoplasm that moves into other tissues is said to metastasize and is referred to as malignant. A malignant neoplasm is commonly referred to simply as a cancer by medical personnel and lay persons alike.

Cancers traditionally have been classified in 2 types. Carcinoma affects epithelial tissue, which lines tubes and cavities and encloses and protects other structures of the body. Sarcoma affects connective tissue, which supports and secures structures of the body. As examples, consider the term squamous cell carcinoma, which is a cancer of epithelial cells in areas exposed to sunlight, as on the face; or the term osteogenic sarcoma, which is a cancer commonly occurring in the growing area of a bone, particularly around the knee. Today, in addition to the traditional classification, a cancer is often named by what its cells resemble and where they arise. A pancreatic cancer implies that it arises in the pancreas and its cells resemble pancreatic cells.

Cancer, a malignant tumor characterized by potentially unlimited cellular growth with ability to invade local tissue and then to attack other parts of the body, strikes 1 of every 3 older Americans, killing more than 1 in 5. With related complications, it is the second leading cause of death among the elderly, second only to cardiovascular disease. Oncologists (cancer specialists) refer to cancer as a broad spectrum of diseases, with a few characteristics in common but with many different causes, some predominantly related to lifestyle, as smoking. In addition to those mentioned above, there are numerous kinds of cancer in the group assaulting the elderly, some more serious than others: Paget's disease (characterized by destruction of bone), leukemia, non-Hodgkin's lymphoma, chronic lymphatic leukemia.

Cancer usually manifests itself after a long latent period. Without observable symptoms, a cancer can develop in any organ and grow into an abnormal mass in which the cells develop in irregular cycles of rest and proliferation and spread by way of the bloodstream and the lymphatic system.

Screening for cancer, ranging from physical inspection to employment of highly sophisticated technology, is recommended on a continual basis for everyone 55+, as is training in recognizing warning signs and symptoms of cancer. Indications which call for investigation include bleeding from an orifice, sores which do not heal, a sudden change in body conditions as mole enlargement or lump in a breast. A smoker's lungs should be promptly checked in case of symptoms like shortness of breath and chronic coughing.

Detection of malignancy, particularly among the elderly, can be crucial because some cancers common in older adults, such as those of the breast and colon, when caught early are potentially curable if the therapy itself is not too aggressive for an aged body to tolerate. Generally, effectiveness of cancer treatment does not lessen with increasing age. Exceptions are among the oldest-old, whose life expectancy may not be so long as the time between detection of cancer and death from the disease.

Not all cancers in the elderly run a fast course, perhaps because oxidants within the body and cancer-causing chemicals in the environment have taken a long time in which to cause malignancy. Longevity of the elderly victim provides a cancer with an incubation period extended enough for full development. This is apparently so with many instances of prostate malignancy, which may take years and years to develop with or without symptoms, so that even when it is discovered both the old patient and his physician find little value in attempts at treatment. Many cancers are detected only at postmortem examination, and even then they are not thought to be the immediate cause of death.

Cancer specialists say that their aims remain constant. They would remove the cancer and prolong life, in the process relieving pain and other unpleasant symptoms. A cure is generally regarded as the patient's being alive and free of the cancer five years after diagnosis. Oncologists do not employ procedures with whose results a patient cannot cope: poor vision may contraindicate a colostomy. Today, appropriate use of analgesics and anesthetic techniques assure almost all cancer victims of significant relief from pain.

Cancer treatment is continually evolving. Here again, education and supportive care are essential. Oncologists maintain that active patient participation in and cooperative acceptance of diagnostic tests and follow-up treatment are of first importance.

Currently, five types of treatment are usually available to elderly cancer patients. While no surgery is without risk and the risk increases with age, in general, older people tolerate elective surgery satisfactorily, as to remove a tumor or to unblock an obstruction resulting from colon cancer. In cases of emergency surgery or surgery where other diseases in addition to cancer are present, risk to the elderly increases significantly. Radiation by means of machines or application of radium may be used alone or in combination with surgery. Radiation often helps to control metastasis and to reduce pain by shrinking tumors. Chemotherapy, as the name implies, employs chemicals to obliterate cancer cells. Because chemotherapy is not truly selective, normal cells may also be affected by the chemicals. Patients may have to cope with anorexia, hair loss and other body changes. Side effects, such as drops in blood count, weakness, nausea and diarrhea, are often too much for older patients who are already suffering physical and emotional pain, and chemotherapy is discontinued. Hormone therapy, which attempts to strengthen the immune system and make it more efficient, is an attractive treatment for the elderly because of fewer side effects.

Patients with cancer are interested in anyone or anything promising a cure or significant pain relief. They particularly fear suffering although many cancers produce little or no pain except in advanced stages. Even then, drug therapy for relief of pain is usually effective in almost all patients. But victims and their families pay a great price, emotional as well as financial, for nostrums potentially dangerous and worthless as cures although guaranteed by salesmen of what turn out ultimately to be false hopes. Anybody other than a reputable physician should not be trusted to advise about and to deal with serious illness.

Apparently, nutrition does influence some forms of cancer. Biomedical researchers administering a diet with normal or better quantities of minerals, proteins and vitamins but low in calories have retarded or eliminated cancer in laboratory rats. In consequence, unscrupulous purveyors of so-called health foods are promising miracles—at advanced prices. Something similar is happening with antioxidants, Vitamins E and C among others, because when animals are given them the appearance of cancer seems to be postponed. Starving or gobbling of vitamins in anticipation of a cure for cancer, to put the matter gently, is not a good idea. Authorities estimate that over-reliance on vitamin and mineral supplementation costs Americans more than $10,000,000,000 a year.

In 1900, principal causes of death were infectious diseases. Today, diphtheria, typhoid fever and smallpox appear so rarely in the United States that the public has almost forgotten them. Tuberculosis and pneumonia are still being fought vigorously and with much success. Greater understanding of cancer at fundamental levels has improved tests and therapies. Researchers are developing new drugs and treatments. More, much more, can be done by way of prevention if people will change their lifestyle, particularly in regard to eating a healthful diet, exercising regularly and maintaining normal body weight.

There is some reason for optimism. Years have been added to the lives of many patients and life to those years. Increasingly certain that there is a genetic basis for cancer, some researchers are designing drugs that thwart mutations in genes, biochemical errors that distort normal controls in body cells, making them susceptible to invasive cancerous growth. Other researchers are beginning to report success in shrinking and eradicating cancer in laboratory mice through blocking blood supply of tumors. By the end of the 21st century, perhaps as a result of ongoing ceaseless research, cancer–the infamous scourge that has taken so many lives after years of intense pain and has cost innumerable families their life savings–will have been conquered and almost forgotten.

Researchers agree that in the meantime it is wise to reduce risk in the diet by eating a wide variety of whole grains, fruits and vegetable and cutting back on fats. To reduce risk in the lifestyle, include at least 30 minutes of moderate physical activity in the daily routine.

POSSIBLE CANCER WARNINGS
NO ONE SHOULD IGNORE

Change in size and/or shape of a mole
A lump in the breast and/or a discharge from the nipple
A sore that does not heal and/or that bleeds continually
A sudden change in bowel and/or bladder habits
Continual indigestion and/or difficulty swallowing
Shortness of breath
Chronic coughing
Persistent unexplained skeletal pain
Fatigue and general weakness
Recurrent episodes of nausea and vomiting
Women: postmenopausal bleeding
On the ear, a small irregular lump with heaped up borders
Weight loss
Painless jaundice
Ulcerated sore(s) in the mouth
Continual abdominal discomfort and/or pain
Scaly or ulcerated skin

BREAST CANCER

As in her breast the wave of life
Kept heaving to and fro.

Thomas Hood

Breast cancer is the most prevalent of all invasive malignancies in women. So great is the fear of breast cancer that symptoms possibly suggesting the disease cause innumerable women to seek medical advice, as any doctor in practice can attest. Not that the fear is without cause. For a woman with a close relative who has succumbed to the disease the risk is ever-present. About 180,000 new cases of breast cancer in women and 1,500 in men, which may metastasize to almost any organ in the body, are reported annually in the United States. Every year approximately, 45,000 women and 1,400 men die of the disease.

Estimates are that some 15,000,000 asymptomatic women, because of worry over contracting breast cancer, consult a doctor at least once a year. For every woman newly diagnosed as having breast cancer, at least 5-10 others endure biopsies that turn out to be benign, whether or not a growth is present. Why so much concern? A man who is the victim of a prostate cancer that has metastasized is facing the prospect that the surgeon may decide as a life-saving technique to remove the testicles, a dreadful prospect. Not only will he be emasculated, he worries, he will be a eunuch, an object of scorn or derisive pity, a butt for contemptuous jokesters. A woman who is the victim of breast cancer, whether or not it has metastasized, is facing the prospect that the surgeon may decide to remove one or both breasts, a dreadful prospect. Not only will she lose proof of her femininity, she will also lose the signs of motherhood. She will be scarred and misshapened, so that she no longer considers herself attractive. She may be concerned about the reaction of her husband. And she knows that, if she survives, she will have problems with prostheses and clothing for the rest of her life.

For many men and women, fear of what the surgeon will do is worse than fear of death. Physicians and nurses and social workers, aware that the man and woman worry intensely about a horrible future, will do what they can by way of reassurance. Support groups, invaluable resources, are also available.

After menopause begins at or about the 50th year of age, a woman undergoes hormonal changes. There are modifications of breast tissues. Ligaments stretch and muscles lose tone, so that contours of the breasts are altered. Cysts, small sacs containing fluid or semifluid, commonly occur. Under probing fingers they may feel like small, slippery peas. Also common in occurrence are bits of lumpiness and breast pain. Physicians refer to these conditions as *fibrocystic disease*. Although neither abnormal nor malign, they can be frightening. More than 90% of women having nipple discharge, whether milky or bloody, are cancer-free. All these conditions are close, too close, to what appear to be symptoms of breast cancer. Elderly women are especially concerned, for 2/3 of all breast cancers occur in women 55+.

Lifetime risk of suffering breast cancer is a bit more than 10%, somewhat more for women with late menopause, and even more for women age 75+. Those women 75+ in whom breast cancer is diagnosed have a shorter survival time than women 55+, possibly because a number of doctors are unwilling to let them undergo the rigors of cancer testing and therapy since breast cancers in older women are usually slower in growth and less aggressive in development. For women 65+ who are diagnosed as having breast cancer, hormone medication is recommended either as an alternative to surgery or to prevent a recurrence of malignancy. If hormone therapy is ineffective, chemotherapy may be tried despite side effects.

Since a woman cannot alter a risk factor like having a close relative with the disease, the best chance for reducing mortality is through early detection. More than 80% of cancers are brought to light after discovery of a lump in the breast by a woman herself. (Other warning signs include change in color, shape and texture of the breast or discharge from the nipple.) Accordingly, doctors recommend that older women examine their breasts regularly for asymmetry and/or lumps. Tumors found this way are more easily treated and have a better prognosis. Instruction by a nurse or by a doctor will make the procedure clear.

For women 55+, a routine recommended by the American Cancer Society that can reduce mortality significantly consists of monthly self-examination, annual mammography and examination by a doctor. Because of medical science's increasing ability to recognize difficulties, many physicians recommend that women start getting mammograms much before the age of 55. Also recommended are exercising, limiting alcohol intake, maintaining a desirable weight and eating a diet low in fat and high in fresh fruit and vegetables. Prognosis for older women with breast cancer depends on the extent and rate of growth of the malignancy.

Ultrasound is not employed routinely in screening for breast cancer although it can discriminate between a cyst (for which treatment is usually not necessary, especially if there are no disturbing symptoms) and a solid mass (which generally needs biopsy). Such screening is not deemed necessary for women 75+. Doctors hope that high-resolution ultra-sound imaging, a relatively new technique for evaluating breast lumps, will reduce the need for biopsies by about 40%.

If a lump is found, if a mass appears in a mammogram or if a warning sign such as pain or tenderness appears, two kinds of biopsy may be performed. The patient is given a local anesthetic, and a hollow needle is inserted into the breast at the suspected site. If no abnormal cells are found, no other action may be taken. If the laboratory report is positive, tissue from the suspected site (possibly a lump) is excised surgically. If the ensuing laboratory report indicates cancer, the patient should discuss treatment options with her doctor, including possibility of breast removal, with or without breast reconstruction, and possible breast-conservation surgery by utilizing lumpectomy rather than mastectomy. If at all possible, the patient should get a second opinion.

At least 8 out of 10 biopsies reveal that the breast tissue is not cancerous. If cancer is discovered to have metastasized, treatment hardly affects survival rates but can palliate symptoms. The usual treatment is surgery, but there are several modalities. Survival rates for patients undergoing a mastectomy (removal of the entire breast) and those undergoing breast-conserving surgery and radiotherapy seem comparable.

If the tumor is large, breast-conserving surgery may be impractical. Choice of treatment is the patient's.

Therapy in this situation should be individualized. Many women opt for breast-conserving surgery plus radiotherapy because of its cosmetic value: some shrinkage does occur in the treated breast, but the effects of radiotherapy are temporary and mild.

COLON and RECTAL CANCER

All prejudice may be traced back to the intestines.

Nietzsche

After digestion of food has been completed in the small intestine, enzymes and various secretions along with water and undigested material pass into the large intestine, which begins with a small pouch, the cecum. From there the colon, the last 5-6 feet of the digestive tract, the major section of the large intestine, extends all the way to the rectum, the last segment of the colon. As material is pushed through the colon, feces are formed and then stored in the rectum. A variety of ailments and disorders can assail these portions of the digestive tract, among which are cancers of the colon and the rectum.

The incidence of colon and rectal cancer in the United States rises sharply with age, reaching a peak for both sexes from 60-75 years. About 135,000 cases are diagnosed annually, 95,000 for the colon, 40,000 for the rectum. Some 55,000 deaths result from the disease despite the fact that colorectal cancer can generally be prevented or dealt with successfully through health education, screening programs and early detection. Prognosis depends largely on the size and extent of spread of the tumor when it is detected. When colorectal cancer is discovered at an early stage, the cure rate is near 90%.

Excluding prostate cancer, colon and rectal cancers are the most common malignancies among the elderly. Colon cancer is more prevalent. In the United States, where the population consumes a diet low in fiber and calcium and high in animal protein, refined carbohydrates and fat, there is an elevated incidence of colon and rectal cancer. Perhaps carcinogens are ingested in the diet. Perhaps they result from bacterial action on dietary substances. The exact causes and mechanisms are unknown. Other factors include heredity, wherein colorectal cancer occurs across generations, and colitis, wherein chronic inflammation of the colon results in abdominal pain and diarrhea and increases the risk of colon cancer.

Symptoms depend on the site, type and extent of the malignancy. On the right side of the colon, abdominal pain, anemia, fatigue, and weight loss may be the only complaints.

Bleeding is commonly occult; that is, it is present in very small amounts. It can be detected by means of a simple, inexpensive stool test that should be done annually. On the left side, occult bleeding and altered bowel habits are the usual symptoms. But a developed malignancy on either or both sides may cause constipation and hemorrhage. If rectal bleeding occurs with defecation, the possibility of colorectal cancer should be checked carefully by testing of the feces even when the person has quite obvious hemorrhoids. By means of a digital rectal examination that should be done annually on the elderly, a doctor can often make a diagnosis. Barium enema X-ray inspection is used in diagnosis of colon but not rectal cancer.

Surgery is often the recommended treatment, both in attempt to cure and to relieve symptoms. Polyps, masses of tissue growing out from the intestinal wall, can usually be detected through an in-office procedure, endoscopy, which is observation of the interior of the intestine by means of a long, flexible, telescope-like tube inserted through the anal sphincter and manipulated through the colon. The two most common endoscopic examinations are sigmoidoscopy which checks about 2 feet of the colon, and colonoscopy, which inspects the entire 5 feet or so. Because polyps often become cancerous, physicians surgically remove them and then have them biopsied. Studies indicate that removal generally prevents further cancer formation for at least 5 years. Even so, many physicians recommend that after surgery a person should have an endoscopy every 3 to 5 years.

In some cases of cancer, it becomes necessary to cut part of the large intestine and create an opening (*stoma* is the medical term) through the abdomen to the outside of the body for the removal of waste. Such surgery is named for the part or parts of the body involved, in this instance a *colostomy* or a *coloproctostomy* (colon and rectum).

Chance of cure is highly dependent on the stage of the cancer at the time of surgery. Early stage colorectal cancer can often be cured with surgery alone. For patients with more advanced tumors in the colon and rectum, chemotherapy or chemotherapy with radiation may increase the chance for cure. Surgical treatment is feasible in about 70% of colon and rectal cancers. Depending on the extent of the malignancy, 5-year survival rates vary from 30-90%. If the cancer has been found to have metastasized at the time of diagnosis, treatment is rarely curative and is often used solely to palliate symptoms.

Who can disagree with Joseph Conrad's dictum that "You can't ignore the importance of a good digestion. The joy of life depends on a sound stomach, whereas a bad digestion inclines one to skepticism, incredulity, breeds black fancies and thoughts of death."

LEUKEMIA

May your own blood rise against you, and the sweetest
drink you take be the bitterest cup of sorrow.

Traditional Wexford Curse

Although leukemia is often referred to as a blood malignancy, it is really a cancerous disorder of the organs that produce blood cells, mainly bone marrow and the lymph system. Despite usage of the word *leukemia* (from the Greek for white blood) to refer to a malignancy involving rapid growth in the number of white blood cells, there is a leukemia of red blood cells but it is much less common. Whether red or white, leukemia usually impacts on all blood cells to some degree.

Advanced age is a major risk factor for developing leukemia. About 28,000 new cases occur annually among the elderly in the United States. Nearly 21,000 persons die from leukemia every year Precise causes of the disease have not been determined although various viruses have been linked to several types of leukemia, and radiation is believed to be a predisposing factor.

Doctors divide the many types of leukemia into 2 major groups, acute and chronic, terms which refer to cell development. Acute leukemias consist predominantly of undifferentiated cell populations; chronic, of mature cells. Acute leads to quick development of anemia; chronic, to slow development. Acute leukemia is the the most common malignancy in children, with a peak incidence among youngsters 3-5 years of age. It does occur in adolescents and young adults but less frequently. It often appears as though an infection with a quick onset and high fever. There has been tremendous progress in treatment, so much so that cure is now an achievable goal for many child victims of this dread disease. Not so with the elderly, for whom incidence of the cancer is 4 times higher than in children.

Chronic lymphocytic leukemia is the most common form of blood cancer afflicting the elderly in the United States, appearing 2-3 times more frequently in men than in women. In general, initial symptoms of chronic leukemia are fatigue, pallor, diminished tolerance of exercise and a general decline of well-being. About 1 in 4 patients are asymptomatic, the disease being discovered at the yearly physical examination or from the laboratory test for blood count. Definitive diagnosis is by inspection of cells in bone marrow. The disease gradually involves lymph tissue with increasing penetration of bone marrow and blood circulation.

Because symptoms may be vague, resembling those of several less serious medical disorders, detection of chronic lymphocytic leukemia is difficult in its early stages. Later on, infections become a problem because of lessened immune function. Many elderly victims of the disease who show low-grade blood abnormality are not given chemotherapy because complications of the treatment may be more harmful than the disease itself. They are monitored instead. Some of these persons live for from 10-15 years, not particularly troubled by the disease. For others, prognosis is unfavorable because the disease has metastasized. Prolonged lessening or disappearance of symptoms, what doctors refer to as *remission,* is not likely in such cases, perhaps because of the high-dose chemotherapy required with various combinations of drugs employed in sequence or because of poor functioning in such organs as the kidneys. The 5-year survival rate is about 50%, death often occurring within 2 years. .

LUNG CANCER

He never saw, never before today,
What was able to take his breath away.

Robert Browning

Despite the fact that it is largely preventable, lung cancer–predominantly refractory to available therapy–is still responsible for more deaths in the United States than any other form of cancer. About 180,000 cases are diagnosed annually, with about 160,000 deaths expected. Warning signs include chest or shoulder pain, repeated episodes of bronchitis, persistent coughing, wheezy breathing.

Most prevalent in adults aged 40-70, lung cancer caused by smoking is accountable for some 90% of all cases in men, about 70% in women. The percentages may draw even soon, for the incidence of lung cancer has been rising rather rapidly in women the past few years; the number of women dying with lung cancer has surpassed the number of women dying with breast cancer each year in the United States.

Preventing lung cancer caused by smoking seems easy: all one has to do is quit cigarette smoking before the disease reaches an advanced stage, giving injured bronchial lining time and chance to heal itself. When smokers quit smoking, however, their risk of developing lung cancer remains high for years and only very slowly declines. This is different from heart disease, where the cessation of smoking fairly quickly diminishes the risk of coronary disease. Exposure to dangerous levels of radon gas at home and/or to carcinogenic agents at work is responsible for most of the remaining cases of lung cancer. The precise role of air pollution is unknown.

Lung cancer is broken down into 2 broad categories, and both are exceedingly difficult to detect early on. Physical examinations are not revelatory. Chest X-rays may locate an abnormality but not metastasis. By the time smoker's cough, wheezing of breath, weight loss and weakness manifest themselves, the patient may have advanced disease. Non-small-cell lung cancer includes squamous cell, large cell, and adenocarcinoma. The other broad category of lung cancer is small-cell carcinoma, the most aggressive of the lung cancers, which more often than not kills patients within 2 years of diagnosis. For non-small cell lung cancer caught early on, surgery is the treatment of choice. Treatment with radiation or chemotherapy and radiation is often used in more advanced disease. For small-cell carcinomas, chemotherapy is the primary therapy, but radiation may also be employed. Although some success with medications has been reported, there is as yet no established regimen for the treatment by drugs of either small-cell carcinoma or non-small cell. The 5-year survival rate is not high, and survivors need careful follow-up because second lung cancers have been known to develop.

Lung cancer can be extremely aggressive in the elderly. Treatment is often palliative and may include chemotherapy and radiation and, when deemed absolutely necessary, surgery

The tragedy is that lung cancer need not be so widespread. The Elizabethan playwright, Ben Jonson, pointed out the danger some 4 centuries ago but to no avail: "The lungs of the tobacconist are rotted, the liver spotted, the brain smoked like the back side of the pig-woman's booth here, and the whole body within black as her pan. . . ."

OVARIAN CANCER

In the dark womb where I began
My mother's life made me a man.

John Masefield

About 27,000 new cases of ovarian cancer are diagnosed annually, with about 15,000 deaths to follow. As the statistics indicate, ovarian cancer is less prevalent than some other cancers affecting women, but it is the most common cause of death from a gynecological cancer. There is no screening test for ovarian cancer. The earliest symptoms are nonspecific, often nothing more than vague digestive complaints and lower abdominal discomfort. There may be enlargement of the abdomen. Abnormal vaginal bleeding is a definite warning sign, but it appears in only 1 of 4 cases. Risk factors include advancing age and a personal or familial history of breast cancer.

Most ovarian tumors are benign. If a malignancy is suspected, actual determination of cancer is by means of a biopsy. When the malignancy occurs in premenopausal women, the likelihood of a cure is much greater than when it strikes after menopause. Treatment of choice is surgery to remove the ovaries, followed often by chemotherapy and/ or radiation therapy. Doctors attribute the relatively low survival rate, about 45-60%, to non-appearance of symptoms until the cancer has reached an advanced stage.

Ovarian cancer patients who have had surgery are followed closely for at least 2 years. Frequent pelvic examinations are performed and continuing diagnosis attempted.

PANCREATIC CANCER

> Asthma and other annoyances
> I have tolerated for years; but
> I cannot put up with cancer.
>
> John Davidson

After breast, colorectal, lung and prostate cancers, pancreatic cancer is the 5th most common cause of cancer deaths in the United States. The incidence of pancreatic cancer increases with age, the vast majority of malignancies appearing at or after 55 years. Over and above 25,000 cases are reported each year, with many more men affected than females, more blacks than whites.

There are several types of pancreatic malignancies, 80% occurring in the head of the pancreas, 20% in the tail. Specific causes have not been determined. Chief risk factors, both dietary and environmental, include coffee in excess and diets high in animal fat, diabetes mellitus, and smoking.

Symptoms generally occur late and may not be noticed at first by the patient. The usual indication for cancer of the head of the pancreas is jaundice, the yellow discoloration hardly noticeable on the skin that results from blockage of the bile duct system, appearing more clearly perhaps in the white of the eyes. There may be nausea and vomiting. In time, weight loss and itching of the skin may occur, along with darkening of the urine to a reddish color and lightening of stools from a brown to a clay color. While developing, cancer in the body of the pancreas may cause back pain and abdominal swelling–the symptoms vague and hardly noticeable at the outset. As the symptoms worsen, pain management varies all the way from aspirin to a neural block for incessant severe aching. Otherwise, drugs neither prolong life nor enhance its quality. Chemotherapy provides no long-term benefits. Radiation therapy may help relieve pain.

Laboratory tests at the yearly physical examination usually appear normal. As a result, early determination of pancreatic cancer, when the growth is still in curable stages, is highly unlikely. Making diagnosis difficult even after symptoms have become apparent is the fact that several diseases, as hepatitis, may produce jaundice. Spread of the cancer to other organs may generate still other symptoms. Although a CT scan may visualize the pancreatic mass and endoscopy detect the cancer in many cases, absolute determination may require abdominal surgery. In approximately 90% of the cases the cancer has so metastasized by the time of diagnosis that death follows within 6 months. The overall 5-year survival rate after surgery is less than 2%.

PROSTATE CANCER

> *Many a time a man cannot be such as he would be,*
> *if circumstances do not admit of it.*
>
> Terence

More than 1/2 of older adult males have prostate difficulties. Unlike almost all other body tissues, the testicles for instance, the prostate gradually increases in size in many men, if not all, as they age from the year 40 on.

For reasons not understood, a number of prostate diseases develop as men age. It is not uncommon to find a tumor, a growth of glandular elements, in the prostate. If not cancerous, the condition is referred to as *benign prostatic hypertrophy* (BHP), even though it may result in complications from bladder obstruction that produces symptoms usually associated with cancer, such as blood in the urine, frequent urination, especially at night, burning sensations while urinating at any time and difficulty when trying to urinate. Neither is *prostatitis* cancerous, an infectious condition in which the prostate gland enlarges from an accumulation of fluid, so that pressure on the bladder neck results in diminished urine flow and symptoms like those of *benign prostatic hypertrophy*. Except in cases of blockage, recurrent urinary tract infections or severe urinary retention, drug therapy has been the treatment of choice for both conditions despite possible undue side effects. With a new procedure labeled TUNA (transurethral needle ablation), urologists can now treat BHP by shrinking the prostrate in the office, using a local anesthetic and a tiny needle, with controlled bursts of radio-frequency radiation that seemingly cause no side effects.

Prostate cancer, the most frequent malignancy of older men, the cause of which is unknown, strikes more than 115,000 older adult males every year. About 40,000 die. Incidence increases with age. Approximately 1/3 of prostate cancers reveal themselves during a person's lifetime to such an extent that treatment is deemed necessary. Warning signs include back pain, a frequent need to urinate, painful urination, weak urine flow although many patients at time of diagnosis are asymptomatic.

Present only in males, the prostate gland is composed of both muscular and glandular tissue. About the size of a walnut, the prostate–located between the bladder and the penis, and above the rectum–is wrapped around the urethra, the tube that empties the bladder. All functions of the prostate are not known except that it secretes an alkaline viscid liquid with which sperm mix during ejaculation. Although prostatic secretion is not necessary for sexual intercourse by the male, the result of its absence is infertility.

As with other cancers, early diagnosis is important although prostate cancers often grow so slowly that researchers estimate 2/3 of them go unnoticed, present no immediate danger and especially in the elderly hardly affect an individual's life expectancy. They may take decades to metastasize. These are some of the reasons that not all researchers favor screening for prostate cancer. Others insist that because prostate cancer may not cause obvious symptoms, an annual checkup is advisable.

Many doctors perform at the annual physical examination of aging male patients a digital rectal examination, a procedure which consists of pressing with a finger to determine if the prostate gland has hard areas or nodules or any other potential signs of cancer. Ultrasound technology is frequently used to check diagnosis of malignancy. As yet, the simple blood test, Prostate-Specific Antigen (PSA), which more accurately than ever before detects prostate cancer early on, cannot differentiate between slow-growing and aggressive cancers, so that neither doctor nor patient can tell just when surgery or radiation will be necessary. The result is an as yet unsolvable dilemma if the test is positive: remove the cancer at once or wait to find out if it is slow-growing? There is a lack of definitive evidence indicating advantages from early treatment. In addition, the PSA test does not always give an accurate result. Even so, the American Cancer Society is recommending yearly PSA measurements and digital examinations beginning at 50 years of age.

Because of cancerous enlargement, the prostate gland squeezes the urethral tube and substantially interferes with the passage of urine. Medications may relieve the situation, but they sometimes have serious side effects. In some men, Saw Palmetto apparently improves symptoms and urinary flow with few adverse effects. Radiation therapy is not always relied on because it can result in bladder difficulties. Chemotherapy has not proved to be so effective as doctors would like. Surgery may be recommended to remove part or all of the prostate gland.

The prostate cancer victim's decision involves a gamble. Is he willing to trade off possibility of improved outcome from therapy versus probability of harm from treatment?

A surgeon, asked about a patient with a localized case, will recommend a nerve-sparing operation, pointing out that chance of impotence resulting is minimal although retrograde ejaculation may occur. If the disease has spread, however, surgery may result in removal of testicles. A radiation therapist will recommend radiation, particularly when the cancer has metastasized to bone, an exceedingly painful condition. Radiation therapy causes fewer cases of impotence than surgery but other side effects, such as bowel irritation, can occur. Radioactive seed implantation, a relatively new option in the fight against early-stage prostate cancer, spares adjacent areas from damage. Well tolerated by patients, seed implant therapy is performed in an outpatient setting, with few untoward side effects.

When the disease is more advanced, many men are concerned that surgery will surely result in impotence, and so they often choose hormonal therapy. It is known that if testosterone levels are greatly reduced, in all likelihood cancer cells will die and further growth of the cancer will be inhibited. But there is a real possibility of such side effects as enlarged breasts, hair loss, muscle weakness and, ironically, drug-induced castration.

Prostatic cancer patients should thoroughly discuss the various methods of treatment with their urologist and explore *all* options before deciding on a specific therapy. Obtaining a second opinion is wise. In the elderly, metastasis may preclude such an attempt at a cure, so that doctors will feel compelled to rely on drugs for palliation of symptoms even though drug therapy is expensive and must be employed unceasingly.

There are urologists who maintain that frequent sexual intercourse will help keep the prostate gland healthy and even overcome some of the difficulties resulting from enlargement. Jokester urologists tell patients to remember the three important gradations of sexual activity: 1. tri-weekly; 2. try weekly; and 3. try weakly, no matter what. Alfred Baxter, half serious, complains:

> *Prostate, prostate, burning right*
> *Up there where the plumbing's tight,*
> *What in hell persuaded thee*
> *To plug the pipe through which I pee?*

DENTAL CONCERNS

All joys I bless, but I confess
There is one greatest thrill:
What the dentist does when he stops the buzz
And puts away the drill.

Christopher Morley

The prospect for tooth health has improved markedly. As placement of fluoride in the water supply and other preventive measures have proved successful, each succeeding generation has become increasingly dentate—a fact that makes tooth loss from a condition which dentists call *periodontal disease*, a catchall term for inflammation of structures around the teeth, a compelling reason for semiannual examination and prompt treatment. Periodontia is one of the more prevalent chronic oral afflictions, the effects being cumulative and revealing themselves with age. Gum disease can develop for years with virtually no indications. Symptoms include bleeding, inflammation, sensitivity. Periodontia results in acceleration of proportion of a tooth seen, the so-called *long tooth* of folklore. Increasingly, evidence demonstrates that if the lesions have not deteriorated drastically, periodontal disease can be treated successfully in the aged even when there is bone loss. The health of gums can be sustained in addition. Victims of gingivitis, which is an inflammation of the gums, can be helped considerably by antibiotics.

The present generation of elderly, raised in years before preventive dentistry was developed and practiced widely, have a higher level of unmet dental needs than any other age group: at least 40% have no natural teeth; 60% have some tooth decay; 90% have some form of periodontal (gum) disease, and almost 100% have lost one or more teeth. Dental caries, a chronic disease that destroys mineralized tissue, is a prevalent problem. A form of decay from not limiting sugar intake and from eating sticky, sweet food like dried fruit between meals, caries can cause painful root cavities sensitive to cold as well as to sweets. David Bates (a writer known as "Old Mortality"), obviously a victim of caries, asks:

Is Dr. Jones, the dentist in?
An aching tooth has made me fret;
But something seems to lull the pain—
Perhaps, sir, you can save it yet.

The tooth is out; once more again
The throbbing, jumping nerves are stilled;
Reader, would you avoid this pain?
Then have your crumbling teeth well filled.

Hopefully, because of fluoride in the water supply and other preventive measures, caries and cavities will soon be things of the past.

Teeth differ from many of the body's other structures in that regenerative capability is quite limited. Teeth are subject to much wear, especially from abrasion. To help save them and prevent buildup of plaque (the invisible film of live bacteria coating teeth and gums), dentists advise daily procedures such as brushing and flossing on awakening, after meals and at bedtime. With age, teeth frequently become brittle to the extent that many elderly suffer from tooth fracture despite no indication of prior trauma. Deterioration of soft-tissue gum attachments from infection or wounds results in loosening even of healthy teeth. More than half of the present generation of elderly have at least one replacement tooth to close a gap and prevent surrounding teeth from moving and possibly causing bite problems and periodontia.

Full dentures, in effect a compromise, are always an approximate fit because of shrinkage of gum and palate. About 1 in 4 older persons has varying degrees of difficulty, often because of reduced tissue tolerance resulting from an improper diet. When not used for chewing at mealtime or for snacks, dentures should be kept apart in the mouth to avoid grinding down bare teeth. Many dentists now advocate that instead of removing dentures for the entire night (approximately 8 hours), wearers take them out for 4 hours of every 24, so that neither bones nor gums are adversely affected by long absence of teeth in the mouth.

When removed, dentures should be kept in a cleansing solution to make sure that they become odorless and do not transmit a yeast infection. For dentures to be thoroughly clean, it is advisable to have 2 pair in order to permit alternate use.

Adaptation to dentures is critical to chewing and speech, as well as to self-esteem and social functioning. Unless the plates fit properly, speech will be slurred. Denture wearers must chew food about 4 times as long as people with natural teeth. It is best to let food get wet with saliva immediately before chewing. Elderly people often worry that a denture may slip in public or that a space left by missing teeth will show. They complain of soreness and inability to chew all kinds of food. They fear that dentures will be expelled from the mouth, as after a sneeze or a yawn. They may be embarrassed when as an overnight guest they have to remove a denture and place it in a glass for cleaning.

Because baby boomers will be living longer than previous generations and keeping more of their teeth owing to improved dentistry, they will undoubtedly need restorative and reconstructive procedures. To obtain a dental restoration that looks and feels as though a natural part of the mouth, many persons rely on implants which anchor artificial (the technical term is *prosthetic)* teeth into the jawbone, usually the lower jaw because often dentures do not fit well there.

Although effective, dental implants are not for everyone. There must be enough jawbone, or bone grafts will be necessary. The procedure may take 3 months or more. Because insurance companies do not pay for anything that can be labeled cosmetic, a person may have to make a large financial commitment. In addition, a patient must resolve to have frequent checkups and to practice excellent dental hygiene since dental implants often create hard-to-reach surfaces in the mouth.

Anyone who has lost teeth will agree with Cervantes that "Every tooth in a man's head is more valuable than a diamond."

DIABETES

Every sweet has its sour.

Ralph Waldo Emerson

Diabetes mellitus, usually referred to simply as diabetes, is a disease characterized by inability of the body to properly metabolize glucose, a sugar the body can utilize to generate energy. Because carbohydrates, starches and sugars in food are metabolized to glucose, the diabetic cannot put these substances to proper use. As a result, blood levels of glucose from digested food may build to unsafe levels and seriously injure body organs.

The fifth most prevalent of disease-related deaths in the United States, diabetes is one of the chief risk factors for cardiovascular disease, cataracts, glaucoma and a variety of kidney disorders. The disease is the chief cause of amputation in the United States because diabetics are so susceptible to skin ulcers and gangrene.

The incidence of maturity-onset diabetes increases with age, appearing in about 10% of elderly 65+ and in about 25% of the 85+ group. Physicians refer to diabetes as a silent disease because it so often goes undetected. Many victims are unaware that they have diabetes. Obesity is a leading predisposing factor. Smoking and high blood pressure apparently hasten development of the disease.

There are essentially two types of diabetes. In Type I diabetes, also called juvenile diabetes, the pancreas cannot synthesize insulin, a hormone required for metabolism, and victims of the disease are dependent on injections. In Type II diabetes, also called maturity-onset diabetes, the prime problem is insulin resistance by the tissues. Although the pancreas synthesizes insulin, the body is under-responsive, exhibiting defective glucose-uptake into cells, thereby starving tissues such as muscle. Drugs are available that act by stimulating the pancreas to release more insulin to compensate for resistance, but after long use the over-worked pancreas may fail and the body then require insulin administration, essentially converting Type II diabetes into Type I. Research is in progress for therapies that will increase tissue insulin sensitivity.

Because kidney functions and thirst responses lessen somewhat with age, the elderly do not necessarily exhibit classical symptoms of diabetes–secretion and excretion of excessive amounts of urine, as well as undue thirst and hunger–and so cases may go unnoticed. The best safeguard is a regular checkup, including blood and urine testing. The exact incidence of diabetes in the elderly is unknown. Blacks are twice as likely to fall victim to diabetes as whites. About 3,000,000 blacks are recognizably diabetic, but many more are probably undiagnosed even though they have the disease. Black women 55+ are particularly vulnerable: approximately 1 in 4 is a diabetic.

Type II diabetes can be quite difficult to identify in the elderly without a blood test. Many late-life diabetics are unaware that they have the disease. Some physicians, to make certain of the diagnosis, administer a glucose-tolerance test. Although late-onset diabetes can lead to blood-vessel diseases, cataracts, impotence, loss of limbs and even death, symptoms like slow-healing cuts may be so mild that they are not recognized or, as happens quite often at a checkup, an ophthalmologist detects visual deterioration, referred to as diabetic retinopathy, indicating presence of the disease.

A chronic condition, Type II diabetes requires a permanent adjustment in lifestyle. Although drugs can help to control the disease, the recommended immediate course of treatment is by way of diet and exercise because diabetics are usually overweight. Research studies indicate that as many as half of persons with mild late-onset diabetes can quit medication without ill effect by adopting a sensible program of diet, about 50% of daily calories coming from such complex carbohydrates as cereals and pasta. Moderate daily exercise, such as walking at a good pace (not sauntering) for 20-30 minutes, is also effective. Activity, which exercises the large muscles, reduces insulin resistance, helps the body's cell receptors become more sensitive to blood sugar and burns glucose quickly. In addition, losing even a small amount of weight often markedly restores blood sugar control. Thereafter, blood sugar levels should be checked weekly. Simple mechanisms are available at medical supply stores for this purpose.

Family physicians should ensure that all obese elderly, in addition to the victims of diabetes, are screened annually. Patient education is essential if the ongoing regimen of therapy is to be effective. They should be taught to be alert to mental and physical conditions. Changes, especially in regard to feet, should be promptly reported to the physician in charge. Intense diarrhea and impotence can occur in the elderly who have had diabetes for a long time. Severe cases require insulin injection. Negligence in regard to its administration, such as overdosing or neglecting to eat, can cause shock and coma, a grave emergency with brain damage and death to follow unless quick and knowledgeable action is taken. For an emergency, diabetics who are ingesting insulin should carry a source of glucose (orange juice or candy) at all times

Although long-term complications of diabetes are numerous among the elderly, most diabetics can and do survive a long time with the disease and without disablement. Those elderly with diabetes can affect what happens to them. They themselves can control diet, exercise and medications. Even so, the doctor's orders need to be followed carefully, with full recognition that the disease is lifelong and potentially dangerous. Diabetics should be immunized against pneumonia and get yearly vaccinations against influenza, as well as a tetanus booster injection every ten years.

But the outlook can be bright. With a proper regimen, full compliance by the diabetic and periodic checkups by a physician, elderly diabetics can expect to lead a normal life.

WARNING SIGNS AND SYMPTOMS OF DIABETES

Type I: Insulin Dependent (the body does not synthesize sufficient insulin)
1. Blurring vision
2. Dramatic weight loss
3. Frequent urination
4. Excessive thirst
5. Extreme hunger

6. Irritability
7. Nausea and/or vomiting
8. Weakness and/or fatigue

Type II: Non-Insulin-Dependent (the body exhibits insulin resistance)
1. Any of the insulin-dependent symptoms listed above
2. Drowsiness
3. Itching
4. Numbness or tingling in hands or feet
5. Slow healing of wounds and infections

GUIDELINES FOR MANAGING SYMPTOMS OF DIABETES

1. Eat Sensibly
   Consult a dietitian for a diet that fits your lifestyle.
   Accustom yourself to a low-fat, balanced diet with a variety of fruits and vegetables.
   Try to eat foods that supply approximately the same number of calories every day.
   Arrange meals to suit the time(s) of medication.
2 Exercise regularly
   Check with your physician for a suitable program.
   Try to exercise at the same time every day.
   Test your blood sugar level before exercising.
   Carry a sugar source in case of hypoglycemia (low blood sugar).
   Warm up before exertion and cool down after.
   Stop exercising if you feel dizzy or weak.
3. Prepare for Illness
   Learn from your physician when it is best to telephone him/her.
   Keep handy instructions for blood-sugar and urine-ketone testing.
   Be aware of possible changes due to medications.

GASTROINTESTINAL DISORDERS

You can't ignore the importance of a good digestion.
The joy of life . . . depends on a sound stomach.

Joseph Conrad

The gastro-intestinal system—consisting of many interrelated organs: the oral cavity, esophagus, stomach, liver, gallbladder, pancreas, small and large intestines and the rectum—takes in food, breaks it down, absorbs it and then excretes the remainder. As just one indication of the complexity of the entire system, consider the act of swallowing, which involves not only coordinating movement of the tongue, mouth muscles and pharynx but also initiating contractions moving food down the gastro-intestinal system.

As people age many changes, both specific and general, take place in the digestive system. Among them are decreased production of digestive juices, reduction in peristalsis and motility of the intestines, loss of muscular strength. Researchers do not know the magnitude of the changes nor how to deal with many of them. But they recognize that dysfunction of the gastro-intestinal system is common among the elderly.

Dyspepsia, known to lay people as indigestion, usually does not begin in late life but shows up more commonly then. Uncomfortable but seemingly minor gastrointestinal symptoms like occasional indigestion and heartburn increase with age. About 50% of older adults report an attack at least once a month, briefly unpleasant but not damaging. For about 10%, heartburn is a chronic condition, a continual threat to quality of life. Medical treatment is trial-and-error: what succeeds in one person may fail in another.

Evaluation of the symptoms of indigestion, as is the case with so many other disorders the elderly suffer, is difficult. The organs of the digestive tract are interrelated, so that discomfort complained of as coming from the stomach may in reality be referred from the small intestine lower in the tract. Disorders outside the digestive system, both cardiovascular and neurologic, may alter esophageal motility. Physicians know that chronic complaints of the elderly about the digestive system or parts thereof bear investigating: mortality from diseases of the gastrointestinal tract is second in the elderly to lung cancer. Mortality rates of surgery for serious gastro-intestinal problems are 15% and higher, not because of age, but because of related medical conditions and opportuneness of surgery.

Some complaints are easy to deal with. Occasional esophageal distress causing chest pain can largely be relieved by eating smaller and more frequent meals and by avoiding foods like citrus fruits and spiced fatty meats that cause difficulties. But food choice should not be severely limited. While like that of other age cohorts the stomach of the elderly is not particularly finicky, with the result that almost any food is satisfying, very few persons of any age can remain for long on a restricted dietary regimen–if only because emotional significance permeates food habits. Much gastrointestinal discomfort is psychologically based; indigestion, for example, is commonly associated with stress. Fast relief can often be obtained by way of over-the-counter medications like Maalox.

Gas production can result from eating beans, onions, raw fruit and high-fiber foods; from swallowing air while chewing; from not properly absorbing carbohydrates, which are then fermented by bacteria in the colon. Dietary change may help reduce production of gas, but passage that seems excessive to one person may be normal to another. For adults, expulsion of gas from 10-18 times a day is considered normal.

Other complaints may be difficult to act on. Abdominal pain can be an indication either of serious illness or of a minor problem. Symptoms of stomach cancer are non-specific, but fatigue, weight loss, and blood in the stool may be indications of trouble. Colon cancer is common in the elderly 70+, accounting for as much as 1/2 of all gastrointestinal malignancies. Incidence of gallstone disease jumps after 65, its symptoms being chronic indigestion and nausea. Treatment involves acceptance of a fat-free diet and/or surgery. Lithotripsy, a method for shattering the stones, is continually being improved. Hemorrhoids, ruptured blood vessels at the anus, which can usually be reduced by drinking 8 glasses of water a day and following a bulk-producing diet, are present in many persons 65+. Diverticula, sacs projecting through the intestine, appear more in elderly women than men, causing spasms of abdominal pain and alternating periods of constipation and diarrhea. The condition can usually be controlled by increasing dietary fiber, as advised by a dietitian. Of itself, fiber is not a panacea. Constipation, a symptom and not a disease, probably the most common gastrointestinal complaint of the elderly because of concern with regularity, can be overcome with diet and exercise regimens.

Supposedly, more than half of the elderly 65+ have hiatus hernia. About 50% of older hiatus hernia patients are asymptomatic, while others complain of indigestion and loss of appetite. As discussed more fully immediately below, rather than hiatus hernia, improper closure of the one-way valve that keeps stomach liquids from flowing back into the mouth is often the primary cause. Hiatus hernia results from protrusion of the stomach or portions thereof above the diaphragm and into the chest. Although diagnosis is usually based on barium-contrast study and endoscopy, X-rays generally can reveal the condition.

There are two main types of hiatus hernia. Sliding hiatus hernia, although almost always asymptomatic, is detectable through barium contrast studies and endoscopy. Treatment is conservative: antacids, a bland diet and elevation of head and chest in bed at night are recommended. Paraesophageal hernia is more serious. Symptoms may include flatulence and chest discomfort exacerbated by meals but relieved somewhat by belching and vomiting. Diagnosis can be made by x-rays and barium contrast studies. The hernia can be immense, with the stomach entirely in the chest. Surgery is the treatment of choice.

Reflux esophagitis, backflow of stomach liquids into the esophagus (referred to by doctors as GERD for Gastro Esophageal Reflux Disorder), may accompany hiatus hernia or occur independently. When the muscular ring at the bottom of the esophagus does not close quickly after food or drink is swallowed, some of the acid contents of the stomach occasionally flow back (reflux) into the esophagus. Symptoms may include abdominal or chest pain, difficulty in swallowing and heartburn. Some persons complain only of morning hoarseness while others suffer from coughing and wheezing when lying down to sleep at night. Abdominal pain can signal a minor problem; if accompanied by bleeding, it is a serious condition and the person involved should consult a doctor promptly. There is a relatively new approach, laparoscopic fundoplication, which in many cases allows a surgeon–utilizing only a tiny incision–to form a barrier between stomach and esophagus.

Heartburn may produce feelings of distress in the chest ranging from a mild burning to a sharp or crushing pain not easily distinguishable at first from that of heart disease. It is important to recognize that occasional heartburn occurs in young and old and is a normal phenomenon treatable by over-the-counter antacids carefully chosen to avoid side effects and conflict with other medications. Modifications of lifestyle are advisable. Eating smaller meals, reducing body weight, stopping smoking, avoiding alcohol and coffee and very hot drinks will help lessen symptoms.

Peptic ulcers, including duodenal and gastric, are frequent problems among the elderly, with at least 150,000 new cases a year. Symptoms are not always specific. Pain is often described by patients as a gnawing or burning sensation. Frequent indigestion when accompanied by such pain and/or abdominal discomfort may indicate a duodenal ulcer, which is an open sore in the lining of that part of the small intestine nearest the stomach. About 4 of 5 ulcers are duodenal, with the majority susceptible of cure as described below. Not treated, a duodenal ulcer may perforate and cause a fatal hemorrhage. Gastric ulcers, ulcers of the stomach lining, are generally larger than duodenal.

Since most ulcers are caused by H. pylori bacteria or frequent use of NSAIDs, they are increasingly coming under pharmacologic control. Any of several antibiotics approved by the FDA accompanied by a physician-prescribed dietary regimen will cure almost all such ulcers within a few weeks. There is a new noninvasive diagnostic procedure based on the discovery that most peptic ulcers are caused by bacteria. Rather than endoscopy with biopsy, the new and faster procedure, the Meretek Breath Test, relies on detecting the ulcer-causing bacteria in a person's breath. The test is a boon because it permits early diagnosis: gastric ulcers are likely to turn cancerous if left untreated.

Mixing hype with hope, an exceedingly large number of supposed cure-all's for immediate relief of all kinds of gastrointestinal distress is advertised daily on TV at the most unappetizing of times like the dinner hour. About 1,000 over-the-counter medications exist, none perfect, none harmless. All such drugs have side effects, and many are of questionable efficacy. Aside from the high cost of daily usage, some of these "medicines" do little but mask symptoms. If unrecognized complications set in, the result could be dangerous indeed.

Maalox is among the safest and most effective of antacids. Not so for the many ointments and suppositories advertised for hemorrhoids, which respond best to hot sitz baths 3-4 times a day. There is no evidence that mouth washes get rid of mouth odors which originate, not in the oral cavity, but far down the digestive tract. Instead, the so-called washes may contribute to drying of delicate membranes. The mechanisms underlying many of the symptoms of nonulcer dyspepsia (indigestion, with bloating and gas), an ailment common among the elderly, are unknown. After suitable tests, the recommended procedure is verbal assurance that no cancer is present.

Roy Atwell was more than half-serious when he wrote:

> In these days of indigestion
> It is oftentimes a question
> As to what to eat and what to leave alone;
> For each microbe and bacillus
> Has a different way to kill us,
> And in time they always claim us for their own.

HEARING

He that hath ears to hear, let him hear.

Mark, IV, 9

Hearing loss is the 3rd most prevalent adverse chronic condition of the elderly, exceeded only by arthritis and hypertension. In many older persons hearing loss may result from age-related deterioration of the auditory system, disease and frequent exposure to intense noise. Estimates are that of the more than 10,000,000 hearing-impaired Americans the vast majority are elderly—about 1/3 of those 65-74 undergoing a loss of some 25% and probably 1/2 of those 75-84 losing as much as 40%. Yet levels of so-called normal hearing for the elderly have not as of now been defined. Nor is it known why men lose their hearing 2 times as fast as women.

Hearing loss can occur gradually or suddenly. In either case, it is important to seek medical help as soon as possible. If the loss occurs a little at a time, a person may not be aware that ability to hear is changing. In an attempt at compensation, so doctors assume, the brain tries to use stored memories of sounds. But such memories fade, with the result that a person can no longer fit words and sounds together as well as before. If the hearing loss occurs suddenly, the victim should consult a physician immediately, preferably an otologist, because the first 24 hours can be critical for treatment.

Although not life-threatening, the effect of hearing loss on the activities of daily living and the quality of life is profound unless quickly corrected. Pitch discrimination abates as does response to sounds in higher frequencies. Understanding of speech decreases as the upper range of the human voice is affected. Use of the telephone is difficult. Social intercourse is awkward because of embarrassment from misunderstandings. Even worse, when answered inappropriately, people act as though cognitive ability of the hearing impaired is also impaired. Mental health suffers as the victim of auditory loss increasingly suspects that others are conspiring to keep conversations secret. The hearing impaired, as a result, can easily fall into depression caused by isolation, loneliness, paranoia. This in combination with one of the many diseases, such as diabetes or stroke, that contributed to the hearing loss!

There are 3 major types of presbycusis, the term physicians use to designate the progressive hearing loss that occurs with aging of the auditory system: conductive, sensorineural and mixed. Sensorineural hearing loss occurs with dysfunction of the auditory nerve or with damage in the inner ear. Degeneration of nerve cells can result in permanent hearing loss in both ears. Conductive loss happens because of impairment of mechanisms of the middle ear, as from wax blocking the ear canal. A mixed hearing loss results from some combination of the 2 types of presbycusis. At the present time, it is exceedingly difficult if not impossible to separate in any of the 3 such causative factors as climate, industrial noise and toxins from conditions solely attributable to aging.

Nerve deafness can quite often be treated with amplification by means of a hearing device. Surgical correction of mechanical difficulties can generally be performed safely and successfully on the elderly. In cases of mixed loss, surgical correction and a hearing aid will often enable a person to overcome much of the difficulty.

Many combinations of events and things can cause bilateral loss of hearing in the elderly. Childhood infections may have resulted in perforation of a membrane. Medication given to an adult, particularly for renal disease, can prove harmful to structures within the ear. Too often the elderly themselves either dismiss the problem or are unaware of its seriousness because of the slow development of symptoms and their expectation that hearing loss occurs with aging. Partial deafness is not easily perceived by the sufferer or a physician. Frequently, the victim of hearing loss complains, not of hearing difficulties, but of problems in understanding speech, saying: "I hear you, but I don't understand you." In actuality, the real problem is hearing loss. While some evaluation of such a hearing difficulty can be attained by so-called ticking watch or whispering tests, only audiometry can ascertain exact levels of the hearing loss.

A hearing aid should usually be worn in both ears, so that sound can be localized. A person desiring to wear an aid in just one ear should be tested with a single aid and then with aids in both ears. Behind-the-ear models are usually more durable and more easily adjusted. In-the-ear models may be much less visible but more difficult to adjust. Unfortunately, the smaller the device, the less power it can contain and therefore the less sound fidelity it may develop.

Even more unfortunately, there is much charlatanism in sale of hearing aids. Not all problems can be solved by means of a hearing aid. It cannot restore normal hearing. A hearing aid amplifies background sounds in addition to speech, so that a person may not hear accurately or distinctly what someone else is saying. Many hearing aids include noise-reduction circuitry, but efficacy is moot. If the auditory nerve is dead, no hearing aid will help.

The otologist can almost always recommend a reputable company which will permit purchase on a trial basis. Training in cleaning, maintenance and operation of the aid should be included with the fitting. Those elderly with limitations of fine-motor dexterity may need extra training and easily manipulated controls. Medicare does not reimburse for hearing aids although estimates are that about 1/3 of the elderly who need the devices do not have them.

Tinnitus, perception of a whine or ringing or buzz in one or both ears, is fairly common among the elderly. It is subjective; that is, it is heard by the afflicted person only, as distinguished from outside noise that the examining physician hears. Tinnitus becomes acute at night and in a quiet environment. Usually, it is accompanied by some degree of hearing loss. It may result from infection, medication, trauma or tumor. Mechanisms involved remain obscure. If an underlying condition, as clogging of the auditory canal by earwax, is treated successfully, tinnitus may be ameliorated. When nerve deafness is the cause of tinnitus, there is no cure despite attempts at utilizing biofeedback, hypnosis, masking devices, medication and surgery. In time, most people learn to tolerate tinnitus.

Communication can be particularly frustrating for the hearing-impaired. But many concert halls and public auditoriums have special hearing systems, Assistive Listening Devices, for which a person can borrow or rent a receiver. ALDs are amplification systems which deliver sound directly to the listener via wire or a technique like infrared transmission. Closed-captioned TV is common as are interactive services on computer networks.

Telephone companies will provide assistive devices, such as a light signal, at no additional charge. Available also are courses in speech reading through observation of lip movement and facial expression in addition to auditory training that enable the hearing impaired to discriminate between sound stimuli. Family members can help by making sure that someone when conversing faces the deaf person squarely from nearby, gains attention before speaking, enunciates slowly and clearly and in cases of incomprehension tries alternative wording, not repetition.

Almost 300 years ago Matthew Henry warned that there is "None so deaf as those that will not hear."

ADAPTIVE STRATEGIES TO COMPENSATE FOR HEARING LOSS

In the Home:
> Install flashing lights on doorbell and telephone
> Add telephone amplification devices and volume control

By the Speaker:
> Gain the person's attention before speaking
> Enunciate words clearly and slowly
> Keep facial expressions and lips visible
> Use low tones
> Speak slightly louder, but avoid shouting
> Use short, simple sentences

By the Older Person:
> Reduce background noise during conversation
> Ask people to write vital information

Source: Lustbader, W. and Hooyman, N.R., *Taking Care of Aging Family Members* (NY: The Free Press, 1994), p. 165.

HEART DISEASE

Heart disease before 80 is our own fault, not God's or Nature's will.

Paul Dudley White, MD

The leading cause of death in the elderly, as in the entire population, is coronary artery disease (whose acronym is CAD), which encompasses a broad spectrum of heart and circulation disorders referred to as atherosclerosis, congenital defects, congestive heart failure, heart attack, rheumatic heart disease, or stroke. While death rates from coronary artery disease have declined in the last 40 years, CAD is responsible for almost 50% of deaths of those elderly 65+. Nevertheless, CAD does not inevitably accompany aging. Physicians are certain that most heart attacks are preventable, much within a person's control. Diet, exercise, relaxation, and management of stress are important.

As people grow older, the incidence of heart disease rises sharply. Probably 1 of every 2 persons 65+ has distinct coronary artery narrowing, often without revelatory symptoms, such as fatigue, shortness of breath, chest pain, weakness. Risk factors for both sexes include diabetes, high cholesterol levels, high-fat diet, hypertension, sedentary lifestyle, smoking and a family history of heart trouble.

Mortality rates for men are considerably higher than for women, particularly at younger ages. But ten years after menopause, women are just as likely as men to suffer heart attacks, and they are more likely to die from the attacks. After menopause, CAD becomes the single largest killer of women, whose arteries are small and therefore susceptible to dangerous narrowing. About 235,000 women die annually from heart attacks, more deaths than from breast and lung cancer combined. Doctors recommend estrogen/progestin therapy within 4 years of menopause to restore hormone heart-protecting benefits.

Heart muscles are fed by a network of arteries encircling the heart like a crown, thus the name *coronary*. Reduced blood flow (ischemia) may result in heart trouble or a disease characterized by brief episodes of not pain so much as pressure in the chest that may radiate as pain to the left arm or jaw when insufficient oxygen reaches the heart muscles after such exertion as climbing a flight of stairs. An elderly person, a victim of arthritis, may not be active enough to cause anginal symptoms and yet still be at risk of CAD.

A heart attack without serious damage, a single episode of angina pectoris, is usually considered a warning of CAD. If rhythmic beating of the heart is disturbed as a result of injury to a heart muscle, a pacemaker can be safely installed because such surgery is well tolerated in late-life adults. If episodes recur with increasing frequency, the situation is regarded as more serious, and any of several methods of treatment described below may be recommended.

Myocardial infarction, obstruction of a coronary artery by a thrombus (the medical term for a clot) and/or the growth of plaque over the years, can lead to a heart attack and death of heart muscles. More than 1/4 of the time the first heart attack is fatal. Unfortunately, physicians are not always certain as how to treat myocardial infarction patients in the oldest-old age cohort because research studies and clinical trials have usually dealt with young men while aged heart-attacks victims are predominantly women.

Most fatal heart attack victims die within 2 hours of the beginning of symptoms of dizziness, nausea, pain in arms and shoulders, sense of fullness or pressure in the chest. Fatigue and weakness in the legs often warn of an impending attack. According to the American Heart Association, about 1 in 4 heart attack victims do not experience arm and shoulder pain but have such atypical symptoms as neck pain and profuse sweating.

Pain syndrome is not conclusive evidence of a heart attack: noncardiac disorders, as in the musculoskeletal system, can mimic cardiac symptoms. Because coronary arteries can narrow as much as 90% before symptoms are apparent, a heart attack may be without discomfort or other signs, what doctors call a silent attack.

The most prevalent form of arteriosclerosis, a generic term doctors use for several disorders involving hardening and stiffening of the arteries, is atherosclerosis, a disease that narrows or closes off both medium and large arteries as plaque (calcium, cholesterol, fats and other deposits) builds up on the inner surfaces of blood vessels. The disease usually starts relatively early in life. Non-renewable in structure, arteries are subject to irreversible damage. Walls of arteries gradually become thicker, hard and inelastic. A clot or clots can suddenly form and block flow of blood to various organs, such as the brain, heart, kidneys.

Congestive heart failure, a result of atherosclerosis, is inability of the weakened heart to maintain normal blood circulation by pumping out blood that was returned to it through the veins. Blood congests in tissues, and fluid accumulates in the lungs. Symptoms include ankle, leg, abdominal swelling and weight increase. Most elderly cases respond well to treatment administered promptly and maintained.

In the past, functional declines in cardiovascular performance were considered to be largely age-related. Stress testing, though, reveals that for those elderly who remain physically fit, maximal work capacity can easily double that of sedentary young adults. The fit have a much lower percentage of body fat than do couch potatoes, thus a lower risk of heart failure. Strange as it may seem, the heart of an 80-year-old healthy, fit man works about as well as that of a 20-year-old. Autopsies performed on people in their 90's often expose hearts that show few signs of wear and tear. The implication is that heart disease is not a direct result of aging. The heart rate at rest is about the same for the elderly as for the young, but the heart of the older person needs more time for recovery after strenuous exertion or severe stress. There is one age-related change, though, that an old person probably would not notice: the old heart fills somewhat more slowly with blood, but each contraction is somewhat more powerful than it was when the heart was young; and so compensation occurs.

With their annual checkup, the elderly should have a blood pressure test, an electrocardiogram and a cholesterol reading. The American Heart Association refers to a "desirable" total cholesterol level as under 200. Other types of safe, noninvasive cardiovascular investigations of the elderly are now possible. There are imaging techniques to scrutinize the anatomy and determine functional effectiveness of the heart in three dimensions and in time. Thallium scanning permits diagnosis of blockage or obstruction of blood. Echocardiography is used to discover valve disorders. Ultrasound helps diagnose disorders of peripheral blood vessels.

Age alone should not be a contraindication for more invasive techniques. The cardiologist may try catheterization of the cardiac chambers. Angioplasty, insertion of a catheter with a balloon tip that can be expanded in a blood vessel to open it, is especially useful in older heart patients who have other medical conditions, such as diabetes, that increase the risk of more severe procedures like open-heart surgery during coronary bypass operations in which surgeons use veins from elsewhere in the body to replace narrowed arteries. Valvuloplasty, like angioplasty, utilizes a balloon to open narrowed heart valves without surgery.

More elderly women than elderly men undergo a coronary bypass operation. Mortality rates for such surgery are low. Elderly persons without serious complicating illness have a much lower mortality rate than other aged patients with coexisting illness(es) or who require emergency surgery. While duration of the hospital stay after a coronary bypass operation has shortened, the elderly need a longer period of hospitalization than do the young.

Exercise, good nutrition and management of stress help prevent heart trouble—as does taking a child's-size aspirin daily. Seneca, Roman statesman and philosopher, was right in the main when he said, " Man does not die: he kills himself."

HIGH BLOOD PRESSURE

O Altitudo in the bloodstream swims.

Conrad Aiken

Diagnosis, evaluation and treatment of hypertension (high blood pressure) are of considerable importance to the elderly because for many, if not most, hypertension can be readily controlled through medication. In addition, treatment of an underlying disorder may slow or turn the course of hypertension and reduce the risk of catastrophic complications. For example, renal atherosclerosis (thickening and stiffening of the inner walls of kidney arteries) may be treatable by angioplasty, thereby lowering arterial pressure. But there is no absolute cure for high blood pressure itself.

Doctors have been known to pursue a policy of benign neglect with the elderly rather than one of intervention and prevention. Observers of the medical scene insist that this is true especially in regard to hypertension, the leading remediable risk factor for CAD in the elderly, because doctors believe that blood pressure tends naturally to rise with age.

Other observers in defense of doctors point out that hypertension is not always clearly detectable, for it may exist without symptoms but with such complicating factors as bloodshot eyes, nosebleeds, continual headaches, dizziness, fatigue.

Untreated, hypertension places victims 65+ at great risk for disabling or fatal organ failure, such as heart disease, kidney disease, retinal hemorrhage and stroke. Yet many older persons who have high blood pressure are unaware of their having succumbed to the disorder and evince no signs of the disease. This is why hypertension is often referred to as *silent*.

In industrialized societies of the West, blood pressure tends to increase with age until about the years 60-65. From then on, pressure of blood returning to the heart tends to stabilize or even decline whereas pressure of the blood pumped from the heart may continue to increase.

In the United States, more than half of persons 65+ have abnormally elevated blood pressure

Blood pressure is the force exerted when the heart contracts and pumps blood to the various parts of the body or when the same organ relaxes and blood returns to the heart. Blood pressure is expressed as 2 numbers, for example,---- (130 over 80). The upper number, called *systolic,* indicates pressure in the arteries while the heart pumps out blood. The lower number, called *diastolic,* indicates pressure when the heart is filling with blood to be pumped out at the next beat. While the American Heart Association considers systolic pressure above 140 to be abnormal, the National Heart, Lung and Blood Institute recommends that those elderly with systolic pressure above 160 and diastolic pressure above 90 be considered hypertensive. In either case, most physicians would advise that immediate treatment for high blood pressure be taken into consideration. But neither organization specifies any number above which blood pressure is absolutely too high. Generally, normal pressure is considered by physicians to be within the following range:---- (90-140 over 60-90). A blood pressure reading above—(140 over 90) is usually considered to indicate hypertension.

The exact mechanisms at work in causing hypertension are not clear. High blood pressure in the elderly may have any of several causes. With age, elasticity of blood vessels in most persons declines while stiffness increases and ability to dilate is reduced. Making matters worse in many of the aged is the clogging of blood vessels by fatty substances which are deposited on interior blood vessel walls. Additionally, changes in bodily regulation of salt and water may be significant in causing high blood pressure.

The test for blood pressure is painless and simple but not infallible. Frequently in a doctor's office a patient may become nervous, so that the reading is falsely elevated–what physicians refer to as *white coat* hypertension. To ensure exactitude, the test can be administered at home by a family member who is under careful instruction and supervision of a health care professional. Administration of the test is easily learned. But sometimes placement of the testing apparatus, as when attached by lay persons, is improper The apparatus itself should be calibrated periodically. Because blood pressure can vary widely during the day, readings should be taken at the same hour but several days apart, while for one test the patient sits and then for another stands.

Successful treatment of hypertension in the elderly relies largely on changes in lifestyle and on medications which are best administered at first in low doses. Treatment for mild hypertension which may help a patient avoid drugs involves maintaining proper body weight, decreasing alcohol intake, lessening dietary salt, engaging in suitable exercise and giving up smoking–a regimen that contributes to well-being and should be maintained even with drug therapy. Hypertensive drugs can help bring more difficult cases into control

When complications are present or probable, drug treatment ought not be delayed. Because many elderly have multiple chronic diseases, physicians need to check for prior medications, including vitamin supplementation, before prescribing drugs useful in reducing hypertension. In general, the elderly respond well to anti-hypertensive medications although such side effects as depression and sleep difficulties may accompany drug treatment.

It is better to try to lower blood pressure over a long period (weeks or months) rather than a short, just as it is better to seek a moderate lowering and not a sharp decline. The elderly should not arbitrarily cease therapy after blood pressure apparently is under control because hypertension is likely to recur.

IMPOTENCE

Of ugly age and feeble impotence
And cruel disintegration of slow years.

Hans Zinsser

Many women have postmenopausal difficulties that interfere with sexual intercourse, but these have nothing to do with impotence, a condition to which only males are subject. As old as mankind, impotence is referred to in the Old Testament and in the writings of Hippocrates. The fears, misunderstandings and superstitions of ancient times continue today.

At one time or another, almost all men experience at least temporary impotence, termed erectile dysfunction by physicians, inability to achieve erection for penetration of the vagina or to maintain an erection for the time necessary to complete sexual intercourse. There are many possible causes. Some are physiological, as nerve deterioration or blockage of blood vessels in the penis. Others are medical, as certain prescription drugs to reduce high blood pressure or to relax muscles. Still others are psychological, as anxiety. Impotence may be due to urinary complications or to prostate surgery. Older men with diabetes mellitus may experience impotence. Impotence may be situational due to poor choice of time and place, lack of self-confidence, or annoyance or boredom with a partner.

The Porter in Shakespeare's play, *Macbeth,* warns: "Drink, Sir, is a great provider of three things . . . nose painting, sleep and urine. Lechery, Sir, it provokes and unprovokes; it provokes the desire, but it takes away the performance."

There are several kinds of treatment for impotence, ranging from injections, implants and surgery to changes in lifestyle to vacuum therapy and other mechanical devices for maintaining an erection. Surgery is never without risk, and in the case of the elderly chronic illnesses may increase the risk and complicate the operation. Although lifestyle modifications, such as a good diet and exercise in addition to counseling and sex therapy, are usually effective for men whose impotence problem does not have physical cause, impotence is not an ailment to which home remedies should be applied. Nor is it a matter to be taken lightly. A urologist should be consulted for treatment methods, ilncluding prescription of Viagra. Despite sniggering in popular culture (Comedians refer to Viagra as "Better loving through chemistry"), sexual activity fulfills deeply persisting physical and psychological needs of the elderly.

An erection can result from erotic stimulation like daydreams or from direct tactile stimulation. With age, sexual fantasies diminish in recurrence and tension until in most men 65+ erotic reveries virtually cease. But impotence is not inevitable, even among the oldest-old who retain capacity for erection although the amount and force of ejaculated fluid decrease. With age, more and more time spent in direct genital stimulation is needed for the older man to have and to maintain an erection.

There are several ways for a physician to arrive at a diagnosis without resorting to all kinds of laboratory tests. If the elderly man complaining of impotence has erections during sleep (a device attached to the penis can monitor whether erections occur) or upon awakening in the morning or if he admits to temporary difficulty, as from a situation, psychological counseling may be helpful, especially if the spouse is willingly included. The same is true if it can be ascertained that onset of impotence was sudden. Slow onset implies an underlying disorder, in which case the urologist will attempt to determine the causal condition, be it prescription drugs or an illness such as diabetes mellitus or vascular disease, from the complainant's medical history or from laboratory testing. If succeeding therapy fails, a prosthesis may be implanted, with success possible but not guaranteed.

Reasonably healthy males maintain the ability for penile erection throughout their lives. Those to whom sex mattered much in early adulthood and middle age, will presumably continue to be active in old age although the experience will be softer and calmer, and perhaps in some ways more satisfying.

PLEASE NOTE: Viagra, the contra-impotence drug, was introduced in 1999. Although frequently derided as better loving throgh chemistry, Viagra has definitely helped many men. Other helplful medications will be available soon.

INCONTINENCE

Circumstances over which I have no control.
                                               Duke of Wellington

It is a silent epidemic. Probably more than 10,000,000 Americans, fearing the malodorous social stigma of urinary incontinence, have hid the condition so successfully that neither doctor nor family have been fully aware of their succumbing to the embarrassing disorder despite the monetary costs (nearly $8,000,000,000 every year) and the disturbing social predicaments. About 1 in 3 elderly 65+ who reside in the community suffer from urinary incontinence to some degree, with twice as many women victims as men.

Most persons urinate from 4-6 times every 24 hours, chiefly in the daytime. Not incontinence sufferers. They can leak urine at any time, especially when experiencing a sudden cough, laugh, sneeze or strain. Incontinence sufferers of both sexes feel a need to run to the bathroom so frequently that they are often reluctant to be away from home for any length of time.

If not properly treated, severe incontinence may predispose victims to bladder or kidney infection, depression and loss of independence because of institutionalization. Yet incontinence is not a disase but a symptom of an underlying condition. In the vast majority of sufferers incontinence can be lessened or cured entirely, even in frail individuals.

Prevention is another matter. Although incontinence is not normal, even at age 90, there is no known way to prevent incontinence or to postpone its onset. Gynecologists recommend maintaining a normal weight because obesity may weaken pelvic muscles and cause involuntary urine leakage. Perhaps practicing Kegel exercises (discussed below) will prevent incontinence, but as yet there is no completed research study investigating the matter. Men should have regularly scheduled prostate examinations. If caught early on, most prostate difficulty can be successfully treated.

Until recently, even the relatively small number of persons who sought help had difficulty finding it because a large number of doctors, regarding incontinence as a social rather than a medical crisis, as a quality-of-life difficulty rather than as a life-debilitating disorder, did not try to evaluate the problem. TV changed all that. Commercials for adult diapers have recently appeared everywhere on the tube, day and night, with the result that almost everyone has become aware of the problem and almost no one is too embarrassed to talk about it. Adult diapers do restore confidence to a large degree although many men are ill at ease wearing them. Unfortunately, the TV ads give the impression that a leak-proof pad-envelope is the only solution to the problem. This is definitely not the case. Drugs, surgery, exercise and behavioral therapy (changes in lifestyle) are among the treatments available today that can significantly lessen incontinence and in many cases produce a cure. For the lucky ones, about 10% of women and 30% of men, urinary incontinence disappears on its own.

People need to understand urinary incontinence and its causes. That the condition is solely an inescapable result of aging is a myth. Health problems that increasingly affect older persons—Parkinson's and stroke among them—can be responsible. Beverages laden with caffeine, highly spiced foods and even milk may contribute to bladder leakage, as may intake of after-dinner fluids. But incontinence can result from infections and from medications like sleeping pills that have negative side effects on the nervous system.

There are several types of urinary incontinence. Urge incontinence, the most common, is a sudden need to urinate without enough time to reach a toilet. Originally caused by infection, irritation or deteriorated reflexes, urge incontinence results in involuntary loss of urine ranging in volume from a few drops to a large amount. Such accidents can occur during the day or night. Stress incontinence causes involuntary leaks. There is little or no warning. Women, because of pregnancy and menopause, are more often victims than men. Pregnancy stretches pelvic floor muscles, so that as a result of childbirth the bladder shifts its position. Urine may leak out when a sudden or unexpected jar, such as a cough or a laugh or a misstep, causes a rise in abdominal pressure.

Menopause brings a decrease in estrogen, partially disabling the urethral sphincter, which controls both letting urine out of the bladder and keeping it in. Stress incontinence in men generally occurs after surgery or a urinary tract infection. Unlike urge incontinence victims, stress incontinence sufferers usually remain dry during the night. Overflow incontinence results from inability of the bladder to empty, a condition caused by an obstructing prostate gland or inadequate bladder contractions. There may be a continual loss of small amounts of urine and the urinary stream may appear weak.

Gynecologists treat incontinence in women; urologists, in men. Finding the cause may take time. The physician will order lab tests for urinary infection, diabetes and physiological abnormality–perhaps for cancer. Technology–including cystoscopy, uroflow and urodynamic studies–may be employed. If the incontinence is caused by disease or is a result of side effects of medication, the condition in both men and women can be alleviated or eliminated by treating the disease or changing the drug. In other instances, the disorder can be corrected in men and women, with different therapies for the sexes. A strategy everyone can practice is restriction of food and beverages, such as highly spiced eatables and caffeinated drinks, which irritate the bladder or contribute to bladder leakage. Sympathetic understanding and support by family and health-care personnel are essential, as when clothing becomes wet and malodorous or the bathroom floor is stained.

A large number of doctors recommend that women interested in behavior modification therapy–the simplest, safest and least expensive treatment–consult a physical therapist who uses feedback to teach correct methods of performing Kegel exercises, which strengthen the urethral sphincter and tighten pelvic-floor muscles. But patients should be aware that pain and sexual stimulation may develop from performing the exercises. In addition to practicing the exercises, women should train themselves to urinate every 3 hours to make certain that a too-full bladder does not leak after a cough, laugh or sneeze. Crossing the legs tightly and bending at the waist when about to cough can be helpful and effective.

Sadly, Kegel exercising, bladder training and posture changing help only about 50% of women with stress incontinence, about 15% with urge incontinence. Persistence is needed since the program is for life. Such physical therapy and biofeedback regimens are generally not covered under Medicare. These may be the major reasons so many women quit behavior modification in favor of other therapies involving drugs and surgery.

Physicians usually discuss options with patients. Some doctors let patients choose. Others make forceful specific recommendations. Drugs, the treatment of choice for seriously annoying urge incontinence, can cure about 80% of men and women patients but at a cost: lifelong expense (currently about $50 a month) and ongoing side effects, such as blurred vision, constipation, dry mouth, heart rhythm irregularity. Careful monitoring of dosage is essential. When urge incontinence is a result of menopause, estrogen is considered a reliable treatment with a high cure rate although at an increased risk of uterine cancer. A pessary (rubber ring inserted into the vagina) is often recommended for stress incontinence suffererers. For severe stress incontinence, patients may choose drugs or surgery. The drugs may have such bothersome side effects as dry mouth and constipation, but they do help about 70% of stress incontinence sufferers.

While surgery offers an excellent chance at cure of incontinence, it requires a hospital stay and procedures similar to those of other major surgery, including general anesthesia. Unfortunately, complications for both men and women may follow. Women, especially, may need further surgery. There is a relatively new method utilizing collagen injections to strengthen the urethral sphincter, but the procedure may have to be repeated several times over a time span of about a month, at additional expense and discomfort. Collagen treatment is more successful with women than men. Men who have had a prostatectomy have special problems which are described in the essay on the prostate in the cancer section of this volume. Surgery for men and women is covered by Medicare and most private insurance.

As with all medical conditions, it is wise to get information and advice from doctors and from reliable persons who have themselves undergone different forms of treatment, in addition to obtaining infor-

mation from the various organizations concerned with urinary incontinence. It will then be possible to make an informed choice regarding
success rate, risk and price.

Less common than urinary incontinence, bowel incontinence can
be far more annoying–particularly to caregivers. Bowel incontinence
may be the result of prolonged laxative usage, illness or surgery. But
the usual cause is constipation so severe that the bowel is blocked and
liquid leaks around the obstruction and out of the anus.

Bowel incontinence is treatable in many instances. A physician
should be consulted as soon as possible. When administered under
proper supervision, a high-fiber diet, exercise and adequate intake of
water can help restore regularity. Biofeedback may enable a person to
regain anal muscle control.

MENTAL DISORDERS

When Nature her great masterpiece design'd,
And fram'd her last, best work, the human mind. . . .

Robert Burns

Chronic physical diseases are almost universal among the elderly of today, sometimes obscuring distinctions between mental and physical illness. Not all complaints of physical distress are of psychosomatic origin, nor are all emotional disorders of physical origin. Physicians today plan treatment programs on the basis of comprehensive physical workups and psychological evaluation. This approach is especially important when tending to elderly patients with a condition such as a broken hip that can easily generate feelings of depression and confusion and be taken by family and friends as the onset of Alzheimer's disease.

Statistics on the mental health status of the elderly should be regarded with some caution. Diagnosis is frequently difficult. There is a tendency to overestimate the incidence of dementia and underestimate that of depression.

Nevertheless, it is possible to classify in general terms mental illness among the aged. Psychoses, such as paranoia and schizophrenia, are uncommon among the aged. Mental disorders with special importance in old age based on frequency of incidence and severity of complaint can be divided into 2 groups, functional and neurologic. Of the functional, depressive disorders make up some of the most common psychiatric complications of old adults. Of the three major neurologic disorders, Alzheimer's disease accounts for much of the dementia, the permanent, progressive physical impairment of the brain that is the fourth leading cause of death in those 65+; cerebrovascular disease, usually a sudden injury to brain cells and tissues referred to as stroke, kills more than 100,000 elderly annually and leaves over the years millions more unable to function well at work, in the home and out in the community; Parkinson's disease is a motor disorder, a combination of involuntary tremors, rigidity of muscles and disturbances in bodily posture, which disables about 50,000 elderly each year so that at present there are about 1,000,000 victims in the United States.

Advances in research, technology and therapy are ameliorating to some extent psychiatric disorders among the aged. As the number of old people increases and the incidence of psychiatric disorders with them, more and more attention is being paid to acquiring knowledge of the nervous system and to solving the problems of its diseases which in monetary cost and the expenditure of natural and human resources threaten society. Many mental ailments, formerly thought to be purely psychological, are now known to be the result of chemical imbalances in the brain. A good number of these disorders respond well to new psychoactive drugs, such as Prozac and Paxil, which provide much relief, if not always an outright cure. Ultimately, researchers hope to find the exact causes of mental illness, whether from alterations in the genes or in the brain.

There is no schema for exact delineation of neurological disorders. Physicians use the term *dementia* (from the Latin *de* without and *mens* mind) to signify not a disease but a wide range of symptoms of permanent or progressive decline in brain function involving memory loss and reasoning capacity. Generally, the confusion and disorientation characteristic of dementia are of insidious onset and slow progression. Diagnostic examinations for dementia include not only complete physical workups but also brain imaging and various kinds of neuropsychological studies. Illnesses causing dementia have been called family diseases on the grounds that caregiving required of the family, incessant and demanding, is overwhelming. Because the brain breaks down in patients with dementia, skilled health care professionals are often needed to take care of patients. Not quite 20% of dementias are reversible. Intellectual capability deteriorates in the other 80%, with a significant negative impact on occupational, personal and social functioning. Confusion, disorientation and hallucinations may give way to dementia if left untreated. In contrast, many supposed cases of mental infirmity among the elderly turn out to be age-related changes, such as hearing loss, which are usually eminently treatable.

Dementia is not a natural endstage in the process of aging. Further research is needed if efficacious treatment is to be found.

ALZHEIMER'S DISEASE

> *Young men have a passion for regarding their elders as senile.*
>
> Henry Adams

A deadly disease afflicting the brain, Alzheimer's is a permanent, progressive senile dementia, whose behavioral hallmarks are impaired learning, memory and thinking accompanied by confusion, disorientation, mood swings and deterioration of personality and speech . (The term *senile* when used by lay persons is less an expression of diagnosis and more an epithet of abuse. When used by physicians, it means pertaining to old age.) Alzheimer's is generally considered the major cause of dementia.

There is no known cause or cure for Alzheimer's. Victims die, generally from an accident or an infection. But Alzheimer's itself is not contagious. Emotional and economic burdens are staggering. Approximately 2,000,000 persons 65+ are believed to be victims of Alzheimer's, and about $40,000,000,000 or more is spent on them. The pain and suffering of victims and families and friends is incalculable.

Chance of succumbing to Alzheimer's increases with age: the condition occurs in approximately 1% of persons 65-74, 7% of those 75-84, 20% of those 85+. It is important to remember that 4 of 5 persons 85+ have normal or nearly normal intellectual functioning. Alzheimer's afflicts more women than men, probably because women live longer.

As yet there is no definitive treatment or cure for Alzheimer's disease although research is proceeding apace and there are palliative drugs on the market. Preliminary studies, still controversial however, indicate that medications many elderly women take regularly, estrogen/progestin after menopause and anti-inflammatories for arthritis, may significantly reduce the risk of Alzheimer's. Men who take anti-inflammatories regularly also may reduce the risk. Researchers postulate that persons who remain mentally active as they age build a reserve of brain synapses that helps stave off the disease.

Alzheimer's, especially in the early stages, is particularly difficult to diagnose. Because Alzheimer's can develop so slowly, even family members may not realize for some time that their loved one is deteriorating. Oddly, Alzheimer's is singular among diseases in that a person with the illness does not suspect that anything is wrong: neurologists say, "If you think you have the disease, then probably you do not." Doctors state that Alzheimer's has an insidious onset, meaning that it progresses so gradually as to be established before it is perceptible. But a CAT scan, blood studies and psychological tests enable a doctor to be reasonably certain of the diagnosis. Absolute certainty can be achieved only by means of autopsy.

It is sometimes hard indeed to distinguish Alzheimer's from such other conditions as Parkinson's because of overlapping features. This may be why it is often said that approximately 60-70% of all demented individuals have Alzheimer's. Even more important is the fact that virtually all the changes in the brain that distinguish Alzheimer's are found, but not to the same degree, in the brains of elderly persons who do not have the disease. It is possible that Alzheimer's is really a number of closely related diseases caused by different factors, such as tiny unnoticed strokes that in the aggregate do the bulk of damage.

Scientists reason that Alzheimer's is a threshold illness, one that occurs when cell and tissue death exceed a certain limit or threshold. In what way, if any, this fact is tied to the fact that chance of becoming a victim of Alzheimer's increases with age is not known.

Personality change with loss of sensitivity even to intimates may be the first sign. Another early symptom is accelerating difficulty in naming objects of all kinds, what physicians call dysnomia. Increasingly debilitating, Alzheimer's may last as little as 2 years or as long as 20. Emotional difficulties, as anxiety and agitation, become more and more conspicuous. Eventually, incontinent and unable to recognize family and friends, the victim becomes incapable of performing even the simplest of activities of daily living, such as eating or dressing.

Thomas Jefferson in a letter to John Adams declared: "Bodily decay is gloomy in prospect, but the most abhorrent of all human contemplation is body without mind." Nevertheless, in 1999David Troxel, MPH, executive director, Santa Barbara, California, chapter of the Alzheimer Association, asserted: "People's [active] lives don't end the minute they're diagnosed with Alzheimer's. Take former President Reagan. His diagnosis was announced in 1994, but he still goes to his office every day, still works out, still greets old friends. People with this disease can have satisfying lives for years."

It is important for families to assist patients in staying independent as long as possible, but such caregiving is an exceedingly difficult and frequently thankless task as the patient loses awareness. Geriatricians say that there are two victims of Alzheimer's disease, the patient and the caregiver, because the one becomes totally dependent upon the other, not just during the day, but also at night. The devastating effects of Alzheimer's on intellect, personality and control of body functions eventually reduce victims to complete helplessness and the family caregivers to frantic frustration. Many a patient is awake at night and may wander away and become lost. A caregiving family finds itself stretched to the absolute limit in providing physical, emotional, social and financial help to an Alzheimer's victim. Geriatricians strongly advise a family to plan ahead with a lawyer and investment counselor in regard to finances, guardianship, eventual placement in a nursing home for an Alzheimer victim if care becomes too difficult for non-professionals to provide .

DEPRESSION

You were not born to be depressed.

Epictetus

Although depression is the most common psychiatric disorder in the elderly, most old persons never experience an episode of significant depression, a mood sustained for weeks or longer. At worst, the risk for medically identifiable depression in late life ranges between 10 and 15%, a span lower than that for either the young or the middle-aged.

The intense feelings which seemingly everyone has at times, whether from disaster or good fortune, do not of themselves cause depression but may simply be a realistic emotional reaction to an unusual circumstance. There has to be predisposition, psychological or physical, for depression to occur. Repressed rage may be an underlying cause. Someone who has broken a hip may worry so intensely and long that a bout of depression occurs. Loneliness and chronic illness may result in depression.

Depression does not of itself indicate insanity or a serious flaw in character. An illness, it does not have a single symptom. Mostly treatable, depression is part chemical, part environmental, part genetic.

Depression really encompasses a broad range of disorders. Symptoms include apathy and inactivity, sadness and dejection, changes in appetite and sleep patterns, neglect of vital Activities of Daily Living, expression of feelings of worthlessness, difficulty in concentrating, thoughts of death. Moods can vary all the way from deep sadness to psychotic with delusional guilt and severe sleep loss. Depression may adversely affect almost all parts of the body. Weight loss in severe depression is sufficient to change mouth anatomy and damage the fit of dentures.

While culture, class and race are not predisposing factors, depression is prevalent among the unmarried old and those who have medical problems. The disorder is not always easy to recognize. Drugs, codeine and digitalis among them, can cause symptoms much like those of depression. Often misdiagnosed, depression among the elderly is without doubt seriously underdiagnosed. Sometimes indications of depression are dismissed as signs of old age or are misinterpreted by relatives as indicative of dementia although a depressed person, unlike a demented, can explain when the condition had its onset and why the impairment causes unhappiness. Depression itself is frequently masked in older people by appearance of other disorders, somatic and/or neurotic. The physical and the mental are inextricably interwoven. Elderly people may exhibit what psychologists call conversion symptoms—that is, physical for emotional, such as nausea, headaches and bowel problems in the case of depression. As a consequence, the depression goes unrecognized.

Early diagnosis and treatment of depression in older people are imperative. As statistics make clear, suicide can result from depression: at least 20% of all suicides occur in persons 65+. The subgroup of elderly most at risk, those 85+, is growing about 6 times faster than the rest of the population, and most of that subgroup consists of unmarried women. Elderly women, who have more chronic illnesses than old men, are especially vulnerable to depression although they may not openly reveal the condition. But elderly men are in more danger from depression-triggered suicide.

Psychiatrists discriminate between bipolar (both depressed and elevated or animated) and unipolar (depressed alone) disorders. Unipolar depression generally lasts from 6-9 months although it may continue for a year or two. Bipolar disorder usually strikes teenagers or young adults and lasts a shorter time, from 3-6 months, with episodes alternating over a long period of time. In contrast, in unipolar depression there may be only one or a few episodes during a lifetime. In those young-old who suffer a period of depression for the first time, episodes may recur. Nevertheless, depression is eminently treatable.

Treatment is by way of support (as from a social worker, friend or family members), drugs or psychotherapy (individual or group) or electroconvulsive therapy (ECT). Alcohol and over-the-counter drugs which may interact adversely with other drugs are to be avoided. The most common treatment is through use of such antidepressant drugs as Prozac, Effexor and Zoloft. Psychotherapist Marlin S. Potash says: "The drugs open a window of opportunity. Often we can use them to go further, faster than 'talking therapy' alone can do, and help people get back to having satisfying lives more quickly." People chronically depressed for some time respond well in about 70% of the cases. Even so, negative side effects of antidepressant medications, such as oversedation or confusion and dizziness, are more likely to occur in elderly patients unless the drug contents have been carefully adjusted with age and illnesses in mind.

Enlisting support of relatives and friends, who should try to maintain as normal a relationship as possible without being critical or disapproving, is crucial to success of psychotherapy. Misunderstanding of depression and its symptoms can poison relationships quickly, hurting both the sick person and would-be caregivers .

Electroconvulsive therapy, which is frequently employed when depression becomes severe or life-threatening to old people, deals successfully with mood disturbance and seems in many cases to improve cognitive performance as well. Side effects are minimal, and the procedure is remarkably safe. Usually, about 10 treatments are needed.

The consequences of unrecognized and untreated depression can be dire. Feeling isolated and unworthy, the victim of depression may turn to excessive use of tranquilizers and alcohol for relief. The risk of suicide is high. Even so, recognized early and treated in timely fashion, depression can almost always be conquered.

DEPRESSION: DANGER SIGNS

Agitation	Change in appetite
Disinterestedness or loss of concentration	Fatigue
Feelings of worthlessness	Guilt
Inattentiveness	Loss of pleasure in activities
Melancholy	Sleeplessness
Suicidal aims	Vacillation
Thoughts of death	Significant weight loss or gain

PLEASE NOTE: Anyone with 4 or more of the symptoms listed above needs help. A physician should be consulted.

PARKINSON'S DISEASE

Unstable as water, thou . . .

Genesis, XLIX,4

Parkinson's, another progressive, degenerative disorder, attacks mainly the elderly. About 50,000 new cases appear annually. Onset generally occurs from 50-60 years, culminating at about 75. When no cause is found, the condition is called primary Parkinsonism. When the cause is evident, the condition is termed secondary Parkinsonism. Carbon monoxide poisoning, tumors and head trauma are known causes—as are various tranquilizing medications. (When the drugs are stopped, Parkinson's almost always stops or subsides.)

Parkinson's is a general term for movement disorders characterized by tremor at rest, muscular rigidity, lack of facial expression, postural instability, difficulty in beginning and in coordinating movement. Parkinson's starts insidiously. Along with depression and anxiety, any of the five symptoms mentioned above may emerge alone or in combination. Or nonspecific complaints, such as a vague sense of not feeling well, may develop and continue for a long time. With progression of the disease, many victims evince greater rigidity while their tremor becomes less pronounced. Others stoop and display quivering in the hands and jaws. Generally, Parkinson's sufferers find it difficult to start walking. They proceed with short, shuffling steps. Activities of daily living become increasingly arduous. At this stage, it is relatively easy to diagnose the difficulty as Parkinson's, not arthritis.

There is no cure for most cases. Therapy is lifelong. Although the cause may not be known, the biochemical defect leading to symptoms is well understood. Treatment for Parkinson's involves replenishment of dopamine, a chemical needed for transmission of messages between neurons of the brain to ensure smooth, coordinated muscle activity, with the result that some patients return to nearly normal behavior. Others who do not respond favorably receive different drugs in various combinations to modify brain function so as to compensate for dopamine deficiency. Physical therapy and a carefully designed exercise program may help constrain symptoms and serve somewhat to restore mobility.

STROKE

Little strokes fell great oaks.

Benjamin Franklin

A major cause of disability leading to institutionalization of those old people who survive, stroke ranks third behind heart disease and cancer as a cause of death. Estimates are 400,000-500,0000 new stroke patients and 100,000 deaths annually. Of the 3,000,000 survivors, more than 1/2 have serious physical and functional impairment ranging from speech difficulty to paralysis. Total cost, direct and indirect, in the United States alone is estimated at $30,000,000,000 every year. To the afflicted, stroke may seem a condition worse than death—robbing them of movement, speech, independence. Onset is sudden, but effects are long-lasting. Depression often follows.

Like a heart attack, a stroke is not so much an illness as a response of the body to something else, usually narrowing of arteries. Stroke is a cerebrovascular disorder, the result of a sudden, marked disruption, generally by a clot or hemorrhage, of blood flow in or to the brain. A leading predisposing condition of stroke is arteriosclerosis, a disease with thickening and hardening of artery walls that markedly slows or interrupts blood flow. Deprived of nutrients and oxygen, cranial neurons die and are not regenerated. Severity of the stroke is determined by the brain area affected and the extent of the damage.

Though incidence has dropped considerably because of effective treatment of high blood pressure and of daily use of a low dose of aspirin to prevent formation of blood clots, strokes continue to afflict the elderly. Risk factors include a sedentary lifestyle, elevated cholesterol, cigarette smoking, diabetes mellitus, heart trouble, hypertension,.

There are warning signs, especially if they occur on only one side of the body. A person experiencing for about 2-30 minutes any of the following disorders should consult a doctor at once: weakness or clumsiness on one side of the body, paralysis of the face, unexpected loss of vision or speech, a severe headache seemingly without cause, dizziness and a fall. A person may undergo several attacks of this nature daily or encounter just 2 or 3 episodes over a period of several years. No matter what the frequency, such attacks should not be ignored. Delay in diagnosis can be disastrous.

A major stroke is often preceded by such mini-strokes (the medical term is transient ischemic attacks, TIAs for short), which are a result of a brief but sharp reduction of blood flow to the brain or parts thereof. How often mini-strokes foreshadow a major stroke is not known. Estimates are that 5% of TIA victims will suffer a stroke within a month, about 10% within a year, about 25% within 3 years. But TIAs are reversible. Anti-coagulants are standard therapy followed by surgery if needed to clear the arteries. To be most effective, treatment should begin within 3-6 hours.

Recent developments in stroke treatment indicate that researchers are on the verge of astonishing breakthroughs. If a victim can be brought to an emergency room quickly, doctors can administer blood thinners to dislodge the clot responsible for the stroke, thereby interrupting the attack and markedly limiting brain damage. In the case of a bleeding stroke, surgeons may be able to repair the vessel oozing blood into the brain. None of these treatments is without risk. Blood thinners, for example, may cause further bleeding into the brain. But research continues in an effort both to prevent strokes from happening and to give doctors in the event of a stroke adequate time to repair damage and restore normal blood flow.

In the instance of a major stroke, brain tissue dies and some paralysis of limb or side of torso, memory loss and difficulty in using words generally result. Ambidextrous persons are the exception: they do not lose word sense because handedness determines which side of the brain controls speech. But there may be performance and spatial difficulties.

Stroke is usually sudden in onset, reaching maximum impact in minutes. For the elderly, stroke may be a devastating shock psychologically. Not all survive, approximately 20% dying in the hospital. The death rate increases with age. Some patients recover to a large extent and live for years. For some, prognosis is good: they will be able to perform activities of daily living independently. But others will have another stroke within 10 months. A recent Gallup survey done for the National Stroke Association found that most patients are unaware that they are at high risk for a second stroke.

A lengthy rehabilitation program may be required after a stroke to obtain some improvement of disabilities, such as achieving proficiency in walking. The earlier such a regimen is started, the better—especially if it is combined with encouragement and increasing contact with the world outside to help overcome the depression that is a common consequence of stroke. The brain has suffered damage but not necessarily intellectual deterioration. Bystanders sometimes do not know or else forget that a speechless stroke victim may understand the speech of others. The patient, relatives and friends need to learn the nature of the handicaps imposed by stroke and to be made aware that because improvement may take time and effort, patience and perseverance are essential.

The toll that Parkinson's, Alzheimer's and stroke take on body and mind rank them amid the foremost scourges ever inflicted on great numbers of human beings. They are brain attacks, and should be given the same publicity and urgency of treatment as heart attacks. As confronting every momentous challenge does, struggling with these illnesses calls forth the physical and spiritual best in human nature, not only of the friends, relatives, nurses, doctors and support groups who care for and treat victims and their families, but also of the researchers whose unstinting efforts have made a brave start in the struggle against these enemies of humanity.

WARNING SIGNS OF AN ONCOMING STROKE

Balance: difficulty walking, lack of coordination, vertigo.
Comprehension: inability to understand conversation of other persons.
Consciousness: restlessness, sleepiness and stupor or coma.
Control: vomiting.
Memory: some impairment of immediate past memory.
Pain: unexpected harsh headaches, often with pain at back of head.
Sensation: numbness, inability to maintain control of one side of body or face, weakness of limbs.
Speech: blurring syllables in speech, inability to speak.
Vision: blurred or dimmed sight, seeing double, loss of sight in one or both eyes.

PLEASE NOTE: Consult a doctor immediately if you experience one or more of the symptoms listed above!

OSTEOPOROSIS

Can these bones live?

Ezekiel, 37:1-14

Primarily affecting women, osteoporosis is a progressive disease characterized by gradual thinning and weakening of bones resulting in skeletal weakness and fractures. More than 17,000,000 women are at immediate risk, and about 5,000,000 more are directly affected. But, as the folklore phrase "little old men" indicates, quite a few males are victims of osteoporosis.

Women are at a dual disadvantage. Their bones are not so dense as men's, and hormone changes at menopause help thin them even further. About 40% of females have such significant loss by age 60 that the thinner bone structure is no longer fully able to withstand the weight-bearing mechanical stresses encountered in daily living. The skeleton is at severe risk of fractures, especially of the ankle, hips, vertebrae and wrist. In time, the vertebrae may become so fragile that they give way and cause debilitating spinal curvature. The cost in human misery is incalculable; in dollars, more than $4,000,000,000 annually to pay for about 1,500,000 bone fractures.

Physicians when dealing with the elderly refer to two classifications of osteoporosis, the most common of all metabolic bone diseases. Primary osteoporosis, consisting of Type I and Type II, accounts for 95% of all cases. Type I osteoporosis, also referred to as postmenopausal osteoporosis, largely responsible for fractures of the vertebrae, occurs in adults 50-70 years of age, affecting 6 times as many women as men. Bone loss can be fairly rapid. Type II osteoporosis, also referred to as senile osteoporosis, more gradual in development, occurs in the elderly 70+, affecting 2 times as many women as men, resulting at times in fracture of the pelvis and/or of the vertebrae. Secondary osteoporosis, neither postmenopausal nor age-related, has many possible causes, including poor nutrition, drug-inducement (as anti-inflammatory drugs given for rheumatoid arthritis), immobilization, hyperthyroidism. It affects 5% of all cases, and it produces much the same damage as that accounted for by both types of primary osteoporosis.

Because symptoms of osteoporosis in the first stages of the disorder are difficult to separate from those of normal aging, early diagnosis is difficult. Just about everyone suffers bone loss with age. Many women are unaware that they have been affected by osteoporosis. X-rays do not reveal the condition until at least 30% of bone mass has been lost. Abnormal biochemical findings have to be determined and evaluated by careful laboratory analysis. Attempts at diagnosis are often made on the basis of structural change in the spine, where osteoporosis typically first occurs and compresses vertebrae into a curvature known as dowager's hump.

Some patients remain asymptomatic, vertebral fractures developing for no apparent reason and with no trauma even though bones have been seriously weakened. Then acute pain arrives, subsiding generally within a few weeks. Other patients may undergo vertebral fractures with dull, aching pain and curvature of the spine. Still others, especially women in their 70's and 80's, fall and fracture a hip when reaching out for something, as a dress in a closet. As many as 1 in 5 victims of hip fracture die within 6 months of complications like pulmonary embolism or pneumonia resulting from the imposed immobility. Not a few victims of osteoporosis suffer tooth loss and find it difficult to keep dentures fitting well. But there appears to be an inverse correlation between osteoporosis and osteoarthritis; that is, persons with osteoporosis seemingly do not endure osteoarthritis.

At the present time, treatment of choice for primary osteoporosis involves prevention, alleviation of symptoms and inhibition of further development of the disorder. Analgesics, heat and massage help assuage acute back pain, especially if combined with an orthopedic garment and an exercise regimen. Bone loss can be slowed and risk of fracture decreased, especially in milder cases, by a combination of weight-bearing exercise and daily dietary supplementation of calcium and vitamin D. Probably the best supplement for the elderly, who commonly suffer from decreased stomach acid, is calcium citrate, about 1,200 milligrams a day, taken with meals. But it should be accompanied by extra fluid intake to avoid kidney trouble. (Calcium carbonate , a less expensive supplement, may cause gas and constipation.) For prevention of osteoporosis, at least 2 glasses daily of fortified skim milk with a high-calcium diet (as salmon and sardines) and a small supplement of vitamin D are recommended from puberty onward. Intake of coffee should be limited, for caffeine may increase bone loss.

Doctors for some years have endorsed giving women with progressive or somewhat more severe osteoporosis estrogen/progestin therapy within 4-6 years of menopause even though it increases risk of endometrial and breast cancer. Estrogen/progestin therapy usually has positive effects on calcium but only relatively mild side effects, such as bloating and nausea. Epidemiological studies indicate the success of the therapy, for it decreases occurrence of hip fractures by about 1/2. Osteoporotic men receive calcium and vitamin D supplementation at levels carefully monitored by their physician. Both men and women at risk from osteoporosis can reduce the likelihood of a hip fracture from a fall by wearing regularly an external plastic appliance built into special underwear available at medical supply houses.

Recent studies of several years' duration on the effects of oral alendronate, a chemical in the aminobisphosphonate group, on women with postmenopausal osteoporosis conclude that daily treatment increases bone mass in the total body, decreases incidence of vertebral fractures and reduces progression of height loss. Alendronate, sold as Fosamax, has been approved by the Food and Drug Administration. Several other aminobisphosphonates have been under investigation for treatment and prevention of postmenopausal osteoporosis; indications are that when properly administered they provide an effective therapy. Doctors, awaiting the outcome of further studies on these and other drugs aimed at prevention and treatment of osteoporosis, remain cautiously optimistic that although a number of effective drugs have already been found, researchers will discover even better ones. But they advise that in combating osteoporosis other factors like exercise and a calcium-rich diet should not be neglected.

Even though much research into prevention and treatment of osteoporosis is under way, doctors are concerned that as the baby boomers get older osteoporosis may be come an epidemic. Dr. Robert P. Heaney, professor of medicine at Creighton University in Omaha, says: "There is good evidence that at least the last two generations of American women have consumed an inadequate amount of calcium, beginning in puberty." The present generation of elderly are also at risk. Their diet has been deficient in dairy products and vegetables which contain noteworthy amounts of calcium; and their sedentary lifestyle has resulted not only in year-round lack of exposure to sun rays which help body synthesis of vitamin D but also in lack of exercise necessary to induce bone formation and maintenance.

Some 1,700 years ago, Pilpay cautioned that "What is bred in the bone will never come out of the flesh."

RESPIRATORY COMPLAINTS

Breath's a ware that will not keep.

A.E. Housman

Among the elderly living in the community the most frequent infections are respiratory: influenza, pneumonia, emphysema and bronchitis. Despite widespread availability of safe, inexpensive vaccines for some of these disorders, thousands and thousands of deaths from respiratory infections occur every year.

The old, particularly those suffering from chronic diseases, have a higher death rate from influenza (commonly referred to as flu or grippe) and are at greater risk for complications than the young. Disorders often follow because the weakened patient easily falls prey to other infections, such as bronchitis, sinus trouble and pneumonia. About 90% of deaths caused by influenza occur in persons 65+. This highly contagious infectious disease is usually prevalent in the form of winter epidemics resulting from importation of the virus via travelers aboard ships and airplanes.

Owing to repeated changes in composition of the influenza virus, doctors advise annual vaccination of the elderly and of health care professionals unless allergic to eggs or egg products. When the influenza vaccine matches closely the virus of an epidemic, efficacy rates for the elderly living in the community are well over 90%. When the immunizing and infecting viral strains do not match, little or no significant protection results from vaccination. Treatment of influenza victims includes generous fluid intake, bedrest and drugs.

Afflicting the elderly more than any other age cohort, the most common cause of death in the oldest-old, pneumonia is an infectious disease of the lungs especially prevalent in winter. Signs of pneumonia are evident in about half the autopsies of all persons 85+. Elderly who are hospitalized or in a nursing home are about 50 times more likely to fall victim to pneumonia as contrasted with older people living at home. Causes of pneumonia include breathing in of the pneumococcus group of bacteria, of the influenza virus, of the organisms of tuberculosis and of various other kinds of bacteria and viruses Pneumonia is transmitted by exhalations from the nose and mouth of infected persons which are then inhaled by other persons. It may begin suddenly or as a complication of other diseases. No wonder many physicians strongly recommend that everyone 65+ receive the preventive vaccine once every 5 years (the span of time for which it is effective) unless allergic to any of its components. As is the situation with the influenza vaccine, the pneumonia vaccine is not administered to anyone suffering from a respiratory infection, no matter how minor, or from illness producing fever. The efficacy rate is said to be approximately 60% among the elderly although this figure is deemed high by many physicians. As with so many other diseases, symptoms of pneumonia differ between young and old persons, the elderly usually not evincing fever, chest pains and chills, with the result that diagnosis of pneumonia can easily be missed. Physicians emphasize the importance in treatment of nutrition and fluid intake as well as that of drugs.

If different locations on the body are used, pneumonia and influenza vaccines can be administered at the same time with no reduction in efficacy of the vaccines or increase in side effects.

Chronic obstructive pulmonary disease (COPD), really a group of diseases including bronchitis and emphysema, impedes expiration of air from the lungs. A major source of illness and death among the elderly, the incidence of COPD increases with age. The chief environmental risk factor for both bronchitis, characterized by a chronic coughing up of sputum (also called mucus or phlegm), and emphysema, characterized by severe impairment of breathing, is cigarette smoking which in time is followed by inflammatory changes in the lungs that destroy small air spaces although pollution can also contribute to the development of the diseases. At least 50% of long-time smokers have one or the other disease, most with a combination of both. Progress of symptoms is generally so slow that doctors may not recognize the disease for years. Because the disorders often coexist, physicians may encounter difficulty deciding whether bronchitis or emphysema is more responsible for the obstruction of the airways. Intensive rehabilitation programs for victims may help improve the quality of life, but the survival rate once emphysema is detected is usually less than 5 years.

As more and more women have taken up smoking, so Thomas Hood's lines, though in another context, have become peculiarly appropriate:

> One more unfortunate,
> Weary of breath,
> Rashly importunate,
> Gone to her death.

SPASMS and OTHER PAINFUL SLEEP SENSATIONS

Where Life becomes a Spasm . . .
If that is not Sensation,
I don't know what it is.

Lewis Carroll

Involuntary movement, painful cramps and "creepy crawly" sensations troubling the legs are relatively common in older people in whom they are not only uncomfortable, they are painful and sleep-robbing. Causes are unknown. Researchers theorize that for about 1/2 of the sufferers the disorders are familial in origin: they derive from an inherited imbalance of chemicals in the nervous system, probably of such neurotransmitters as dopamine and serotonin. Other possible causes have been attributed to alcohol and caffeine, diabetes, certain prescribed medications, mineral or vitamin deficiency, pregnancy.

The "creepy crawly" syndrome strikes most often when a person lies down to sleep. But it can occur to a diner in a restaurant or to the driver of an automobile. It is as though something were crawling on the surface of the legs or moving deep within the legs and causing fidgeting and pain. In an attempt at gaining relief, victims get out of bed or chair and press the soles of their feet hard against the floor or walk around and around, sometimes for as much as 5 minutes or more.

Many elderly suffer from restless leg syndrome, also referred to by physicians as nocturnal myoclonus, a condition in which recurrent involuntary jerking and kicking of the legs disturbs sleep of victims and may awaken them time and again. Relatively common is the condition in which muscles, generally in the foot, calf or thigh, contract involuntarily in sleep or as one lies down to sleep, producing agonizing cramps.

Women are more generally afflicted than men. Sufferers desirous of preventing the condition are often advised to move gently when getting into or turning in bed. Massaging the afflicted part, pressing the foot hard on the floor and stretching may bring relief as may contracting muscles opposite the muscle in spasm. Often, the sufferer walks until the spasm ceases, seemingly of its own accord.

Preventive measures against these leg disorders include for people who sleep on their backs using a frame to keep covers above the legs, and for people who sleep on their stomachs letting feet hang over the edge of the bed. Quinine, a muscle relaxant, is prescribed for leg cramps but there is a possibility of serious side effects. Some sufferers report relief from supplements of Vitamins E and C and magnesium. Most recently, calcium citrate has been recommended but with warnings that high doses (like 1200 milligrams) may cause gall bladder trouble or kidney stones. Helpful is active participation in a support group.

Persons afflicted with painful sleep sensations think that Auden's description is apposite:

> Cramp rack their limbs till they resemble
> Cartoons by Goya.

STRESS

Who knows when thou mayest be tested.
So live that thou bearest the strain.

R.A. Hopwood

An inevitable aspect of living, stress is psychological or physical–often a mixture of the two. Stress is a state of tension triggered by events, whether positive or negative, that upset body and mind equilibrium.

Different kinds of stress vary in degree. Driving a car which is skidding on snow causes a temporary strain, mild and soon recovered from. Although positive and relatively moderate in impact, the stress undergone by a mother making arrangements for a daughter's wedding lasts longer and is not so easy to deal with. An expected stressful event, as taking the bar examination, can be handled relatively easily, but an unexpected event, as sudden loss of a job, may create a severe strain difficult to endure. Chronic, dangerous, debilitating illness can result from such severe stress as loss of a mate or of a close friend.

Not always harmful, stress can add zest and spice to an activity. This is one reason people enjoy a sport, such as tennis. By challenging people and keeping them alert, stress helps people grow and achieve objectives, as a would-be doctor striving to pass the state licensing examination. Stress can be a kind of work aphrodisiac says Paul Rosch, professor of medicine at the American Institute of Stress: "It's a question of setting goals that are appropriate, beyond your grasp but within reach."

There is more than a simple connection between body and mind. Stress can profoundly affect physical systems as well as mental. The endocrine system, which controls responses to stress, and the immune system are interdependent, so that what affects one is reflected in the other. Adrenaline, known as the "fight or flight hormone," which makes it possible for a person to respond at once to stress, if called upon too often will lead to deleterious consequences. In many instances, grieving widowers experience a depressed immune response because white blood cells needed to fight disease-producing agents are reduced in number.

Excessive, prolonged stress among the elderly can cause a variety of psychological and physiological disorders–including anxiety, depression, forgetfulness, headache, elevated blood pressure, damage to connective tissue, heart trouble, raised blood sugar levels, sleeplessness, stomach aches. Liable to continual environmental and social stress, the old fear financial decreases, loneliness, loss of independence, physical and mental disability. Responses of older persons aimed at coping with stress may be healthy, as exercise and meditation, or unhealthy, as alcohol abuse and overeating. Most of the elderly do adapt, often rating their health as good although physicians' ratings may be distinctly lower. The elderly have found it better to cope with stress, not by trying to change circumstances, but by accommodating themselves to the demands of the outer world.

Stress is as necessary as it is inevitable. In response to stress, people learn how to adjust to challenges to themselves and their environment. Older persons traveling to China with Elderhostel, for instance, encounter lectures, literature, language training and tests. They work hard and they travel hard, and return home having enjoyed themselves thoroughly. It is obvious that if effective coping mechanisms are employed to ameliorate stress, a person–no matter what the age–will view success in managing stressful situations as significant and in so doing find a source of intense emotional gratification.

Because change, whether for better or worse, is always stressful, successful management calls for continual adaptation to change throughout the life span. But whether a change is beneficial or harmful may be less important than perception of difficulties involved in alteration of life-style or than confidence in ability to adapt to different circumstances. Some elderly because of fear of risks involved in trying to alter a situation resist any change in circumstance. Although having difficulty with such activities of daily living as shopping and transportation, a widowed oldster may insist on continuing to live in an apartment absolutely familiar after decades of residence. Another, faced with the same problem, viewing the situation as demanding immediate action, may insist on moving to an institution where cooking, cleaning and transportation are provided although satisfaction with one-room living quarters is unlikely and having to adjust to an entirely new group of companions of unknown quality may prove uncomfortable. Both choices by elderly persons seeking to avoid future change will likely result in dissatisfaction and increased levels of stress.

Inability to manage elevated levels of stress may result in pathological symptoms and unbecoming behavior, such as back problems and snapping at others. Stress may even accelerate the aging process. Swallowing alcohol or tranquilizers has for decades in the United States been regarded as a simple, easy way for adults to reduce stress, to smooth over life's rough edges brought on by whatever difficulties of the day, whether work related or familial. For the elderly, this solution is anything but simple and definitely not easy. With age, ability to tolerate alcohol and many medications—which are metabolized more slowly than in youth—is severely reduced to the point that addiction may become a severe, even deadly, problem. Precise effects of chronic addiction on an elderly individual cannot be gauged beforehand. Loss of control may be one result, sometimes giving the appearance of depression or senility Another result, much more dangerous, may occur because of interaction of medications or of alcohol with medications. Toxic effects with permanent damage to the brain and other organs cannot be ruled out. In grave danger, the elderly addict needs help.

Stress incontinence, the involuntary leakage of small to moderate amounts of urine, is not unusual in older women who have had multiple vaginal births and in older men who have had prostate surgery. It often occurs with coughing, laughing, sneezing or the sudden picking up of heavy weights. Stress incontinence may respond to drug therapy or to behavioral intervention, such as feedback. Sometimes surgery is beneficial. Manufacturers sell special undergarments to help victims of stress incontinence avoid embarrassment.

Although perception of problems and the scope and intensity of stress may vary over time, a chronic situation of strain can produce a sense of entrapment or a feeling of being overwhelmed, thereby increasing the level of stress. Learned helplessness, a condition in which a person stops trying to cope and relies on others, may result. Psychologists consider the burdens of such stress to have subjective and objective aspects. The subjective burden is the mental outlook and feelings concerning the extent of the stress. An elderly woman who has fractured her hip may worry constantly that she will never again be ambulatory even though the therapist has helped her begin to walk again. The objective burden is the effect on a person's resources, namely family and friends, income and health status. An older person with a heart condition, such as *angina pectoris*, concerned with ongoing care, may tax unnecessarily the patience of friends and family, waste income on unneeded medications and lower health status by imagining emergency after emergency.

Inclusion of an impaired old person into an established family unit can be traumatic, particularly so when grown children are leaving the household and the caregiver is anticipating a period of increased freedom of activity. There are significant levels of stress for both the impaired or disabled elderly and their care-giving children as a result of reversed dependency relationships. Such parent-child relationships are frequently guilt-ridden. Much of the emotional stress to a care-giver results from isolation with decreased opportunity for friendship and participation in community social life. The unrelenting chronic stress on children forced into parental care-giving by family responsibilities is reflected in exacerbation of health problems and sometimes in elder abuse. Burdens on a care-giving spouse advanced in years are even heavier, largely because of age, health and financial limitations. In the United States, ironically, one of the two federal programs providing support to care-giving families is the IRS; the other is the Veterans Administration.

Studies invalidate the hypothesis that aging women are more susceptible than older men to life stresses. This although women in the later stages of life are more vulnerable than the men to loss of a spouse, lessening of financial resources and chronic health problems. Coping patterns in response to health-related stressors are virtually the same for elderly men and women except that females call on health-care services more often than males. Reliance on faith as a coping mechanism increases with age and is seemingly depended on more by women.

For both sexes, role shifts which occur at a period of life in which that kind of event is generally to be expected are less stressful than those that happen unexpectedly. Those who experience the death of a spouse in old age have less stress than those who in early or mid-life are suddenly subjected to widowhood.

It is wise for the elderly to undergo a stress test periodically as part of the basic physical examination, not just as a vehicle of clearance to exercise. Studies indicate that stress tests are more valid in the old than in the young. Knowledge of symptoms produced by stress tests is helpful to both the physician and the elderly patient in preventing or in dealing with disorders. "Stress reduction and treating the mind and body as a single entity," adds Dr. I. Rosenfeld, professor of clinical medicine at New York Hospital–Cornell Medical Center, "can have a significant impact on the prevention and management of disease."

Dr. James S. Gordon, director of the Center for Mind-Body Medicine in Washington, DC, recommends a helpful procedure for a person to deal with feelings and regain perspective: "Set aside a little time daily to be with just yourself. Breathe deeply to quiet yourself." Books found in every public library explain in simple terms how to practice relaxation techniques, such as breath control, guided imagery, meditation. Physicians and psychologists teach special techniques–progressive muscle relaxation, biofeedback and self-hypnosis among others–to help patients reduce levels of stress.

Nevertheless, Dr. Hans Selye, respected stress researcher, cautioned that of itself stress is not harmful. "Man," Selye maintained, "should not try to avoid stress any more than he would shun food, love or exercise." As always, the golden mean applies.

SUICIDE

*Just as I shall select my ship when I am about to go on a
voyage, or my house when I propose to take a residence,
so I shall choose my death when I am about to depart
from life.*

Seneca

*a suicide is a person who has
considered his own case and decided
that he is worthless and who acts
as his own judge and jury and executioner
and he probably knows better
than anyone else whether there is justice
in the verdict*

Don Marquis

Complete information about suicide is impossible to obtain. Under-reporting because of family and other pressures is the rule. Yet it is known that self-destruction is the 3rd leading cause of death by injury in the old-age cohort, higher than in any other age group, probably double that of the general population. Suicide rates increase markedly with age. Suicide talk or threats by an older person should not be taken casually. The elderly are usually successful in realizing suicide plans.

Suicide rates among the elderly may be much higher than statistics denote. Intentional taking of overdoses of prescribed medications may not be recognized as such. Physicians dislike reporting a suicide. Families often destroy suicide notes out of shame, compassion and sentiment.

According to a study by the Centers for Disease Control and Prevention, the short-term trend in the rate of suicide has steadily increased among persons 65+ since 1980. In 1990, the National Center for Health Statistics, Mortality Branch, reported that there were about 85 suicides a day, almost 20 of which by persons 65+.Late-life adults, less than 15% of the total population, committed about 25% of all suicides 1980-

1992 The numbers and percentages are undoubtedly larger for would-be suicides because there are probably at least 6 survivors for an incomplete suicide and at least 8 attempts for every completed suicide. Future trends are difficult to foresee, some researchers arguing for much higher rates when the baby boomers reach old age, others arguing for lower rates—both agreeing that size of the cohort will be the most important factor in determination of actual numbers.

There is a gender gap in regard to suicide. Firearms are the method of choice of males; poison or overdose of medication, of females. Males account for more than 80% of suicides among those 65+. White men 85+ have a higher rate of suicide than that of any other age group. Among women 65-74, suicide rates seemed in recent decades to be declining—only to rise again among those 75+. Females make more attempts; males prevail more often.

Research studies on suicide of the aged may be scarce, but to sociologists it is apparent that suicide by the elderly is of multidimensional causation. Many years ago, Seneca declared:

I will not relinquish old age if it leaves my better part intact. But if it begins to shake my mind, if it destroys my faculties one by one, if it leaves me not life but breath, I will depart from the putrid or tottering edifice. I will not escape by death from disease so long as it may be healed, and leaves my mind unimpaired. I will not raise my hand against myself on account of pain, for so to die is to be conquered. But if I know that I must suffer without hope of relief, I will depart, not through fear of the pain itself, but because it prevents all for which I would live.

Psychologists maintain that suicide is not a matter of self-hatred or of aggression directed inward. Suicide is self-inflicted, intentional cessation of life, an attempt to find release from internal and/or external stress. The elderly suicidal person, feeling helpless and hopeless, trapped in a situation of unbearable pain, seeing no alternative to despair, has a sense of withdrawal from life—a condition the French call *anomie*.

Aging and the deterioration it can entail are often accompanied by losses at the very time the elderly are least able to handle them. Jobs are unavailable. There may be financial difficulties. Friends and family move away or die. No longer is there a confidant with whom to share problems. Driving a car is difficult or impossible. Loneliness and isolation begin to predominate as social status and action decline with lessened mobility. Chronic illnesses take away independence and pain-free activity: there is a direct link between physical health and incidence of suicide. Feelings of worthlessness begin to pervade the empty days, and the sense of having become a burden increases.

For the elderly, swift-moving technological change increases the sense of being outside the life around them. Society, giving the old no role to play, devalues them because they have lost their beauty, health and youth. Depression, involved in more than 1/2 of suicides, results. Researchers have found that often a suicide attempt is an impulsive act occurring during a mood of dark emotion.

Suicide behavior involves both *attempted* and *completed* suicide. There are several kinds of attempted suicide, also known as *parasuicide.* When a suicide scheme and action to implement it are implausible and hardly possible, psychiatrists term them a *gesture*, a cry for help. Both *gesture* and *attempt* should be taken seriously. Early intervention to prevent suicide could save many an elderly life. Every attempt and gesture increases risk for future successful suicide. More than 70% of *completed* suicides are by individuals who gave much warning. They communicated intent to at least one person. Many consulted a doctor just hours or days before acting. But some elderly are unaware of suicidal tendencies. If completed, such suicide is called *subintentional.*

The pain of existence is unbearable to someone suicidal, but physicians know that such suffering is remediable. Psychiatric treatment is aimed at relief of distress and wretchedness, at providing comfort and at prevention of other *gestures* and *attempts,* especially since about 20% of intended suicides try again within a year and 10% actually complete the act.

Some aged may commit so-called *passive* suicide: having lost the will to live, they stop caring for themselves by postponing treatment for illness or not taking prescribed medications or gradually cutting down on food and drink. Some elderly are considered *rational* suicides, persons committing an act of thought-out choice rather than of unreasoning impulse. Although marriage is generally associated with a lower rate of suicide, a husband, victim of an illness increasingly debilitating and expensive to treat, such as cancer, may prefer death to leaving his widow worn out from taking care of him and destitute from paying medical bills. Others suffering from a terminal illness, such as crippling stroke, may seek a quick end rather than try to put up with years of steady deterioration. Assisted suicide for relief of suffering in cases of terminal illness or unbearable pain appears to be slowly winning ethical and legal public approval, so the activities of Dr. Kevorkian indicate.

In this connection, recommendations of the 16th century English humanist and devout Catholic, Sir Thomas More, often called the Father of Euthanasia, remain timely:

If the disease be not only incurable, but also full of continual pain and anguish, then the priests and magistrate exhort the man that . . . he will determine with himself no longer to cherish that pestilent and painful disease. . . . And in doing so they tell him he shall do wisely, seeing by his death he shall lose no happiness, but end his torture. . . . They that be convinced finish their lives willingly, either by fasting, or else they are released by an opiate in their sleep without any feeling of death. But cause none such to die against his will.

Scientists are trying to discover effects of normal aging on the brain, so as to detect biological in addition to psychological markers for suicide but conclusions as yet are tentative. Research indicates that psychiatric disorder, especially depression, is a large factor in more than 1/2 of elderly suicides. Acceptance of self and joy in one's life, affirmation rather than rejection, are central to existence. Although depression is not a normal consequence of aging—instances appear in less than 3% of community-dwelling elderly—some symptoms occur at one time or another in about 15-30% of all those 65+.

Depression in institutional settings, wherein dwell the elderly who have lost their home, freedom and privacy, is more usual.

To prevent many suicides among the elderly, it is necessary to recognize depression for what it is and to treat it effectively. Neither is easy. The symptoms of depression overlap those of physical illness and the effects of medications as well as those of dementia. While there is a range of therapies for depression, not all elderly respond except, perhaps, to shock treatments. After successful treatment, other problems arise. A physician cannot change social roles for the aged or transfer them to more healthful surroundings or give them coping skills to meet new stresses. A comprehensive welfare follow-up, utilizing services of support groups and psychotherapists, is important. To a large degree, a concerned family and network of friends can help although they themselves will need assistance in overcoming intense feelings of guilt, remorse, shame and sorrow.

Spinoza wrote: "Those who commit suicide are powerless souls, and allow themselves to be conquered by external causes repugnant to their nature." In sympathetic agreement is Arthur Eaton:

> His heart was breaking, breaking,
> 'Neath loads of care and wrong;
> Who blames the man for taking
> What life denied so long?

VARICOSE VEINS

Stiffen the sinews, summon up the blood.

William Shakespeare

Varicose veins, blood vessels close to the surface of the skin that have become abnormally twisted and enlarged, can start early (even in children) and then grow progressively worse with age. At least 20% of all American adults have this painful and unsightly condition. Many elderly have medium to excessively large varicose veins. Authorities think that women sufferers outnumber men by at least 2 to 1; the estimate is inexact because so many men prefer not to make much of the condition.

Risk factors for varicose veins include advancing age, constipation, estrogen-replacing drugs, extended bed rest after major surgery, family history, lifting heavy objects, lack of exercise, obesity, past episodes of clots in the veins (thrombophlebitis), continual sitting with legs crossed, prolonged sitting or standing in one place. Presumably, lifestyle plays an important role: incidence of varicose veins is about the same among white and black Americans while Africans rarely are troubled by them.

When a person sits or stands, pressure pushing blood up the veins of the lower extremities to return the vital fluid to the heart is barely enough to counter the force of gravity pulling it down. Many veins, therefore, have one-way valves to prevent backflow. Varicose veins result when valves in veins weaken or malfunction. Blood pools in affected veins, especially in the legs. The veins become enlarged, so that they can be seen as bluish extended bulges just under the skin. Often at the beginning of the process and/or in smaller veins there are fine "spiderlike" bursts on the skin. Later on, sores, cramps and a feeling of heaviness in the legs are relatively common symptoms.

In most cases, varicose veins are a minor affliction. But there can be serious complications, as when an open ulcer occurs. In especially severe cases, varicose veins may lead to deep-vein thrombosis, a potentially life-threatening disorder in which blood clots form. But many persons have no symptoms other than unsightly veins. Unfortunately, by the time a victim notices the disorder, the varicosity has been under-way for a long period, and extent of the condition is usually larger than simple inspection reveals.

Sufferers themselves usually make the first diagnosis of varicose veins. Before concurring, the doctor will try to rule out other possible conditions, such as nerve irritation, muscle trauma and osteoarthritis. The doctor can obtain a venogram, an X-ray of the vein, and/or an ultrasound test to determine whether or not there are complicating problems.

Some persons with varicose veins seek relief from discomfort as well as cosmetic treatment by way of surgery–traditionally either de-struction of the vein by way of injection or removal by cutting, tying and then pulling the strip of vein out of the leg. A relatively new outpa-tient procedure called ambulatory phlebectomy requires only local an-esthesia and seems to present minimal risks by utilizing tiny punctures to access, clamp off and pull out offending veins. Laser treatment to cause the vein to fade away is also available. Unfortunately, veins that are normal at the time of an operation can become varicose later on.

Because varicose veins generally present no immediate danger, geri-atricians usually recommend instead of surgery elevation of the legs (lie down on a couch or bed and raise the limbs above chest level for a few minutes several times a day) and wearing of special hosiery to provide relief from the nagging aches and pains by compressing lower parts of legs more than the upper. Such stockings should be put on first thing in the morning when legs are least swollen. The elderly are also advised to exercise, especially to engage in brisk walking, control their weight and eat high-fiber foods to promote regularity and avoid constipation be-cause straining on the toilet transmits pressure to the legs, stay out of sunlight because heat promotes blood pooling. Raising the foot of the bed 2-4 inches can be helpful. Constrictive apparel at the waist, groin, leg should not be worn. Women should be careful with such items as girdles, garters and stockings with tight elastic tops; men, with trouser belts and close-fitting briefs.

Geriatricians warn that in general any treatment of varicose veins will not completely relieve the problem, and dermatologic surgeons add that continued medical observation and treatment with as conservative measures as possible will be necessary for life. Both recommend that anyone who must sit or stand in one place for a long time, flex feet and legs periodically, so that blood does not pool in the lower limbs.

VISION

They shall see eye to eye.

Isaiah, LII:7

Low vision is a common problem of the elderly, who have the highest rates of cataract, diabetic retinopathy, glaucoma and macular degeneration. Risk of blindness is about 10 times that of the young.

Late-life adults should have regularly scheduled ophthalmologic examinations, biennially at the very least. Simple problems can usually be solved with eyeglasses. More serious problems can be avoided by early detection, increasing the need for periodic testing because there may be no external symptoms of severe problems that lead to blindness. Such visual disorders, age-related but seemingly not a result of normal aging, are due to disease, drugs or injury.

Although visual decline is common in aging, about 10% of 80-year-olds retain 20-20 vision. Fewer than 20% of the oldest-old have visual acuity of 20/20 with or without glasses. Impairment of vision, inability to read newsprint, even with eyeglasses, is more prevalent as people age. Probably, about 3,000,000 of those persons 65+ are visually impaired. Seemingly, as with muscles, the admonition *Use it or lose it!* is true of some aspects of eyesight. Barring untoward circumstance, practice and experience can slow some types of vision loss, as in visual contrast, and may prevent it.

Vision loss and disorders can lead to many kinds of problems with activities of daily living and with social interaction. A person may see a spot on a bedspread yet bump into a chair at the side. All directions should be in large print. Bottles of medication should be color coded. Fluorescent tape around keyholes, light switches, electric outlets, and thermostats will help prevent accidents. Victims of vision loss may be embarrassed to be with strangers as well as fearful of leaving a well-known room.

With age come many changes in and around the eyes. Some are not at all serious, as the appearance of fat pouches (bags) beneath the eyes. Others need attention. Some late-life persons experience increased dryness and occasional itching as tear production declines. Vitreous spots, which the French call *flies*, seem to float about the eye but are not hazardous unless accompanied by what seem to be flashes of light— in which case the afflicted person should be checked immediately by an ophthalmologist for the possibility of a detached retina. Risk of retinal detachment increases with age, especially in nearsighted persons and those who have undergone cataract surgery.

Most age-related vision changes which negatively affect daily functioning of the elderly are due to structural alterations in the pupil, lens and retina. Both eyes do not always react identically, so that vision can deteriorate in one eye at a more rapid rate than in the other. As the pupil size diminishes, response of the eye diminishes, especially in dark places, and as the lens becomes more opaque, the eye suffers increased inability to deal with areas of low-light levels. Depth perception and judgment of distance decline. So, too, does ability to see separately events occurring closely in time as when in an automobile moving rapidly past people or such objects as road signs. Because of different rates of hardening in various areas of the lens, there is uneven refraction of light. Combined, these deficiencies are especially troubling to older drivers, particularly at night when they must face the glare of approaching headlights and quickly go from a brightly lit area to a darker one or the opposite. A similar situation can occur in daylight when sunbeams bounce in and out through leaves and limbs of trees overhanging the road. Sunglasses put on when an elderly person is about to leave a dark place, such as a movie theater or a tunnel, may help, as may eyeglasses that lighten and darken automatically.

Because of yellowing of the lens and changes in visual and neural pathways, the elderly are not always able to discriminate between blues, blue-greens and violet. Handrails, therefore, should be marked with yellow, orange or red. In presbyopia, a condition which accompanies aging, the lens loses elasticity and ability to accommodate to near vision. The person becomes farsighted and needs eyeglasses, usually bifocals, in which the upper segment focuses for distance and the lower segment focuses for near vision, as when reading a newspaper or book.

Some age-related disorders of the retina, the actual visual receptor, a sensory membrane at the innermost back part of the eye, are quite serious. Consisting of blood vessels interspersed among a sheet of nerve cells, rods and cones which respond to light with electrical impulses transmitted into the central nervous system by way of the optic nerve and thence to the brain, the retina is extremely sensitive. Approximately half of vision problems of the aged involve disorders of the retina.

Diabetic retinopathy, which primarily affects victims of diabetes who have had the disease for some time, may result in detachment of the retina and blindness. In early stages, blood vessels leak into the retina and blur vision. In later stages, blood vessels grow into the retina and impede or destroy vision. If detected early enough, the condition through laser treatment can be prevented somewhat from worsening, resulting in preservation of sight although therapy may be difficult and not completely satisfactory.

The leading cause of visual decline among the elderly is a cataract, an opacity in one of the refracting elements of the eye, usually the lens, seriously impairing its function to focus light on the retina. The problem often begins in 1 eye, moving later on to the other. Estimates are that at least 2/3 of the population 65+ have lens opacity to some degree. Obstruction, distortion and diffusion of light into the eye from opacity blur and dim vision, as though there were a milky film over the eye. Possible causes include diabetes, exposure to ultraviolet radiation of sunlight, injury, long-term use of steroids, smoking. (Sunglasses may be incapable of warding off harm if they do not filter UV and near UV wavelengths.) Loss of vision is painless unless the cataract swells and induces glaucoma.

Treatment for a cataract is by way of surgery, often under local anesthesia. Quite common among the elderly, the procedure is quick and inexpensive. Indeed, cataract surgery is the most frequently performed operation in the United States. Timing of surgical removal depends on the degree of impact of the cataract on the eye, such that visual impairment is not corrigible with eyeglasses. The lens is removed and a plastic replacement implanted to prevent blindness. In some cases, the afflicted person may rely on contact lenses or eyeglasses. Surgery is almost 100% successful since development of micro-surgical technique. Not long ago, cataract surgery involved a week's hospital stay and a long recuperation period at home. Today, such procedures are routinely performed on a same day basis, so that often the patient is at home that evening. Recovery usually takes 2-4 weeks, many a patient then able to see as well as when he was young.

More than 70% of the legally blind from any of a number of diseases grouped together as glaucoma are 65+. Glaucoma occurs when faulty drainage of eye fluids causes an abnormal but painless increase in pressure on blood vessels and the optic nerve, leading to loss of vision, ranging from slight declines to total blindness. Experts fear that half the 2,000,000 persons who have glaucoma are unaware of it. Symptoms of glaucoma, as trouble adjusting to changes of light, are usually not experienced until after the optic nerve has been irreversibly damaged. If caught early enough, the effects of most cases can be prevented, reduced or delayed with medication, lasers or surgery. The key to glaucoma diagnosis is periodic testing, preferably begun as early as the 4th decade, performed annually thereafter. Screening for glaucoma should be routine during every eye examination, utilizing both the puff-of-air test and a detailed retina and visual field examination.

Age-related macular degeneration (AMD) is the principal cause of irreversible visual impairment and legal blindness among the elderly. Macular degeneration can cause different symptoms in different persons. Generally affecting both eyes with symptoms of darkened or distorted vision and loss of sharp, central sight, macular degeneration can progress rapidly. Patients at risk are given a grid (called the Amsler Grid) to look at daily as a test for visual distortion. They are advised to notify the ophthalmologist at once should this or any other sudden change in vision occur.

Vision is composed of 2 essentials which people are accustomed to treating as 1. The rather imprecise sight of much of the retina is useful for orientation and navigation, allowing people to move around in the physical world. In the center of the retina is a small yellowish spot, the macula, which is for perception of fine details and the central field of vision. Hardly noticeable because so free of pain, macular degeneration occurs in about 20% of those 65-74, and in about 40% of those 75+. Etiology is unknown. Exposure to solar radiation may be a cause. (It is advisable for everyone, young and old, to obtain prescription sunglasses or to have regular eyeglasses coated to filter out UV light.)

There are two types of macular degeneration. Dry occurs when light-sensitive cells of the eye break down and distort vision, so that letters seem to blur. Blank spots are left in the field of vision. A person may also see wavy lines on the Amsler Grid. There is no effective treatment. Wet occurs when blood vessels leak and cause dark spots in the field of vision and straight lines look wavy. Some patients are helped by laser therapy to seal off blood vessels. Others who have good peripheral vision and color determination remaining should be made aware that they will not lose all eyesight although they may be legally blind (20/200 vision).

Researchers are seeking to perfect devices to make it possible for anyone with peripheral vision to read normally. Meanwhile, many persons learn Braille, so as to be able to read. Even for persons free of severe eye ailments, visual impairment becomes increasingly prevalent with age: about 5% of those 65-74, about 15% of those 75-84, and about 25% of those 85 +. For them and for victims of eye disease, a variety of implements to help with close work is available. Magnifying glasses enlarge recipes in cookbooks or needles and thread for sewing. Large-print attachments can be used to cover the small numbers on a telephone base. There are signature guides to help with filling out and signing checks. Talking books and calculators take the place of printed materials. Special timers and watches are made with large black numbers on white backgrounds. Increasingly available are computers that utilize voice synthesizers to vocalize words. Optical character readers that scan pages of text and send them to a computer for enlargement or vocalization are also on the market. Especially helpful are video magnifiers (closed-circuit television devices) which use a video camera to magnify pictures or printed materials as much as 45 times.

Such low-vision aids and professionals to explain how to use them can be located in the yellow pages of the local telephone book under the heading, *blind institutions.*

Unfortunately, there is no standard, successful cure for severe visual loss. It is easy to be a Pollyanna when you yourself are not affected, but it is good to remember that John Milton composed one of the world's great epics after having become blind. With the support of family and friends, those elderly with severe vision loss can continue to perform normal activities of daily living, including socializing, with only minimal changes in lifestyle.

Alice Cary wrote:

> My soul is full of whispered song,–
> My blindness is my sight;
> The shadows that I feared so long
> Are full of life and light.

ADAPTIVE STRATEGIES TO COMPENSATE FOR VISION LOSS

Lighting
> Night Lights placed throughout the house
> Multiple light sources, evenly distributed
> Horizontal blinds to control light and glare
> More intense light over work areas and stairs

Safety
> Edge of steps marked with nonskid colored tape
> Throw rugs removed, clutter reduced
> Objects kept in same place

Daily Tasks
> Color codes on medication bottles
> Raised number templates for telephones
> Stove and washer controls marked with colored dots
> Talking clocks which announce the time
> Adapted clothing, such as Velcro or large buttons
> Magnifiers for close-up activities
> Drinking glasses with painted rims

Source: Lustbader, W. and Hooyman, N.R., *Taking Care of Aging Family Members* (NY: The Free Press, 1994), p.161.

Amsler Grid

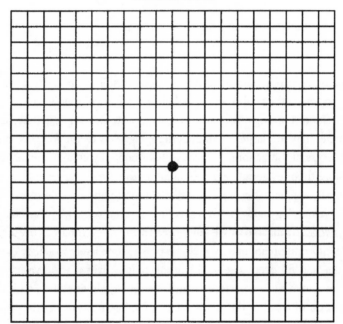

AFTERWORD

No thing great is created suddenly, any more than a bunch
of grapes or a fig. If you tell me that you desire a fig, I answer
you that there must be time. Let it first blossom, then bear
fruit, then ripen.

Epictetus

After the harvest, golden sheaves.

George Cooper

Because research on aging and the aged is still at an early stage of development, the final chapters in **Aging: An Encyclopedia** have yet to be written. Findings from a flurry of new studies suggest that gene changes may to a large extent underlie aging. New technology involved in success of the genome project will undoubtedly enable scientists to explore theories about causes of aging at the molecular level through analysis of gene patterns at various stages in the human life span.

Gerontology and geriatrics are dynamic, complex fields–ever-changing, ever-growing. No single volume can adequately impart all the available information about aging. Nor is one volume likely to satisfy every reader and fill every need. This book ranges over a wide variety of topics drawn from an extensive and ever-enlarging literature, with the intention of treating the many facets of aging, from factual to philosophical, controversial to accepted, goals to means–always focusing on presenting information in readable form while maintaining accuracy and balance. There is no squeezing or twisting of facts and subjects. As the field of aging becomes more mainstream, research in the various disciplines becomes more sophisticated. Future editions will hold new information based on breakthroughs and research not now envisaged.

We are in a revolution of incomparable consequence in world history. Future elderly cohorts will probably be larger than anticipated in current projections. Today's is the oldest population that has ever existed. And it is growing older.

Aging, considered an ecological phenomenon shaped by chance, genetics, environment (physical, psychological and social) and individual behavior, undoubtedly will be studied more and more from a multidisciplinary focus. Humanity will then cease wasting one of its most valuable resources, know-how of the elderly.

As the aged become an integral part of society, philosophic studies will contribute to an understanding of the best ways to conduct one's life in the later years. Needed is recognition of exactly what biological aging entails, of the capabilities of the aged, of what services will be necessary, of the directions gerontological and geriatric research should take. The elderly lack realistic role models. Too often they are given as exemplars extraordinary persons with exceptional artistic, athletic or intellectual ability who attain fame and by chance achieve extreme longevity.

The over-all goal of this volume is pragmatic: to improve the quality of life, not just for the elderly, but for the young as well. Built into it is the assumption that what is learned about aging through reading and experience will be translated into improved prospects for the growing numbers of survivors into late maturity. Specific goals include: increasing life expectancy, making life healthy by preventing or alleviating illness, helping late-life years become productive, lifting the spirit by brightening moods.

The struggle to prevent disease and to promote and preserve health has hardly begun. Health may be regarded as a relatively stable state of physical, psychological and social well-being that includes bodily and mental reserves necessary to maintain equilibrium—in toto, a complex, dynamic set of conditions that change continually in the face of environmental challenges, such as 100° days in summer and flu epidemics in winter. The goal of optimum functioning for all is not much talked about—as yet. But it will be once the degenerative processes associated with the passage of years are slowed and physiological and cognitive capabilities are improved.

In the 20th century, the most significant modification in the history of the health of human beings occurred. Medicine proved largely successful in curing and/or preventing acute diseases. Life expectancy jumped, and old age was postponed for many. Will medicine in the 21st century prove successful in curing and/or preventing chronic diseases? Will people cooperate by changing personal health habits? If so, life expectancy will jump again and old age will be postponed even further.

But even more fundamental modifications may be in the making. Will researchers learn how to control the rate and extent of aging by altering the intrinsic makeup of human beings? At present, genetic engineering and hormone implementation are only 2 of the approaches deemed feasible in the hunt for mechanisms of immortality. Many scientists regard aging as culminating in a death sentence which they should counter with every means at their disposal, including the reworking of evolution and its programs. .

Already, aging research is coping unsuccessfully with success. Throughout history humankind has sought longevity; now that we have it, we as yet do not know how to deal with it properly. As the war against disease and injury continues on a winning basis, a new stage of human life has emerged. The National Long-Term Care Study at Duke University's Center for Demographic Studies shows a steady decline in disability in old age cohorts. Contrary to popular belief and standardized tests accepted as valid and reliable, a large number of the aged now exhibit excellent functioning even into their 80's and 90's, as the many 80-year-old marathoners and 90-year-old ice skaters prove. There will be more, many more.

What will the elderly do with the gift of another 20-30 years of active life? What will society permit them to do?

T.S. Eliot put it well: "We shall not cease from exploration."

GLOSSARY

If you would converse with me, you must first define your terms.

Voltaire

Part One: In General

Accidental Fall: Unintentional drop to a lower level or to the floor from a standing, sitting or even supine position.

Active Euthanasia: Deliberate termination of the life of a nonfunctional or incurably ill person.

Activities of Daily Living (ADL): Skills basic to living at home independently, as eating, bathing, dressing, toileting.

Acupuncture: A system of oriental medicine using needles to puncture the skin in order to stimulate energy points and influence specific parts of the body.

Acute Illness: An ailment of temporary duration characterized by rapid onset and good response to therapy.

Adaptation: Adjustment to the environment.

Adult Day Care Center: A community facility designed to prevent premature institutionalization of older persons by providing professional support and means of socializing.

Adult Education: Education of older adults, formal and informal, for credit as well as noncredit, varying from discussion groups in libraries to courses for learning while traveling.

Adulthood: Period of life span after maturity.

Advance Directive: An Advance Directive, which can include an Instruction Directive and/or a Proxy Directive, is the most effective plan for making medical decisions ahead of time and for choosing someone who will make decisions in the future with you or for you if you are unable. An Instruction Directive states a person's express wishes. A Proxy Directive names the persons(s) designated to carry out those wishes.

Aerobic Conditioning: Improved endurance, as well as increased stroke volume and cardiac output, because of lowered heart rate during exercise.

Affective Illness: A psychiatric term for a mood disorder, as depression.

Age : Can refer to the number of years a person has lived, to a stage of life, or to a period in history as The Age of Longevity.

Age Roles: Behavior expected of persons at different stages, as widow-hood or retirement.

Ageism: Discrimination against an individual or group because of age.

Aging : Process of change from a young organism to an old one occurring as persons advance in years. (Cf. Senescence.)

Allopathy: Treatment of a disease by using therapies to produce effects opposite those of the illness.

Alternative Medicine: Also referred to as Mind-Body Therapy as, for instance, Meditation. Utilization of unconventional therapies.

Alzheimer's Disease: A disorder with slowly progressive dementia.

Amsler Grid: A self-test for visual distortion.

Anaerobic Conditioning: Physiologic adaptations which increase tolerance to oxygen debt and increased lactate levels.

Analgesic: a medication producing a state in which pain is not felt although the patient remains conscious.

Androgynous: Pertaining to a person with both male and female traits.

Anesthetic: A substance which induces a loss of sensation in addition to eliminating pain.

Angina Pectoris: A disease characterized by brief episodes of pressure in the chest after exertion.

Angioplasty: Insertion of a catheter with a balloon tip that can be expanded in a blood vessel to open it.

Anorexia: Eating disorder, characterized by severe reduction of appetite for food.

Anthropometry: Study of human body measurements.

Antihistamine: A drug used to counter allergic reaction to a condition, such as hay fever.

Antioxidant: An enzyme or micronutrient that inhibits effects of free radicals.

Arteriosclerosis: A disorder characterized by thickening, hardening and stiffening of arterial walls.

Arthritis: Disease involving inflammation and/or degeneration of a joint or joints.

Assisted Living: Residential setting of private apartments with such support services as meals, social activities and protective oversight.

Assisted Suicide: Obtaining for a person means needed to end his or her life.

Ataxia: A term applied to uncoordinated movements that may influence posture and gait.

Atherosclerosis: Disease of the inner walls of arteries with thickening and loss of elasticity owing to deposits of calcium, cholesterol, fat and other such substances, leading to blockage of the blood vessels.

Baby Boomers: Persons born between 1946 and 1964, approximately 76,000,000 individuals.

Barrio: A Mexican-American urban community.

Basal Cell Carcinoma: Slow-growing cancer of the skin.

Basal Metabolic Rate (BMR): Measurement of energy needed to maintain the body at rest.

Benign Prostatic Hypertrophy: A non-cancerous tumor in the prostate.

Bereavement: Period of grief following loss of a loved one.

Beta Blocker: A substance that blocks action of norepinephrine at its receptor in the heart or other tissues.

Bioelectromagnetics: Electricity to help with bone repair and nerve stimulation.

Biofeedback: Technique for conscious control of involuntary body functions, such as blood pressure and temperature.

Biomarker: A descriptive or predictive variable of an attribute, so far undiscovered, helpful in measuring age or aging and/or capable of predicting remaining life span.

Biomedicine: Mainstream medicine.

Biopsy: Removal of body tissue for examination.

Body Mass Index: An approximate estimate of body fat, expressed as a ratio of weight in kilograms over height in meters.

Brain Death: Death as indicated by cessation of activity in the brain.

Bronchitis: See Chronic Obstructive Pulmonary Disease.

CAD: See Coronary Artery Disease.

Calorie: Unit of heat used to measure energy produced by food in the body; amount of heat needed to raise 1 gram of water 1° Centigrade.

Cancer: A malignant tumor with potentially unlimited cellular growth.

Carcinogen: A cancer-producing substance.

Carcinoma: A cancerous growth composed of epithelial cells. .

Caregivers: Family members, volunteers of service organizations and professionals who help older persons to achieve and maintain an optimal level of independence.

Caries: A chronic disease that destroys mineralized tooth tissue.

Cartilage: Tough, elastic tissue acting as a shock absorber at joints.

Cataract: A visual disorder characterized by opacity of the eye lens.

Cecum: A small pouch in the large intestine.

Centenarian: A person who has lived 100 years or more.

Chiropractic: A form of healing which, to normalize body functions, utilizes manipulation of the spine and joints.

Cholesterol: A steroid alcohol in animal fats of the diet and in many body tissues.

Chorea: A nervous condition producing rapid jerky movements.

Chronic Illness: Characterized by a gradual onset, an incurable ailment that lasts a long time, usually at least 3 months.

Chronic Obstructive Pulmonary Disease: A group of diseases that impair breathing.

Chronotherapeutics: Study of biochemical rhythms predisposing the body to conditions affecting medications.

Circadian Rhythms: Biological activities occurring daily at approximately the same hour, such as the time a person usually falls asleep.

Circuit Training: An exercise regimen utilizing various kinds of bodily exertion.

Cognition: The mental processes involved in comprehension, perception, reasoning and recognition.

Cohort: a group of persons with the same demographic characteristics, as being born within a particular period of time, so that they experience the same temporal range and similar life patterns.

Colitis: Chronic inflammation of the colon.

Colon: The last 5-6 feet of the digestive tract.

Colonoscopy: Observation of the interior of the colon by means of a tube inserted through the anal sphincter.

Colostomy: Surgical removal of part of the colon. See Stoma.

Complementary Medicine: See Alternative Medicine.

Congestive Heart Failure: Impaired pumping action permits too much blood to remain in the heart and other tissues.

Congregate Housing: semi-independent arrangement of individual units for tenants but with such group services as meals in a common dining room.

Continuing Care Community: A housing complex for those elderly who cannot live on their own but do not need a high level of care. Usually requires an entrance fee or lump sum payment.

Conventional Medicine: See Mainstream Medicine.

Conversion Symptom: Substitution of physical for emotional problems, as bowel difficulties for feelings of depression.

COPD: See Chronic Obstructive Pulmonary Disease.

Coping: A process by means of which a person reduces stress.

Coronary Artery Disease: Reduced blood flow to the heart resulting from narrowing of arteries supplying the heart.

Coronary Bypass Operation: Surgeons use veins from elsewhere in the body to replace narrowed arteries.

Cross-Linkage: Theory of aging that deleterious connections between cell molecules are produced as by-products of metabolism.

Cross-Sectional Study: A research design in which a group (or 2 or more groups, each from a different age cohort) is studied at one point in time.

Cyst: Saclike structure in the body which contains liquid and/or disease materials.

Cytogerontologist: Scientist who studies cells of the body in regard to aging.

Death: The immediate result of irreversible cessation of all functions of the brain and the circulatory and respiratory systems.

Dehydration: Excessive loss of water from the body.

Dementia: A progressive, lasting deterioration in mental capacity that has a negative impact on such functioning as language, memory, thinking.

Demography: Study of population characteristics and changes through statistics relating to birth, death, disease, distribution, and other vital statistics of a population.

Denture: A full or partial set of artificial teeth.

Depression: A mood disorder characterized by deep sadness and hope-lessness in addition to appetite deterioration, sleeping difficulty and energy loss.

Diabetes Mellitus: Disorder of carbohydrate utilization.

Diabetic Retinopathy: Visual deterioration that is a result of diabetes.

Diastolic: Pertaining to measurement of pressure in arteries during the relaxation phase of the heartbeat. Cf. Systolic.

Dietary Reference Intake (DRI): A level of nutrient intake that optimizes health.

Digital Examination: Probing with a finger to determine a medical condition, as enlargement of the prostate.

Diuretic: Drug promoting urine excretion.

Diverticula: Sacs projecting through the intestine.

DNA (Deoxyribonucleic acid): A cell component that transmits patterns of heredity.

Double Blind Study: To prevent experimental bias in an experiment, subjects and researchers do not know who receives a drug, who receives a placebo.

Double Standard of Aging: A term for the different ways older men and women are considered in society.

Duodenal Ulcer: An open sore in the lining of the small intestine nearest the stomach.

Durable Power of Attorney: A competent person gives over legal rights to someone else. See Power of Attorney.

Dysnomia: Difficulty in naming objects of all kinds.

Dyspepsia: Indigestion.

Echo House (ECHO): A free-standing removable unit allowing elderly to live with children but in a separate dwelling.

Edema: Swelling in cells, cavities or tissues of the body.

Elder Abuse: Mistreatment, whether financial, mental or physical, of older persons by caregivers.

Elderhostel: An organization offering college-level courses at moderate cost through a network of educational institutions.

Electroconvulsive Therapy (ECT): Use of electric shock to restore normalcy in the brain.

Emphysema: See Chronic Obstructive Pulmonary Disease.

Endorphin: A neuropeptide that influences emotions positively.

Entitlement Rights: Obligation of the government to provide goods or services to certain individuals.

Enzyme: A protein that speeds up a biochemical reaction in the body.

Epidemiology: Study of occurrence or non-occurrence of causes, effects and manifestations of disease in a population.

Ergonomics: Study of how people adjust to the environment.

Estrogen: Female hormone.

Estrogen-Replacement Therapy: Medication therapy for osteoporosis.

Ethics: A system for standards of behavior and moral judgments.

Ethnic: Pertaining to a person or group within a population distinguished by customs, language, national origin, race, religion.

Euthanasia: To end suffering by causing death as painlessly as possible, whether in accord or not with a person's wish.

Extended Family: A family in which the generations live apart but are closely connected by mutual aid and affection.

Family: A basic social unit consisting of a group of persons related by ancestry or marriage. Because of emerging lifestyles, the traditional definition of the family is changing.

Fat Soluble Vitamins: Vitamins that can be dissolved in fat.

Free Radical Theory of Aging: Aging is a result of accumulation of damage to cells by free radicals.

Free Radical: An atom or molecule containing one or more unpaired electrons capable of binding to and damaging cellular components.

Frostbite: Freezing of a body part because of exposure to below-freezing temperatures.

Frostnip: Near freezing of a body part because of exposure to temperatures close to freezing.

Gallstone: Insoluble stone formed in the gallbladder.

Gastric Ulcer: An ulcer of the stomach lining.

Gastrointestinal System: Body system that takes in food, breaks it down, absorbs it and excretes the remainder.

Gay: Term used interchangeably for lesbians and homosexuals.

Gender Role: Cultural behavior widely regarded as appropriate for a gender.

Gene: A cell component responsible for determining and transmitting hereditary characteristics.

Generation Gap: Differences in values and lifestyles of cohorts separated by birth date.

GERD: See Reflux Esophagitis.

Geriatrician: A medical doctor specializing in geriatrics, especially one certified by the American Board of Internal Medicine and the American Board of Family Practice.

Geriatrics: A specialty of internal medicine and/or family practice dealing with ailments and health problems of the elderly.

Gerodesign: See Gerontechnology.

Gerontechnology: Multidisciplinary field aiming through art and technology to design a safe and comfortable environment for the elderly.

Gerontology: The scientific study of the process of aging and of the problems of older persons.

Gingivitis: An inflammation of the gums.

Glaucoma: Disease of the eye characterized by increased but painless intraocular pressure and gradual loss of vision.

Gout: Painful ailment associated with urea deposits in joints.

Guardianship: A legal device for declaring a person incompetent, so that an overseer can be appointed.

Gustation: Sense of taste.

Gynecologist: Physician who treats diseases specific to women.

Hayflick Limit: The finite number of times a cell can divide.

Heart Failure: Inability of heart to pump blood efficiently results in fluid accumulating in tissues and in shortness of breath.

Heartburn: Varies from a mild burning sensation to a sharp pain in the chest.

Hemorrhoid: Painfully dilated or ruptured veins in the anal region.

Hiatus Hernia: Protrusion of the stomach or parts thereof above the diaphragm and into the chest.

Hip Fracture: a break in the part of the thigh bone nearest the pelvis.

HMO (Health Maintenance Organization): A health-care provider offering medical services for a fixed, prepaid monthly fee.

Homeopathy: An Alternative Medicine therapy for curing a disease by administering to a patient small dosages of drugs that in large doses in a healthy person produce the same disease symptoms as those of the patient.

Hormone: A substance produced by the endocrine glands which is circulated in body fluid to an organ or tissue at a distance where it influences cellular activity.

Hospice: A place for the terminally ill and their families run by health professionals and lay volunteers where the priority is to control disease symptoms and provide emotional support but not to extend the life span.

Hype: Writing or speech publicizing in a sensational manner.

Hypertension: High blood pressure.

Hyperthermia: Abnormally high body temperature.

Hypnosis: A state of altered consciousness resembling sleep in which the patient responds to suggestions of the hypnotist.

Hypothermia: Abnormally low body temperature.

Iatrogenic: Of'an ailment or symptom caused inadvertently by medical treatment.

Immune System: Purpose is to protect the body from infections and to eliminate foreign and potentially damaging materials.

Impotence: Inability to achieve an erection for penetration of the vagina or to maintain an erection for the time necessary to complete sexual intercourse.

Incidence: Number of new cases of a disease occurring during a specific period in a given segment of the population.

Incontinence: Inability to hold back excretion of urine from the body.

Insidious: Developing in a slow or not easily noticed manner.

Instruction Directive: See Advanced Directive.

Instrumental Activities of Daily Living (IADL): Fairly complex set of self-care activities, such as skills needed for community living: preparing meals, doing laundry, managing money.

Interval Training: Exercising at intermittent periods of low and high demand.

Insulin: Hormone enabling the body to utilize sugar and other carbohydrates.

Ischemia: Reduction or obstruction of blood flow.

Kegel Exercises: Exercises to strengthen the urethral sphincter so as to reduce or to stop incontinence.

Kinesthesia: awareness of the position and movement of the body and limbs in space.

Learned Helplessness: A condition in which a person, feeling incapable, has ceased all attempts at coping with difficulties.

Leisure Activity: Any activity freely chosen for relaxation, excitement, rest.

Leukemia: A cancerous disorder of the organs that produce blood cells; a condition often referred to as cancer of the blood.

Life Expectancy: An actuarial value derived from population tables indicating the average remaining lifetime for a person of a given age.

Life Review: A process, supposed to be initiated by anticipation of death, in which older persons reflect on their past.

Life Span: Number of years an individual will survive under ideal conditions. Maximum life span is that of the longest lived individual for whom credible records exist.

Lithotripsy: A technique for shattering gallstones without harming the patient.

Living Will: Sometimes referred to as a Right-to-Die Will, instructs physicians to cease invasive measures of treatment or to remove life-sustaining equipment in a case of terminal illness.

Long-Term Memory: Memory thought to be an unlimited capacity system of the brain which contains all the information a person has accrued.

Longevity: Often used as a synonym for life span, is the duration of an individual's life.

Longitudinal Study: A research design in which an age cohort is studied at more than one point in time.

Lumpectomy: Surgical removal of a lump, as from a breast.

Lymph system: A system in the body of vessels that by way of channels and ducts carries a liquid to bathe the tissues.

Macronutrient: Nutrient essential to the body in a large amount.

Macular Degeneration: Deterioration of the central portion of the retina, with consequent diminution of vision.

Mainstream Medicine: An organized empirical discipline of diagnostic and therapeutical skills making use of the findings of scientific research.

Malignancy: A disease that will kill or is likely to kill an organism.

Malignant Melanoma: A cancer originating in the skin.

Mastectomy: Surgical removal of a breast.

Medicaid: A federal-state welfare program providing health insurance coverage to persons based on their poverty level.

Medicare: A federal program making available basic hospital and medical insurance to everyone 65 years of age or older.

Medication: a drug or other substance, prescribed or over the counter, for curing, healing or relieving pain.

Medigap Insurance: Insurance that supplements Medicare.

Meditation: A self-directed way of reducing stress, as by concentrating solely on a word or phrase for a period of time.

Menopause: Cessation of menstruation, generally near the age of 50.

Mental Healing: See Prayerful Healing.

Metabolism: A collective term for physical and chemical body processes by which food is broken down and utilized and then excreted as waste.

Metastasis: Spread of disease in the body from one site to another or others.

Micronutrient: Nutrient essential to the body in trace amounts.

Mind-Body Medicine: See Alternative Medicine.

Mini-Stroke: See Transient Ischemic Attacks.

Minority: A population group discriminated against because of ethnic background.

Modality: Employment and/or method of a therapeutic treatment.

Morbidity: Term used by physicians to indicate a state of illness.

Mortality Rate: Number of deaths per 100,000 of a specific population or portion thereof per year.

Musculoskeletal: Body system of bones, cartilage, joints, ligaments, tendons.

Myocardial Infarction: Heart attack due to blockage of blood flow to heart muscle.

Naturopathy: A system of therapy that relies largely on nutrition and a healthy lifestyle to prevent disease.

Neoplasm: A new growth of tissue.

Neurotransmitter: A biochemical substance that, released from nerve endings when a nerve fires, transmits impulses from one cell to another.

Nocturia: Disturbance of sleep by need to urinate during the night.

Nocturnal Myoclonus: A sleep disorder characterized by twitching or jerking of leg muscles.

Nonsteroidal Anti-Inflammatory Drugs (NSAIDs): Drugs administered to counteract inflammation.

Nostrum: A quack medicine.

Nuclear Family: Basic unit consisting of husband, wife and immediate children.

Nursing Home: A term for a residential facility, usually required to be licensed, that offers nursing care.

Nutrient: Anything useful as a food substance.

Nutrition: Processes by which a person takes in and utilizes food.

Olfaction: Sense of smell.

Oncologist: Physician whose specialty is cancer.

Ophthalmologist: Physician whose specialty is the eyes.

Orthopedist: Physician whose specialty is treatment of the skeleton.

Osteoarthritis: A degenerative joint disease occurring mainly among the elderly.

Osteoporosis: A bone disorder distinguished by loss of bone density and mass and increased susceptibility to bone fracture.

Papule: A small, firm, conical elevation of the skin.

Paranoia: A mental disorder characterized by delusions of persecution.

Parasuicide: An incomplete attempt at suicide.

Parkinson's Disease: A chronic brain disorder characterized by tremors and impaired posture.

Passive Euthanasia: Allowing a person to die naturally without resorting to extraordinary means to sustain life.

Pathology: Branch of medicine dealing with disease.

Peptic Ulcer: See Duodenal Ulcer and Gastric Ulcer.

Periodontia: Inflammation of the gums and tissue surrounding teeth.

Peristalsis: Contractions and dilations of muscles that move contents of nutrients down the digestive tract.

Pharmacology: Study of interaction of the body and therapeutic medications.

Physiatrist: Physician whose specialty is movement of the body and limb.

Placebo Response: Improvement in condition of an ill person who is administered an innocuous substance, such as a sugar-pill, as if it were a real medication.

Plaque: Deposit of calcium, cholesterol and other substances on inner arterial walls. In dentistry: a thin film on a tooth surface.

Polyp: A mass of tissue growing out from the intestinal wall.

Post-Fall Syndrome: Fear of falling, usually characterized by tendencies to stagger or to show alarm at walking without help.

Power of Attorney: Device allowing a person to designate another to act legally for him/her.

Prayerful Healing: The healer supposedly conveys a mystical sensation, termed a flow of "cosmic" energy, to the healee.

Presbycusis: Progressive loss of hearing associated with advancing age.

Presbyopia: An eye defect in advancing age, such that the lens loses elasticity and ability to accommodate to near vision.

Primary Aging: The age-related changes observable in all members of a species Sometimes referred to as normal aging.

Progeria: A rare disease causing children to resemble very old, small persons.

Programmed Theory of Aging: Idea that aging is controlled by action of the genes.

Prostate: A partly muscular gland surrounding the urethra in males.

Prostatitis: An infectious non-cancerous condition in which the prostate enlarges.

Prosthesis: An artificial replacement for a part of the body, as a tooth or a limb.

Proxy Directive: See Advanced Directive.

Psychoactive Medication: A medication that affects the mind.

Psychogenic: Originating in the mind.

Psychophysiological Therapy: Treatment concentrating on the interrelationship of mental and bodily processes.

Psychosomatic: A physical disorder originating in or worsening as a result of psychological aspects of a patient. In general, pertaining to relationship of body and mind.

Psychotherapy: Treatment utilizing talking and/or personal interaction with a patient.

Reaction Time: Time elapsed between a stimulus and response.

Recommended Dietary Allowance (RDA): Amount of vitamins and minerals in the diet needed daily to maintain a healthy body.

Reflux Esophagitis: Backflow of stomach liquids into the mouth.

Religion: A formal system of belief and practice organized to interpret and respond to what is regarded as sacred and/or supernatural.

Remission: Prolonged lessening or disappearance of symptoms.

Renal Atherosclerosis: Thickening and stiffening of inner walls of kidney arteries.

Restless Leg Syndrome: See Nocturnal Myoclonus.

Retina: A sensory membrane at the back of the eye, the actual visual receptor.

Retirement: A period of life after a worker has withdrawn from employment.

Rheumatoid Arthritis: A severe chronic inflammatory condition affecting connective tissue.

Right-to-Die Will: See Living Will.

Sacrum: The thick triangular bone at the base of the spine.

Schizophrenia: A mental disorder characterized by delusions and hallucinations, often without diminution of basic thought processes.

Sciatica: A painful condition down the hip, buttock and rear of the thigh to below the knee.

Sebum: A fatty lubricant in the skin.

Secondary Aging: Changes, neither universal nor inevitable, that occur in the presence of disease, stress and toxins.

Senescence: Old age. Period of progressively reduced ability of an older person to respond adaptively to change both within and without.

Senile Dementia: Alzheimer's Disease.

Senior Center: A community facility for the elderly that provides a wide variety of activities and services.

Sensory Receptors: Body parts, such as the eyes, which pass information about the world to the central nervous system and thence to the brain.

Shared Housing: A home wherein a room or rooms is provided in exchange for services and/or rent.

Short-term Memory: A limited capacity system which keeps information available in the brain for a short period of time.

Sigmoidoscopy: Examination of part of the colon.

Silent Disease: Patient, unaware of having succumbed, evinces no sign of disease

Sitz Bath: A bath in which hips and buttocks are under water

Sleep Apnea: A sleep disorder in which the sleeper stops breathing temporarily.

Somatic: Pertaining to the body, not the mind.

Somatogenic: Originating in the body.

Spinal Disc: A rounded, flattened structure with a gel-like center that appears between spinal segments.

SRO: A single room of an inner-city hotel, where kitchen units are unavailable.

Stereotype: A fixed notion, usually negative, attributed to all members of a group and allowing of no variation; individuals are labeled and described in accord with the belief.

Stoma: An opening through the abdomen to the outside of the body for removal of waste. The opening is named for the part of the body involved, as colostomy for the area of the colon.

Stress: Tension resulting from the difference between demands placed on an individual and that person's ability to adjust to them.

Stroke: Onset of a neurological deficiency owing to blockage or rupture of an artery in the brain.

Suicide: Self-inflicted, intentional taking of one's life.

Support Group: An organization offering help/advice to patients and caregivers.

Synapse: Point of contact between neurons, where impulses are transmitted.

Syndrome: A pattern of symptoms characteristic of a disease or disorder.

Systolic: Pertaining to measurement of pressure in arteries during the contraction phase of the heart.

Tai Chi: A graceful form of Chinese martial arts.

Telomere: The end of a chromosome (currently being studied for its possible connection with the process of aging).

Terminal Drop: A theory holding that a distinct drop in intelligence precedes death by a few years.

Testosterone: Male hormone.

Threshold Illness: Disease that occurs when cell and tissue death exceed a certain limit.

Thrombosis: Formation of a blood clot within a blood vessel

TIA: See Transient Ischemic Attacks.

Tinnitus: Perception of noise in the ear, as a buzzing, but not from an external stimulus.

Tissue: A group of cells composing one of the structural materials of the body, as muscle tissue.

Trace Elements: Vitamins and minerals.

Transient Ischemic Attack: A brief reduction in blood flow to the brain, often called a mini-stroke because it can result in dizziness and unsteadiness and may be a precursor of a major stroke.

Tumor: A growth with no physiologic function.

Urinary Incontinence: See Incontinence.

Urologist: Physician whose specialty is treatment of the bladder, kidneys and male sex organs.

Valvuloplasty: Utilization of a balloon to open narrowed heart valves without surgery.

Vertebrae: Bony or cartilaginous segments of the spinal column.

Vitamin: An essential compound acting as a catalyst in various body processes.

Water-Soluble Vitamin: A vitamin, as C, that can be dissolved in water.

Werner's Syndrome: A disorder characteristicc of young persons who experience cataracts, hardening of the arteries and osteoporosis.

Western Diet: A characteristic diet of Western societies, high in fat, refined carbohydrates and processed food but low in dietary fiber.

Xerostomia: A dry or burning sensation in the mouth.

Yoga: A Hindu philosophy utilizing dietary prescription and exercise to achieve good health.

RESOURCES

Help me with knowledge–.

Robert Browning

Although comprehensive, this list does not identify all agencies and organizations pertaining to the elderly. The Eldercare Locator (800-677-1116) gives free referrals to local Offices on Aging anywhere in the country. Each state Administration on Aging, the telephone number of which is listed in the telephone directory, can also provide information on local agencies and organizations. The National Association of Professional Geriatric Care Managers (520-881-8008) specializes in making long-term care arrangements. Additional information is available from neighborhood hospitals' Social Service or Patient Case Management departments.

Part One: In General

Accidents

AAA Foundation for Traffic Safety, 1440 New York Ave. NW, Suite 201, Washington, DC 20005.

Dizziness and Balance Disorders Association Resource Center, 1015 Northwest Ave., Portland, OR 97210.

National Safety Council, 1121Spring Lake Dr., Itasca, IL 60143.

U.S. Consumer Products Safety Commission, 4330 East-West Highway, Bethesda, MD 20814

Activities of Daily Living

Geri-Wear, P.O. Box 780, South Bend, IN 46624.

Independent Living Aids, 27 East Mall, Plainview, NY 11803.

Life Safety Systems, 2100 M St. NW, Washington, DC 20037

National Association for Home Care, 519 C St. NE, Stanton Park, Washington, DC 20002.

Visiting Nurse Associations of America, 3801 Florida Ave.E, Denver, CO 80210.

Age

The Gerontological Society, 1 Dupont Circle, Washington, DC 20036.

American Society on Aging, 833 Market Street, San Francisco, CA 94103.

Ageism

Gray Panthers, 3700 Chestnut St., Phila., PA 19104.

National Academy for Teaching and Learning about Aging, Univ. of Texas, Denton, TX 13438.

Older Women's League, 730 11th Street NW, Washington DC 20001.

Agencies and Organizations

Administration on Aging, 330 C St. SW, HEW, Washington, DC 20201.

National Association of Area Agencies on Aging, 600 Maryland Ave. SW, Washington, DC 20024.

The Age of Longevity: An Overview

Alliance for Aging Research, 2021 K St. NW, Washington, DC 20006.

American Psychological Association, 1200 17th St. NW, Washington, DC 20036.

National Council on the Aging, Inc., 409 Third St. SW, Washington, DC 20024.

National Institute on Aging Info. Center, P.O.Box 8057, Gaithersburg, MD 20898.

Alternative Medicine

American Association of Naturopathic Physicians, 2366 Eastlake Ave. E, Seattle, WA 98102.

American Holistic Medical Association, 4101 Lake Boone Trail #201, Raleigh, NC 26707.

American Osteopathic Association, 142 E. Ontario St., Chicago IL 60611.

American Society of Clinical Hypnosis, 2250 East Devon Ave., Des Plaines, IL 60018.

Biofeedback Society of America, 10200 West 44th Ave., Wheatridge, CO 80033.

Committee on Pain Therapy and Acupuncture, American Society of Anesthesiologists, 515 Busse Highway, Park Ridge, IL 60068.

Beating the Cold and the Heat

Information Office, National Institutes of Health, U.S. Dept. of Health and Human Services, P.O. Box 8057, Bethesda, MD 20205.

Crime

Federal Crime Insurance Program, P.O. Box 6301, Rockville, MD 20849.

National Consumers League's National Fraud Information Center, 1522 C St., NW, Suite 406, Washington, DC 20005.

National Council Against Health Fraud, P.O. Box 1276, Loma Linda, CA 92354.

National Organization for Victim Assistance, 717 D St. NW, Washington, DC 20004.

Death

AARP Widowed Persons Service, 601 E St. NW, Washington, DC 20049.

Choice in Dying, 200 Varick St., N.Y., NY 10014.

National Hospice Organization, 1901 N. Moore St., Arlington, VA 22209.

Continental Association of Funeral and Memorial Societies, 2001 S St. NW, Washington, DC 20036.

Declines and Losses

National Association for Human Development, 1424 16th St. NW, P.O. Box 100, Washington, DC 20036.

Diet and Nutrition
>The American Dietetic Association, 216 West Jackson Boulevard, Chicago, IL 60606.
>Food and Drug Administration, 5600 Fishers Lane, Rockville, MD 20856.
>Food and Nutrition Information Center, 10301 Baltimore Blvd., Dept. of Agriculture, Beltsville, MD 20705. National Association of Meal Programs, 101 North Alfred St., Alexandria, VA 22314.

Discounts
>Mature Outlook, 6001 North Clark St., Chicago, IL 60660.
>National Alliance of Senior Citizens, Inc., 1700 Eighteenth St. NW, Washington, DC 20009.
>National Council of Senior Citizens, 1511 K St. NW, Washington, DC 20005.

Doctor: A Checklist for Choosing
>American College of Medical Quality, 9005 Congressional Ct., Potomac, MD 20854.

Doctors: Specialties
>American Board of Medical Specialists, 47 Perimeter Center E., Atlanta, GA 30346.

Education
>Adult Education Association, 1225 19th St., Washington, DC 22036.
>Elderhostel, 80 Boylston St., Boston, MA 92116.
>Institute of Lifetime Learning, AARP, 601 E St. NW, Washington, DC 20049.
>National University Extension Association, 1 Dupont Circle NW, Washington, DC 20036.

Ethics

> Joseph and Rose Kennedy Institute of Ethics, National Reference Center for Bioethics Literature, Georgetown University, 1421 37th St. NW, Washington, DC 20057.
>
> The Hastings Center, 360 Broadway, Hastings-on-Hudson, NY 10706

Ethnic and Minority Elderly.

> National Association for the Hispanic Elderly (Asociacion Nacional Pro Personas Mayores), 3325 Wilshire Blvd., Los Angeles, CA 90010.
>
> National Caucus and Center on Black Aged, 1424 K Street NW, Washington, DC 20005.
>
> National Indian Council on Aging, Inc., 6400 Uptown Blvd., NE, Albuquerque, NM 87110.
>
> National Asian Pacific Center on Aging, Melbourne Tower, 1511 Third Ave., Seattle, WA 98101.

Exercise

> American College of Sports Medicine, P.O. Box 1330, Indianapolis, IN 46206.
>
> National Senior Sports Association, 317 Cameron St., Alexandria, VA 22314.
>
> President's Council on Physical Fitness and Sports, 701 Pennsylvania Ave., NW, Washington, DC 20034.
>
> U.S. National Senior Olympics, 14323 S. Outer Forty Rd., Chesterfield, MO 63107

Family

> Children of Aging Parents, 2761 Trenton Rd., Levittown PA 19056.
>
> Family Service Association of America, 44 East 23rd St., N.Y., NY 10010.
>
> National Coalition against Domestic Violence, 1757 Park Road NW, Washington, DC 20010.

Financial Matters

Institute of Certified Financial Planners, 2 Denver Highlands, 10065, E. Harvard Ave., Denver, Co 80231.

Office of Public Inquiries, Social Security Administration, 6401 Security Blvd., Baltimore, MD 21235.

Tax-Aide Program, AARP, 601 E St., NW Washington, DC 20049.

Friendly Environment

Access Foundation, 1109 Linden St., Valley Stream, NY 11580.

National Rehabilitation Information Center and ABLEDATA, 8455 Colesville Rd., Silver Spring, MD 20910.

Gender

Older Women's League, 666 Eleventh St. NW, Washington, DC 20001.

Task Force on Older Women, National Organization for Women, 3800 Harrison St., Oakland, CA 94611.

Geriatrics, Anyone?

The American Geriatrics Society, 10 Columbus Circle, N.Y., NY 10019.

Grandparenthood

Foundation for Grandparenting, 53 Principe de Paz, Santa Fe, NM 87505.

Grandparents Rights Organization, 555 S. Woodward Ave., Birmingham, MI 48009.

National Federation of Grandmother Clubs of America, 203 North Wabash Ave., Chicago, IL 60601.

Health-Care Costs

American Health Care Association, 1201 L St. NW, Washington, DC 20005.

Information Office, National Institute on Aging, National Institutes of Health, U.S. Dept of Health and Human Services, 6325 Security Blvd., Baltimore, MD 21207.

National Committee to Preserve Social Security and Medicare, 2000 K Street, NW, Washington DC 20006.

Hormones and Aging: Breakthrough?

American Association of Clinical Endocrinologists, 701 Fisk St., Jacksonville, FL 32204.

Hospitals: Classification, Function and Personnel

American Hospital Association, 840 North Lake Shore Drive, Chicago, IL 60611.

Housing

American Association of Homes and Services for the Aging, 901 E St., NW, Washington, D.C. 20004.

Council of State Housing Agencies, 400 North Capital Street NW, Washington, DC 20001.

Hope House Fix-It Program, 1921 Belmont Ave., Dover, N.J 07801.

Hype

AAF Education Services, 1101 Vermont Ave. NW, Washington, DC 20005. Advertising Research Foundation, 641 Lexington Ave., N.Y., NY 10022.

Legal Matters

National Association of Elder Law Attorneys, 1604 North Country Club Rd., Tucson, AZ 85716.

Legal Counsel for the Elderly, AARP, 601 E St., NW, Washington, DC 20049.

Legal Services for the Elderly, 132 West 43rd St., N.Y., NY 10036.

National Senior Citizens Law Center, 2025 M St. NW, Washington, DC , 20036.

Library

American Library Association, 50 E. Huron St., Chicago 60611.

Marriage

Institute of Marriage and Family Relations, 6116 Rolling Rd., Springfield, VA 22152.

Medications

American Pharmaceutical Association, 2215 Constitution Ave., NW Washington, DC 20037.

The Food and Drug Administration, Center for Drugs and Biologics, Division of Regulatory Affairs, 5600 Fishers Lane, Rockville, MD 20857.

Liberty Health Care, 300 Hamilton Ave., Lobby, White Plains, NY 10601.

Memory

Information Center, National Mental Health Association, 1021 Prince St., Alexandria, VA 22314.

Nursing Home

American Health Care Association, 1201 L St. NW, Washington, DC 20005.

National Citizens Coalition for Nursing Home Reform, 1825 Connecticut Ave. NW, Washington, DC 20009.

Pain

American Academy of Pain Medicine, 5700 Old Orchard Rd, Skokie, IL 60077.

American Pain Society, 4700 W. Lake Ave., Glenview, IL 60025.

Prevention

American College of Preventive Medicine, 1600 L St., Washington, DC 20036.

Centers for Disease Control and Prevention, 4770 Buford Highway NE, Atlanta, GA 30341.
Health Information Center, Office of Disease Prevention and Health Promotion, P.O. Box 1133, Washington, DC 20013.
National Eldercare Institute on Health Promotion (AARP), 601 E St. NW, Washington, DC 20049.

Religion and Spirituality
National Interfaith Coalition on Aging, P.O. Box 1924, Athens, GA 30603.

Retirement
American Association of Retired Persons, 1909 K St. NW, Washington, DC 20006.
Association of Part-time Professionals, Flow General Building, 7655 Old Springhouse Rd., McLean, VA 22102.
Pension Rights Center, 918 16th St., NW, Washington, DC 20006.
U.S. Dept. of Health and Human Services, 200 Independence Ave., SW, Washington DC 20201.

Senses
Multidisciplinary Institute for Neuropsychological Development, 48 Garden St., Cambridge, MA 02138.

Sex
American Association of Sex Educators, Counselors and Therapists, 1 East Wacker Drive, Chicago, IL 60601.
Gay and Lesbian Outreach to Elders, 1853 Market St., San Francisco, CA 94103.
Sex Info.and Ed.Council of the U.S., 1855 Broadway, N.Y., NY 10023.

Skin
American Academy of Dermatology, P.O. Box 4014, Schaumberg, IL 60168.

Sleep

American Sleep Disorders Association, 604 2nd St.NW, Rochester, MN 55092.

National Sleep Foundation, 1367 Connecticut Ave. NW, Washington DC, 20036.

Support Groups

American Self-Help Clearinghouse, 25 Pocono Rd., St. Clare's Riverside Medical Center, Denville, NJ 07834.

Elder Support Network, P.O. Box 248, Kendall Park, NJ 08824.

National Support Center for Children of the Aging, P.O. Box 245, Swarthmore, PA 19081.

Travel

Access America, Inc., P.O. Box 90311, Richmond, VA 23230.

International Association for Medical Assistance to Travelers, 417 Center St., Lewiston, NY 14092.

Seniors Abroad, 12533 Pocato Circle North, San Diego CA 92128.

Travel Assistance International, 1133 Fifteenth St. NW, Suite 400, Washington, DC 20005.

Use It Or–

Fitness Motivation Institute of America Association, 5521 Scotts Valley, CA 95066.

National Association of Governor's Councils on Physical Fitness and Sports, 201 South Capital Ave., Indianapolis, IN 46225.

Veterans

Dept. of Veterans Affairs, 810 Vermont Ave.NW, Washington, DC 20420.

Yoga and Tai Chi

The American Yoga Association, 513 South Orange Ave., Sarasota, FL 34236.

Part Two: Diseases and Disorders:

Ailments

>American Geriatrics Society, 10 Columbus Circle, N.Y., NY 10019.
>
>American Medical Association, 535 North Dearborn St., Chicago, IL 60610.
>
>National Health Information Center, P.O. Box 1133, Washington, DC 20013.
>
>United Seniors Health Cooperative, 1331 H St., NW, Washington, DC 20005.
>
>Office of Communications, National Institute of Allergy and Infectious Disease, 9000 Rockville Pike, Bethesda, MD 20892.
>
>Wellness Community National Headquarters, 2200 Colorado Ave., Santa Monica, CA 90404.

Arthritis

>Arthritis Foundation, P.O. Box 7669, Atlanta, GA 30357.
>
>Information Office, National Institute of Arthritis and Musculoskeletal and Skin Diseases, 9000 Rockville Pike, Bethesda, MD 20892.

Back Problems

>American Chiropractic Association, 1701 Clarendon Rd., Arlington, VA 22209.
>
>North American Spine Society, 6300 North River Road, Rosemont, IL 60018.

Cancer

>American Cancer Society, 1599 Clifton Road, NE, Atlanta, GA 30329.
>
>CanCare, 2929 Selwyn Ave., Charlotte, NC 28209.
>
>Cancer Guidance Institute, 5604 Solway St., Pittsburgh, PA 15217.
>
>Cancer Information Service, National Cancer Institute, 9000 Rockville Pike, Bethesda, MD 20892.
>
>Cancer Support Network, 802 East Jefferson, Bloomington, IL 61701.

Breast Cancer
>   Breast Cancer Advisory Center, 11426 Rockville Pike, Rockville, MD 20859.
>   Encore, YWCA of the U.S.A., 726 Broadway, N.Y., NY 10003.

Colon and Rectal Cancer
>   Colon Cancer Support Group, UCSF/Mt. Zion Cancer Center, 2356 Sutter St., San Francisco, CA 94120.
>   United Ostomy Association, 36 Executive Park, Irvine, CA 92714.

Leukemia
>   Leukemia Society of America, 600 Third Ave., N.Y., 10016.
>   National Leukemia Association, Inc., 585 Stewart Avenue, Garden City, NY 11530.

Lung Cancer
>   American Lung Association, 1740 Broadway, N.Y., NY 10019.
>   National Heart, Lung and Blood Institute, 3733 Bethesda Ave., Bethesda, MD 200814.

Ovarian Cancer
>   Ovarian Cancer Prevention and Early Detection Foundation, 841 Bishop St., Honolulu, HI 96813.

Pancreatic Cancer
>   American Pancreatic Association, VA Hospital, 16111 Plummer St., Sepulveda, CA 91343.

Prostate Cancer
>   American Foundation for Urologic Disease, Inc., 300 West Pratt St., Baltimore, MD 21201.
>   American Prostate Society, 1340 Charwood Rd., Hanover, MD 21076.

Dental Concerns

> American Dental Association, 211 E. Chicago Ave., Chicago, IL 60611.
>
> American Society for Geriatric Dentistry, 1121 W. Michigan St., Indianapolis, IN 46202.
>
> Public Reports and Inquiries Section, National Institute of Dental Research, 9000 Rockville Pike, Bethesda, MD 20892.

Diabetes

> American Diabetes Association, 1 West 48 St., N.Y., NY 10020.
>
> National Diabetes Information Clearinghouse, P.O. Box NDIC, 9000 Rockville Pike, Bethesda, MD 20892.

Gastrointestinal Disorders

> National Digestive Diseases Information Clearinghouse, 2 Information Way, Bethesda, MD 20892.

Hearing

> American Tinnitus Association, P.O. Box 5, Portland, OR 97207.
>
> National Information Center on Deafness, Gallaudet University, 800 Florida Ave., NE, Washington, DC 20002.
>
> Self-Help for Hard of Hearing People, Inc., 7800 Wisconsin Avenue, Bethesda, MD 20814.

Heart Disease

> American Association of Cardiovascular and Pulmonary Rehabilitation, 7611 Elmwood Ave., Middleton, WI 53562.
>
> American Heart Association, 7272 Greenville Ave., Dallas, TX 75321.

High Blood Pressure

> High Blood Pressure Information Center, P.O. Box 30105, Bethesda, MD 20814.

Impotence

> Impotence Institute of America, 119 Ruth St., Maryville, TN 37803.

Incontinence Help for Incontinent People, P.O. Box 544A, Union, SC 29379.

Simon Foundation for Continence, P.O. Box 815, Wilmette, IL 600091

Mental Disorders

American Psychiatric Association, 1700 18th St. NW, Washington, DC 20009.

Information Office, National Mental Health Association, 1021 Prince St., Alexandria, VA 22314.

Alzheimer's Disease

Alzheimer's Association, 919 North Michigan Ave., Chicago, IL 60611.Also known as the Alzheimer's Disease and Related Disorders Association.

Alzheimer's Disease Education and Referral Center, P.O. Box 8250, Silver Spring, MD 20907

Depression

National Depressive and Manic Depressive Association, 730 North Franklin St., Chicago, IL 60610.

National Foundation for Depressive Illness, P.O. Box 2257, N.Y., NY 10016.

Parkinson's Disease

American Parkinson's Disease Association, Inc., 60 Bay St., Staten Island, NY 10301.

National Parkinson's Foundation, 1501 N.W. Ninth Ave., Miami, FL 33136.

Stroke

National Institute of Neurological Disorders and Stroke, 31 Center Drive, MSC 2540, Bethesda, MD 20892.

National Stroke Association, 300 East Hampden Ave., Englewood CO 80112.

Osteoporosis
>National Osteoporosis Foundation, 2100 M Street, NW, Washington, DC 20037.

Respiratory Complaints
>American Lung Association, 1740 Broadway, N.Y., NY 10019.

Spasms and Other Painful Sleep Sensations
>National Center on Sleep Disorders Research, National Heart, Lung and Blood Information Center, P.O. Box 300105, Bethesda, MD 20824.
>Restless Legs Syndrome Foundation, Inc., 304 Glenwood Ave., Raleigh, NC 27603.

Stress
>American Institute of Stress, 124 Park Ave., Yonkers, NY 10703.

Suicide
>American Association of Suicidology, 2549 S. Ash, Denver, Co 8022.

Vision
>Eye Care Helpline (National Eye Care Project), Foundation of the American National Association for the Visually Handicapped, Inc., 22 West 21st St., N.Y., NY 10010.
>The Lighthouse National Center for Vision and Aging, 111 East 59 St., New York, NY 10022
>National Eye Institute, 9000 Rockville Pike, Bethesda, MD 20892.

Afterword
>American Health Care Association, 1201 L St., NW, Washington, DC20005.

BIBLIOGRAPHY

Books are keys to wisdom's treasure.

Emilie Poulsson

Part One: In General

Accidents

Massie, D.L. and Campbell, K.L., *Analysis of Accident Rates by Age, Gender and Time of Day* (Ann Arbor: Univ. of Michigan Transportation Research Institute, 1993).

U.S. Consumer Products Safety Commission, *Home Safety Checklist* and *Safety for Older Consumers* (Washington, DC 20207). No date.

Activities of Daily Living

George, L.K. and Binstock, R.H. eds., *Handbook of Aging and the Social Sciences* (San Diego: Academic Press, 1995), 4th ed.

Keddie, Kenneth M.G., *Action with the Elderly* (New York: Pergamon Press, 1978).

O'Quinn, J. et al., *A Survey of Assistive Devices, Behavioral Management and Environmental Modifications for Use with the Cognitively Impaired Elderly* (Oxford, MS: Living Systems, 1986).

Siebers, M.J., et al., eds., *Coping with Loss of Independence* (San Diego: Singular Pub. Group, 1993).

Age

Cole, T.D., *Longevity* (New York: Oxford University Press, 1993).

Fraser, J.T., *Time, the Familiar Stranger* (Amherst: Univ. of Massachusetts Press, 1987).

Kertzer, D.L. and Schaie, K.W., eds., *Age Structuring: Comparative Perspective* (Hillsdale, NJ: Erlbaum, 1989).

Ageism

Bagnell, P.et al., *Perceptions of Aging in Literature* (Westport, CT: Greenwood Press, 1989).

Butler, R.N., *Being Old in America: Why Survive?* (New York: Harper and Row, 1975).

Bytheway, B., *Ageism* (Phila. and Buckingham: Open University Press, 1995).

Davis, R.H. and Davis, J.A., *TV's Image of the Elderly* (Lexington, MA: D.C. Heath, 1985).

Hudson, R. B., ed., *The Future of Age-Based Public Policy* (Baltimore, MD : Johns Hopkins University Press, 1997).

Agencies

Day, C.L., *What Older Americans Think: Interest Groups and Aging Policy* (Princeton, NJ: Princeton Univ. Press, 1990). Van Tassel, D.D. and Meyer, J.E.W., eds., *U.S. Aging Policy Interest Groups (New York: Greenwood Press, 1992).*

Wallace, S.P. and Williamson, J.B., *The Senior Movement: References and Resources* (New York: G.K. Hall, 1992).

The Age of Longevity: An Overview

Martin, L.G. and Preston, S.H., eds., *Demography of Aging* (Washington, D.C.: National Academy Press, 1994).

Minois, George, *History of Old Age* (Chicago: Univ. of Chicago Press, 1989).

Rose, M.R. *Evolutionary Biology of Aging* (New York: Oxford University Press, 1991).

Siegel, J., *A Generation of Change: A Profile of America's Older Population* (New York: Russell Sage Foundation, 1993).

Alternative Medicine

Berman, B.M. and Larson, D.B., eds. *Alternative Medicine* (Washington, DC: U.S. Govt. Printing Office, 1992).

Choosing Medical Treatments, Item 549D, and *Unproven Medical Treatments Lure Elderly,* Item 560D, (Consumer Information Center, Pueblo, CO 81009).

Beating the Cold and the Heat

National Institute on Aging, *Heat, Cold and Being Old* (Bethesda, MD 20205).

Hopkins, P.M., and Ellis, F.R., *Hypermetabolic Disorders, Exertional Heat Stroke, Malignant Hyperthermia and Related Syndromes* (Cambridge: Cambridge Univ. Press, 1996).

Wilkerson, J.A., et al., eds., *Hypothermia, Frostbite and Other Cold Injuries: Prevention, Recognition, Pre-Hospital Treatment* (Seattle, WA: Mountaineers, 1986).

Crime

Moore, M.A. and Deneen, S., eds., *Crime-Proof: Protecting Yourself, Your Family and Your Property* (Kansas City, MO: Andrews and McMeel, 1994).

Moschis, G., *Marketing to Older Consumers* (Westport, CT: Quorum Books, 1992).

Tonry, M. and Morris, N., eds., "Age and Crime" in *Crime and Justice: An Annual Review of Research* (Chicago: Univ. of Chicago Press, 1986), vol. 7, pp. 189-250.

Death

Byock, I., *Dying Well: The Prospect for Growth at the End of Life* (NY: Putnam's, 1997). Hayslip, B. and Leon, J., *Hospice Care* (Newbury Park, CA: Sage, 1992).

Kastenbaum, R., *Death, Society, and Human Experience* (Boston: Allyn & Bacon, 1995), 5th ed.

Lopata, H.Z., *Current Widowhood: Myths and Realities* (Newbury Park, CA: Sage, 1996).

Peck, M. Scott, *Denial of the Soul: Spiritual and Medical Perspectives on Euthanasia* (NY: Crown, 1997).

Declines and Losses

Schneider, E.L. and. Rowe, J. W., eds., *Handook of the Biology of Aging* (San Diego: Academic Press, 1996), 4th ed.

Bonder, B.R. and Wagner, M.B., eds., *Functional Performance in Older Adults* (Phila.: F.A. Davis Co.,1994).

Diet and Nutrition

Morley, J.E., et al., eds., *Geriatric Nutrition: A Comprehensive Review* (New York: Raven Press Ltd., 1990).

Anderson, J. and Diskins, B. *The Nutrition Bible* (New York: William Morrow and Co., 1995).

Discounts for Seniors

Bowman, L., *Freebies (& More) for Folks over Fifty* (Chicago: Probus, 1991).

Heilman, J.R. *Unbelievably Good Deals and Great Adventure That You Absolutely Can't Get Unless You're Over 50* (Chicago: Contemporary Books, 1997).

Mandell, J. *Golden Opportunities: Deals & Discounts for Senior Citizens* (Charlottesville, VA: Platen Press, 1991).

Doctor: A Checklist for Choosing

National Institute on Aging, *Finding Good Medical Care for Older Americans* (9000 Rockville Pike,Bethesda, MD 20014).

Doctors: Specialties

Haug, M., ed., *Elderly Patients and Their Doctors* (New York:Springer, 1981).

Education

Lamdin, L. and Fugate, M., *Elderlearning: New Frontier in an Aging Society* (Phoenix, AZ: American Council on Education and Oryx Press, 1997).

Manheimer, R.J., Snodgrass, D. and Moskow-McKenzie, D., *Older Adult Education: A Guide to Research, Policy, and Programs* (Westport, CT: Greenwood Press, 1995).

Peterson, D.A., *Facilitating Education for Older Learners* (San Francisco: Jossey-Bass, 1987).

Ethics; Medical

Jecker, N., ed., *Aging and Ethics* (Clifton, NJ: The Humana Press, 1991).

Ethnic and Minority Elderly

Harel, Z., et al., eds., *Black Aging* (Newbury Park: Sage, 1990).

Keith, J., et al., *The Aging Experience: Diversity and Commonality across Cultures* (Thousand Oaks, CA: Sage, 1994).

Stanford, E.P. and Torres-Gil, F.M., eds., *Diversity: New Approaches to Ethnic Minority Aging* (Amityville, NY: Baywood Publishing Co., 1992).

Exercise

AARP, *Pep Up Your Life: A Fitness Book for Seniors,* 3200 East Carson St., Lakewood, CA, 90712. Free.

Choate, S., *Exercising with Dorothy* (Chicago: Terra Nova Pub., 1996). An exercise video featuring a workout designed for all elderly persons.

Cooper, R., MD, *Health and Fitness Excellence* Boston: Houghton Mifflin, 1989).

Sallade, J.R. *Exercise for Health* (Alexandria, VA: American Physical Therapy Assn., 1986).

Family

Bennett, G. and Kingston, P., *Elder Abuse: Concepts, Theories and Interventions* (London: Chapman & Hall, 1993).

Blieszner,, R. and Bedford, V., eds., *Handbook of Aging and the Family* (Westport CT: Greenwood Press, 1995).

Rossi, A.S. and Rossi, P.H., *Of Human Bondage: Parent-Child Relations Across the Life Course* (New York: Aldine de Gruyere, 1990).

Financial Matters

Cutler, N.E., Gregg, D.W., and Lawton, M.P., eds., *Aging, Money, and Life Satisfaction: Aspects of Financial Gerontology* (New York: Springer, 1992).

Schulz, J.H., *The Economics of Aging* (Westport, CT: Auburn House, 1985).

Friendly Environment

Bouma, H. and Graafmans, J.A.M., eds., *Gerontechnology (Amsterdam:* IOS Press, 1992).

Coleman, R. and Pullinger, D.J., eds.,"Designing for Our Future Selves," *Applied Ergonomics,* 1993, 24 (1).

A Consumer's Guide to Home Adaptation, Adaptive Environments Center, 374 Congress St., Boston MA 02210. No date.

Gender Roles

Arber, S. and Ginn, J., eds., *Connecting Gender and Ageing: A Sociological Approach (*Buckingham: Open University Press, 1995).

Garner, J.D. and Mercer, S.O., *Women as They Age* (Binghamton, NY: Haworth Press, 1989).

Ory, M. and Warner, H., eds., *Gender, Health and Longevity* (New York: Springer, 1990).

Geriatrics, Anyone?

Hazzard, W.R., Andres, R. et al, eds., *Principles of Geriatric Medicine and Gerontology* (New York: McGraw-Hill, 1990).

Journal of Geriatrics

Grandparenthood

Bengston, V.L. and Robertson, J.F., eds., *Grandparenthood* (Newbury Beach CA: Sage Pubs., 1985).

Cherlin, A.J. and Furstenberg, F.F., Jr. , *The New* American *Grandparent: A Place in the Family, a Life Apart* (New York: Basic Books, 1986).

Health-Care Costs

Lewis, C.B., ed., *Aging: The Health-Care Challenge* (Phila: Davis, 1996), 3rd ed.

Manton, K.G., Singer, B.H. and Suzman, eds., *Forecasting the Health of Elderly Populations* (New York: Springer-Verlag, 1993).

Health Care Financing Administration, *The Medicare Handbook.* 7500 Security Blvd., Baltimore, MD 21244-1850. Free.

Hormones and Aging: Breakthrough?

Morley, J.E and Korenman, S.G., eds., *Endocrinology and Metabolism in the Elderly (*Oxford: Blackwell Scientific Publications, *1992).*

Timiras, P.S., et al, eds., *Hormones and Aging* (Boca Raton, Fl: CRC Press, 1995).

Hospitals: Classification and Function

Council of Better Business Bureaus, Inc., *Tips on Choosing a Hospital* (Arlington, VA 22209).

Housing

Golant, S.M., *Housing America's Elderly: Many Possibilities,Few Choices* (Newbury Park, CA: Sage Pubs, 1992).

Hype

Haug, M. and Lavin, B., *Consumerism in Medicine* (Beverly Hills, CA: Sage, 1983).
Food Label Close-up, Pub. 529 D (Pueblo, CO 81002: Consumer Information Center, Box 100).

Legal Matters

Abramson, B. and Groom, M., *Senior Citizens and the Law* (Madison, WI: Center for Public Representation, 1984).
Arnason, S., Rosenzweig, E. and Koski, A., *The Legal Rights of the Elderly* (N.Y.: Practising Law Institute, 1995).
Kapp, M.B., *Geriatrics and the Law* (New York: Springer, 1992), 2nd ed.

Library

Brevick, P. and Gee, E.G., *Information–Literacy Revolution in the Library* (New York: Macmillan, 1989).
Budd, J.M., *Library and Its Users: The Communication Process* (Westport, CT:Greenwood Press, 1992).

Marriage

AARP, *Divorce after 50: Challenge and Choices,* 601 E St. NW, Washington, DC 20049.

Adams, J.E., *Marriage, Divorce and Remarriage* (Phillipsburg, NJ: Presbyterian and Reformed Pub. Co., 1980).

Johnson, C.L., "Divorced and Reconstituted Families: Effects on the Older Generations," *Families and Aging,* Summer, 1992, 17-40.

Medications

Colvin, Rob, *Prescription Abuse: The Hidden Epidemic* (Omaha, NE: Addicus Books, 1996).

Swonger, A.K. and Burbank, P.M., *Drug Therapy and the Elderly* (Boston: Jones and Bartlette, 1995).

Memory

Haight, B.K. and Webster, J.D., *The Art and Science of Reminiscing: Theory, Researching, Methods, and Applications* Washington, DC: Taylor & Francis, 1995).

Kausler, D.H., *Learning and Memory in Normal Aging* (San Diego: Academic Press, 1994).

Morley, J.E., et al., *Memory: Function and Aging-Related Disorders* (New York: Springer, 1992).

Nursing Home

Johnson, C.L. and Grant, L.A., *The Nursing Home in American Society* (Baltimore: Johns Hopkins Univ. Press, 1985).

Vladeck, Bruce C., *Unloving Care: The Nursing Home Tragedy* (New York: Basic Books, 1980).

Pain

Wall, P.D. and Melzack, R., eds., *Textbook of Pain* (Edinburgh: Churchill Livingstone, 1994).

Prevention

Kennie, D.C., *Preventive Care for Elderly People* (Cambridge: Cambridge Univ. Press, 1993).

Tarlov, A. and Pope, A., *Disablity in America: Toward a National Agenda for Prevention* (Washington, DC: National Academy Press, 1991).

Religion and Spirituality

Health Advocacy Series, AARP, 1909 K ST., NW, Washington, DC 20049.

Kimble, M.A., et al., eds. *Aging, Spirituality, and Religion: A Handbook* (Minneapolis, MN: Fortress Press, 1995).

Koenig, H. G, *Is Religion Good for Your Health?* (Binghamton, NY: Haworth Press, 1997).

Thomas, L.E. and Eisenhandler, S.A., eds., *Aging and the Religious Dimension* (Westport, CT: Auburn House, 1994).

Retirement

Achenbaum, W.A., *Social Security: Visions and Revisions* (Cambridge: Cambridge Univ. Press, 1988), 4th ed.

Doyle, R.L., Tacchino, B., et al., *Can You Afford to Retire?* (Chicago: Probus Pub., 1992).

Haffeman, J.S., *Pension Answer Book* (N.Y.: Panel Pubs., 1990).

Senses

Verrillo, R.T. *Sensory Research: Multimodal Perspectives* (Hillsdale, NJ: Erlbaum, 1993).

Murphy, C., et al., eds., *Nutrition and the Chemical Senses in Aging* (New York: Academy of Sciences, 1989).

Sex

Butler, R.N. and Lewis, M.I., *Love and Sex after 60* (New York: Ballantine Books, 1993), rev. ed.

Guam, J.K. and Whitford, G.S. "Adaptation and Age-Related Expectations of Older Gay and Lesbian Adults," *The Gerontologist,* 1992, 32 (3), 367-374.

Skin

Kligman, A.M. et al., eds., *Cutaneous Aging* (Fort Collins, CO: Colorado Univ. Press, 1989).
Leveque, Jean Luc and Agache, *Aging Skin* (N.Y.: Dekker, 1992).

Sleep

Cooper, R., ed., *Sleep* (N.Y.: Chapman and Hall, 1993).
Morgan, K. *Sleep and Aging: A Research-Based Guide to Sleep in Later Life* (Baltimore, MD: Johns Hopkins Univ. Press, 1987).

Support Groups

National Council on the Aging, 409 3rd St. SW, Washington, DC 20024, *Ideabook on Caregiver Support Groups,* Publication #2010.
Sher, B. and Gottlieb, K.A., *Teamworks: Building Support Groups that Guarantee Success* (N.Y. Warner Books, 1989).
Wuthnow, R. *Sharing the Journey: Support Groups and America's New Quest for Community* (N.Y. Free Press, 1994).

Transportation

Committee for the Study on Improving Mobility and Safety for Older Persons, Transportation Research Board, U.S. National Research Council, *Transportation in an Aging Society: Improving Mobility and Safety for Older Persons* (Washington, DC: U.S. National Research Council, 1988), vols. 1 and 2, 1988.

Travel

International Society of Travel Medicine Clinic Directory, Immodium A-D, 1675 Bwy., N.Y., NY 10019. No date.

Ginnis, Christopher, *202 Tips Even the Best Business Travelers May not Know* (Burr Ridge, IL: Irwin Prof. Pub., 1994).

Massow, R., *Travel Easy: The Practical Guide for Persons over 50* (Washington, DC: AARP Books, 1985).

Use It Or–

Kelly, J.R., *Activity and Aging: Staying Involved in Later Life* (Newbury Park, CA: Sage Pubs., 1993).

Perls, T.T., "The Oldest-Old," *Scientific American, 1994,* 274,70-72.

Suzman, R.M., et al., eds. *The Oldest Old* (New York: Oxford University Press, 1992).

Veterans

Kubey, C. and Snyder, K.D., *Veterans Benefits: The Complete Guide* (N.Y.:Harper Collins, 1994).

VA (Dept. of Veterans Affairs), *Federal Benefits for Veterans and Dependents* (Pittsburgh: Govt. Printing Office 15250.

Yoga and Tai Chi

Bell, L., *Gentle Yoga* (Berkeley, CA: Celestial Arts, 1990).

Bender, R., *Yoga Exercises for Every Body* (Avon, CT: Ruben, 1975).

Carradine, D. and Nakahara, D., *David Carradine's Tai Chi Workout: The Beginner's Program for a Healthier Mind & Body* (New York: Holt, 1995).

Part Two: Diseases and Disorders:

Ailments:

Division of Health Promotion and Disease Prevention, Institute of Medicine, National Academy of Sciences, *The Second Fifty Years* (Washington, DC: National Academy Press, DC, 1990).

Hazzard, W.R., et al., eds., *Principles of Geriatric Medicine and Gerontology* (N.Y.: McGraw-Hill, 1994).

National Institute on Aging Information Center, 2209 Distribution Center, Silver Spring, MD 20910. Ongoing series providing information on health problems of the elderly. Write to be placed on the mailing list. Free.

Arthritis

McCarty, D., Jr., ed., *Arthritis and Allied Conditions* (Phila.: Lea and Febiger, 1993).

Schumacher, H.R., ed., *Primer on the Rheumatic Diseases* (Atlanta: Arthritis Foundation, 1993), 10th ed.

Back Problems

Salmans, S., *Back Pains: Questions You Have–Answers You Need* (Allentown, Pa.: People's Medical Society, 1995).

Cancer

Yaancik, R. and Yates, J.W., eds., *Cancer in the Elderly: Approaches to Early Detection and Treatment* (N.Y.: Springer, 1989).

Breast Cancer

Pederson, L.M. and Trigg, J.M., *Breast Cancer: A Family Survival Guide* (Westport, CT.: Greenwood Press, 1995).

Baum, M. et al., *Breast Cancer: A Guide for Every Woman* (N.Y.: Oxford University Press, 1994).

Colon and Rectal Cancer

Gray, R., *Colon Health Handbook* (Reno, NV: Emerald Pub., 1991).
MacKeigan, J.M. and Hillary, R.M., *Colon and Rectal Cancer* (Grand Rapids, MI: Ludann, 1990).

Leukemia

Siegel, D.S. and Newman, D.E., *Leukemia* (Danbury, CT: Watts, 1994).

Lung Cancer

Williams, C., *Lung Cancer* (N.Y.: Oxford University Press, 1995).
Della Cruz, C.M. and Hambimi, K, *Lung Cancer Handbook* (Newark, NJ: Gordon and Breach, 1993), 4th ed.

Ovarian Cancer

Sharp, F. and Blackett, T. *Ovarian Cancer* (N.Y.: Chapman and Hall, 1996), 4th ed.

Pancreatic Cancer

Buechler, M.M., ed., *Pancreatic Disease: New Horizons* (N.Y.: S. Karger, 1994).

Prostate Cancer

Walsh, P.C. and Worthington, J.F., *Prostate Cancer: A Guide for Men and the Women who Love Them* (Baltimore, MD: Johns Hopkins, 1995).

Dental Concerns

Papas, A.S., et al., eds., *Geriatric Dentistry: Aging and Oral Health* (St. Louis: Mosby Yearbook, 1991).

Diabetes

Brisco, P. *Diabetes: Questions You Have–Answers You Need* (Allentown, PA: People's Medical Society, 1993).

Gastrointestinal Disorders

Yamada, T., ed., *Textbook of Gastroenterology* (Phila.: J.B. Lippincott, 1995).

Hearing

Willott, J.F., *Aging and the Auditory System: Anatomy, Physiology and Psychophysics* (San Diego: Singular Pub. Groups, 1991).

Heart Disease

Martin, A. and Camm, A.J., eds., *Heart Disease in the Elderly* (Somerset, NJ: Wiley, 1989).

High Blood Pressure

Schulman, N., *High Blood Pressure* (N.Y.: Dell, 1989).

Impotence

Bennett, A.H., ed., *Diagnosis and Management of Erectile Dysfunction* (N.Y.: Saunders, 1993).

Farrell, A.D. *Impotence: Index of Modern Information* (Washington, DC: Abbe Pubs.Assn., 1991).

Incontinence

Hahn, S., *Incontinence* (Chicago: Univ. of Chicago Press, 1993).
HIP Report, Help for Incontinent People, P.O. Box 544, Union, SC 29379. No date.

Mental Disorders

National Mental Health Association, 1021 Prince St., Alexandria, VA 22314. Publications on psychological problems. Free.
Turner, F.J. *Mental Health and the Elderly* (N.Y.: Macmillan, 1992).

Alzheimer's Disease

Powell, L.S. *Alzheimer's Disease: A Guide for Families* (Reading, MA: Addison: Wesley, 1992), rev. ed.

Depression

Blazer, D.G., *Depression in Late Life* (St. Louis: C.V. Mosby, 1993).
Schneider, L.S. et al., eds. *Diagnosis and Treatment of Depression in Late Life* (Washington, DC: American Psychiatric Press, 1994).

Parkinson's Disease

Duvoisin, R.C., *Parkinson's Disease: A Guide for Patients and Family* (Phila., PA: Lippincott Raven, 1991) 3rd ed.

Stroke

Hay, J., Stroke: *Questions You Have–Answers You Need* (Allentown, PA: People's Medical Society, 1995).

Osteoporosis

Heaney, R.P., "Bone Mass, Nutrition and Other Lifestyle Factors," *American Journal of Medicine*, 1993, 95, 29S-33S.

Respiratory Complaints

Connolly, M., *Respiratory Disease in the Elderly Patient* (N.Y.: Chapman and Hall, 1995).

Howder, C.L., *Respiratory Care: Know the Facts* (Phila. PA: Lippincott and Raven, 1989).

Sleep

Spasms and Other Painful Sleep Sensations Hartmann, Ernest, *The Sleep Book: Understanding and Preventing Sleep Problems in People Over 50* (Washington, DC: AARP Books, 1987).

Stress

McQuade, W. and Aikman, A., *Stress: What It Is, What It Can Do to Your Health, How to Handle It* (N.Y.: NAL, 1993), rev. ed.

Suicide

Gomez, C., *Regulating Death* (N.Y.: Free Press, 1991.

Leenaars, A.A., et al., eds., *Suicide and the Older Adult* (N.Y. and London: Guilford Press, 1992.

Vision

Bagnoli, P. and Hodos, W., eds., *The Changing Visual System: Maturation and Aging in the Central Nervous System* (N.Y.: Plenum Press, 1991).

Rosenbloom, A.J. and Morgan, M.W., *Vision and Aging* (Newton, MA: Butterworth and Heinemann, 1993).

Afterword

Collins, L.M. and Horn, J.L., *Best Methods for the Analysis of Change: Recent Advances, Unanswered Questions, Future Directions* (Washington, DC: American Psychological Association, 1991.

Lonergan, E.T., ed., *Extending Life, Enhancing Life* (Washington, DC: National Academic Press, 1991).

Part Three:

A HOME MEDICAL LIBRARY FOR THE ELDERLY
AND THEIR CHILDREN

Books

Advice for the Patient: Drug Information in Lay Language (Taunton, MA: Rand McNally, 1995), United States Pharmacopeial Convention, Inc., vol.2, 15th ed. Advice on many different aspects of drugs and drug therapy.

The American Medical Association Pocket Guide to Emergency First Aid (New York: Random House, 1993). A compact, clear guide—excellent for travel.

Berkow, R., MD, et al., eds., *The Merck Manual of Medical Information, Home Edition* (Whitehouse Station, NJ: Merck Research Laboratories, 1997). Clear expression in lay terms of almost every ailment known to humankind.

Exercises for Prevention and Treatment of Illness edited by L. Goldberg and D.L. Elliot (Phila.: Davis Co., 1994). Sensible, moderate approach to fitness and wellness.

Griffith, H.W., *Complete Guide to Prescription and Non-Prescription Drugs* (Los Angeles: Body Press, Perigee Books, 1992). Reasonably up to date, a handy reference.

The Johns Hopkins Handbook of Drugs Specially Edited & Organized by Disease for People Over 50, edited by Simeon Margolis (New York: Random House, 1993). An excellent easy-to-follow handbook.

The Johns Hopkins Medical Handbook: The 100 Major Medical Disorders of People Over the Age of 50 by Johns Hopkins University

Staff (New York: Random House, 1992). As is its companion listed immediately above, an excellent, easy-to-follow handbook.

A Medical Handbook for Senior Citizens and Their Families by H.A. Thornton (Dover, MA: Auburn House, 1989). Clear statement of disorders and therapies.

Natural Health, Natural Medicine: A Comprehensive Manual for Wellness & Self-Care by Andrew Weil, MD (Boston: Houghton Mifflin, 1991). Descriptions and explanations of alternative medicine therapies.

The PDR Family Guide to Prescription Drugs, no author listed (Montvale, NJ: Medical Economics Data, 1994). Easily understood version of the technical *Physician's Desk Reference.*

The Second Fifty Years: Promoting Health and Preventing Disability edited by Robert L. Berg and Joseph Cassells (Wash., DC: National Academy Press, 1990). Practical, authoritative recommendations.

Symptoms by Isadore Rosenfeld, MD (New York: Bantam, 1990). An excellent aid in determining what ails a person.

Periodicals

Aging (Washington, DC: Administration on Aging), information on legislation, programs and services at state and federal levels, aimed at both geriatricians and the elderly.

Bulletin and *Modern Maturity* (Lakewood, CA: American Association of Retired Persons), for the lay person, sources of information and explanatory articles.

Geriatrics (Cleveland, OH: Advanstar Communications,) for physicians, but much of material presented is utilizable by the general public.

Remedy (Westport, CT: Rx Remedy, Inc.), up-to-the-minute, reliable information in easily understood articles for lay persons. Free on request

INDEX

In such indexes . . . there is seen
The baby figure of the giant mass
Of things to come at large.
William Shakespeare